This book is a vital part of an ever-growing mov scholarly and multidisciplinary focus to crime in book adds a significant new chapter to the rural crime in a region of the world where rural crin before – Sweden. Yet, the book is international in her analysis her own background, having grown parative perspective based on her own extensive knowledge of the rural crime literature from around the world.

Joseph F. Donnermeyer, *Professor Emeritus, School of Environment and Natural Resources, Ohio State University, USA*

What a book! This is one of the most comprehensive texts on the topic of crime in rural areas that has ever been written. An amazing and important book about a neglected topic. With impressive engagement and skill, Vania Ceccato challenges a number of stereotypes and prejudices about crime and security in rural areas. With the use of a huge data set, the author presents us with a rich amount of evidence for a more qualified understanding of crime in rural areas.

Gunnel Forsberg, *Professor in Human Geography, Stockholm University, Sweden*

Rural crime and safety is an under-researched area and Vania Ceccato's book is a welcome addition to the emerging literature in the field. Its detailed case studies from Sweden provide a strong empirical foundation, whilst its analysis and arguments will be of interest to criminologists, geographers, and sociologists everywhere.

Michael Woods, *Professor of Human Geography, Aberystwyth University, UK*

Rural Crime and Community Safety is an important and timely addition to the growing literature on rural criminology. This thorough examination of contemporary issues in farm crime, environmental and wildlife crime, gendered violence, youth problems, and crime prevention in rural Sweden is compared and contrasted with research from other countries. The book provides further evidence that rural communities are not always the safe, crime-free places they are often perceived to be and that rural criminology is a vitally important area for enquiry for students, researchers, policy makers, police, and other criminal justice practitioners.

Elaine Barclay, *Associate Professor, School of Behavioural, Cognitive and Social Sciences, University of New England, Australia*

Rural Crime and Community Safety

Crime is often perceived as an urban issue rather than a problem that occurs in rural areas, but how far is this view tenable? This book explores the relationship between crime and community in rural areas and addresses the notion of safety as part of the community dynamics in such areas.

Rural Crime and Community Safety makes a significant contribution to Crime Science and integrates a range of theories to understand patterns of crime and perceived safety in rural contexts. Based on a wealth of original research, Ceccato combines spatial methods with qualitative analysis to examine, in detail, farm and wildlife crime, youth related crimes, and gendered violence in rural settings.

Making the most of the expanding field of Criminology and of the growing professional inquiry into crime and crime prevention in rural areas, rural development, and the social sustainability of rural areas, this book builds a bridge by connecting Criminology and Human Geography. This book will be suitable for academics, students, and practitioners in the fields of criminology, community safety, rural studies, rural development, and gender studies.

Vania Ceccato is Associate Professor at Housing and Safety Research Group at Royal Institute of Technology (KTH), Stockholm, Sweden. Her current interests are urban and rural crime, transit safety, housing and community safety, gendered violence, crime prevention, and spatial analysis.

Routledge studies in crime and society

Rural Crime and Community Safety

Vania Ceccato

Routledge
Taylor & Francis Group

LONDON AND NEW YORK

First published 2016
by Routledge
2 Park Square, Milton Park, Abingdon, Oxfordshire OX14 4RN

and by Routledge
711 Third Avenue, New York, NY 10017

First issued in paperback 2017

Routledge is an imprint of the Taylor & Francis Group, an informa business

British Library Cataloguing in Publication Data
A catalogue record for this book is available from the British Library

Library of Congress Cataloging-in-Publication Data
Ceccato, Vania.
Rural crime and community safety / Vania Ceccato. – First Edition.
    pages cm. – (Routledge studies in crime and society ; 18)
    1. Rural crimes. 2. Women–Crimes against–Sweden–Case studies.
    3. Crime prevention–Sweden–Case studies. I. Title.
    HV6791.C43 2015
    364.109173'4–dc23   2015004168

ISBN 13: 978-1-138-06591-8 (pbk)
ISBN 13: 978-0-415-85643-0 (hbk)

Typeset in Times New Roman
by Wearset Ltd, Boldon, Tyne and Wear

I dedicate this book to Anders

Contents

Figures

Boxes

Tables

About the author

Vania Ceccato is Associate Professor at Housing and Safety Research Group at Royal Institute of Technology (KTH), Stockholm, Sweden. Her current interests are in urban and rural crime, transit safety, gendered and intersectionality in safety issues, housing and community safety, crime prevention, and spatial data analysis. Ceccato has published in international journals, mostly in Criminology, Geography and Planning and is the author of *Moving safely: Crime and perceived safety in Stockholm's subway stations* (2013), the editor of the book *The urban fabric of crime and fear* (2012) and co-editor of *Safety and security in transit environments: An interdisciplinary approach* (2015).

Preface

Why are you writing a book about crime in rural areas? This was a common question I got while writing this book. The quick answer to this question was, Why not? On top of the motivations I will put forward in this book, I usually answered this question by saying that I felt the need to spell out the multiplicity of rural realities I came across in my life.

I have had the opportunity to experience country-specific contexts in which both safety and rurality can take different expressions. I grew up in the countryside in the state of São Paulo, Brazil, and have lived half of my life in urban Europe, coming in contact with different levels of ruralities in Sweden, the United Kingdom, and, to a much lesser extent, in Austria and the Baltic states when visiting these countries. With regards to rural, what fascinates me is that although these places might look different, they share a number of commonalities. Of course, nobody can be fooled by the idea that what is rural in these countries can be boiled down to a single common denominator. Yet it seems to me that there are some common recurring issues that are latent; some of them have to do with nature, others with people, culture, and not less safety. I will try to highlight some of them in the next few paragraphs.

Rural areas are dynamic places and, obviously, what I encountered as a child in Brazil is no longer there to be experienced nowadays by my children. I wonder if any parent today would dare to let seven-year-old kids walk three kilometers to school by themselves along a dirt road. But that was what children did in the late 1970s. Rural roads were safe. My parents' concerns were of a more mystic kind: We were instructed to stay away from voodoo dolls and other signs of black magic left at the crossroads on our way to school. Thoughts about safety or traffic accidents (we rarely met a car anyway, horses were still the main means of transportation) did not cross one's mind in those days, even if one lived in an urban area. Although things were about to change, I experienced life as usual: cows were milked, carts went to the fields, lampposts were repaired after a torrential rain, and, on the weekends, social gatherings were populated by families coming from far and wide, allowing space for dancing and fighting between neighbors and local drunks. At the edges of these country gatherings, young people discussed better opportunities in the city under the scrutiny of adults and the elderly. Young people, alone, could hardly be blamed. The truth was that general economic conditions were steadily improving in the cities in relation to the countryside, which heavily impacted on people's decisions to sell farms and move to the city. The newly acquired TV sets were showing how schools and industries were offering a ticket for an appealing urban life. After all, monetary incentives were no longer in place to support small farmers to continue what their parents and grandparents once manage to do: to produce staple food for the local and regional market. Government investments were being redirected to mechanized large-scale plantation, such as sugar cane, giving little chance to small farmers to survive on small properties. Banks made it easy for large landholders to shift to monoculture. An increase in mechanization, a growth of cattle farming and changes in rural labor relations made it difficult for small farmers to remain in the countryside.

By the late 1970s, we moved to the city, as did 40 percent of the Brazilian rural population. Although it sounded like a smooth course of events, in reality it was a process characterized by conflict and violence. The skills of farmers were not tradable in the city; instead of working in the fields, now they had to learn from scratch to control machines and to stay indoors in poorly ventilated hermetic industrial sheds for eight hours a day. For sanitary reasons, farmers who moved to the urban fringe had to sell their carts, horses, tractors and animals, dispossessing them of many of their means of production. This made it difficult for former farmers to go back to farming if they changed their minds. On a collective level, the rural exodus led to land conflicts in different parts of the country, environmental degradation in both rural and urban areas, and massive pressure on ill-prepared infrastructure in the cities, small or big. Metropolitan cities such as São Paulo and Rio de Janeiro became synonymous with high rates of violence by any standards in the 1980s. At that time, crime and safety seemed like an unlikely problem for a recently graduated geographer like me to take on, but I begged to differ. Crime and perceived safety were important dimensions of the quality of life in my hometown as assessed in my master's thesis in the early 1990s.

I believed much of my rural experience would be left behind when I emigrated from Brazil to Sweden to pursue PhD studies in the mid-1990s. I was wrong. The rural issues were catching up with me. Soon I realized that rural depopulation was also a national concern in Sweden. In contrast to the situation in Brazil, though, the exodus was considered an old, and perhaps well-managed, problem. First, Sweden had suffered a period of emigration (one-fifth of the country's population migrated abroad, mostly to the United States) which only stopped in the 1930s when resources started to keep pace with population growth. In the following decades, rural–urban flows were caused by factors similar to those in Brazil: simply put, better life opportunities and modernization of agriculture. By the 1960s, the majority of the Swedish population was regarded as urban, reaching 84 percent in the beginning of the 2000s. It was then I had the opportunity to learn about Swedish rural areas as a researcher by taking part in the European joint research project "Dynamics of rural areas" (grant number FAIR6-CT98-4162) which aimed at investigating the reasons why some rural communities performed better than others. It was during this time that the Swedish welfare system took a significant market-oriented turn, opening up for funding from the European Union structural funds. The fieldwork of this research project allowed me to meet entrepreneurs, priests, politicians, police officers, and local residents in 13 Swedish rural municipalities, in northern and southern Sweden. By analyzing information from interviews and secondary data, we found that, compared with lagging areas, the successful ones had more vigorous local (small-scale) entrepreneurship and that their success was often associated with tangible structural and institutional factors (such as demography, public funding, universities) but also linked with less tangible ones (such as local history, culture, and attractiveness of the rural landscape). This book draws on experience from this project and the wonderful exchange of ideas I had with Lars Olof Persson at Nordregio and other team members in Greece, Germany, and Scotland, particularly Professor John Bryden.

Thirteen years on, despite divergent economic performance, 15 percent of Swedes still live in rural areas. What is different today compared with the time I first came in contact with rural Sweden is the recent interest of the media in incidents of crime. The picture of the countryside as deviant from the cities, something out of the ordinary, is often powered by a few murders, some related to organized crime and others a result of violence at home. Violence in intimate relationships has long been known as a problem in some rural communities in Sweden but until recently has been tolerated as part of the "local culture."

Another example of differences today is the acceptance of members of motorcycle gangs (some of them with police records of theft and organized crime) as part of the local culture. Added to this abnormal image of Swedish rural life are conflicts between local rural residents and seasonal foreign workers. On one hand, locals blame seasonal workers for committing petty crimes. On the other hand, seasonal workers file complaints of poor working and living conditions while employed by fraudulent entrepreneurs. Although these issues often hit the national news, they rarely awaken any interest among the urban population, who are often too distant to understand and become concerned with any of these rural realities.

Closer to the urban reality are youth-related problems in rural areas, such as violence and addiction, and cases of environmental and wildlife crimes against nature. The increase in cases of fraud – a problem that affects both urban and rural populations – has become a concern as the use of the Internet and information and communication technology (ICT) has become widespread. Surely, these issues inspired me to investigate further urban and rural crime rates and trends in the research project entitled "Social sustainability in rural Sweden: Crime, fear of crime and crime prevention in rural communities" (FORMAS, grant number 2007-1954). I knew that official police statistics showed that some rural areas had become more criminogenic in the past decades, but it was unclear whether this development had any effect on people's perceptions of safety (which was later revealed when the first national crime victim survey was published in 2006). Using Crime Science principles (Laycock, 2005), I investigated whether crime levels in rural municipalities reflect the demographic and socioeconomic changes that took place during 1996 and 2006. This was followed by an analysis of differences and/or similarities of local crime prevention councils in rural communities. The intention was to identify "good practices" (what can be learned from eight municipalities) that could guide crime prevention efforts in other rural communities. This book gathers material adapted from three articles produced in collaboration with Lars Dolmén, from the Swedish Police Academy, and Adriaan Uittenbogaard, at the Royal Institute of Technology (Ceccato and Dolmén 2011, 2013, and Ceccato and Uittenbogaard 2013).

Part of my rural experience comes from the United Kingdom, as daily experiences while living there: interacting with people and walking and cycling in the countryside on the weekends with my family. In England, more than anywhere else I have lived, a plethora of issues about safety come up daily, in street corner conversations as well as in mainstream media (this was prior to the 2011 riots in major English cities but contemporary with the 2005 London bombings). Minor events such as youth anti-social behavior in the neighborhood combined with contemporary urban myths mixed with what was on TV: from historical documentaries about Jack the Ripper, to fictional pieces, starring no less a personality than Sherlock Holmes. I believe it is easy to capture the many types of rural areas that exist in the UK despite the oversimplified, perhaps stereotypical, image portrayed in the media. Differences between rural and urban get blurred by the high density of the urban structure, particularly in southern English towns. Roads pass through small villages, creating a net of interconnections that surely has an impact on criminogenic conditions in these places. Street violence, thefts, and addiction are often recognized rural problems. It is also commonly known that the number of burglaries has increased more in rural areas in the past two decades than in suburban or urban areas. Still the fear of crime is less likely to have an impact on people's quality of life in a rural area. More important than actual statistics, the fear of crime is fed by particular cases of crime, especially in rural contexts. Individual cases create scars and damage the reputations of villages that no outsiders knew were there before the event. Time passes, but these individual cases remain in people's minds for a long time and often unfairly characterize the image of rural Britain. The Norfolk murder is a good example. Two young men entered a property in a rural village, and the owner shot at them, killing one. The case was openly discussed by the media and was highly controversial. Although this case was unique, it did raise a number of issues related to current social developments about people's attitudes toward intruders (the homeowner's decision to shoot at the young men and the possession and use of guns to protect property) and the criminal justice system in Britain (why the sentence was changed after the first judgment, as the house owner was imprisoned for murder but his sentence was later reduced to manslaughter).

With this preface, I position myself in relation to the ample field of Rural Studies, Criminology, and Crime Science and to give you the chance to understand the starting point and the approach adopted in this book. Thus, it offers chapters with the best analysis I managed to put together, assembling findings from modeling, spatial data analysis using Geographical Information Systems (GIS), and official statistics. However, I believe that some relevant questions on crime and rural safety demanded a qualitative approach, calling for an analysis of phenomena based on deep interviews as well as email surveys. Another important feature of this book is the final chapters devoted to crime prevention practices, which I think can be of interest to those who deal with crime and safety issues in rural environments in Sweden but also elsewhere.

I would certainly not be able to write this book and turn my back on issues that occupy my mind daily. Gendered violence is one of these topics. I have consciously strived to adopt a gender-informed approach to violence in rural environments in this book, taking into account other types of vulnerabilities that intersect gender, such as ethnic belonging. I regard women as active agents who, under certain circumstances, are faced by imposed layers of vulnerability, namely, by their place of residence and by discrimination because of age, ethnic belonging, or income. Two chapters in this book are devoted to violence against women in private realms.

Finally, it is important to mention that my personal experiences from Brazil, Sweden, and the UK in no way made me an expert on these countries. But my life experiences may provide you, as a reader, clues to why this book is shaped the way it is. Except for Brazil, my experience in writing this book reflects the view of an "outsider," someone from Latin America who decided to migrate to Sweden and the UK and write about crime and safety in rural contexts.

Stockholm, January 2015
Vania Ceccato

The author at age five in rural Brazil

References

Ceccato, V., & Dolmén, L. (2011). Crime in rural Sweden. *Applied Geography, 31*, 119–135.

Ceccato, V., & Dolmén, L. (2013). Crime prevention in rural Sweden. *European Journal of Criminology, 10*, 89–112.

Ceccato, V., & Uittenbogaard, A. (2013). Environmental and wildlife crime in Sweden. *International Journal of Rural Criminology, 2*, 23–47.

Laycock, G. (2005). Defining crime science: New approaches to detecting and preventing crime. In N. Tilley & Melissa J. Smith (Eds.), *Crime science* (pp. 3–24). Cullompton, Devon: Willan Publishing.

Acknowledgements

There are many people whom I wish to thank as they have helped me in the development of the research and preparation of the manuscript. Thanks go to Lars Olof Persson (in memoriam) who introduced me to rural Sweden as an object of study through a research project we developed together in the early 2000s. I am also grateful for the fruitful discussions I had with my colleague Lars Dolmén, from the Swedish Police Academy, during the research project "Social sustainability in rural Sweden: Crime, fear of crime and crime prevention in rural communities." Some of the joint work we produced in the project is referenced in this book. I would like to thank FORMAS, the Swedish Research Council for Environment, Agricultural Sciences and Spatial Planning, which financed part of the Swedish case study (Grant 251-2007-1954).

In the genesis and writing of this book, I was inspired by those who for decades have devoted their research to rural areas and rural crime and community safety, just to name a few: Joseph Donnermeyer, Elaine Barclay, Ralph Weisheit, Kerry Carrington, Rob Mawby, Richard Yarwood, and Walter DeKeseredy. Along the years, I came across a number of studies from the United States, United Kingdom, Canada, and Australia that inspired me.[1] This book is a humble contribution to this existing body of knowledge. I hope that, by framing old and new questions of rural crime and community safety using Sweden as a case study, new insights can be brought to the table that can expand knowledge in this area.

Many authors in this book's bibliography shared their knowledge in an international workshop entitled "Rural crime and community safety," organized by the Housing and Safety Research Group at KTH, which took place in Stockholm in October 2014. Most of the papers presented in that workshop were included in a special issue of the *Journal of Rural Studies* in 2015. Many thanks go to Professor Mike Woods. First, as the editor of the journal, Mike recognized the issue of rural crime and community safety as relevant to the journal's audience. Second, he actively supported the special issue by acting as moderator at the Stockholm workshop, a step that was fundamental to the process of eventually publishing the articles. Third, Mike was a patient steward during my time learning the editorial system as guest editor for the special issue. The author is also grateful to all participants and audience members, who made that seminar an

Acknowledgements xxvii

open arena of discussion. On a financial note, I would like to thank the Swedish Research Council (VR) and the Swedish Research Council for Health, Working Life and Welfare (FORTE) for sponsoring the workshop. The workshop provided me with an overview of the field while I was writing this book.

My deep gratitude must also go to those who made this research possible by providing the data or participated in the surveys and interviews for the research project. The Swedish National Council for Crime Prevention (BRÅ) provided the police-recorded data, crime survey data, and project database of the funded projects driven by local crime prevention councils. Martina Johansson from the Rikspolisstyrelsen (Swedish National Police Board) kindly provided employment data of the police.

Thanks also to all those who gave permission for me to reproduce previously published material in this book. This includes Sage, BRÅ (the Swedish National Council for Crime Prevention), BJS (Bureau of Justice Statistics), the *International Journal of Rural Criminology*, the newspapers *Ångermanland Dagbladet* and *Västerbottens Kuriren*, APU (Anti Poaching Unit Sweden), Peter Lindström, Nikolaus Koutakis, Carin Lennesiö, TT News Agency, Elsevier, Crimestoppers, NCJRS and CAN (Swedish Council for Information on Alcohol and Other Drugs).

The documentation on crime prevention activities from the case studies was provided by representatives of local crime prevention councils when the interviews were performed. My thanks also go to those who kindly took the time to answer the email survey and/or participated in the face-to-face interviews conducted by Carin Lennesiö, whose dedication resulted in high-quality material for this research. I also interviewed a number of experts and researchers working with crime and safety in rural areas in Sweden, rural policing, and rural development. I am particularly grateful for the time and trouble people took to provide me with information about and interpretations of their perspectives. Thanks go to colleagues who have shared their insights the past few years – over lunch, by email, or over the phone: Björn Furuhagen, Peter Lindström, May-Britt Öhman, Anders Johannesson, John Bryden, colleagues at BRÅ, and, more recently, the representatives of the Women's Shelter organization, the Federation of Swedish Farmers, Swedish Transport Administration, and Magnus Rydhult (Crimestoppers Sweden).

I would like to thank my colleagues and students at the School of Architecture and the Built Environment (ABE), Royal Institute of Technology (KTH), especially the Housing and Safety Research Group: Adriaan Uittenbogaard, Asifa Iqbal, Bridget da Costa, Mats Wilhelmsson, and Roya Bamzar.

I am grateful to Rebecca Foreman who proofread the manuscript and made valuable comments on the structure of sentences, paragraphs, and chapters. Remaining shortcomings are, of course, entirely this author's responsibility.

I would also like to thank my publisher, Routledge, for their support. I particularly wish to acknowledge Heidi Lee, Amy Ekins-Coward and Sally Quinn for their stewardship of this project. Thanks for your encouraging words and patience during the process of writing and making it into the final product.

Finally, thanks for all the love and support I received from my family, on both sides of the Atlantic, especially my husband, Anders Karlsson, and my children, Amanda and Filip, my parents, Luiza and Lidio, and my three brothers and two sisters, who lived most of their lives in the countryside, where I was born.

Note

1 The references listed below are the most important, but not limited to them.

References

Barclay, E., & Donnermeyer, J. F. (2002). Property crime and crime prevention on farms in Australia. *Crime Prevention of Community Safety, 4*(4), 47–61.

Barclay, E., & Donnermeyer, J. F. (2007). Farm victimisation: The quintessential rural crime. In E. Barclay, J. F. Donnermeyer, J. Scott, & R. Hogg (Eds.), *Crime in rural Australia* (pp. 57–68). Sydney: Federation Press.

Barclay, E., Donnermeyer, J. F., Doyle, B. D., & Talary, D. (2001). Property crime victimisation and crime prevention on farms. Report to the NSW A.-G. C. P. Division (Ed.), Institute for Rural Futures, University of New England.

Barclay, E., Donnermeyer, J. F., & Jobes, P. C. (2004). The dark side of Gemeinschaft: Criminality within rural communities. *Crime Prevention and Community Safety, 6*(3), 7–22.

Barclay, E., Hogg, R., & Scott, J. (2007). Young people and crime in rural communities. In E. Barclay, J. Donnermeyer, J. Scott, & R. Hogg (Eds.), *Crime in rural Australia* (pp. 100–114). Sidney: Federation Press.

Barclay, E., Scott, J., & Donnermeyer, J. (2011). Policing the outback: Impacts on integration in an Australian context. In R. Mawby & R. Yarwood (Eds.), *Rural policing and policing the rural: A constable countryside?* (pp. 33–44). Farnham: Ashgate.

Barclay, E., Scott, J., Hogg, R., & Donnermeyer, J. (Eds.). (2007). *Crime in rural Australia.* Sydney: Federation Press.

Bull, M. (2007). Alcohol and drug problems in rural and regional Australia. In J. F. D. E. Barclay, J. Scott, & R. Hogg (Eds.), *Crime in rural Australia.* Sydney: Federation Press.

Carrington, K. (2007). Crime in rural and regional areas. In J. F. D. E. Barclay, J. Scott, & R. Hogg (Eds.), *Crime in rural Australia* (pp. 27–43). Sydney: Federation Press.

Cunneen, C. (2007). Crime, justice and indigenous people. In E. Barclay, J. Donnermeyer, J. Scott, & R. Hogg (Eds.), *Crime in rural Australia* (pp. 142–154). Sydney: Federation Press.

DeKeseredy, W. S., Donnermeyer, J. F., & Schwartz, M. D. (2009). Toward a gendered second generation CPTED for preventing woman abuse in rural communities. *Security Journal, 22*, 178–189.

DeKeseredy, W. S., Donnermeyer, J. F., Schwartz, M. D., Tunnell, K., & Hall, M. (2007). Thinking critically about rural gender relations: Toward a rural masculinity crisis/male peer support model of separation/divorce sexual assault. *Critical Criminology, 15*(4), 295–311.

Donnermeyer, J. (1995). Crime and violence in rural communities. Columbus, OH: National Rural Crime Prevention Center.

Donnermeyer, J., DeKeseredy, W. S., & Dragiewicz, M. (2011). Policing rural Canada and the United States. In R. Mawby & R. Yarwood (Eds.), *Rural policing and policing the rural: A constable countryside?* (pp. 23–32). Farnham: Ashgate.

Donnermeyer, J., & Kreps, G. M. (1986). *The benefits of crime prevention: A comparative analysis*. Columbus, OH: National Rural Crime Prevention Center.

Donnermeyer, J. F. (2007). Rural crime: Roots and restoration. *International Journal of Rural Crime, 1*, 2–20.

Donnermeyer, J. F., & Barclay, E. (2005). The policing farm crime. *Practices and Research, 6*(1), 3–17.

Donnermeyer, J. F., Barclay, E. M., & Mears, D. P. (2011). Policing agricultural crime. In R. I. Mawby & R. Yarwood (Eds.), *Rural policing and policing the rural: A constable countryside* (pp. 193–204). Farnham: Ashgate.

Donnermeyer, J. F., Jobes, P., & Barclay, E. (2006). Rural crime, poverty and rural community. In W. S. DeKeseredy & B. Perry (Eds.), *Advancing critical criminology: Theory and application* (pp. 199–213). Oxford: Lexington Books.

Donnermeyer, J. F., Plested, B. A., Edwards, R. W., Oetting, G., & Littlethunder, L. (1997). Community readiness and prevention programs. *Journal of the Community Development Society, 28*(1), 65–83.

Falcone, D. N., Wells, L. E., & Weisheit, R. A. (2002). The small-town police department. *Policing, 25*(2), 371–384.

Gilling, D. (2011). Governing crime in rural UK: Risk and representation. In R. I. Mawby & R. Yarwood (Eds.), *Rural policing and policing the rural: A constable countryside?* (pp. 69–80). Farnham: Ashgate.

Halfacree, K. (2011). Still "out of place in the country"? Travellers and the post-productivist rural. In R. I. Mawby & R. Yarwood (Eds.), *Rural policing and policing the rural: A constable countryside?* (pp. 124–135). Farnham: Ashgate.

Mawby, R. (2011). Plural policing in rural Britain. In R. Mawby & R. Yarwood (Eds.), *Rural policing and policing the rural: A constable countryside?* (pp. 57–67). Farnham: Ashgate.

Mawby, R., & Yarwood, R. (Eds.). (2011). *Rural policing and policing the rural: A constable countryside?* Farnham: Ashgate.

Scott, J., Carrington, K., & McIntosh, A. (2012). Established-outsider relations and fear of crime in mining towns. *Sociologia Ruralis, 52*(2), 147–169.

Websdale, N. (1995). Rural woman abuse: the voice of Kentucky women. *Violence against women, 1*, 309–338.

Websdale, N., & Johnson, B. (1998). An ethnostatistical comparison of the forms and levels of woman battering in Urban and rural areas of Kentucky. *Criminal Justice Review, 23*, 161–196.

Weisheit, R. A., & Donnermeyer, J. F. (2000). Change and continuity in rural America. In G. LaFree (Ed.), *The nature of crime: Continuity and change* (Vol. 1). Washington, DC: National Institute of Justice.

Weisheit, R. A., & Donnermeyer, J. F. (2000). Changes and continuity in crime in rural America. In G. LaFree (Ed.), *Criminal justice 2000: The nature of crime of crime, continuity and change* (pp. 309–357). Washington, DC: US Department of Justice.

Weisheit, R. A., Falcone, D. N., & Wells, L. E. (2006). *Crime and policing in rural and small-town rural America.* Prospect Heights, IL: Waveland Press.

Weisheit, R. A., & Wells, L. E. (2004). Youth gangs in rural America. *National Institute of Justice Journal, 251*, 2–6.

Weisheit, R. A., Wells, L. E., & Falcone, D. N. (1994). Community policing in small town and rural America. *Crime and Delinquency, 40*(4), 549–567.

Woods, M. (2005). Defining the rural. In *Rural geography* (pp. 3–16). London: Sage.

Woods, M. (2011a). Policing rural protest. In R. Mawby & R. Yarwood (Eds.), *Rural policing and policing the rural: A constable countryside?* (pp. 109–122). Farnham: Ashgate.

Woods, M. (2011b). *Rural.* London/New York: Routledge.

Yarwood, R. (2001). Crime and policing in the British countryside: Some agendas for contemporary geographical research. *Sociologia Ruralis, 41*(2), 201–219.

Yarwood, R. (2010a). An exclusive countryside? Crime concern, social exclusion and community policing in two English villages. *Policing and Society, 20*(1), 61–78.

Yarwood, R. (2010b). Risk, rescue and emergency services: The changing spatialities of mountain rescue teams in England and Wales. *Geoforum, 41*(2), 257–270.

Yarwood, R., & Edwards, B. (1995). Voluntary action in rural areas: The case of neighbourhood watch. *Journal of Rural Studies, 11*(4), 447–459.

Yarwood, R., & Gardner, G. (2000). Fear of crime, cultural threat and the countryside. *Area, 32*(4), 403–411.

Part I
Introduction

1   Aim, scope, and book structure

This book is about crime and community safety in rural areas. Crime is often regarded as an urban rather than a rural issue. Is this because rural areas are safer than urban areas? We suggest in this book that even if they are, this is just a partial view of what safety in rural communities is or what it is perceived to be. The relationship between crime and community characteristics is complex, determined by a set of interdependent factors that, together, create nuanced differences of what is thought to be safety in rural areas. The chapter defines the aim, scope, and structure of the book.

Aim and scope

The aim of this book is to make a contribution to the knowledge base on crime and perceived safety as well as crime prevention in rural areas. This is important because these issues are neglected fields in both criminology and in rural studies. One reason they are neglected is that safety in rural areas is often regarded as synonymous with low crime rates. If crime rates are low, safety is not a problem and thus not an issue. Another reason is that patterns of crime are far too often considered to be homogeneous across rural areas, because "rural" is everything that is not urban. The implication of this rural–urban dichotomy is that it disregards the impact of different rural contexts on crime and safety and neglects the dynamics of rural areas and residents' agency.

The novelty of the book is to put safety in rural areas in focus by: (1) arguing why we should care about crime and community safety in rural areas; (2) addressing safety as part of the dynamics of rural areas across countries; (3) placing crime and safety in Swedish rural areas in an international context; (4) reporting on crime prevention experiences in rural contexts; and, without going beyond the main aim of the book, (5) interpreting the intersectionality of safety and gender as a social construct experienced by those who suffer violence in the private realm in rural areas.

The book is an example of *Crime Science* because it integrates theories from different disciplines to understand patterns of crime and perceived safety in a rural context. Crime Science is "the application of the methods of science to crime and disorder" (Laycock, 2005, p. 4). Crime Science focuses on crime from a wide range of sciences and disciplines using a number of tools. It brings knowledge together into a functional and coordinated response to crime. Crime Science depends on different contexts, addressing not only what works but where, how, and when (Pawson & Tilley, 1997).

The Swedish case is analyzed in a systematic and detailed way by depicting not only levels but also patterns of crime. It also contributes to Crime Science by testing hypotheses to reveal mechanisms and relationships that can help understand crime patterns and actions to reduce crime. Moreover, as any product of Crime Science, the book makes use of scientific methods, combining quantitative and spatial methods (spatial analysis techniques, regression analysis) with qualitative approaches (interviews, vignette analysis). An important part of the book focuses on action taken against crime in crime prevention initiatives in rural areas. Using data and evidence from interviews, the discussion in Part V broadens the scientific base for understanding, analyzing, and preventing crime in rural contexts.

The book provides an overview of crime and safety issues in rural areas using a Scandinavian country as a case. This is important because most of the literature on crime and perceived safety in rural areas is based on cases from North American and British studies. It is worth noting that the Swedish case study is presented against this background as a framework of analysis rather than a reference for drawing conclusions or making generalizations across countries.

Finally, and importantly, this book builds a bridge connecting Criminology and Human Geography – lacking in the international literature – by making the most of the expanding field of criminology and of the growing professional inquiry into crime and crime prevention in rural areas, rural development, and the social sustainability of rural areas. I hope this book will act as a starting point for those who are carrying out or are interested in research on crime and perceived safety, rural geography, and comparative research in criminology. By approaching a number of issues never before addressed in the Swedish rural context, such as gendered safety and crimes against the environment and wildlife, this book fills a growing niche and will satisfy demand from an expanding discipline for years to come. This book does not claim to provide a complete and detailed picture of patterns of victimization and safety in Swedish rural areas. Instead, the book's goal is to show a variety of facets that characterize a set of core issues that are perceived to be relevant in the Swedish rural context with regards to crime, perceived safety, and crime prevention practices, so far inexistent in the international literature.

This book is intended to reach a wide group of professionals, scholars, criminal justice practitioners, and policy makers interested in safety issues as well as people working with rural areas (criminologists, geographers, rural experts, people working directly with safety interventions at the community and regional levels). This is an ideal book for undergraduate students in criminology.

Book structure

The book is divided into seven parts and 15 chapters. In Part I, Chapter 1 introduces the aim, scope, and structure of the book. Chapter 2 presents 10 reasons that crime and community safety are relevant to criminology and rural research. Chapter 3 builds the theoretical background for the book and introduces the issues discussed in Parts IV to V. The chapter presents a number of theories of crime prevention drawing on the paradigm of Crime Science. Here the focus is on crimes (situations) and not on offenders. Some of these theories identify societal processes at the macro level (e.g., social crime prevention) that lead to crime, while others focus on micro aspects. What is fundamental is the discussion of the most important theories that, taken together, help explain why crime happens. Are they enough to reveal the nature of crime in a rural context? The chapter also highlights the focus of criminology on certain theories that neglect the nature of rural areas. In urban areas, lack of social control leads to crime, according to social disorganization theory. The opposite is often taken for granted: less crime in rural areas means more social control and social cohesion. Chapter 3 calls these assumptions into question. The chapter also discusses how rural change has affected victimization and perceived safety.

In Part II, Chapter 4 illustrates trends and patterns of crime in rural areas. Are rural areas becoming more criminogenic? Or are big cities still synonymous with big danger? Crime victimization disproportionately affects more urban than rural residents, regardless of country or differences in rural–urban definitions. Although some would claim that crime is eminently an urban phenomenon, recent changes in rural–urban relationships have affected regional criminogenic landscapes, making individuals living in some rural areas more exposed to crime than in the past. The chapter shows that this trend often goes undetected, because changes do not affect rural areas evenly across the board. As a result, victimization may be selective and unequal across social groups and environments. Finding evidence on how these changes affect criminogenic conditions is difficult because, as we will discuss, actual change may be hidden under generally "decreasing" or "stable" trends or data sources showing contradictory crime developments.

Chapter 4 compares crime rates in Sweden with those found in the United States and the United Kingdom. In all these countries, urban crime rates are greater than rural ones, regardless of definitions of crime type and how rural areas are conceptualized. An alternative to official police statistics is to complement them, as much as possible, with data from national crime victim surveys, as is done in this chapter. Despite the limitations of these sources of data, it is the most reliable data available for representing the geographical distribution of crime in Sweden and elsewhere. An analysis of the available data appears in the two chapters that follow. First, trends in crime rates and prevalence are compared in a select number of countries as a background for the Swedish case. The chapter discusses evidence about the so-called "convergence hypothesis" of urban and rural crime rates. Then, the analysis focuses on specific types of violent and property crimes in rural areas, drawing conclusions for rural areas across countries when possible.

Chapter 5 focuses on the geography of property and violent crime in Sweden. The analysis focuses first on trends and geographical differences between urban areas, accessible rural areas, and remote rural areas, made feasible by the use of Geographical Information Systems (GIS). Then, crime rates are cross-sectionally modeled as a function of municipalities' characteristics. An important change in the regional geography of crime is the shift of clusters of high rates of theft and residential burglary, from Stockholm to Skåne (Skåne, the southernmost area of Sweden). Modeling results show links between spatial variations in property crime rates and the regions' demographic, socioeconomic, and locational characteristics, both in 1996 and 2007. Evidence from regression models also indicates that accessible rural municipalities, particularly those located in southern Sweden, were more criminogenic in 2007 than they were a decade previous. Changes in routine activities associated with existing and new social disorganization risk factors are highlighted as potential causes of increased vulnerability in accessible rural areas during the past decade.

Perceived safety in rural areas is the theme of Part III of the book. People fear crime less in rural areas than they do in urban areas. This fact represents a partial picture of perceived safety, because people can fear greatly even if they perceive little chance of a crime occurring. It is likely that the experience of crime in rural areas differs qualitatively as well as quantitatively from urban areas. This part looks beyond actual statistics on perceived safety in rural and urban areas to shed light on the nature of fear among those living in rural areas. It also suggests why we should care about perceived safety in rural areas. In Chapter 6, instead of reducing the issue of fear of crime to risk of victimization, we turn to a discussion in which fear can be discussed in a broader context of rural areas, with particular attention to the Swedish case. The chapter highlights the need for knowledge in different areas of research on fear of crime in rural contexts. Chapter 7 concentrates on examples of what fear of crime statistics show in different countries about rural and urban environments and concludes with examples from Swedish rural areas.

In Part IV, Chapter 8 presents crime in a rural context with a focus on farm and environmental and wildlife crimes, youth-related problems, and violence against women. Chapter 8 indicates how previous literature on rural crime suggests that crime in rural areas is more varied now than it once was. Rural crime includes thefts of fertilizer and tractors as well as environmental offenses, such as illegal dumping of oil. The chapter also reviews the current literature on farm and environmental crimes in Sweden. The Swedish case study is based on an analysis of both police-recorded data and Swedish print and Internet media coverage (newspapers) on farm and environmental crimes in rural Sweden. Chapter 8 concludes with a discussion of the barriers to detecting and prosecuting offenders who commit farm and environmental crimes.

Chapter 9 focuses on youngsters living in rural areas as well as youth-related disorder. Youth-related crime is often regarded by those working with crime prevention in rural areas as the main safety problem (Ceccato & Dolmén, 2013). This chapter characterizes what are considered "youth problems" in rural areas in different country contexts (United States, United Kingdom, Australia, and Sweden).

The chapter about violence against women touches on the barriers women living in rural areas face in reporting violence. In Chapter 10, the Swedish case study is discussed by highlighting urban–rural trends, geographical patterns, and a discussion of determinants of violence against women. To provide a basis for the analysis of the Swedish case, Chapter 10 also lists individual and structural factors pointed out in the international literature as determinants of violence against women in rural areas.

Part V is about policing and crime prevention in a rural context. Chapter 11 starts with an international overview of what "policing" has been, with particular focus on the historical development of the rural police as an institution. The chapter also provides detailed historical development of policing in Swedish rural areas and discusses examples of police officers' contemporary daily work with crime, crime prevention, and community safety. The chapter ends with a discussion of future challenges for policing in the Swedish countryside as the commodification of policing has become a reality and the police organization is becoming centralized.

Chapters 12–14 present the challenges of those working in local crime prevention in rural areas. Although this chapter draws upon empirical work done in Swedish rural municipalities, the analysis also reports on experiences from the United States, United Kingdom, and Australia. Here actions are directed to three types of crime. Chapter 12 concerns farm crime and crimes against nature and wildlife, Chapter 13 deals with prevention of youth-related crime, and Chapter 14 is devoted to the challenges in preventing women abuse in rural communities.

Part VI summarizes the most important issues related to crime, perceived safety, and crime prevention in Swedish rural areas, and, more importantly, Chapter 15 defines an agenda for future research.

References

Ceccato, V., & Dolmén, L. (2013). Crime prevention in rural Sweden. *European Journal of Criminology, 10*, 89–112.

Laycock, G. (2005). Defining crime science: New approaches to detecting and preventing crime. In N. Tilley & Melissa J. Smith (Eds.), *Crime science* (pp. 3–24). Cullompton, Devon: Willan Publishing.

Pawson, R., & Tilley, N. (1997). *Realistic evaluation*. London: Sage.

2   Crime and safety in rural areas

This chapter starts by listing 10 reasons why crime and safety in rural areas is a subject worth examining in its own right. These 10 reasons guide the themes discussed in this book and are developed in detail in Chapters 3–14.

Why care about crime and safety in rural areas?

Low crime rates in rural areas are often taken as a sign that crime in rural areas is not a major concern. This recognition is not particularly original but does reflect negligence by different disciplines and society in general concerning issues outside the urban realm – not less in rural crime and safety. One of the reasons for this lack of attention to rural crime is perhaps the widespread belief in a dichotomy between urban and rural, the former being criminogenic, the latter problem-free, idyllic, and healthier and friendlier than the urban. This chapter challenges such ideas about crime and safety in rural areas. Drawing upon international literature and the Swedish context, the chapter presents the following 10 reasons why crime and safety are relevant issues in a rural context.

1 Crime is not just an "urban problem."
2 Low crime rates in rural areas do not equate to "no problems."
3 Rural areas are heterogeneous entities.
4 Rural areas are in constant transformation.
5 The nature of rural areas influences crime.
6 Perceived safety is unequal.
7 Commodification of security in rural areas is taking place.
8 Crime prevention is urban-centered.
9 An intersectional gendered perspective of safety in rural context is needed.
10 Crime and safety are important dimensions of sustainable rural development.

These 10 reasons are discussed in detail in the following pages.

1 Crime is not just an "urban problem"

The claim that "crime is an urban problem" may not sound unreasonable, but it assumes that crime is primarily an urban feature – which surely it is not. To explore this issue, the idea of *rural idyll*, another rural myth, can be helpful. *Rural idyll* (Bell, 2006) conceptualizes the perceptions that rural areas are safe, quiet places without conflict. People's perceptions of rural areas as being free of crime are important in defining rurality. Common ideas concerning a rural idyll, encouraged by "country living" magazines, for example, are beliefs that keep the idyllic image alive. The idea of rural myth can be found anywhere on the globe: from England to Argentina, from Sweden to Australia. In Australia, for instance, rural idyll is reinforced by ideas of "the rural" consisting of simple, harmonious, cohesive, and homogeneous communities surrounded by a hinterland of farmers and ranchers, with little or no conflict (Lockie & Bourke, 2001; Squire, 1993; Wangüemert, 2001). Thus, these rural areas are thought to be, by nature, immune to crime and superior to urban areas.

The idyllic image of rural has been both reinforced and contested in fiction (art and moving pictures) as well by media coverage of our everyday lives. In Sweden, Astrid Lindgren's books depict the idyllic side of the Scandinavian countryside, while various contemporary works of fiction from around the country have challenged this idyllic image. Recent examples include a series of novels by Åsa Larsson, who defies the idyll in direct relation to the hectic capital city of Sweden. Her main character leaves the career-driven life of a Stockholm lawyer for a supposedly idyllic village in northern Sweden. Soon she is hit by the reality of the place. The landscape is vast between human settlements and deadly cold, priests are murdered, sects are revealed, victims are found on top of and under the ice. Internationally, perhaps one of the most well-known works of fiction that clearly illustrates the pitfalls of assuming "crime is an urban problem" is Sir Arthur Conan Doyle's *The Adventure of the Copper Beeches*,[1] a Sherlock Holmes story. The excerpt below is a conversation between Sherlock Holmes and his assistant Dr. Watson, traveling by train through the English countryside.[2]

All over the countryside, away to the rolling hills around Aldershot, the little red and grey roofs of the farm-steadings peeped out from amid the light green of the new foliage.

"Are they not fresh and beautiful?" Watson cried with all the enthusiasm of a man fresh from the fogs of Baker Street.

But Holmes shook his head gravely. "Do you know, Watson," said Holmes, "that it is one of the curses of a mind with a turn like mine that I must look at everything with reference to my own special subject. You look at these scattered houses, and you are impressed by their beauty. I look at them, and the only thought which comes to me is a feeling of their isolation and of the impunity with which crime may be committed there."

"Good heavens!" Watson cried. "Who would associate crime with these dear old homesteads?"

"They always fill me with a certain horror. It is my belief, Watson, founded upon my experience, that the lowest and vilest alleys in London do not present a more dreadful record of sin than does the smiling and beautiful countryside."

"You horrify me!" replied Watson.

Fiction writers and journalists are not the only parties guilty of propagating images of the rural idyll. In a recent article using Sweden as a case study, Jansson (2013, p. 91) illustrates how the media plays a key role in the hegemonic process to define the centers (the urban) and the margins (the rural) of society. The survey shows that the countryside is understood as misrepresented by the media, whereas the city is understood as much too positively represented: "whereas life in the countryside is predominantly associated with *high quality of life, local engagement, solidarity*, and *work ethics*, life in Swedish cities is associated with *openness to new ideas* and *global engagement*." The author also shows how the hegemony of the urban–rural divide is constructed through social practices, notably mobility and place making, and examples of everyday culture and media.

In academia, the distorted image of the rural is far from new. Research of the rural has been dominated by romantic images of the countryside (for a review, see e.g., Woods, 2011). In criminology research, for instance, the duality between rural and urban has long been attributed to studies based on Tönnies' (1887) distinction between *gemeinschaft* and *gesellschaft*. This pair of concepts is normally translated as "community" and "society." *Gemeinschaft* is associated with more "community-oriented" values and virtuous, cohesive communities, while *gesellschaft* is linked to more "individualistic" forms of thought and practice (Inglis, 2014). As suggested by Donnermeyer and DeKeseredy (2008), *gemeinschaft* interpretations of rural space draw on the "rural idyll." They misinterpret crime in the rural context as either exceptional or a lagged effect of urbanization, never endemic to rural culture or rural communities. Moreover, Cloke and Little (1997) indicate that research on the rural has been fascinated with the neat morphological unit of the nucleated village and by an obsession with *gemeinschaft* social relations. According to Owen and Carrington (2015), these images compress the richness of rurality into a homogenizing template, neglecting the existence of "other rurals" that embody different dimensions of the rural as suggested by Philo (1997, p. 22). As illustrated in this book, particularly in Chapters 8–10, there is a need to put into perspective the rural–urban dichotomy and to go beyond the naïve assumption of rural places as being free of crime. It is also worth investigating the potential "second myth" in the Swedish context, which portrays the countryside as dangerous and malevolent (Bell, 1997). While the rural idyll creates rural space as an object of desire because it is not urban, rural space may also be presented as an object of dread because it is not urban (Bell, 1997; Scott & Biron, 2010). This myth works to exaggerate rural "strangeness" and, in doing so, works to broaden the assumed gap which separates rural and urban life (Donnermeyer, Scott, & Carrington, 2013).

2 *Low crime rates in rural areas do not equate to "no problems"*

Another reason for caring about crime in rural areas is the assumption that "because there is less crime in the countryside, crime is not a problem for people living there" (Yarwood, 2001, p. 206). The problem is the way issues of rural crime and safety have been approached by their own discipline. Criminology is urban-biased, and it is no surprise that rural crime consistently ranks among the least studied social problems in criminology (DeKeseredy, 2015; Donnermeyer, 2012).

Although the risk of some crimes appears to be much greater in urban areas, other crimes, such as theft from motor vehicles, may be more of a problem for rural than urban residents (Marshall & Johnson, 2005). In Sweden, Ceccato and Dolmén (2011) also show a differentiated pattern of violent and property crime between urban and rural areas as well as within rural areas. In the 1990s, violent crimes, including homicides and assault, were also prevalent in some rural areas in the Baltic states of Estonia, Latvia, and Lithuania (Ceccato & Haining, 2008; Kerry, Goovaerts, Haining, & Ceccato, 2010). Rural areas in Australia show a higher rate of violent crime than property crime. Carcach (2000) found that in rural Australia, street violence was particularly prevalent in some remote rural regions.

Again, lower rates do not measure the impact crime and perceived safety have in a rural community. Even if they did, crime rates alone might be poor indicators of the problem encountered in rural areas. This is because the rate may be low because of low reporting rates, triggered by a number of factors. Long distances may affect reporting rates in rural areas. In Sweden, for instance, there are indications that police presence has declined since the mid-2000s. Lindström (2014) suggests that, from 2006 the number of police officers per capita declined nearly 10 percent in rural areas, while it increased by 3 percent in the rest of the country. For certain types of crime, the lack of anonymity in rural areas determines whether or not a crime is reported by a battered woman, for example (DeKeseredy, Dragiewicz, & Rennisson, 2012). In Australia, Barclay, Donnermeyer, and Jobes (2004) show that the reporting rate is lower because farmers have a high tolerance for several criminal behaviors. More important perhaps is to consider types of crime that most affect rural communities and how they individually impact particular groups. For some groups, an increase in crimes against property leads to a sense of insecurity regardless of the level of crime. For instance, the recent increase in thefts from farmers in Sweden is bound to have an impact on group behavior, their propensity to seek more protection, their perception of safety, and their trust in local authorities, especially the police (Lantbrukarnas Riksförbund, 2012).

Yet, it is not only quantity that matters but also the types of crime that occur in rural areas. A significant increase in thefts or vandalism in a rural municipality may have less of an effect on people's perceived safety than a single case of crime in the village. Individual serious crimes, such as murder, have a long-term effect on people's perceptions of safety and on the image of the community (see, for instance, Peste, 2011). Moreover, long-term neighbor disputes (Mackay & Moody, 1996) and chronic problems of social disorder (Coomber et al., 2011), while they may not turn into an act of crime, may damage the social capital of communities as much as crimes do.

3 Rural areas are heterogeneous entities

Rural areas in Europe are quite diverse not only geographically but also in terms of the different challenges they face (European Communities, 2008). This is just an example that it is a mistake to assume that patterns of crime are homogeneous across rural areas (Wells & Weisheit, 2004). The rural as a homogeneous entity is a notion commonly fed by mediated images of what is expected of urban and rural. In this context, Jansson (2013) argues that the problem is not to recognize what can be urban or rural in the traditional sense but to identify forgotten places that fall outside the dichotomous image of urban and rural: suburbs, small towns, and other in-between spaces. In a globalized media society, these landscapes seem to be the real "other places" and yet may be rural in some aspects and urban in others.

Another way to check the heterogeneity of rural areas is to assess the way crime comes about in these areas. The dynamics of rural areas vary according to their economic basis and socioeconomic composition (e.g., Persson & Ceccato, 2001), and through these characteristics crime may be seen as the tip of the iceberg of a number of other problems. In Sweden, predictors of crime in rural areas are not the same as those in urban areas. For instance, the proportion of foreign-born population and the population growth rate tend to explain theft rates in urban areas but not in rural areas (Ceccato & Dolmén, 2011). In the United States, Osgood and Chambers (2003) found a feature of non-metropolitan counties that distinguished them from metropolitan counties, namely, that poverty and population mobility were negatively correlated in rural areas, whereas the relationship was positive in the urban setting. In rural areas, rates of juvenile violence varied markedly with population size: counties with the smallest juvenile populations showed exceptionally low arrest rates. Social factors, such as family structure, are more important as predictors of crime than economic ones are in non-urban areas (for a review, see Wells and Weisheit, 2004). In Germany, Entorf and Spengler (2000) also found different crime patterns in west and east Germany, where some criminal activities are triggered by distinct criminogenic conditions over time and space.

Nevertheless, some of these patterns may reflect something more fluid than place-centered explanations of crime such as population composition or poverty. Crime may be influenced by criminogenic networks that connect individuals without paying attention to territories or geographical borders. Some are local networks, such as drugs commercialized by youth gangs; others can be large regional criminal networks. In Italy, for instance, regional patterns of crime have to be assessed taking into account the existence of regional crime organizations, with a north and south divide (Cracolici & Uberti, 2009). Along similar lines, differentiated patterns of violence particularly in the United States have been suggested to reflect cultural differences in values, norms, and beliefs held by members of groups or subgroups (Messner & Rosenfeld, 1999). It is believed that some subcultures provide greater normative support for violence than others (Corzine, Corzine, & Whitt, 1999). The existence of differences in violence between ethnic groups is the subject of controversy among researchers (Farrington, Loeber, & Southamer-Loeber, 2003) but has been suggested as one explanation for large regional differences in homicide rates in some countries (Ceccato, 2014a).

Rural areas are not homogeneous entities, because rural crime also varies over time. Rural touristic municipalities tend to experience seasonal variations in crime rates, often depending on visitor inflows. Such municipalities also tend to have a number of service sectors (restaurants, hotels) that are not found in municipalities with a more traditional "old" economic structure (mining, forestry). Ski resorts in the winter and summer destinations and municipalities are examples of this dynamic illustrated by Ceccato and Dolmén (2013) and are further discussed in Chapter 4.

4 Rural areas are in constant transformation

As much as 41 percent of the European population lives in urban regions, 35 percent in intermediate regions, and 23 percent in rural regions (Eurostat, 2012).[3] The shift from agricultural production toward a multifunctional landscape and the increasing value assigned to environmental values has affected European rural areas. Even in the predominantly rural regions nowadays agriculture contributes less than 15 percent to the total production and income generated (van Leeuwen, 2010). Eurostat, the statistical office of the European Union, recently published figures on the distribution of the European population across 27 countries based on a new urban–rural typology that analyzes population density and total population. Interestingly, the highest population growth in urban regions was observed in Scandinavia; the highest rates were in Sweden (an increase of 17.3 percent per capita), Finland (10 percent), and Denmark (5 percent). The Baltic countries showed an increase in the opposite direction, from urban to non-urban areas. The rural population in the United States, United Kingdom, and Australia was last measured at 19, 18, and 11 percent, respectively, according to the World Bank (2012).

Rural areas are undergoing a number of changes, often dictated by forces far beyond their local reality (Shortall & Warner, 2012; Woods, 2011). In the United States, Krannich, Luloff, and Field (2011) illustrate how aesthetic values of rural landscapes have been coupled with the forces of commodity industry. In some cases the restructuring process has forced rural communities to move away from traditional economies toward more diversified local employment bases. Crime is part of the transformation occurring at different paces and on various scales around the rural world. The urban–rural relationship is changing (Johansson, Westlund, & Eliasson, 2009). In Sweden, the redistribution of the population from small villages to larger cities that has taken place in the past three decades affects people's routines and their risks of becoming a target for crime. In Sweden, it seems that such a development does not follow urbanization or counterurbanization or gentrification processes in the strict sense, as has been found in the United Kingdom and elsewhere (Amcoff & Westholm, 2007; Johansson et al., 2009). Ceccato and Dolmén (2011) suggest that the population redistribution can be associated with crime in several ways. In the long run, population shifts affect density of "acquaintanceship," that is, the degree to which members of the community know each other (Weisheit & Donnermeyer, 2000). If people move out, such ties are broken, which may generate socioeconomic instability and, in the long run, support conditions favoring crime (Kim & Pridemore, 2005). Community life may be particularly affected when emigration is selective (young people, female), often leaving behind poorly educated middle-aged or elderly males.

Rural areas are becoming more similar to urban areas both socially and economically (Ceccato & Dolmén, 2011). As in other parts of the world, Sweden shows signs of an emergence of a "post-productivist countryside" that differs from the agri-industrial landscapes of "conventional" agriculture (Ilbery & Bowler, 1998; Marsden, 1998). The exchange that occurs through media, migration, and daily commuting, connecting people near and far (Westholm, 2008), are examples of this new economic landscape. Moreover, urban–rural relationships are being redefined by the use of ICT, such as the Internet and cell phones, making crime less dependent on physical space. In 2010, as many as 91 percent of Swedes had access to the Internet at home, compared with 79 percent in 2004. ICT has meant new opportunities but also new dangers. This development imposes new challenges for crime prevention, because law enforcement authorities have to deal with offenders and victims who may reside far from their territorial jurisdiction. On the other hand, social media (Twitter, Facebook) have become a tool for community policing, allowing the residents themselves to engage in daily police work.

These transformations are not specific to the Global North (Siwale, 2014; Tapiador, 2008; Woods, 2011). Scorzafave, Justus, and Shikida (2015) show for example that, although less than 14 percent of the Brazilian population lives in rural areas today this population is experiencing an increase in violence. They show that, in some cases, violence growth rates are steeper in rural areas. Attempted robbery is the crime for which the highest growth rate was observed, but high growth rates were also registered for other crimes. The development process in Brazil is integrating rural and urban areas. Criminality is spreading to rural areas. This poses new challenges to public safety policy, because most public services are centralized in large cities. Small towns and rural areas need more investment to change this situation. Scorzafave et al. (2015) suggest that small towns and rural areas need more public services that help prevent crimes (e.g., schools, cultural centers) and more law enforcement services (e.g., police stations, video surveillance equipment, police officers).

5 The nature of rural areas influences crime

Rural crimes are crimes that take place in rural contexts. Some are ordinary crimes such as burglary and fights, while others are more specifically related to the opportunities for crime that only occur in rural areas. Rural crime includes farm crime, such as the theft of tractors or cattle, but also crimes against nature and wildlife. The reasons why people commit crime in rural areas are certainly not different from the reasons in urban areas. Yet, some opportunities for crime will be more typical in rural areas than in urban, and vice versa.

Certain crime opportunities or targets may only be present in rural areas, such as forests and farms. It is no surprise that hot spots of diesel theft from tractors are concentrated in farm-based municipalities. In other cases, a lack of presence of people or poor surveillance makes certain crimes easier to commit in rural areas. Low population density affects crime opportunities and detection. As Felson (2013) suggests, population density and population movement during the course of the day transmit information about crime events quite independently of mass media or personal networks.

If people are not present, some crimes may go undetected for some time, for instance, the dumping of garbage in forests (Ceccato & Uittenbogaard, 2013). Other conditions that may promote crime in rural areas is the high tolerance for certain types of behavior and crime itself among individuals of the local community (Barclay et al., 2004; Barclay, Scott, Hogg, & Donnermeyer, 2007). Distance from police stations as well as cultural factors are behind such differences in the willingness to report an offense. The population's willingness to report crime in Sweden is relatively high (BRÅ, 2008), but there are differences in reporting practices by type of crime (violence often being less reported than property crimes) and by region, with urban areas having the highest propensity to report offenses (BRÅ, 2008). Farmers avoid reporting if the offense is not serious (Lantbrukarnas Riksförbund, 2012). Because of a perceived lack of anonymity in rural areas, victims may refrain from contact with local authorities, including the police.

In rural areas, women are less likely to report violence, for numerous reasons (e.g., DeKeseredy, Donnermeyer, Schwartz, Tunnell, & Hall, 2007). For instance, long distances create isolation to a greater degree than in urban areas. This book discusses in detail the barriers that women living in rural areas face when reporting violence when the perpetrator is known to the victim. Internationally, the literature suggests that such social isolation can be particularly problematic for ethnic minority groups when seeking advice and reporting racial discrimination and abuse (Chakraborti & Garland, 2011; Garland & Chakraborti, 2006, 2012; Greenfields, 2014; Robinson & Gardner, 2012). These issues call for better knowledge of the nature of crime in rural areas.

6 Perceived safety is unequal

It may be no surprise that people living in rural areas declare overall that they feel safer than people living in urban areas do. Higher rates of victimization in larger cities are often pointed out as an explanation of lower perceptions of safety (BRÅ, 2011; Skogan, 1990). Yet, looking more closely at this phenomenon, perceived safety shows a patchier pattern, with a nature that is harder to grasp than expected, something that can be heterogeneous across space and time and between groups. One way forward is to assume that, as suggested by Hope and Sparks (2000), people's responses to risk are formed not only in relation to their sense of place, where place refers to the immediate settings and conditions of their daily life, but also in relation to their sense of its place in a larger societal set of stories, conflicts, troubles, and insecurities. Yet, why do people declare lower fear of victimization in rural areas?

A reason for high declared safety in rural areas might be the low population density that characterizes them. Felson (2013, p. 356) recognizes that associating population density and crime rates is not problem-free, as many low-density cities might show high crime rates, though places with higher population density are often perceived as more dangerous and problematical. Felson points out that "perception has a structure" based on density of people. He adds:

> two cities have identical population sizes and crime rates. The first city is a "convergent city" ... the second one is characterized by urban sprawl ... in the convergent city crimes will impinge on a larger number of persons because the sights and sounds about those crimes will reach people.

Following this reasoning, individuals living in rural areas would be less affected by crime and its consequences, including the "buzz" suggested by Felson (2013), than those living in highly dense places, such as urban areas. Zaluar (2012), discussing levels of fear in urban *favelas* in Brazil, suggests that, even within urban areas, the "noise" that triggers fear is uneven. She notes that even when the sound of gunfire is heard more than seen, the noise, and the fear it produces, is unevenly distributed between neighborhoods. The richest areas are the ones where gunfire is heard less. Some of the poorest areas, where trafficking gangs dominate most of the *favela*, are those with the most gunfire noise and where people declare feeling most in fear.

Yet, some factors that impact perceived safety are more tangible, such as victimization. Inequality in victimization between groups reveals a picture different from this homogeneous pattern of rural safety. Fear reflects unbalanced levels of victimization, in which the poor are overrepresented among crime victims (BRÅ, 2014; Nilsson & Estrada, 2006; Tseloni, Mailley, Farrell, & Tilley, 2010). Thus, individuals' fears reflect their immediate settings and conditions of their daily life, but also their sense of their place in a larger societal context (Hope & Sparks, 2000). In Sweden, for instance, the poor who are victims of crime reveal more anxieties than wealthier groups in Sweden (Nilsson & Estrada, 2006). Although the poor are overrepresented in some large Swedish cities, such as Stockholm, Malmö, and Gothenburg, little is known about fear of crime and other potential anxieties that go under the label "poor perceived safety" among vulnerable groups living in rural areas. In Sweden, Bäckman, Nilsson, and Fritzell (2008) show that the mortality rate is higher among socially excluded young adults in rural areas than their counterparts in big cities. International literature confirms that this process goes along with long-term social and economic exclusion and discrimination that occur by gender, ethnicity, and residents versus newcomers (Babacan, 2012; Chakraborti

& Garland, 2011; Jensen, 2012; Scott, Carrington, & McIntosh, 2012). Fear, in this case, as suggested by Pain and Smith (2008), is central to the terrain of everyday lived experience, rather than a straightforward relationship between the individual and a variety of societal structures; it is embedded in a network of moral and political geographies.

Perceived safety is also impacted by the environments in which we spend time. In Sweden, for instance, in the past few decades a shrinking labor market in smaller municipalities has imposed changes on people's routines. Some choose to move to larger municipalities where the jobs are. Changes in people's routine activities may affect their risk of victimization and perceived safety. The situation becomes especially problematic in remote rural areas that are relatively far from the major labor markets. Safety is also relevant, as one in five employees in Europe spends at least one hour traveling to and from work each way. This means many hours are spent on trains and buses or in transit (Ceccato, 2014b).

Fear can also be revealed by silence. Examples in this book discuss the differences in reported rates of domestic violence across Sweden as a sign of differences in gender contracts. Low rates of reported violence against women can be associated with a silence code imposed by patriarchal community values and a fear of ostracism if violence becomes public (DeKeseredy et al., 2012).

There might be other sources of fear that generate silence. One example is the despair of police authorities, as victims and witnesses rarely cooperate with them when they know crimes have been committed by organized gangs. Motorcycle groups, typical of some rural areas in Sweden, are examples of these criminal groups. In summary, Part III of this book attempts to look beyond actual statistics on perceived safety between rural and urban areas in order to shed light on the nature of fear among groups of people living in rural areas.

7 *Commodification of security in rural areas is taking place*

Commodification of rural areas is perhaps more often associated with rural tourism and the inflow of temporary population. How can the rural be commodified? As Woods (2011, p. 95) suggests, "an object becomes a commodity when its exchange value, the price that consumers are prepared to pay for the object, exceeds its use value"; "it also takes place when entities that have not traditionally been considered in economic terms are ascribed with an economic value." Commodities can take different shapes, such as paying for observing a landscape or patting animals. Rural commodification has been occurring since the 1980s across the globe relying on global capital flows and a complex network of local and global actors (Mackay & Perkins, 2013; Woods, 2011; Woods, Flemmen, & Wollan, 2014).

Rural tourism has a safety dimension on top of the economic, social, and environmental ones. Rural tourism can be defined as "touristic activities that are focused on the consumption of rural landscapes, artifacts, cultures, and experiences, involving different degrees of engagement and performance";

"rural tourism involves the consumption of rural signifiers as participants seek connection with an imagined idea of the rural" (Woods, 2011, p. 954). New criminogenic conditions are created with these activities that would not otherwise occur in these places. For instance, people create new routine activities in these places; they gather in newly created leisure centers where festivities take place and they leave their cars in adjacent parking lots. Extra police forces are often called from neighboring cities to support big events that attract many people.

Another dimension of the rural commodification is the development of residential neighborhoods in rural areas targeting a specific demand from buyers. This may take the form of counterurbanization, as people leave cities in a search for the attractions of the countryside (Brown & Glasgow, 2008) but also gentrification of the rural. In extreme cases, new housing developments are built to satisfy the demands of certain groups. Countries in the Global South show examples where gated communities are not only found in urban areas but have also increasingly become a part of the countryside (Spocter, 2013). The extraction of amenity value from the rural landscape happens as people are willing to pay extra to enjoy the quiet of rural gated communities. The so-called "free-of-crime zones" are ensured by high walls, private guards, and modern security systems.

Finally, a third dimension of the commodification of rural areas is privatization of security provision. As discussed in Chapter 11, private security companies provide services for private enterprises and the state as well as municipalities and individuals. Private security is not a new phenomenon, nor has its expansion gone unnoticed, but nowadays private security organizations have taken over a number of responsibilities that used to be associated with the public sector, in other words, law enforcement. As the presence and impact of commercial security actors increase, the roles and functions conventionally ascribed to the state are being transformed, as new geographies of power and influence take form (Berndtsson & Stern, 2011).

In Sweden, the centralization of the police now taking place (Lindström, 2014) is following a parallel process of privatization of security provision. It is uncertain whether this process will affect the nature of security as a public good, because security companies are taking over a number of duties previously ascribed to the police, especially in rural areas. Public goods are provided collectively, partly because their benefits, by definition, are not limited to those who are willing and/or able to pay for them (non-excludability principle). Likewise, to be a real public good, security should satisfy the principle of non-rivalry, which means that the consumption of that public good by any individual will not reduce its availability to others in society (Ceccato, 2014b). However, the way security is provided, produced, and consumed in rural areas (by the development of rural tourism, gated housing settlements, and privatization of policing) puts in doubt the idea of security as a truly public good. As it is now, security in rural areas is instead increasingly becoming a commodity and, as such, not attained by all.

8 Crime prevention is urban-centered

There is no disagreement that crime prevention should fit the nature of the crime and the context of the crime, even as it happens in rural areas. However, for various reasons crime prevention in rural areas tends to deal with problems that are more relevant for large cities than for the rural areas themselves. In Sweden, youth riots, such as those that took place in Stockholm and Malmö in 2013, are never witnessed in rural municipalities, although they constitute youth violence. Yet, youth violence has been considered by local crime prevention councils as the most important crime problem in rural municipalities (Ceccato & Dolmén, 2013). Similarly, neighbourhood watch schemes and safety audits have been important examples of community safety practices in rural areas. Most of these crime prevention models are imported from urban areas to rural ones as examples of good practice, with little concern about potential differences in contexts (Ceccato & Dolmén, 2013). In the Swedish context, the implementation of community safety schemes based on local partnerships (composed of police representatives, the municipality, local business, local associations, individual members of the community) went hand in hand with the overall decentralization of the police in the mid-1990s. Twenty years later, a centralization process is culminating in a new police organization in early 2015, which is bound to have an effect on the way policing takes place across the country. This issue is further discussed in Part V of this book.

The lack of attention at the national level to crime in rural areas and its prevention is not unique to Sweden. In European countries, the rural dimension has been omitted in the evaluation of safety and crime prevention policies in Europe; see, for instance, Robert (2010). This fact may be related to issues that make society as a whole perceive rural areas and rural crime as less important than crime in urban and metropolitan areas, where most people live. The perception, again, is fed by lower crime rates and the idea that rural areas are safe places. Other factors may be structural frameworks in national crime prevention documents that guide intervention toward where the problems are – in other words, urban areas. These are possible reasons for the urban focus that, for the time being, characterizes most local crime prevention councils in Sweden.

9 An intersectional gendered perspective of safety in a rural context is needed

There is a need to investigate intersectionality in victimization in rural contexts. Chapter 10 of this book illustrates how women from minorities seem to be at higher risk for violence than other groups in Australia, the United States, and Bangladesh, just to name a few. There is no doubt about the current need for research that is sensitive to how, when, and why gender intersects with age, class, and ethnic belonging, which together result in poor perceived safety. The intersections of these different dimensions have been studied for some time. According to Thompson (2002), intersectionality of gender, age, ethnicity, and the like was first named by Kimberlé Crenshaw in the late 1980s, though the concept can be traced back to the nineteenth century; it became popular in sociology in the late 1960s and early 1970s in conjunction with the multiracial feminist movement in the United States.

According to Davis (2008), intersectionality as a theoretical framework attempts to explain how race, class, ability, gender, health status – and even other dimensions of identity such as social practices, institutional arrangements, and cultural ideologies – intersect to generate an outcome that goes beyond a one-dimensional perspective of identity. Expressions of intersectionality in violence against women are shown in Chapter 10 of this book. Several authors in different parts of the world report special difficulties of battered immigrant women in rural areas. Yet another author reminds readers that the situation of immigrant women may be more complicated than that of poor native women because often "the domestic violence victim is dependent upon her batterer for her continued residence in the country via a conditional visa." Rural immigrant women may also be hampered by a limited knowledge of the language as well as strong cultural influences in which women are taught to defer to their husbands. For further theoretical guidance, see Treloar (2014). Thus, it is argued in this book that intersectionality as an analytic tool can also be useful to other groups that are overrepresented among victims (and perpetrators): males, the young, poor, and ill. For instance, Chapter 11 illustrates the layers of vulnerability of young individuals who see crime as a form of conflict resolution in places where a sense of belonging is perceived as poor.

10 Crime and safety are important dimensions of sustainable rural development

Researchers and experts have long recognized crime and fear as important challenges in creating sustainable communities. An unsustainable environment is commonly characterized by "images of poverty, physical deterioration, increasing levels of crime, and perceived fear of crime" (Cozens, 2002, p. 131). Despite such importance, the social dimension of sustainable development is underrepresented among the environmental and economic dimensions in rural contexts.

As a process, sustainable development is thought to be dependent on people's attitudes with daily practices, as it is considered the path to amend unsustainabilities (Coral, 2009).

> [Sustainable development] consists of a development process among other things that leads to a society in which all present and future humans have their basic needs met and in which everyone has fair and equitable access to the earth's resources, a decent quality of life, and celebrates cultural diversity.[4]

In practice, Greed (2012, p. 219) believes that so far sustainability-driven policies are working against inclusive, equitable, and accessible places. She notes, "sustainability policy is set at too high a level to engage with the realities of everyday life." Since the 1990s, academic discourse has promoted and challenged the sustainability of rural areas in relation to a number of issues, such as energy, tourism, food production, and ecological entrepreneurship (Butler, 1991; Kaygusuz, 2011; Munday, Bristow, & Cowell, 2011; Tovey, 1997). Research on social sustainable development of rural areas has mostly concentrated on urban agriculture, social capital, and ecotourism (Ferris, Norman, & Sempik, 2001; Woolcock & Narayan, 2000).

It should come as no surprise that crime and safety are neglected in rural research studies that focus on what is called the social dimension of sustainable development (but see Carrington, Hogg, & McIntosh, 2011; Glasson & Cozens, 2011; Smith & McElwee, 2013). Although the studies by Carrington et al. (2011) and Smith and McElwee (2013) do not mention sustainable development as such, the impact of economic development on social and environmental dimensions of the localities is discussed in a way pertinent to sustainable development. The third study by Smith and McElwee (2013) is methodological and explores the coverage of crime and safety issues in the history of Environmental Impact Assessment (EIA) and similar documents, then considers several issues for advancing better practice in crime prevention using an impact assessment framework.

In practice, dealing with the problems of crime and community safety as dimensions of rural sustainable development requires a clearer definition of the roles of public and private actors in providing security as well as a better understanding of the roles of civil society and governments in balancing all goals of sustainability on various spatial scales (local, regional, national, and supranational). Chapters 8 and 12 of this book touch briefly on conflicts between the economic and social dimensions of sustainable development as illustrated in cases of environmental harm and wildlife crime.

Concluding remarks

In contrast to urban areas, rural areas are regarded as a retreat from the problems of urban living, including crime. Such areas are characterized as places where people reside closer to nature, in cohesive communities. This chapter attempts to untangle this simplistic view of rural areas by discussing a number of issues that show facets of rural areas as both safe and criminogenic. For instance, crime and safety in rural areas is a subject worth examining in its own right, because rural areas are in constant transformation across space and over time, and such dynamics sometimes create new opportunities for crime. Another important reason among those discussed previously in this chapter is the nature of perceived safety. Low crime rates, typical of rural areas, do not necessarily mean safety for all if victimization is unequally distributed, perhaps even concentrated among a specific group. Furthermore, safety is a reflexive phenomenon that depends on those who define it, something that goes beyond victimization. Whether or not rural areas are proven to be safer than urban areas, what is important is that low crime rates already put them at a great advantage in terms of attractiveness and sustainability – and this is in itself a good starting point.

Notes

1 See http://bakerstreet.wikia.com/wiki/Story_Text:_The_Adventure_of_the_Copper_ Beeches, retrieved January 30, 2015.
2 The author is grateful to Richard Wortley, a declared Holmes fan, who cordially shared this inspirational quote when this book was in its initial stages of being written.
3 The urban–rural typology is based on a classification of grid cells of 1 km². An area that has a population density of at least 300 inhabitants per km² and a minimum population of 5,000 inhabitants in contiguous cells above that density threshold is classified as urban; the other cells are considered rural. An intermediate region has its population in grid cells that are classified as urban equal 50–80 percent of the total population, while a predominantly rural region comprises a population in grid cells that are classified as rural equal to 50 percent or more of the total population. For further information, see: http://epp.eurostat.ec.europa.eu/portal/page/portal/rural_development/introduction and http://epp.eurostat.ec.europa.eu/statistics_explained/index.php/Regional_typologies_overview (retrieved April 7, 2015).
4 See http://hdr.undp.org/en (retrieved April 7 2015).

References

Amcoff, J., & Westholm, E. (2007). Understanding rural change: Demography as a key to the future. *Futures, 39*(4), 363–379.

Babacan, H. (2012). Racism denial in Australia: The power of silence. *Australian Mosaic, 32*, 1–3.

Bäckman, O., Nilsson, A., & Fritzell, J. (2008). Marginalisering och uppväxtvillkor. *Framtider, 4*, 21–23.

Barclay, E., Donnermeyer, J. F., & Jobes, P. C. (2004). The dark side of gemeinschaft: Criminality within rural communities. *Crime Prevention and Community Safety, 6*(3), 7–22.

Barclay, E., Scott, J., Hogg, R., & Donnermeyer, J. (Eds.). (2007). *Crime in rural Australia*. Sydney: Federation Press.

Bell, D. (1997). Anti-idyll: Rural horror. In P. Cloke & J. Litte (Eds.), *Contested countryside cultures: Otherness, marginalisation and rurality* (pp. 94–108). London: Routledge.

Bell, D. (2006). Variation on the rural idyll. In P. Cloke, T. Marsden, & P. Mooney (Eds.), *Handbook of rural studies* (pp. 149–160). London: Sage.

Berndtsson, J., & Stern, M. (2011). Private security and the public–private divide: Contested lines of distinction and modes of governance in the Stockholm-Arlanda Security Assemblage. *International Political Sociology, 5*(4), 408–425.

Brandth, B. (1995). Rural masculinity in transition: Gender images in tractor advertisements. *Journal of Rural Studies, 11*(2), 123–133.

Brown, D. L., & Glasgow, N. (2008). *Rural retirement migration*. Dordrecht: Springer.

Brottsförebyggande rådet – BRÅ (National Council of Crime Prevention). (2008). Nationella trygghetsundersökningen 2007: Om utsatthet, trygghet och förtroende. Stockholm: BRÅ.

Brottsförebyggande rådet – BRÅ (National Council of Crime Prevention). (2011). The national victims survey. Stockholm: BRÅ.

Brottsförebyggande rådet – BRÅ (National Council of Crime Prevention). (2014). Nationella trygghetsundersökningen 2006–2013. Stockholm: BRÅ.

Butler, R. W. (1991). Tourism, environment, and sustainable development. *Environmental Conservation, 18*(03), 201–209.

Carcach, C. (2000). Size, accessibility and crime in regional Australia. *Trends and issues in crime and criminal justice* (Vol. 175). Canberra: Australian Institute of Criminology.

Carrington, K., Hogg, R., & McIntosh, A. (2011). The resource boom's underbelly: Criminological impacts of mining development. *Australian and New Zealand Journal of Criminology, 44*(3), 335–354.

Ceccato, V. (2014a). The geographic, socioeconomic, and cultural determinants of violence. In P. D. Donnelly & C. L. Ward (Eds.), *Oxford textbook of violence prevention: Epidemiology, evidence, and policy* (pp. 77–86). Oxford: Oxford.

Ceccato, V. (2014b). Safety on the move: Crime and perceived safety in transit environments. *Security Journal, 27*(2), 127–131.

Ceccato, V., & Dolmén, L. (2011). Crime in rural Sweden. *Applied Geography, 31*(1), 119–135.

Ceccato, V., & Dolmén, L. (2013). Crime prevention in rural Sweden. *European Journal of Criminology, 10*, 89–112.

Ceccato, V., & Haining, R. (2008). Short and medium term dynamics and their influence on acquisitive crime rates in the transition states of Estonia, Latvia and Lithuania. *Applied Spatial Analysis and Policy, 1*(3), 215–244.

Ceccato, V., & Uittenbogaard, A. C. (2013). Environmental and wildlife crime in Sweden. *International Journal of Rural Criminology, 2*(1), 23–50.

Chakraborti, N., & Garland, J. (Eds.). (2011). *Rural racism.* Abingdon/New York: Routledge.

Cloke, P., & Little, J. (1997). *Contested countryside cultures: Otherness marginalisation and rurality.* London: Routledge.

Collins, P. H. (2000). Gender, black feminism, and black political economy. *ANNALS of the American Academy of Political and Social Science, 568*(1), 41–53.

Coomber, K., Toumbourou, J. W., Miller, P., Staiger, P. K., Hemphill, S. A., & Catalano, R. F. (2011). Rural adolescent alcohol, tobacco, and illicit drug use: A comparison of students in Victoria, Australia, and Washington State, United States. *Journal of Rural Health, 27*(4), 409–415.

Coral, J. S. (2009). Engineering education for a sustainable future (PhD, Universitat Politecnica de Catalunya, Barcelona).

Corzine, J., Corzine, L. H., & Whitt, H. P. (1999). Cultural and subcultural theories of homicide. In M. D. Smith & M. A. Zahn (Eds.), *Homicide: A sourcebook of social research* (pp. 42–58). London: Sage.

Cozens, P. M. (2002). Sustainable urban development and crime prevention through environmental design for the British city: Towards an effective urban environmentalism for the 21st century. *Cities, 19*(2), 129–137.

Cracolici, M. F., & Uberti, T. E. (2009). Geographical distribution of crime in Italian provinces: A spatial econometric analysis. *Jahrbuch für Regionalwissenschaft, 29*(1), 1–28.

Davis, K. (2008). Intersectionality as buzzword: A sociology of science perspective on what makes a feminist theory successful. *Feminist Theory, 9*(1), 67–85.

DeKeseredy, W. S. (2015). New directions in feminist understandings of rural crime and social control. *Journal of Rural Studies* (in press).

DeKeseredy, W. S., Donnermeyer, J. F., Schwartz, M. D., Tunnell, K., & Hall, M. (2007). Thinking critically about rural gender relations: Toward a rural masculinity crisis/male peer support model of separation/divorce sexual assault. *Critical Criminology, 15*(4), 295–311.

DeKeseredy, W. S., Dragiewicz, M., & Rennisson, C. M. (2012). Racial/ethnic variations in violence against women: Urban, suburban, and rural differences. *International Journal of Rural Criminology, 1*(2), 184–202.

Donnermeyer, D., & DeKeseredy, W. S. (2008). Toward a rural critical criminology. *Southern Rural Sociology, 23*(2), 4–28.

Donnermeyer, J. (2012). Rural crime and critical criminology. In W. S. DeKeseredy & M. Dragiewicz (Eds.), *Routledge handbook of critical criminology* (pp. 290–302). Abingdon: Routledge.

Donnermeyer, J., Scott, J., & Carrington, K. (2013). How rural criminology informs critical thinking in criminology. *International Journal for Crime, Justice and Social Democracy, 2*(3), 69–91.

Entorf, H., & Spengler, H. (2000). Socioeconomic and demographic factors of crime in Germany: Evidence from panel data of the German states. *International Review of Law and Economics, 20*(1), 75–106.

European Communities. (2008). EU rural development policy 2007–2013. Fact Sheet. Office for Official Publications of the European Communities, Luxembourg.

Eurostat. (2012). Urban–intermediate–rural regions [Press release].

Farrington, D., Loeber, R., & Southamer-Loeber, M. (2003). How can the relationship between race and violence be explained? In D. F. Hawkins (Ed.), *Violent crime: Assessing race and ethnic differences* (pp. 213–237). Cambridge: Cambridge University Press.

Felson, M. (2013). Crime's impingement in space. In S. Ruiter, W. Bernasco, W. Huisman, & G. Bruinsma (Eds.), *Eenvoud en verscheidenheid: Liber amicorum voor Henk Elffers* (pp. 341–355). Amsterdam: NSCR & Afdeling Criminologie Vrije Universiteit Amsterdam.

Ferris, J., Norman, C., & Sempik, J. (2001). People, land and sustainability: Community gardens and the social dimension of sustainable development. *Social Policy and Administration, 35*(5), 559–568.

Forsberg, G., & Stenbacka, S. (2013). Mapping gendered ruralities *European Countryside, 5*, 1.

Garland, J., & Chakraborti, N. (2006). "Race", space and place: Examining identity and cultures of exclusion in rural England. *Ethnicities, 6*(2), 159–177.

Garland, J., & Chakraborti, N. (2012). Another country? Community, belonging and exclusion in rural England. In N. Chakraborti & J. Garland (Eds.), *Rural racism* (pp. 122–140). Abingdon/New York: Routledge.

Glasson, J., & Cozens, P. (2011). Making communities safer from crime: An undervalued element in impact assessment. *Environmental Impact Assessment Review, 31*(1), 25–35.

Greed, C. (2012). Planning for sustainable transport or for people's needs. *Proceedings of the ICE: Urban Design and Planning, 165*, 219–229.

Greenfields, M. (2014). Gypsies and travellers in modern rural England. In G. Bosworth & P. Somerville (Eds.), *Interpreting rurality: Multidisciplinary approaches* (pp. 219–234). London/New York: Routledge.

Halfacree, K. (1993). Locality and social representation: Space, discourse and alternative definitions of the rural. *Journal of Rural Studies, 9*(1), 23–37.

Hope, T., & Sparks, R. (2000). *Crime, risk, and insecurity: Law and order in everyday life and political discourse.* London: Routledge.

Ilbery, B., & Bowler, I. (1998). From agricultural productivism to post-productivism. In B. Ilbery (Ed.), *The geography of rural change* (pp. 53–83). Harlow: Addison Wesley Longman.

Inglis, D. (2014). Gemeinschaft and gesellschaft. *The encyclopedia of political thought* (pp. 1438–1440). London: John Wiley & Sons.

Jansson, A. (2013). The hegemony of the urban/rural divide: Cultural transformations and mediatized moral geographies in Sweden. *Space and Culture, 16*(1), 88–103.

Jensen, M. (2012). Rasism, missnöje och "fertile grounds" Östergötland Sverige jämförs med Birkaland Finland: Sverigedemokraterna vs Sannfinländarna (Master's degree, Linköping University, Linköping). Retrieved April 8, 2015, from www.diva-portal.org/smash/record.jsf?pid=diva2:479299.

Johansson, M., Westlund, H., & Eliasson, K. (2009). The "new rurality" and entrepreneurship: Attributes influencing enterprise propensity in rural Sweden. Paper presented at the *Congress of Regional Science Association International*, Lodz, Poland.

Kaygusuz, K. (2011). Energy services and energy poverty for sustainable rural development. *Renewable and Sustainable Energy Reviews, 15*(2), 936–947.

Kerry, R., Goovaerts, P., Haining, R. P., & Ceccato, V. (2010). Applying geostatistical analysis to crime data: Car-related thefts in the Baltic states. *Geographical Analysis, 42*(1), 53–77.

Kim, S.-W., & Pridemore, W. A. (2005). Social change, institutional anomie and serious property crime in transitional Russia. *British Journal of Criminology, 45*(1), 81–97.

Krannich, R. S., Luloff, E., & Field, D. R. (2011). *People, places and landscapes: Social change in high amenity rural areas*. Dordrecht/Heidelberg/London/New York: Springer.

Lantbrukarnas Riksförbund (2012). Brott på landet: En undersökning bland lantbrukare (J. Johansson, Ed., p. 40). Stockholm: Sveriges Lantbruk.

Lindström, P. (2014). Police and crime in rural and small swedish municipalities. *Journal of Rural Studies* (submitted).

Lockie, S., & Bourke, L. (2001). *Rurality bites: The social and environmental transformation of rural Australia*. London: Pluto.

Mackay, M., & Perkins, H. (2013). Commodification and the making of a rural destination: Insights from Cromwell district, Central Otago, New Zealand. In J. Fountain & K. Moore (Eds.), *Tourism and global change: On the edge of something big* (pp. 494–496). Christchurch, New Zealand: Lincoln University.

Mackay, R. E., & Moody, S. R. (1996). Diversion of neighbourhood disputes to community mediation. *Howard Journal of Criminal Justice, 35*(4), 299–313.

Marsden, T. (1998). New rural territories: Regulating the differentiated rural spaces. *Journal of Rural Studies, 14*(1), 107–117.

Marshall, B., & Johnson, S. (2005). Crime in rural areas: A review of the literature for the rural evidence research centre. Jill Dando Institute of Crime Science, University College, London.

Messner, S., & Rosenfeld, R. (Eds.). (1999). *Social structure and homicide: Theory and research* (Vols. 27–34). London: Sage.

Munday, M., Bristow, G., & Cowell, R. (2011). Wind farms in rural areas: How far do community benefits from wind farms represent a local economic development opportunity? *Journal of Rural Studies, 27*(1), 1–12.

Nilsson, A., & Estrada, F. (2006). The inequality of victimization: Trends in exposure to crime among rich and poor. *European Journal of Criminology, 3*(4), 387–412.

Osgood, D. W., & Chambers, J. M. (2003). Community correlates of rural youth violence. *Juvenile Justice Bulletin*, May, 12.

Owen, S., & Carrington, K. (2015). Domestic violence (DV) service provision and the architecture of rural life: An Australian case study. *Journal of Rural Studies* (in press).

Pain, R., & Smith, S. J. (2008). Fear: Critical geopolitics and everyday life. In R. Pain & S. J. Smith (Eds.), *Fear: Critical geopolitics and everyday life* (pp. 1–24). Aldershot: Ashgate.

Persson, L., & Ceccato, V. (2001). Dynamics of rural areas: Sweden *National Report – Sweden* (Vol. 2, p. 168). Stockholm: Nordregio.

Peste, J. (2011). Murder in Knutby: Charisma, eroticism, and violence in a Swedish pentecostal community. In J. R. Lewis (Ed.), *Violence and new religious movements* (pp. 217–229). New York: Oxford.

Philo, C. (1997). Of other rurals. In P. Cloke & J. Little (Eds.), *Contested countryside cultures: Otherness marginalisation and rurality* (pp. 19–48). London: Routledge.

Robert, P. (2010). Evaluation of safety and crime prevention policies in Europe. In CRIMPREV (Ed.), *Assessing deviance, crime and prevention in Europe*. Guyancourt: Groupe Européen de recherche sur les Normativités.

Robinson, V., & Gardner, G. (2012). Unravelling a stereotype: The lived experience of black and minority ethnic in rural Wales. In N. Chakraborti & J. Garland (Eds.), *Rural racism* (pp. 85–107). Abingdon/New York: Routledge.

Scorzafave, L. G., Justus, M., & Shikida, P. F. A. (2015). Safety in the global south: Criminal victimization in Brazilian rural areas. *Journal of Rural Studies* (in press).

Scott, J., & Biron, D. (2010). Wolf Creek, rurality and the Australian gothic. *Continuum, 24*(2), 307–322.

Scott, J., Carrington, K., & McIntosh, A. (2012). Established-outsider relations and fear of crime in mining towns. *Sociologia Ruralis, 52*(2), 147–169.

Shortall, S., & Warner, M. (2012). Rural transformations: Conceptual and policy issues. In M. Shucksmith, D. Brown, S. Shothall, J. Vergunst, & M. Warner (Eds.), *Rural transformations and rural policies in the US and UK* (pp. 3–18). New York: Routledge.

Siwale, J. (2014). Challenging western perceptions: A case study of rural Zambia. In G. Bosworth & P. Somerville (Eds.), *Interpreting rurality: Multidisciplinary approaches* (pp. 15–30). Abingdon: Routledge.

Skogan, W. G. (1990). *Disorder and decline: Crime and the spiral of decay in American neighborhoods*. New York: Free Press.

Smith, R., & McElwee, G. (2013). Confronting social constructions of rural criminality: A case story on "illegal pluriactivity" in the farming community. *Sociologia Ruralis, 53*(1), 112–134.

Spocter, M. (2013). Rural gated developments as a contributor to post-productivism in the Western Cape. *South African Geographical Journal, 95*(2), 165–186.

Squire, S. J. (1993). Valuing countryside: Reflections on Beatrix Potter tourism. *Area, 25*(1), 5–10.

Tapiador, F. J. (2008). *Rural analysis and management: An earth science approach to rural science*. Berlin/Heidelberg: Springer.

Thompson, B. (2002). Multiracial feminism: Recasting the chronology of second wave feminism. *Feminist Studies, 28*(2), 337–360.

Tönnies, F. (1887). *Gemeinschaft und Gesellschaft*. Leipzig: Fues's Verlag. (Translated, 1957 by Charles Price Loomis as *Community and society*, East Lansing, MI: Michigan State University Press.)

Tovey, H. (1997). Food, environmentalism and rural sociology: On the organic farming movement in Ireland. *Sociologia Ruralis, 37*(1), 21–37.

Treloar, R. (2014). Intersectionality. In T. Teo (Ed.), *Encyclopedia of critical psychology* (pp. 995–1001). New York: Springer.

Tseloni, A., Mailley, J., Farrell, G., & Tilley, N. (2010). Exploring the international decline in crime rates. *European Journal of Criminology, 7*(5), 375–394.

van Leeuwen, E. S. (2010). *Urban–rural interactions towns as focus points in rural development.* Heidelberg/Dordrecht/London/New York: Springer-Verlag.

Wangüemert, M. M. (2001). La pampa: Historia de una pasión argentina. *Escuela de Estudios Hispano-Americanos de Sevilla, 357*–369.

Weisheit, R. A., & Donnermeyer, J. F. (2000). Changes and continuity in crime in rural America. In G. LaFree (Ed.), *Criminal justice 2000: The nature of crime of crime, continuity and change* (pp. 309–357). Washington, DC: US Department of Justice.

Wells, L. E., & Weisheit, R. A. (2004). Patterns of rural and urban crime: A county-level comparison. *Criminal Justice Review, 29*(1), 1–22.

Westholm, E. (2008). Vad menas egentlingen med landsbygd? Ska hela Sverige leva? *Ska hela Sverige leva?* (pp. 49–58). Stockholm: Formas.

Woods, M. (2011). *Rural.* London/New York: Routledge.

Woods, M., Flemmen, A. B., & Wollan, G. (2014). Beyond the idyll: Contested spaces of rural tourism. *Norsk Geografisk Tidsskrift, 68*(3), 202–204.

Woolcock, M., & Narayan, D. (2000). Social capital: Implications for development theory, research, and policy. *World Bank Research Observer, 15*(2), 225–249.

World Bank. (2012). Rural population in the United States. *Trading economics.* Retrieved April 9, 2014, from www.tradingeconomics.com/united-states/rural-population-percent-of-total-population-wb-data.html.

Yarwood, R. (2001). Crime and policing in the British countryside: Some agendas for contemporary geographical research. *Sociologia Ruralis, 41*(2), 201–219.

Zaluar, A. (2012). Turf war in Rio de Janeiro: Youth, drug traffic, guns and hyper-masculinity. In V. Ceccato (Ed.), *The urban fabric of crime and fear* (pp. 217–237). Dordrecht: Springer.

3 Definitions, theory, and research making in rural Sweden

This chapter has four sections. The first section offers a number of basic definitions in rural criminology used in this book. In some cases, several definitions are put forward instead of assuming a single definition. The case of "rural" provides an example of this approach. The second section is devoted to a number of theories that provide the theoretical basis for the book. Each theory is introduced in a way that highlights its importance for rural studies, particularly on crime, perceived safety, and crime prevention. In the third section, the chapter takes a practical turn and focuses on the making of research on crime and safety in rural areas. This section discusses issues of measurement and data quality that are used later in the book. Finally, in the fourth section Sweden is introduced as study area.

Definitions

The definitions set out a basis for the concepts referred to throughout the book.

Rural, rurality

There is common agreement that any attempt to obtain a common definition of rural (rural areas, rurality) might not be useful or even possible.[1] There are several reasons why a blunt template around the definition of rural should be avoided, such as:

> Not all rural communities are alike, and defining the concept *rural* is subject to much debate.
>
> > (DeKeseredy, 2015; Donnermeyer, 2012; Websdale & Johnson, 1998)

> The broad category "rural" is obfuscatory ... as intra-rural differences can be enormous and rural–urban similarities can be sharp.
>
> > (Hoggart, 1990, p. 245)

> Rurality is a contested concept that remains somewhat arbitrary and open to debate.
>
> > (Hogg & Carrington, 2006)

Rural areas are not only a residual to urban areas: just because it isn't urban doesn't mean it must be rural.

(e.g., Bosworth & Somerville, 2014; Groves, 2011)

Rural areas are in constant transformation (Woods, 2005, 2011), so any definition of what rural might be depends on the time, the space, and other contexts. The search for a singular definition of rural is illusory.

(Halfacree, 1993)

Traditional images of "rural" compress the richness of rurality into a homogenizing template, neglecting the existence of "other rurals" (Philo, 1997: 22) and images that embody different socialities, sexualities, ethnicities, and subjectivities.

(Owen & Carrington, 2015)

The term "rural" is generally employed to describe non-urban or peripheral regions (Barclay, Scott, Hogg, & Donnermeyer, 2007, p. 3). Rural is composed of a diverse set of communities with different characteristics and needs that share a number of qualities and challenges (Ceccato & Dolmén, 2013, p. 90). In Sweden, there are different definitions of "rural". The one adopted in this book breaks rural areas in two types: Remote Rural (RR) and Accessible Rural (AR) (Swedish National Rural Development Agency, 2008). This definition reflects the municipalities' population size and accessibility – two relevant components to an area's criminogenic conditions (For more details see the last section of this chapter). What do these areas have in common? What does it matter to crime and community safety?

1   *Rural has a spatial dimension.* Hogg and Carrington (1998) suggest that rural can be defined in terms of demography, population size, density, and geographical isolation (Halfacree, 1993; Woods, 2005, 2011). Remoteness is also associated with rural, but as Barclay et al. (2007) observe, the exact distance that designates what places are remote and the exact number of people that distinguishes rural are on a sliding scale. The geographical dimension also involves the economic profile of an area, land use, and productive systems (Woods, 2005). The spatial dimension may be attributed by those who live there or by outsiders through intuitive understandings of rurality. For crime and safety, the spatial dimensions of rural have implications for both research and practice. Crime levels and the nature of crimes may vary, as well as ways that they have to be combated through crime prevention measures. See examples in Chapters 5–6 and 8–14 of this book.

2   *Time is an important dimension when defining rural.* Time is as fundamental to the conception of rural as the spatial dimension is. As well observed by Thrift (1996, p. 47), time and space do not exist alone. Time provides a reference, such that invisible changes might be happening in rural areas but as yet may not be noticeable to the naked eye (Ilbery & Bowler, 1998; Marsden, 1998; Shortall & Warner, 2012; Woods, 2011). "[Rural] space

should be seen as a process and in process: all space is practiced, all space is place." In this respect, any investigation into rural space requires a strongly temporal contextual approach that makes it possible to analyze potential entanglements at play (Halfacree, 2006). For crime, the temporal dimension is crucial, as crimes may not happen if their basic conditions are not in place (Brantingham & Brantingham, 1984; Cohen & Felson, 1979; Rhodes & Conly, 1981; Wikström, Ceccato, Hardie, & Treiber, 2010).

3   *Context matters when defining rural.* The importance of context in rural is also suggested by Halfacree (2006, p. 45), as the author indicates that any analysis of rural space must always be sensitive to the issue of geographical specificity. This argument has been reinforced by many other scholars in the field of rural studies (Woods, 2005; Yarwood & Edwards, 1995), some by focusing on historical context (Mahon, 2007), the social, cultural, and economic change contexts (Holloway & Kneafsey, 2000), regulatory contexts (Marsden, 2008), and geographical ones, from the village up to the national levels (e.g., Barclay et al., 2007; Ceccato & Dolmén, 2011; Scorzafave, Justus, & Shikida, 2015; Weisheit & Donnermeyer, 2000). Focusing on the specificity of a particular context for crime and safety in rural areas requires a new method of interpretation, one that avoids generalization and allows for the richer, more nuanced, and perhaps more meaningful knowledge gained by investigating a particular case study. For practice, context is fundamental to crime prevention, which should be tailored to each local context, avoiding "one-size-fits-all" solutions.

4   *Rural–urban interactions.* The interactions between urban cores and their hinterland are fundamental to understand the contemporary conception of rurality, not only in economic and political terms (van Leeuwen, 2010) but in relation to people's daily mobility and communication patterns as well as lifestyle changes. These interactions and interdependences are not something new (for a review of Von Thunen's and Christaller theories, see Melamid, 1967) but have fairly recently been recognized as important to understand the dynamics of crime across regions (Ceccato, 2007; Ceccato & Haining, 2004; Weisheit, Falcone, & Wells, 2006; Weisheit, Wells, & Falcone, 1994).

Table 3.1 Some rural–urban dichotomies

Author	Urban category	Non-urban category
Becker	Secular	Sacred
Durkheim	Organic solidarity	Mechanical solidarity
Maine	Contract	Status
Redfied	Urban	Folk
Spencer	Industrial	Military
Tonnies	*Gesellschaft*	*Gemeinschaft*
Weber	Rational	Traditional
Bell	Criminogenic	Idyll
Bell, Philo	Normal	Strange, horror

Source: adapted from Reissman (1964) in Halfacree (1993, p. 25).

5   *Rural depends on the eye of the beholder.* The relativism of the concept of rural is apparent in the diverse understandings of rurality, some emphasizing cohesiveness, informality between locals, or idyllic images, others revealing the dark side with retrograde values that allows a process of othering and may be associated with peculiar behavior and horror (Bell, 1997; DeKeseredy, Muzzatti, & Donnermeyer, 2014; Donnermeyer, Jobes, & Barclay, 2006; Philo, 1997b; Scott, Carrington, & McIntosh, 2012; Tönnies, 1887). Rural possesses a dimension of reflexivity (Giddens, 1991): what is rural depends on those who observe and produce it. The dichotomy of perceptions within rural may be relatively new, but for some time it has defined urban versus rural. Dichotomies related to rural–urban environments influenced some of the early studies of rural communities (Halfacree, 1993) and are also noticeable in more recent rural studies (Table 3.1).

Research on crime and community safety can take advantage of these commonalities and make them visible by developing cases, that is, particular studies, and promoting the application of comparative research that can shed further light on rurality in its own right.

Rural space

"Space does not 'just exist,' waiting passively to be discovered and mapped, but is something created in a whole series of forms and at a whole series of scales by social individuals"; space is not one but rather a great diversity of "species of space" (Crang & Thrift, 2000, p. 3). In a few chapters of this book, "spaces" are the spaces experienced and/or perceived by people in rural areas. In other chapters, space is the domestic environment, which can be a safe realm but may be a place of violence. In yet other chapters, rural spaces are arenas of conflict and resistance of imposed macro-scale political and economic social orders in the wilds of northern Sweden. Yet, as this book progresses, the discussion will suggest that rural space is "more than simply the sum of separate relations that comprise its parts" (Smith, 1984, p. 83), tied up with different time frameworks and contexts.

Traditionally, Frey and Zimmer (2001) suggests that there are three elements which can help distinguish an area as "urban" or "rural." First, there is the ecological element, which includes population and density. The second element is economic, which refers to the function of an area and the activities that take place (this tends to increase the number of people commuting into the area and country contexts). The third element which distinguishes urban from rural areas is the social character of an area. Differences appear, for example, in the way urban and rural people live, such as people's behavioral characteristics and values.

Halfacree's model of rural space (2006, pp. 48, 52) is advertised as one "that can be applied to all rural places" yet allows for distinctiveness of contexts. Halfacree's architectural model for rural space is, according to this author, about realizing "what is already there," rather than imposing a new understanding of it.

The first part of his model is composed of what he calls *rural localities* that are inscribed by relatively unique spatial practices, either by production or consumption activities. The second part refers to the *formal representations of the rural* and how "rural" is framed, for instance, within the production process, by capitalist interests, bureaucrats, or politicians; in this case, how the rural is commodified in exchange-value terms. Finally, the third part consists of *everyday lives of the rural* and, as such, is constituted by incoherent and fractured experiences of the rural. These incorporate individual and social elements ("culture") in their cognitive interpretation and negotiation of the rural; in a planning language, this provides a basis for a bottom-up perspective of the rural.

Rural community

One modern definition of rural communities is "places with small population sizes/densities, areas where people are more likely to know each other's business and come into regular contact with each other" (Websdale & Johnson, 1998, p. 102). Also, according to DeKeseredy (2015), they are locales that exhibit variable levels of collective efficacy. The term collective efficacy, although generated originally with urban settings in mind, means "mutual trust among neighbors combined with a willingness to act on behalf of the common good, specifically to supervise children and maintain public order" (Sampson, Raudenbush, & Earls, 1997, p. 1). According to this, rural communities would tend to show these features more often than any other type of environment. Chapters 12–14 show how these features are expressed in the Swedish context by promoting individual and group mobilization to prevent crime and promote safety principles.

Actions, meanings, and practices are also part of the definition of community as proposed by Liepins (2000, p. 30). For the author, a community is a place in which "entities … are produced through relations and interactions between actors and intermediaries which are linked through networks." Spaces and structures relate to the physical and non-physical dimensions, for they enable "the materialization of meanings" and impact on "how practices can occur." Communities are therefore "temporarily and locationally specific terrains of power and discourse." What is particularly positive about this definition is that it goes beyond the space-related definitions of communities that have dominated rural research and defines rural communities as worthy of analysis in their own right.

Up to now, rural communities have been identified as different from urban areas (Rogers, Burdge, Korsching, & Donnermeyer, 1988), which fits into the contrasting notion of urban and rural communities that was previously in vogue. These conceptions drew heavily on Tönnies' (1887) *gemeinschaft* and *gesellschaft*, the former being associated with communities with strong social ties, socially intimate and characterized by strongly shared norms imposing social order. The latter type of community was characterized by the individualistic, formal, and rational. Individuals' standards of behavior are negotiated following rules and contractual obligations and may be expressed in social relations that are more superficial, leading to social isolation (Donnermeyer, 2007; Tönnies, 1887). This is the urban–rural dichotomy that has guided and perhaps dictated the way communities have been framed in twentieth century research. However, there is reason to believe that contemporary social interaction challenges the tyranny imposed by Tönnies' "black and white" definition of *gemeinschaft* and *gesellschaft* and perhaps makes obsolete any type of traditional notion of community. In a digital era, community takes a virtual form and is a much more fluid concept than any other conception of rural community so far, while still connecting with the *gesellschaft* notion of community and individualism. Individuality comes as a result of the fact that people are given more "informed choices" (Giddens, 1991).

The idea of online community has become increasingly widespread. Fernback (2007) found that the concept of "community" in cyberspace is one of convenient togetherness without real responsibility or commitment ... that community is an evolving process, and that commitment is the truly desired social ideal in social interaction, whether online or offline. Yet cyberspace can also build on existing communities and social ties. Lambert (2013, p. x) suggests that "community – no matter the setting – is grounded in belonging, understanding, in plurality."

> When relationships are built and strengthened through storytelling, people feel welcomed and valued, and civic participation is enhanced. There is nothing new in this. What is new is the digital. Indeed, we're awash in such stories.... We're telling it as it is. As we are experiencing it. We are forming communities around our stories.

In the summer of 2014, people in Sweden turned their eyes to the countryside, as a fire spread over an area of 65 km of forest in Västmanland County. The media portrayed the experiences of individual families and their vulnerability in this disaster, which cost more than one billion Swedish crowns.[2] Locals as well as people far from Västmanland saw the involvement of individuals through social media to support those in need. They offered shelter for people and space for both big and small animals, such as cows and horses, using social media.[3] Sweden is not alone. Social media and other online communication tools are becoming a subject of great interest in mass emergency response (Hughes, Lise, Palen, & Anderson, 2014; Palen, Vieweg, Liu, & Hughes, 2009), which helps build new, perhaps solid social networks and temporary communities.

Crime, farm crime, and rural crime

The definition of crime varies by country, but all definitions share the same core. According to the Swedish Penal Code, "Crime is legally an act in contravention of a provision of law for which there is a prescribed punishment" (Ministry of Justice, 1994). The Swedish definition of crime is similar to the one in the *Oxford English Dictionary* (2009): "an offense or a criminal offense and is an act harmful not only to some individual, but also to the community or the state (a public wrong), which is forbidden and punishable by law." Some are directed to persons, other properties, the state or society, and the environment. Overall, to be classified as a crime, the intention has to be part of the action; that is, an act of wrongdoing must usually be accompanied by the intention to commit the wrong.

Rural crimes are crimes that take place in rural contexts. Some are ordinary crimes, such as burglary and fights (crimes against property or a person), while others are more specifically related to the opportunities for crime that only occur in rural areas. Rural crime includes *farm crime*, such as theft of tractors or cattle, often property crimes against the unit of production (farm), but also acts that cause harm to nature or wildlife, also called environmental crimes (excessive levels of air, water, or soil pollution, deforestation in natural reserves, injuries of animals and wildlife). Some violations fit the definition of harmful actions but may not be considered a crime; however, every crime violates the law. Chapter 8 discusses in detail examples and definitions of these rural crimes.

Harm and social harm

A few definitions of harm are "physical or psychological injury or damage," "wrongdoing, evil," and "to injure physically, morally, or mentally" someone and something (*Collins English Dictionary*, 2003). A portion of the research on social harm that is pertinent to this book focuses on whether a social harm is labeled a crime as well as the degree to which that crime or social harm is visible (see e.g., Davies, Francis, & Wyatt, 2014). The authors suggest that uncovering crime may not be easy; realizing that it is a criminal act and defining it as such depends on a number of factors. There must be witnesses, detection, and recognized victims. It is this dynamic that allows crimes and harm to have different degrees of invisibility that stem from the interplay of this range of factors, which overlap and interact to decrease or increase the level of visibility. In this book, the term "harm" is associated with damaging acts against nature and wildlife; some acts are registered as crimes by the police or environmental inspectors, while others refer to cases of destruction of rivers or forests or maltreatment of or injury to animals or wildlife witnessed, but in some cases captured only by radio or newspaper journalists.

Safety and security

The concept of "security" is rooted in the Latin term *securitas*, associated with "peace of mind, freedom from care, and also freedom from danger" (Ceccato, 2013b). Wiebe et al. (2014) defines security as "being free from the risk of being assaulted and security from feeling afraid of being assaulted," while safety is "an individual's perception of how safe they are from the risk of being victimized." Safety and security are contested concepts that remain somewhat arbitrary and open to debate as different disciplines attach different meaning to them. Some use these terms in completely opposite ways (Ceccato & Newton, 2015) or broaden it by including the notion of harm to individuals and nature, such as victimization by natural hazards.

Although in this book safety and security are used interchangeably, *security* will be more often associated with the risk of being the victim of a crime, while *safety* will be linked to an individual's perception of how safe they are from the risk of being victimized. Individuals may also be affected by other anxieties caused by multi-scale factors that may lead individuals to declare feeling unsafe. Thus, perceived safety in this book is an umbrella concept that involves a number of feelings, from fear of crime to emotions and anxieties that may be triggered by current uncertainties and threats that are far from the individual, family, or community scale (see for instance, Giddens, 1991, 2014). In Chapter 6 potential causes of these emotions are discussed in detail in the rural context.

Gender and intersectionality

Safety is defined here as being dependent on the individual and the groups to which they might belong (Giddens, 1991). With regards to victimization and perceived safety, this book puts a special focus on those individuals and groups whose safety is overlooked by police and official statistics. Among the individual factors affecting the perception of safety, gender is perhaps the most important. Violence against women in domestic settings is just one example of a situation that demands a nuanced approach to rural safety. On this subject, see the work done by criminologists in DeKeseredy (2015). As rural is concerned, what does it mean to adopt a gender-informed approach to safety?

Gender can be defined in the context of gender mainstreaming, which is defined by the UN (1997) in terms of a set of strategies for making women's as well as men's concerns and experiences an integral part of policies and programs in all societal spheres, so that women and men benefit equally so inequality is not perpetuated. The main goal is to achieve a society with better gender equality, assuming from the start that there are many spheres of life in which women are at a great disadvantage to men. In the context of safety, this principle should mean that victimization and fear should not depend on the basic characteristics of an individual, such as gender or age. Worldwide, much of what is in place in terms of intervention practices, for instance by the UN Women's initiative *Safe Cities* (UN, 2013), as the name illustrates, focuses on violence against women in public places and is predominantly linked to women in urban areas (but see UN Women, 2014).

Both in research and practice, though, it is important not to overgeneralize between groups and not to overemphasize the gender dimension on top of other individual qualities. A range of factors can influence victimization and fear of crime, including age, gender, ethnicity, economics, behavior, culture, and self-identity. The complexity of gender and safety requires paying attention not just to being a woman or a man but also to the intersections between gender and age, ethnicity, financial resources, individual experiences, and culture, to name a few. These overlaps are essential considerations, because the way they take shape in an individual creates different outcomes: one being of discrimination, weakness, and disadvantage, as opposed to integration, power, and advantage. More interesting, the combination may also have a synergic effect, for instance, being a woman from a minority ethnic group and unemployed.

Intersectionality has been around for some time and became popular particularly in sociology in the late 1960s and early 1970s. It has been adapted to criminology by studies devoted to inequality in victimization, particularly in the United States (e.g., Barak, Leighton, & Flavin, 2010; Peterson & Krivo, 2005). The concept of "intersectionality," "the interaction of multiple identities and experiences of exclusion and subordination," as defined by Davis (2008, p. 67), can also be associated with the environmental justice movement and scholarships that emerged in the 1970s and 1980s in the United States (e.g., Bullard, 1983) and flourished since then as a predominately "urban-centric" field (but see e.g., Bell and Braun, 2010). Chapters 7 and 10 exemplify how these dimensions cross over to emerge as layers of vulnerability and discrimination recognized by experiences discussed in the case of Sami youth, and non-Swedish women.

Othering, otherness, and discrimination

Differences between residents and newcomers in a rural community can be maximized by both groups, giving expression to *us–them* feelings. In the literature, this has been associated to different terms, such as "othering," the process of perceiving or portraying someone or something as fundamentally different from oneself or a group to which the one pertains (as part of *othering* or the process of transforming a difference into *otherness*). Sandercock (2005) suggests that fear of others is often one cause of the animosity between newcomers and locals, previously identified as an expression of the fear of the unknown. This can take different shapes, from fear and neglect, to discrimination and violence of different types (Carrington, Hogg, & McIntosh, 2011; Cloke & Little, 1997; Philo, 1997b; Scott et al., 2012).

Garland and Chakraborti (2006) discuss the process of racial discrimination in rural England against the idyll myth of the rural communities being neighborly and close-knit with strong feelings of belonging. They suggest that this process obscures and marginalizes the experiences of minority ethnic residents who can often feel excluded from village life. Garland and Chakraborti (2006) argue that the intersection of rurality with notions of Englishness and "whiteness" serves to reinforce further the process of marginalization. For a detailed discussion, see Chakraborti and Garland (2011). This book, in particular Chapters 6 and 10, illustrates the process of *othering* and discrimination in the rural Swedish context.

The emergence of rural crime and community safety in criminology

Rural criminology is a multidisciplinary and interdisciplinary field of research (Ceccato, 2015). This cannot be better illustrated than by the special issue on "crime and community safety" recently published by the *Journal of Rural*

Studies in 2015, volume 39. Researchers from different traditions provided a variety of articles, each contributing new research to their own particular disciplines while together approaching the issues of crime and safety in rural communities. These studies stemmed from different, sometimes similar, epistemological and paradigmatic traditions in the social and natural sciences. Their approaches varied, from positivistic, to critical and feminist, from quantitative modeling, to the many different qualitative methods. The volume resulted in an intricate composition of themes at different analytical levels and depth, from country-based to individual-level studies. This book bypasses that rich body of previous theories and methods and instead sets out theories that are more focused on and therefore more pertinent to the scope of this book. The objective of this chapter is to translate these theories into an integrated theory-driven conceptual framework within which crime and community safety in rural areas can be further analyzed. None of these theories is without criticism, and none has been developed strictly for the purpose of explaining crime and safety in rural contexts. Worth noting is the special attention given to rural places as a criminogenic element in the interplay between offenders and victims. If the emphasis is on the environment where crime takes place, then reducing crime, or making places safer, requires initiatives that focus on reducing crime opportunities at those places by taking into account their particular contexts.

Theories that support the study of crime in rural studies

Theories in rural crime research have focused predominantly on the spatial dimension of crime (Donnermeyer, 2007), which is not surprising, as almost any consideration of what "rural" means must consider its geographical dimensions (Hobbs, 1994). Crime opportunities are not random; nor are patterns in fear of crime. One explanation is that crime reflects people's whereabouts, where people spend time. For urban settings, environmental criminology research is populated by examples of how crime geography reflects people's routine activities over time (e.g., Cohen & Felson, 1979; Sherman, Gartin, & Buerger, 1989). But how do these principles work in rural areas? Do rural areas present a particular set of situations unique from other non-rural environments?

According to crime point pattern theory, it is the interaction of the location of potential targets and the criminal's awareness or activity space that culminates in particular patterns of crime occurrence. Brantingham and Brantingham (1984, p. 362) indicate that this happens because individuals' whereabouts affect their chances of coming in contact with other individuals, some of them offenders. In defining the concept of "opportunity space," these authors suggest that offenders learn through experience or social transmission the clues that are associated with "good" victims or places where they can attack. A node is an activity space where people carry out major activities and spend most of their time, for example the office, home, or local pub. It is suggested that around these activity nodes individuals develop awareness spaces, around the settings they become acquainted with. Paths are the routes that individuals take between these nodes.

In rural context they can be the streets individuals take when moving around in the village or when commuting to the neighboring village – a principle that applies both for victims and offenders.

Another concept of crime pattern theory is that of "edges," beyond which persons are unfamiliar with the space. Crimes occur where and when the immediate environment makes the offender feel familiar and safe to act, whilst victims are unfamiliar with certain environments and the risks they face, for instance, when they are traveling in areas they do not routinely go. In rural contexts, edges can be perceived as the boundaries of the village, or for young people or children, it can be their own street. These ideas are corroborated by decades of evidence that indicate that individuals commit crime not far from their current (and previous) place of residence and that their journey is affected by different types of geographical barriers (Bernasco, 2010; Porter, 1996; White, 1932; Wiles & Costello, 2000) but see, for example, Townsley and Sidebottom (2010).

Whether an offender travels far is perhaps not as interesting as asking whether crimes in rural areas are committed by locals and against local residents (Ceccato & Dolmén, 2011; Mawby, 2015) or whether people take advantage of barriers to commit crime elsewhere. For instance, Mawby (2015) examined police data and victim surveys from Cornwall, England, to investigate victims' and offenders' status: long-term residents; recent arrivals; second-home owners; temporary residents, e.g., seasonal workers; visitors, e.g., holidaymakers; or people there on business. Findings provide little evidence whether the offenders or victims were nonresidents or residents. Ceccato and Haining (2004) assessed offenders' mobility at the southern Swedish border after the opening of the Öresund bridge linking Sweden and Denmark and found different results. Data on the total number of suspects committing offenses by citizenship indicates a slight increase since 2000 in the total number of offenders in the Öresund region for all citizenships selected (Danes, Germans, Poles, Latvians, Lithuanians, Estonians). According to the National Police Board, despite the fact that data on offenders' citizenship does not provide an accurate indication of offenders' mobility patterns, since we do not know their home address, the data constitutes "a good proxy." For example, 75 percent of Polish citizens and 45 percent of Danish citizens arrested for committing crime in Swedish Öresund in 1998 did not live in the region. Among Polish citizens, a large number came from deprived areas in northwest Poland. The analysis, however, was not limited to rural areas but covered the whole region of Öresund with large urban agglomerations such as Malmö.

Two other interesting concepts are "crime attractors" and "crime generators" (Brantingham & Brantingham 1995). These concepts help us think about differences in crime concentrations in rural contexts, though they may be more appropriate to explain the geography of crime in urban environments. Crime generators are places where large numbers of people are present, for reasons unrelated to criminal motivation. This convergence in time and space creates new and unexpected criminal opportunities for violence and property crimes. Crime attractors are places that breed crime and many criminal opportunities and may be well known to offenders.

Criminally motivated individuals are drawn to such locations, thus increasing the number of crime and disorder events. For instance, some types of crimes are concentrated in border municipalities or in some parts of them (crime attractors); others are concentrated in villages that receive a large inflow of population during the summer (crime generators). Yet, not all places that attract many people are criminogenic. For certain types of offenses, fewer people around and alert makes the environment more criminogenic, for instance for burglary, rape, domestic violence, dumping of oil in nature. This leads us to reason about the necessary conditions for crime, here indicated by *routine activity theory*. The theory draws attention to the environmental or situational context that influences the offender's decision to commit rape.

Crimes depend on the convergence in space and time of motivated offenders, suitable targets, and the absence of capable guardians (Cohen & Felson, 1979). The "right place" poses opportunities for crime, which for theft might be a crowded place, for rape a secluded place, or where either guardianship is not present or not willing or able to intervene. Felson (2006) exemplifies that guardianship can be produced by multiple actors. Some are what is called *handlers* who control potential offenders (e.g., guards, police, and the rural community in general). Others are *managers*, who control places (e.g., rural transients, those who collect milk at the entrance of a farm daily), and *guardians*, who control targets (e.g., the farmers themselves). For targets, there are two types of guardians: formal guardians whose responsibility is to protect people and property from crime, such as police officers and security guards, and informal guardians, including friends and others who are at the same place as the target. Donnermeyer (2007) indicates that more so than other place-based theories, routine activity theory includes changes of circumstances in its framework. Such changes can be economic, social, or cultural changes that modify the number of motivated offenders and/or suitable targets and increase or decrease guardianship; crime levels will change accordingly. For instance, the location of buildings may affect thefts (close to the road as opposed to far from the view of transients), dogs or other farm security measures may reduce the chances for thefts by improving guardianship on a farm, or thefts might increase if prices on livestock rapidly increase.

As in crime point pattern theory, routine activity principles rely on people's everyday life rhythms: morning, noon, afternoon, night, weekdays and weekends, winter and summer. This means that any type of human activity is limited by the amount of time available each day. Time is both a necessary condition and a constraint for an activity. In this sense, committing a crime (or falling victim of it) is an example of an activity like any other. As Felson (2006, pp. 6–7) indicates:

> The daily life of a city provides the targets for crime and removes them. The sleeping, walking, working, and eating patterns of offenders affect the metabolism of crime.... We must study these rhythms of life if we wish to understand crime.

Whilst routine activity theory defines the necessary conditions for a crime to occur, it does not define the sufficient conditions. Crime does not happen just because victims and offenders happen to share similar spatial awareness and converge at a certain place and time. An understanding of the sufficient conditions for crime begins by considering each individual's perception of their safety and how it affects their movement patterns. Between the residents of different neighborhoods, there are large differences in perceptions of safety that affect individuals' daily movements and people's capacity to exercise social control. The offender may avoid these areas, and, as a consequence, crime becomes concentrated in other areas. Yet, crime varies within rural areas, just as rural areas themselves vary from one another (Lowe, Marsden, Murdoch, & Ward, 2012). Equally, within rural areas, towns appear to experience higher levels of crime than villages and smaller settlements (Mawby, 2015). Community size and population density are not the only factors that affect crime (Carrington, 2007; Ceccato & Dolmén, 2011; Donnermeyer et al., 2006; Felson, 2013; Kaylen & Pridemore, 2013b; Mawby, 2007). Decades of evidence from urban environments have shown that socially disorganized neighborhoods experience disproportionately more crimes.

Social Disorganization Theory (Bursik, 1999; Kornhauser, 1978; Sampson, 1986; Shaw & McKay, 1942) has provided part of the theoretical foundation for many studies that focus on the impact of area (and neighborhood) characteristics on crime. Shaw and McKay linked neighborhood social disorganization (areas that combine deprivation, residential instability, and ethnic diversity) to delinquency and crime. The mechanisms linking socially disorganized neighborhoods and crime relate to people's inability to exercise social control in their neighborhoods and solve jointly experienced problems. In neighborhoods with high population turnover (perhaps linked with people's fear of crime in that area), guardianship decreases further, enhancing the ecological conditions associated with crime. Social disorganization theory suggests that structural disadvantage breeds crime and that offending occurs when impaired social bonds are insufficient to encourage or enforce legitimate behavior and discourage deviant behavior.

Bursik (1999) defines social disorganization as an inability of community members to achieve shared values or to solve jointly experienced problems. In other words, these communities lack social capital. Social capital has been associated with social bonds that create networks that bring a collective benefit to neighborhood residents. Communities with high stocks of social capital are more effective in exerting informal social control through the establishment and maintenance of norms. However, high social capital does not necessarily result in collective benefits. Social capital can be bonding, or exclusive, or bridging, or inclusive (Putnam, 2000, p. 22). Groups may exclude or subordinate other groups (Ceccato & Haining, 2005). Deller and Deller (2012) assessed the role of social capital in explaining patterns of rural larceny and burglary crime rates. They find consistent evidence that higher levels of social capital tend to be associated with lower levels of rural property crime rates.

Nevertheless, Sampson et al. (1997), suggest that action to restrict crime does not necessarily demand "strong local social ties or associations." Action by the group may happen where personal ties and social networks are weak. Collective efficacy is the group-level term used by Sampson et al. (1997) to refer to the situation where there are shared expectations within the group and a willingness to engage in processes of social control.

Two versions of empirical applications of social disorganization theory are recognized in the international literature: *the structural antecedents model* and *the systemic model* (Donnermeyer, 2014). Donnermeyer writes that the structural antecedents model relies on aggregated properties of a specific area (neighborhood, town, city, village, mostly coming from censuses and other sources) as factors affecting crime and delinquency (police recorded data). In the systemic model, the antecedents are only "proxies" and are mediated by more direct indicators of internal social cohesion and control through local networks.

The first test of the antecedents model was the one by Osgood and Chambers (2003). They hypothesized that, as in urban areas, in small towns and rural communities, systems of relationships are relevant to crime and delinquency. The authors found that one or more of the social disorganization variables were significantly associated with arrest rates for all of the violent offenses other than homicide. Rates of crime and delinquency were associated with residential instability, ethnic diversity, and family disruption. For example, a higher proportion of female-headed households was strongly associated with higher rates of arrest for violent offenses except homicide. This was interpreted as the burden of single parenting and joint supervision of children. However, surprisingly, the authors did not find any link between poverty and rates of delinquency. One of the interpretations is that poverty does not strike in rural areas as it does in urban areas, particularly metropolitan areas. Thus, the authors concluded that a high rate of rural poverty that does not affect the delinquency rate appears to be consistent with social disorganization theory.

However, the results of a similar study conducted by Kaylen and Pridemore (Deller & Deller, 2010, 2011; Kaylen & Pridemore, 2011, 2012, 2013a, 2013b) indicate that the association between social disorganization and violence in rural areas is sensitive to how the dependent variable is measured. Authors suggest a search for other data sources and not to rely solely on official crime data from rural areas when testing sociological and criminological theories. On the latter point, they are convincing in Kaylen and Pridemore (2013a), using the British Crime Survey. The study examines data from respondents living in rural areas in 318 postcode sectors and is declared to be the first test of the full social disorganization model in the literature on rural crime. Again, their findings call for a reassessment of the conclusions drawn about how social disorganization and crime are related in rural communities.

Donnermeyer (2014) suggests therefore that the same social networks and social capital that produce social cohesion and collective efficacy can simultaneously constrain some crimes even as the occurrence of other crimes is facilitated. The author suggests that there are multiple forms of social organization, or collective efficacy (instead of social disorganization or anti-efficacy) at the same place and same time, allowing individuals to simultaneously participate in multiple networks, some of which may be criminal. For a detailed discussion of *social organization* and crime, see Donnermeyer and DeKeseredy (2013), Donnermeyer, Scott, and Carrington (2013).

Cultural differences in values, norms, and beliefs held by members of groups or subgroups may also explain variations in crime. The idea of the existence of a subculture for crime has been associated with high rates of violence, particularly in the United States (Messner & Rosenfeld, 1999). In the United States, the evidence for this subculture of violence is the concentration of high rates of murder that have characterized the south. The *subculture of violence* theory is a controversial one (Farrington, Loeber, & Southamer-Loeber, 2003) but has been suggested to be part of the explanation for large regional differences in violence elsewhere (Salla, Ceccato, & Ahven, 2011). Chapter 9 in this book refers to the subculture of crime and violence that characterizes motorcycle gangs in rural Sweden, such as *Hells Angels* and *Bandidos*, and that is intertwined with the local way of life in some municipalities.

The influence of area characteristics on individual offender behavior depends on their mobility. Individuals are mobile and spend time in many settings and environments with differing criminogenic characteristics. *Situational action theory* (SAT) offers a process-based explanation of offending and identifies the sufficient conditions for a crime to occur. This framework attempts to explain why individuals commit crime. It comprises four features: an individual, a setting, a situation, and an action. SAT states that criminal acts in a place are the outcome of a perception–choice process initiated by the interaction between the individual's crime propensity and the discouragements to crime that are present in the area. The outcome (offending or otherwise) depends on two sets of factors: (1) the individual's own moral rules and self-control and (2) the extent to which society's moral rules are enforced in that place (Wikström et al., 2010, p. 56). This means that a rural environment that enforces law-abiding behavior would be less propitious to promote offending. A remaining question is whether rural areas present a distinct set of situations for an individual living there that are different from those for individuals living in urban environments.

Macro theories of crime and rural transformations

Macro theories relating crime to society's structure and organization, such as anomie theory, have also been adopted in rural studies to aid in understanding the levels and patterns of crime. These transformations in rural areas are thought not to be detached from processes suggested by theories of rural change (Ilbery & Bowler, 1998; Marsden, 1998; Ramsey, Abrams, & Evans, 2013). Woods (2011) presents in detail the process of rural transformation, from rural as a space of production, to contemporary products of exploitation of the countryside that characterize the global economy. Similar processes of rural change occur under multiple forces at an unprecedented pace elsewhere, involving rapid and unexpected changes that are bound to have an impact at the micro level, that is, in rural communities. For example, Ravera et al. (2014), drawing upon six context-specific case studies from Asia, Latin America, and Europe, examine the current drivers and pathways of rural change by analyzing examples of new ruralities that are emerging as responses across different world regions. Sweden has also shown signs of rural change as a result of a period of major restructuring under the recent development of the globalized economy (Ilbery & Bowler, 1998; Marsden, 1998). Johansson, Westlund, and Eliasson (2009) suggest that this "new rurality" is imposing new patterns of demographic, socioeconomic, and environmental differentiation at both local and regional levels.

Crime is argued to be linked to rural change, because profound transformations are expected to produce a chronic state of deregulation in society, in which valued goals are reduced and society fails to place normative limits on people's behavior. Durkheim (1897) was the first to suggest that rapid social change creates anomie, which can have a negative impact on society and is linked to increases in crime. Individuals take advantage of anomic conditions, or the insecurity status resulting from a breakdown of standards and values in society. Using the United States as a background, Merton (1938) suggests that anomie is the result of a lack of adequate means to fulfill society's culturally sanctioned goals conceptualized as "the American Dream." Thus, "normlessness" transforms into a lack of or weakening of social controls which are fundamental for preventing crime. Another line of inquiry considers the relationship of strain to criminal behavior (Agnew, 1999). A growing literature has evolved in the past decade linking societal transformations to crime (Ceccato, 2008; Ceccato & Haining, 2008; Kim & Pridemore, 2005; Liu, 2005; Salla et al., 2011) but rarely focusing specifically on rural areas (but see Freudenburg & Jones, 1991; Rephann, 1999). Ceccato (2008) examines how demographic, socioeconomic, land use, and institutional factors relate to crime geography and levels in the Baltic countries after the fall of the Soviet Union and in the transition to a market economy. The author also found that indicators of municipalities social structure, such as divorce rate, predict the variation in crime better than other indicators, such as land use and economic covariates. In rural contexts, Freudenburg and Jones (1991) assessed crime in rural communities that undergo rapid population change due to various types of economic development.

The effect of societal changes may be moderated by the existing safety net, promoted by pro-social institutions. It was Messner and Rosenfeld (1994, 1997) who suggested social institutions tend to be devalued in comparison to economic institutions (which they called "institutional anomie") and lose their power so that criminogenic conditions increase. However, they also suggest that such an effect can be moderated by social institutions in places that invest in formation of social capital. Chapter 5 focuses on shifts in the geography of crime, from the 1990s to the 2000s, and some of these principles are used as a reference. A redistribution of the urban population to larger cities has affected the labor market and affected regional income distribution (Johansson et al., 2009). These changes are expected to have an impact on crime dynamics that might be moderated by pro-social institutions.

Principles of fear of crime and perceived safety

The nature of perceived safety (or the lack thereof – fear) is a phenomenon affected by multi-scale factors (Day, 2009; Los, 2002; Wyant, 2008). Some factors that affect perceived safety are generated locally, and perhaps they are felt as tangible, whilst others may be more difficult to assess but still affect individuals' anxieties and may be produced in all possible geographical dimensions, from global to local. Perceived safety involves more than just fear of crime.

Warr (2000, p. 453) defines fear as "an emotion, a feeling of alarm or dread caused by awareness or expectation of danger." Thus, an increase in crime would hypothetically affect perceived safety. Yet, this simplistic causal relationship rarely matches, as the fear of crime refers to the fear of being a victim of crime, as opposed to the actual probability of being a victim of crime. Fear can be multidimensional, as an individual can fear for oneself (personal fear) and fear for others (altruistic fear) whose safety the person values.

Chapter 6 includes a detailed discussion of why perceived safety (fear of crime and overall anxieties) varies across groups and across rural areas, looking for answers behind individual, local, and global factors. The chapter also separately reviews possible causes of variations in perceived safety, but, of course, in reality perceived safety is bound to be a result of intersections of all these factors: gender, previous victimization, familiarity, physical environment, signs of disorder and crime, mobility patterns, social cohesion and collective efficacy, *othering*, macro-societal changes, commodification of security, and media.

Crime prevention in theory

There are several ways to prevent crime from occurring. One is to intervene before an individual has the choice to consider crime as an alternative. For that, social crime prevention addresses individual- and family-level factors that might lead to offending. Individual-level factors, such as attachment to school and involvement in pro-social activities, decrease the probability of criminal involvement but rely on long-term intervention. Other types of intervention focus on individuals that are already at risk and are in need of targeted intervention.

Crimes cannot be properly explained, or effectively prevented, without a deep understanding of the environments in which they occur (Smith & Cornish, 2006). These interventions adopt techniques focusing on reducing the opportunity to commit a crime. Some techniques include increasing the difficulty of crime, increasing the risk of crime, and reducing the rewards of crime (Clarke, 1997). Situational crime prevention aims to affect the motivation of criminals by means of environmental and situational changes and is based on three elements: (1) increasing the perceived difficulty of crime; (2) increasing the risks; and (3) reducing the rewards. Thus, this book focuses on situational crime prevention but also looks at general actions in rural community policing. As suggested by Yarwood (2015), community policing may engage several actors: police, voluntary organizations, citizens, and private actors. Whilst police are typically assigned to act in specific geographical areas in their jurisdiction, policing may have less distinctive territorial boundaries, as actors are not necessarily restricted on a territorial basis, which is the way the police work to cover large rural municipalities in rural Sweden, particularly in the north. These types of crime prevention strategies are considered in detail in this book in Chapters 12, 13, and 14.

The making of criminological research in rural areas

Quoting Young (2011, p. 58), Joe Donnermeyer made an important point in his presentation at the 2014 Stockholm workshop on crime and community safety. Donnermeyer noted the importance of theories in rural studies, regardless of the methods and tools a researcher may adopt: "It is not more and fancier statistical testing that will solve the problems of numbers in the social sciences. Rather it is theory and conceptualization … that give numbers relevance, utility, and their place." This is certainly accurate, for any field of science. In rural studies, this is especially important as the rural is, and always has been, a dynamic and diverse space (Woods, 2011, p. 293). Theories and conceptual frameworks have to allow for the diversity and complexity of rurality. This complex rural reality is what guides us through the process of inquiry.

In this book, Crime Science principles (see e.g., Laycock, 2005; Pawson & Tilley, 1997) have been adopted to guide the process of inquiry. I have attempted to illustrate why rural areas are worth investigating by taking into account the variability of the term "rural." To do that, principles from Crime Science can be useful, as they promote the integration of theories from different disciplines for understanding patterns of crime and perceived safety. Two examples here illustrate this point. *The first step*, before outlining the theory to be used, is to define the aim of the inquiry. For instance:

1   *Why does farm crime cluster in certain areas of the country?*
    or
2   *What do offenders and victims know about the situational conditions of farm crime?*

While the first research question aims at generalizing the criminogenic conditions of farm crime across the country, the second one aims at teasing out thieves' and farmers' interpretations (of the target and offender) of particular criminal opportunities (situational conditions) and their respective actions for crime perpetration/prevention. Most researchers would agree that despite being two similar research questions, in practice they demand different theoretical frameworks and different – perhaps complementary, at best case, overlapping – research methods and datasets.

The second step in the process of inquiry is to adopt a set of theories that support the search for answers to the research questions. In example (1), routine activity theory may be useful in the interpretation of patterns of farm crime, together with theories of social (dis)organization. Here quantitative indicators may be regressed against rates or cases of police-recorded farm crimes at municipal levels.

In example (2), a combination of positivistic and critical sociological theories is desirable to frame the research question, relying on situational crime prevention and the theory of "othering" analyzed through interviews with farmers and thieves. Each research question is set with specific context descriptors, for instance, temporal and spatial. It is worth noting that spatial analysis can become an integral part of the research process in these examples: in (1) by mapping and statistically analyzing spatial patterns of police-recorded statistics, and in (2) by allowing detailed mental maps drawn by both thieves and farmers. Thus, the argument put forward here is that the research is not data-, method-, or theory-driven. Instead, as common sense as it sounds, it is the (rural) reality materialized by the research questions that guides the researcher's decision-making through the process. These overlapping research questions exemplify different realities of rural seen through the eyes of the researcher. Both are worth investigating, as they are bound to produce different outcomes, providing complementary pictures of the rural. By acknowledging this plurality, Woods (2011) observes that our studies give only partial glimpses of what rural is. He recognizes that it is exactly this complexity of the rural that makes its study challenging and exciting, with much to explore. This leads us to the next issue.

The idea of obtaining a single definition of rural, rural areas/spaces, or rurality – something that has become clearer through this book – appears to be fruitless. Yet, the recognition that rural areas are composed of a diverse set of communities with different characteristics and needs that share a number of qualities and challenges compels us forward in an attempt to capture the nature of rural areas from a particular viewpoint. In this book, rural areas were framed from a criminological perspective using different theoretical frameworks. How was this done?

The focus is on the plurality of crime, victimization, and practices in crime prevention. The book also considers a number of ways of tackling these subject areas, from top-down to bottom-up research approaches. One example of this is the analysis of violence against women. On one hand, official statistics showed general concentrations of gendered violence across the country and within rural areas; on the other hand, violence was investigated considering specific cases of women who, for instance, were brought to the country by their partners and later fell by the partner's brutality. Another example is the assessment of crime prevention practices using cross-triangulation of three data sources: from top-down, a database from the Swedish National Council for Crime Prevention; from bottom-up, an email survey sent to representatives of local crime prevention groups in all rural municipalities in Sweden and interviews with more than 40 agents working with crime prevention in eight rural municipalities. A similar approach was taken when assessing youth-related problems and crime against nature. Overall, this combination of perspectives was successful in illustrating sometimes diverging, other times complementary, views of rural safety.

The multi-method and multi-data approach adopted in this book requires the object of study to be fixed in relation to particular temporal (cross-sectional or longitudinal) and spatial references, as well as other contexts that might be relevant to the studied phenomena. Comparative frameworks can be useful to establish some external reference to a specific case. As Chapters 4–14 illustrate, this approach calls for a development of research and practice in rural crime and community safety that goes beyond the borders of research fields and theoretical perspectives.

The novelty of this approach is to allow the combination of interdisciplinary research questions (for instance, from Psychology and Criminology) into a framework of analysis that shares the same field of inquiry but takes different perspectives. Another advantage is to welcome a diverse array of paradigmatic perspectives, from positivistic to critical perspectives in Criminology (see e.g., Donnermeyer & DeKeseredy, 2013), into a single framework. Traditionally, such diverse approaches are thought to be incompatible and require different research processes. They may do so, but these paradigmatic starting points can, when pursued in parallel, produce complementary views of the same rural reality.

Issues of measuring crime and perceived safety in a rural context

Ten different types of data were used for the analysis in Chapters 4–14 of this book (Table 3.2). The use of multi-methods was a necessity, given the diverse types of data sources. The array of quantitative, qualitative, and spatial methods has proved useful, as the combination allowed new ways to explore new relationships between different scales of analysis of a single-problem (for instance, violence against women or crime against the environment), nation-wide or case-study-based analysis. The use of maps and spatial analysis is a red thread in Chapters 4 to 14.

Table 3.2 Types of data

Data type	Coverage
Official police data	Sweden, municipality, x,y coordinates
National victims surveys and farmers victimization survey	Sweden
Demographic, socio-economic and land use data in GIS	Sweden
Database on local crime prevention projects (BRÅ)	Sweden (selected municipalities)
Health statistics/hospitalization of women victims of violence by hospitals	Hospitals
Women's data shelter database for Sweden	Sweden by women's shelter
CrimeStoppers Sweden database on crime incidence	
Media coverage analysis, newspaper	Sweden
Email survey	Sweden (selected municipalities)
Interviews face-to-face	Sweden (selected municipalities)

Source: Halfacree (1993).

The most important data sources for this book were *recorded police data* and *national victim surveys*, but without other sources the book would not exist. Each of these crime data sources is reliable for most crimes, but none is free of problems. In this section the data quality issues with police-reported statistics and victimization surveys are discussed. Some of the issues discussed below are particularly problematic in rural areas and are discussed in detail in each chapter. Police statistics are based on administrative data (or *x-y* coordinates) generated by reports of crime to the police, and national victimization surveys show the prevalence and incidence of crime based on crime victim surveys.

Police-recorded data

Data reliability is an important issue when working with police crime data or crime-victim survey data. Underreporting is a known cause of lack of reliability in databases of police-recorded offenses. Traditionally, levels of reporting vary with the type of offense and its seriousness. This is particularly important in rural areas, as an individual may face traveling long distances to report a crime. Internationally, burglary and theft of vehicles are far more likely to be reported than many other types of offenses, such as domestic violence. Burglary and theft are often more reported for insurance purposes, while domestic violence is not because the offender is someone whom the victim knows well (see Chapter 10 for more). There are also indications that the offense reporting level may be underestimated in areas where people think that it is not worthwhile reporting them. Chapters 5 and 8 illustrate the low reporting rates for certain types of crimes among farmers in Sweden, as they believe that reporting is "a waste of time."

Other problems of data quality occur during the process of recording. Ceccato (2005) observes that this can be caused by the lack of information about the event from the victim (not knowing exactly where the offense took place) or by the police officer failing to record the event properly (failing to record the exact location). This may create extra cases in those particular locations, which may, if not identified in advance, contribute to "false hot spots." In rural environments, it is common to have crime associated with a single point linked to the center of a polygon; often that location does not match the exact location of the offense (for instance, behind a barn, garage, main house). This inaccuracy can be related to the place of the offense or the time it happened (if the victim was away when it happened). When there is no available information about the time that the event occurred, estimating a range of hours is often the common practice (e.g., 12:00–16:00). However, for analysis purposes, this limits any space–time trend assessment. Aoristic models (Ratcliffe, 2010; Ratcliffe & McCullagh, 1998) are commonly used to interpolate time-related data that are missing.

Despite the fact that there are conventions for recording offenses in many countries, including Scandinavia, differences still occur in practice. Problems of data quality relate to the lack of systematization of procedures when recording an offense. For example, an assessment of the Swedish offense database for Skåne (southern Sweden) has shown that large municipalities often have better offense records than small ones. After an evaluation of thousands of records in small towns, Ceccato and Haining (2004) found that the victims or police officers in small municipalities only approximate the offense's location (such as close to the park, in front of the bus station), which contributes to the poor quality of records.

Inaccuracies in crime data can also be introduced during geocoding. Geocoding is the process of matching records in two databases: the offense addresses database (without map position information) and the reference street map with *x-y* coordinates. The quality of the geocoding process depends very much on the quality of the offense records, the quality of the address dictionary, the chosen method for geocoding (matching), and the experience of the geocoder. Ceccato and Snickars (2000) estimate, for instance, that about 25 percent of all offenses committed in a district were attached not to their "real locations" but to the polygons' centroids of the local commercial area.

Although they constitute a minority, one group of offenses have places or times unknown by the victim or are hard to pinpoint, as people were in motion when the crime happened. A typical example is when a crime takes place on a bus or train traveling between point A and point B. Stations and bus stops are often the reference for these types of crimes but may be indicators of potential false hot spots. A good way to identify potential false hot spots is to check them for long-term patterns. If they are false, they may disappear over time, because the way the offense is reported may change, affecting the choice of "dumping site" (Ceccato, 2005).

In some cases, the location of crime is not geographical but virtual and is difficult to tackle. In many cases such as fraud over the telephone, the victim and offender may never meet. On the Internet, residents living in rural, remote areas in Sweden are potentially as vulnerable to these sorts of crimes as their counterparts living in the Swedish capital, assuming they have Internet access and a computer. The crime can also be committed against a large number of people simultaneously. On a general level, one can speak of a trend away from theft offenses toward more fraud and scams, constituting a new type of crime often using ICT (BRÅ, 2014).

National victims surveys

Most general methodological problems in victimization surveys are related to sampling, measurement, and inference problems (Schneider, 1981) – but they are not limited to these. There are numerous methodological pitfalls in the use of survey data to study violence against women or to analyze fear of crime, for instance (Farrall, Bannister, Ditton, & Gilchrist, 1997; Schwartz, 2000). Schwartz and Pitts (1995) indicate that the major problems in analyzing violence against women are definitional problems, operationalization of concepts, recall bias, underreporting, question order, external validity, and the sex and ethnicity of interviewers.

In terms of sampling, an important problem is the issue of representation. Serious crimes are a relatively rare event. Thus, samples have to be of a considerable size to generate enough incidents of any particular type to permit detailed and meaningful analysis. This is particularly a problem when rural areas are concerned. However, a number of strategies can be used (e.g., weighting) depending on the response rate by groups and classes. See Chapter 10 for the details of this particular problem in the case of the Swedish victims surveys for violence against women in rural areas.

Another challenge when using crime victim survey data is that most research in this area may face problems because of what they assume with the data available. There is a long tradition among criminologists to use casual models using data from a survey cross-sectionally instead of a panel design. The problem grows when victimization is set as an independent variable, because the direction of causality may be difficult to ascertain. The problem is particularly accentuated when these variables designate behaviors and attitudes and are collected at a certain point in time, whereas the assumed victimization occurred prior to the interview. Schneider (1981) noted, for instance, that when victimization is set as an independent variable it is easier to deal with.

The third type of problem with crime victimization surveys is how far one can make inferences for a certain variable. It is difficult to determine how much of the variance in the victimization variable is true variance and how much is error. Whether the error is produced by a lack of reliability or by a lack of validity is not particularly important; what is important is that measurement error can influence the conclusions drawn from research studies.

In summary, the challenges in using police-recorded statistics and/or crime-victim survey data include not only the data itself but the way in which these data resources are utilized and theoretically framed. For instance, in ecological analysis there is a constant risk of so-called ecological fallacy, which occurs when correlated, aggregated values over a specific geographical area are erroneously related to the individual level. There is also the risk that maps, such as the ones presented in this book, may be used to create images that cannot be generalized for the whole group, and a distorted map may turn out to be a tool for exclusionary practices instead of providing a basis for more just actions (Ceccato, 2013a, pp. 20–21). In practice, the quality of data impacts on the quality of safety provided, in a best case scenario guiding evidence-based practices that can be shared by policing actors.

Rural Sweden: The study area

Why study Sweden? Sweden is an interesting case study for several reasons. Sweden is a Scandinavian and Nordic country (Figure 3.1a) with a milder climate than most other European countries. Most of the country is icebound from December to April, which limits, for instance, agriculture.

According to Eurostat, in 2014 there were 9.7 million people in Sweden. Of Sweden's 9.7 million residents, about 200,000 live in remote rural areas. Far

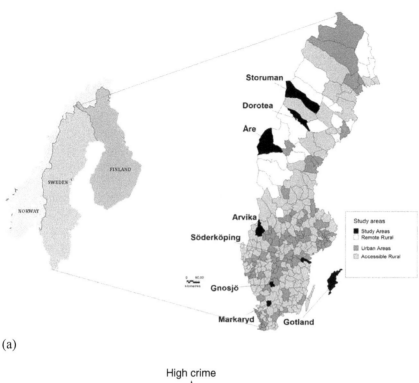

(a)

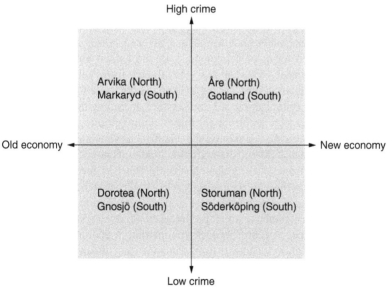

(b)

Figure 3.1 Municipalities in Sweden by type (a) and selection of eight municipalities for evaluating local crime prevention (b).

from being a homogeneous entity, rural in this book is considered here as a diverse set of communities with different characteristics and needs but that share a number of qualities and challenges. In Sweden, rural municipalities can be of two types: Remote Rural (RR) are areas more than 45 minutes by car from the nearest urban neighborhood with more than 3,000 inhabitants and Accessible Rural (AR), is composed of areas 5–45 minutes by car from urban locations with more than 3,000 inhabitants. Municipalities with more than 3,000 inhabitants and reachable in five minutes by car are regarded as Urban Areas (UA)[4] (Swedish National Rural Development Agency, 2008) (Figure 3.1a). Although problematic because it does not incorporate other dimensions of rurality, this definition reflects the municipalities' population size and accessibility, which are important criminogenic factors.

From an European perspective, Sweden is a sparsely populated country (22 inhabitants per km^2; the corresponding figure for Denmark is 125). There are 290 municipalities (*Kommun*) in Sweden, with an average population size of 31,000 inhabitants (from a minimum of 2.6 up to 766,000 inhabitants). In most chapters of this book municipalities are the unit of analysis since it is the smallest administrative unit and it is at this level that most indicators are available for comparisons at national level. There is a clear north–south divide in the population distribution: most remote rural municipalities are located in the mid-northwest of the country (22), whereas accessible rural (156) and urban (112) areas are found in the mid-South.

In addition, Sweden constitutes an interesting case study because most of the literature on crime and perceived safety in rural areas is based on case studies from North American and British studies. There is a need to extend the empirical evidence to include cases studies such as those in Sweden, which are embedded in more socially oriented forms of capitalism. Like the United States and most Western European countries, Sweden has transitioned from being rural and agrarian to urban and industrial/post-industrial state, which has affected not only crime levels but also the organization of basic services, including the police. Yet, welfare system principles play an important role in defining policies in Sweden, but with a more market oriented economy, the country has shown signs of 'rural change' that has imposed different demographic, socio-economic and cultural differentiation at both local and regional levels. In the last few decades the regional population redistribution have decreased but the tendency is towards concentration to a few regions with a decrease of population in rural areas. These developments – as described above – can be linked to the dynamics of crime. In addition, about 14 percent of the Swedish population was born in another country, the 10 largest groups coming from Finland, Iraq, Poland, the former Yugoslavia, Iran, Somalia, Germany, Turkey, and Denmark. Although they tend to be concentrated in the three largest cities in Sweden, certain foreign-born groups may be overrepresented in some parts of the country and/or towns. Foreign-born individuals are more often exposed to crime than natives, which has a direct impact on their perceived safety and quality of life, with marginal differences between urban and rural areas.

Studies reporting experiences with crime prevention (CP) in rural areas are relatively few in the international literature in comparison with those in urban areas. This book makes a contribution to this knowledge basis by looking at CP in rural areas particularly to deal with youth problems, farms and environmental crimes, and gendered violence. In 2010 there were 300 CP groups across the country. In order to evaluate CP in rural areas, a group of eight municipalities were selected representing the new and the old economy chosen based on the percentage of the active population employed in service sectors (Åre, Gotland, Storuman, and Söderköping) and in traditional sectors of the economy (Arvika, Markaryd, Dorotea, and Gnosjö), respectively (Figure 3.1b). High and low crime levels are defined based on the relative rural regional average rate: high-crime municipalities are those with crime rates above the average and low-crime municipalities show a rate below the rural average (Åre and Gotland from the new economy and Arvika and Markaryd from the traditional economy are high-crime municipalities; low-crime municipalities are Storuman and Söderköping from the modern economy and Dorotea and Gnosjö from the old economy). By studying Sweden, this book characterizes rural crime, perceived safety and crime prevention in Scandinavian rural contexts, which was until recently inexistent in the international literature.

Concluding remarks

This chapter highlights some of the most important theoretical markers for the book. It starts with basic definitions in crime and community safety in rural areas with the intention to provide a conceptual framework for the book. Key theories in criminology are discussed in relation to their theoretical power to support the analysis and complexities of rural areas. This includes a short review of the main types of crime prevention models portrayed in Chapters 11 to 14. Finally, a number of issues related to data quality and implications of data sources for the analysis of rural crime, perceived safety, and crime prevention are highlighted, with the focus on official police statistics and national crime victims surveys.

A number of points are worth keeping in mind when reading the next chapters. First, the search for a singular definition of "rural" is illusory, but this does not mean that rural is an indefinable theoretical entity. In reality, rural areas are composed of a diverse set of communities with different characteristics and needs that share a number of qualities and challenges. Their qualities might be worth investigating taking into account both the relativism of the term associated to what is considered to be "rural" according to those that produce and experience the rural (its reflexivity). Rural must be regarded in relation to time and spatial references as well as contexts in which it occurs. This calls for the development of research and practice about rural and safety that crosses the current boundaries between fields, disciplines, and theoretical perspectives.

Another important point is that none of the theories discussed in this chapter is without criticism, and none was developed for the purpose of explaining crime, perceived safety, and crime prevention in rural contexts. However, all these theoretical principles have the potential to support the analysis of rural areas in the next chapters, from routine activity theory to situational crime theory, as well as macro theories such as institutional anomie.

Perceived safety involves more than just fear of crime but it can be captured as such through crime victim surveys. How one defines safety is a result of inter-sections of many factors, some being individual (such as age, gender, sexual identity, disability, previous victimization, familiarity with an environment, mobility), others being related to qualities attributed to the environment where he or she is embedded (such as signs of disorder and crime, social cohesion, and collective efficacy) or macro-scale processes (such as the media, natural hazards, global threats). Safety depends on the individual and the groups' characteristics to which they belong. With regards to victimization and perceived safety, special focus is given in this book to those individuals and groups whose safety is often overlooked by police and official statistics. The book adopts a *gender-informed approach* to safety, avoiding generalization and assessing how victimization *intersects* with other types of individual characteristics.

Emphasis is given to the environment where crime takes place. This means that reducing crime, or making places safer, requires initiatives that focus on reducing crime opportunities at those places by taking into account their par-ticular contexts. Knowledge of what works and what does not work in rural con-texts is necessary. Problems in police data and data from crime victims' surveys are unlikely to be resolved in the short term, by researchers or practitioners, but the use of multi-data and multi-methods, as in this book, will likely become a worthwhile alternative for rural criminology.

Notes

1 For a complete discussion of the different types of definitions, see, for example, Halfa-cree (1993, 2006) and Woods (2005, 2011).
2 *Dagens Nyheter*, Försäkringsbranschen: Förbered Sverige bättre för extremväder, retrieved September 11, 2014, from www.dn.se/ekonomi/forsakringsbranschen-forbered-sverige-battre-for-extremvader/.
3 *Södermanlands Nyheter*, Stort engagemang för skogsbranden i sociala medier, retrieved August 5, 2014, from www.sn.se/nyheter/sormland/1.2537146.
4 An alternative way to classify Swedish rural areas was suggested by Statistics Sweden (H-regions), with six classes of municipalities, from large urban areas to remote rural ones, based on their geographical and economic homogeneity.

References

Agnew, R. (1999). A general strain theory of community differences in crime rates. *Journal of Research in Crime and Delinquency, 36*(2), 123–155.
Barak, G., Leighton, P., & Flavin, J. (2010). *Class, race, gender, and crime: The social realities of justice in America*. Plymouth: Rowman & Littlefield.
Barclay, E., Scott, J., Hogg, R., & Donnermeyer, J. (Eds.). (2007). *Crime in rural Aus-tralia*. Sydney: Federation Press.

Bell, D. (1997). Anti-idyll: Rural horror. In P. Cloke & J. Litte (Eds.), *Contested countryside cultures: Otherness, marginalisation and rurality* (pp. 94–108). London: Routledge.

Bell, S. E., & Braun, Y. A. (2010). Coal, identity, and the gendering of environmental justice activism in central Appalachia. *Gender and Society, 24*(6), 794–813.

Bernasco, W. I. M. (2010). A sentimental journey to crime: Effects of residential history on crime location choice. *Criminology, 48*(2), 389–416.

Bosworth, G., & Somerville, P. (2014). Introduction. In G. Bosworth & P. Somerville (Eds.), *Interpreting rurality: Multidisciplinary approaches* (pp. 1–11). Oxford: Routledge.

Brantingham, P., & Brantingham, P. (1984). *Patterns in crime*. New York: Macmillan.

Brantingham, P., & Brantingham, P. (1995). Criminality of place: Crime generators and crime attractors. *European Journal on Criminal Policy and Research, 3*, 1–26.

Brottsförebyggande rådet – BRÅ (National Council of Crime Prevention). (2014). Police recorded statistics. Stockholm: BRÅ.

Bullard, R. D. (1983). Solid waste sites and the black Houston community. *Sociological Inquiry, 53*(2–3), 273–288.

Bursik, R. J. (1999). The informal control of crime through neighborhood networks. *Sociological Focus, 32*(1), 85–97.

Carrington, K. (2007). Crime in rural and regional areas. In J. F. D. E. Barclay, J. Scott, & R. Hogg (Eds.), *Crime in rural Australia* (pp. 27–43). Sydney: Federation Press.

Carrington, K., Hogg, R., & McIntosh, A. (2011). The resource boom's underbelly: Criminological impacts of mining development. *Australian and New Zealand Journal of Criminology, 44*(3), 335–354.

Ceccato, V. (2005). Tools in the spatial analysis of offences: Evidence from Scandinavian cities. In M. Campagna (Ed.), *GIS for sustainable development* (pp. 267–287). Boca Raton, CA: CRC, Taylor & Francis.

Ceccato, V. (2007). Crime dynamics at Lithuanian borders. *European Journal of Criminology, 4*(2), 131–160.

Ceccato, V. (2008). Expressive crimes in post-socialist states of Estonia, Latvia and Lithuania. *Journal of Scandinavian Studies in Criminology and Crime Prevention, 9*(1), 2–30.

Ceccato, V. (2012). *The urban fabric of crime and fear*. Dordrecht/New York/London: Springer.

Ceccato, V. (2013a). Integrating geographical information into urban safety research and planning. *Proceedings of the ICE – Urban Design and Planning, 166*, 15–23.

Ceccato, V. (2013b). *Moving safely: Crime and perceived safety in Stockholm's subway stations*. Plymouth: Lexington.

Ceccato, V. (2015). Guest editorial. *Journal of Rural Studies, 37*.

Ceccato, V., & Dolmén, L. (2011). Crime in rural Sweden. *Applied Geography, 31*(1), 119–135.

Ceccato, V., & Dolmén, L. (2013). Crime prevention in rural Sweden. *European Journal of Criminology, 10*, 89–112.

Ceccato, V., & Haining, R. (2004). Crime in border regions: The Scandinavian case of Öresund, 1998–2001. *Annals of the Association of American Geographers, 94*, 807–826.

Ceccato, V., & Haining, R. (2005). Assessing the geography of vandalism: Evidence from a Swedish city. *Urban Studies, 42*, 1637–1656.

Ceccato, V., & Haining, R. (2008). Short and medium term dynamics and their influence on acquisitive crime rates in the transition states of Estonia, Latvia and Lithuania. *Applied Spatial Analysis and Policy, 1*(3), 215–244.

Ceccato, V., & Newton, A. (Eds.). (2015). *Safety and security in transit environments: An interdisciplinary approach*. Basingstoke: Palgrave.

Ceccato, V. A., & Snickars, F. (2000). Adapting GIS technology to the needs of local planning. *Environment and Planning B: Planning and Design, 27*(6), 923–937.

Chakraborti, N., & Garland, J. (Eds.). (2011). *Rural racism*. Abingdon/New York: Routledge.

Clarke, R. V. (1997). *Situational crime prevention: Successful case studies*. Monsey, NY: Willow Tree.

Cloke, P., & Little, J. (1997). *Contested countryside cultures: Otherness marginalisation and rurality*. London: Routledge.

Cohen, L. E., & Felson, M. (1979). Social change and crime rate trends: A routine activity approach. *American Sociological Review, 44*, 588–608.

Collins English Dictionary. (2003). Harm. Complete and Unabridged, Collins. Retrieved December 2, 2014, from www.thefreedictionary.com/harm.

Crang, M., & Thrift, N. (2000). Introduction. In M. Crang & N. Thrift (Eds.), *Thinking Space* (pp. 1–30). London: Routledge.

Davies, P., Francis, P., & Wyatt, T. (2014). Taking invisible crimes and social harms seriously. In P. Davies, P. Francis, & T. Wyatt (Eds.), *Invisible crimes and social harms* (pp. 1–25). Basingstoke: Palgrave Macmillan.

Davis, K. (2008). Intersectionality as buzzword: A sociology of science perspective on what makes a feminist theory successful. *Feminist Theory, 9*(1), 67–85.

Day, K. (2009). Being feared: Masculinity and race in public space. In M. L. S. Farrall (Ed.), *Fear of crime: Critical voices in an age of anxiety* (pp. 82–107). New York: Routledge-Cavendish.

DeKeseredy, W., Muzzatti, S., & Donnermeyer, J. (2014). Mad men in bib overalls: Media's horrification and pornification of rural culture. *Critical Criminology, 22*(2), 179–197.

DeKeseredy, W. S. (2015). New directions in feminist understandings of rural crime and social control. *Journal of Rural Studies* (in press).

Deller, S., & Deller, M. (2010). Rural crime and social capital. *Growth and Change, 41*(2), 221–275.

Deller, S., & Deller, M. (2011). Structural shifts in select determinants of crime with a focus on rural and urban differences. *Western Criminology Review, 12*(3), 120–138.

Deller, S., & Deller, M. (2012). Spatial heterogeneity, social capital, and rural larceny and burglary. *Rural Sociology, 77*(2), 225–253.

Donnermeyer, D., & DeKeseredy, W. S. (2013). *Rural criminology*. Abingdon: Routledge.

Donnermeyer, J. (2007). Locating rural crime: The role of theory. In E. Barclay, J. Donnermeyer, J. Scott, & R. Hogg (Eds.), *Crime in rural Australia* (pp. 15–26). Annandale: Federation Press.

Donnermeyer, J. (2012). Rural crime and critical criminology. In W. S. DeKeseredy & M. Dragiewicz (Eds.), *Routledge handbook of critical criminology* (pp. 290–302). Abingdon: Routledge.

Donnermeyer, J., Scott, J., & Carrington, K. (2013). How rural criminology informs critical thinking in criminology. *International Journal for Crime, Justice and Social Democracy, 2*(3), 69–91.

Donnermeyer, J. F. (2014). The social organization of rural america and crime. Paper presented at *Rural Crime and Community Safety*, Stockholm.

Donnermeyer, J. F., Jobes, P., & Barclay, E. (2006). Rural crime, poverty and rural community. In W. S. DeKeseredy & B. Perry (Eds.), *Advancing critical criminology: Theory and application* (pp. 199–213). Oxford: Lexington Books.

Durkheim, E. (1897). *Suicide: A study in sociology*. New York: Free Press.

Farrall, S., Bannister, J., Ditton, J., & Gilchrist, E. (1997). Questioning the measurement of the gear of crime: Findings from a major methodological study. *British Journal of Criminology, 37*(4), 658–679.

Farrington, D., Loeber, R., & Southamer-Loeber, M. (2003). How can the relationship between race and violence be explained? In D. F. Hawkins (Ed.), *Violent crime: Assessing race and ethnic differences* (pp. 213–237). Cambridge: Cambridge University Press.

Felson, M. (2006). *Crime and nature.* Thousand Oaks, CA: Sage.

Felson, M. (2013). Crime's impingement in space. In S. Ruiter, W. Bernasco, W. Huisman, & G. Bruinsma (Eds.), *Eenvoud en verscheidenheid: Liber amicorum voor Henk Elffers* (pp. 341–355). Amsterdam: NSCR & Afdeling Criminologie Vrije Universiteit Amsterdam.

Fernback, J. (2007). Beyond the diluted community concept: A symbolic interactionist perspective on online social relations. *New Media and Society, 9*(1), 49–69.

Freudenburg, W. R., & Jones, R. E. (1991). Criminal behavior and rapid community growth: Examining the evidence 1. *Rural Sociology, 56*(4), 619–645.

Frey, W. H., & Zimmer, Z. (2001). Defining the city. In R. Paddison (Ed.), *Handbook of urban studies* (pp. 14–35). London: Sage.

Garland, J., & Chakraborti, N. (2006). "Race", space and place: Examining identity and cultures of exclusion in rural England. *Ethnicities, 6*(2), 159–177.

Giddens, A. (1991). *Modernity and self-identity: Self and society in the late modern age.* Cambridge: Polity Press.

Giddens, A. (2014). *Turbulent and mighty continent: What future for Europe?* Cambridge: Polity.

Groves, R. (2011). *Rural and suburban America: When one definition is not enough.* Seattle, WA: Washington University.

Halfacree, K. (1993). Locality and social representation: Space, discourse and alternative definitions of the rural. *Journal of Rural Studies, 9*(1), 23–37.

Halfacree, K. (2006). Rural space: Constructing a three-fold architecture. In P. Clocke, T. Marsden, & P. Mooney (Eds.), *Handbook of rural studies* (pp. 44–62). London: Sage.

Hobbs, D. (1994). The context of rising rates of rural violence and substance abuse: The problems and potential of rural communities. In S. M. Blaser, J. Blaser, & K. Pantoja (Eds.), *Perspectives on violence and substance use in rural America* (pp. 115–124). Wilmington, NC: North Carolina Regional Educational Laboratory.

Hogg, R., & Carrington, K. (1998). Crime, rurality and community. *Australian and New Zealand Journal of Criminology, 31*(2), 160–181.

Hogg, R., & Carrington, K. (2006). *Policing the rural crisis.* Sydney: Federation Press.

Hoggart, K. (1990). Let's do away with rural. *Journal of Rural Studies, 6*(3), 245–257.

Holloway, R., & Kneafsey, L. (2000). Reading the space of the farmers' market: A preliminary investigation from the UK. *Journal Sociologia Ruralis, 40*(3), 285–299.

Hughes, A., Lise, A. A., Palen, L., & Anderson, K. N. (2014). Online public communications by police & fire services during the 2012 Hurricane Sandy. Paper presented at the *Proceedings of the SIGCHI Conference on Human Factors in Computing Systems,* Toronto, Ontario, Canada.

Ilbery, B., & Bowler, I. (1998). From agricultural productivism to post-productivism. In B. Ilbery (Ed.), *The geography of rural change* (pp. 53–83). Harlow: Addison Wesley Longman.

Johansson, M., Westlund, H., & Eliasson, K. (2009). The "new rurality" and entrepreneurship: Attributes influencing enterprise propensity in rural Sweden. Paper presented at the *Congress of Regional Science Association International,* Lodz, Poland.

Kaylen, M., & Pridemore, W. A. (2012). Systematically addressing inconsistencies in the rural social disorganization and crime literature. *International Journal of Rural Criminology, 1*(2), 148.

Kaylen, M. T., & Pridemore, W. A. (2011). A reassessment of the association between social disorganization and youth violence in rural areas. *Social Science Quarterly, 92*(4), 978–1001.

Kaylen, M. T., & Pridemore, W. A. (2013a). The association between social disorganization and rural violence is sensitive to the measurement of the dependent variable. *Criminal Justice Review*, 38(2), 169–189.

Kaylen, M. T., & Pridemore, W. A. (2013b). Social disorganization and crime in rural communities: The first direct test of the systemic model. *British Journal of Criminology, 53*(5), 905–923.

Kim, S.-W., & Pridemore, W. A. (2005). Social change, institutional anomie and serious property crime in transitional Russia. *British Journal of Criminology, 45*(1), 81–97.

Kornhauser, R. (1978). *Social sources of delinquency*. Chicago, IL: University of Chicago Press.

Lambert, J. (2013). *Digital storytelling: Capturing lives, creating community* (4th ed.). New York: Routledge.

Laycock, G. (2005). Defining crime science: New approaches to detecting and preventing crime. In N. T. Melissa & J. Smith (Eds.), *Crime science* (pp. 3–24). Cullompton, Devon: Willan Publishing.

Liepins, R. (2000). New energies for an old idea: Reworking approaches to "community" in contemporary rural studies. *Journal of Rural Studies, 16*(1), 23–35.

Liu, J. (2005). Crime patterns during the market transition in China. *British Journal of Criminology, 45*(5), 613–633.

Los, M. (2002). Post-communist fear of crime and the commercialization of security. *Theoretical Criminology, 6*(2), 165–188.

Lowe, P., Marsden, T., Murdoch, J., & Ward, N. (2012). *The differentiated countryside*. London/New York: Routledge.

Mahon, M. (2007). New populations; shifting expectations: The changing experience of Irish rural space and place. *Journal of Rural Studies, 23*(3), 345–356.

Marsden, T. (1998). New rural territories: Regulating the differentiated rural spaces. *Journal of Rural Studies, 14*(1), 107–117.

Marsden, T. (2008). Agri-food contestations in rural space: GM in its regulatory context. *Geoforum, 39*(1), 191–203.

Mawby, R. (2015). Exploring the relationship between crime and place in the countryside. *Journal of Rural Studies* (in press).

Mawby, R. I. (2007). Crime, place and explaining rural hotspots. *International Journal of Rural Crime, 1*, 21–43.

Melamid, A. (1967). Von Thunen's isolated state: An English edition of Der Isolierte Staat by Johann Heinrich von Thunen; Carla M. Wartenberg; Peter Hall; central places in southern Germany by Walter Christaller; Carlisle W. Baskin. *Geographical Review, 57*(4), 574–576.

Merton, R. (1938). Social structure and anomie. *American Sociological Review, 3*, 672–682.

Messner, S., & Rosenfeld, R. (1994). *Crime and the American dream*. Belmont, CA: Wadsworth.

Messner, S. F., & Rosenfeld, R. (1997). Political restraint of the market and levels of criminal homicide: A cross-national application of institutional anomie theory. *Social Forces, 75*, 1393–1416.

Messner, S., & Rosenfeld, R. (Eds.). (1999). *Social structure and homicide: Theory and research* (Vols. 27–34). London: Sage.

Ministry of Justice. (1994). Brott, Lag (1994:458). C.F.R. § kap. 1 § Brottsbalken Regeringskansliets rättsdatabaser (in Swedish). Retrieved April, 9, 2015 from https://lagen.nu/1962:700#K1P1.

Osgood, D. W., & Chambers, J. M. (2003). Community correlates of rural youth violence. *Juvenile Justice Bulletin*, May, 12.

Oxford English Dictionary (2009). Crime. Oxford: Oxford University Press.

Owen, S., & Carrington, K. (2015). Domestic violence (DV) service provision and the architecture of rural life: An Australian case study. *Journal of Rural Studies* (in press).

Palen, L., Vieweg, S., Liu, S. B., & Hughes, A. L. (2009). Crisis in a networked world: Features of computer-mediated communication in the April 16, 2007, Virginia tech event. *Social Science Computer Review, 27*(4), 467–480.

Pawson, R., & Tilley, N. (1997). *Realistic evaluation*. London: Sage.

Peterson, R. D., & Krivo, L. J. (2005). Macrostructural analyses of race, ethnicity, and violent crime: Recent lessons and new directions for research. *Annual Review of Sociology, 31*, 331–356.

Philo, C. (1997a). Across the water: Reviewing geographical studies of asylums and other mental health facilities. *Health and Place, 3*(2), 73–89.

Philo, C. (1997b). Of other rurals. In P. Cloke & J. Little (Eds.), *Contested countryside cultures: Otherness marginalisation and rurality* (pp. 19–48). London: Routledge.

Porter, M. (1996). *Tackling cross border crime*. London: Home Office.

Putnam, R. (2000). *Bowling alone: The collapse and revival of American community*. New York: Simon & Schuster.

Ramsey, D., Abrams, J., Clark, J. K., & Evans, N. J. (2013). Rural geography – rural development: An examination of agriculture, policy and planning, and community in rural areas. *Journal of Rural and Community Development, 8*(1), i–v.

Ratcliffe, J. (2010). Crime mapping: Spatial and temporal challenges. In A. R. Piquero & D. Weisburd (Eds.), *Handbook of quantitative criminology* (pp. 5–24). New York: Springer.

Ratcliffe, J. H., & McCullagh, M. J. (1998). Aoristic crime analysis. *International Journal of Geographical Information Science, 12*(7), 751–764.

Ravera, F., Scheidel, A., dell'Angelo, J., Gamboa, G., Serrano, T., Mingorría, S., Cabello, V., Arizpe, N., & Ariza, P. (2014). Pathways of rural change: an integrated assessment of metabolic patterns in emerging ruralities. *Environment, Development and Sustainability, 16*(4), 811–820.

Reissman, L. (1964). *The urban process: Cities in industrial societies*. New York: Free Press of Glencoe.

Rephann, T. J. (1999). Links between rural development and crime. *Papers in Regional Science, 78*(4), 365–386.

Rhodes, W., & Conly, C. (1981). Crime and mobility: An empirical study. In P. J. Brantingham & P. L. Brantingham (Eds.), *Environmental criminology* (pp. 167–188). Beverly Hills, CA: Sage.

Rogers, E. M., Burdge, R. J., Korsching, P. J., & Donnermeyer, J. (1988). *Social change in rural societies* (3rd ed.). Englewood Cliffs, NJ: Prentice Hall.

Salla, J., Ceccato, V., & Ahven, A. (2011). Homicide in Estonia. In M. C. A. Liem & W. A. Pridemore (Eds.), *Handbook of European homicide research: Patterns, explanations, and country* (pp. 421–437). New York/Dordrecht/Heidelberg/London: Springer.

Sampson, R. J. (1986). Crime in cities: The effects of formal and informal social control. *Crime and Justice, 8*, 271–311.

Sampson, R. J., Raudenbush, S. W., & Earls, F. (1997). Neighborhoods and violent crime: A multilevel study of collective efficacy. *Science, 277*(5328), 918–924.

Sandercock, R. J. (Ed.). (2005). *Difference, fear and habitus: A political economy of urban fear*. Aldershot: Ashgate.

Schneider, A. L. (1981). Methodological problems in victim surveys and their implications for research in victimology. *Journal of Criminal Law and Criminology, 72*(2), 818–838.

Schwartz, M. D. (2000). Methodological issues in the use of survey data for measuring and characterizing violence against women. *Violence Against Women, 6*(8), 815–838.

Schwartz, M. D., & Pitts, V. L. (1995). Exploring a feminist routine activities approaches to explaining sexual assault. *Justice Quarterly, 12*, 9–31.

Scorzafave, L. G., Justus, M., & Shikida, P. F. A. (2015). Safety in the global south: Criminal victimization in Brazilian rural areas. *Journal of Rural Studies* (in press).

Scott, J., Carrington, K., & McIntosh, A. (2012). Established-outsider relations and fear of crime in mining towns. *Sociologia Ruralis, 52*(2), 147–169.

Shaw, C. R., & McKay, H. D. (1942). *Juvenile delinquency and urban areas*. Chicago, IL: University of Chicago Press.

Sherman, L. W., Gartin, P. R., & Buerger, M. E. (1989). Hot spots of predatory crime: Routine activities and the criminology of place. *Criminology, 27*(1), 27–56.

Shortall, S., & Warner, M. (2012). Rural transformations: Conceptual and policy issues. In M. Shucksmith, D. Brown, S. Shothall, J. Vergunst, & M. Warner (Eds.), *Rural transformations and rural policies in the US and UK* (pp. 3–18). New York: Routledge.

Smith, M. J., & Cornish, D. B. (2006). *Secure and tranquil travel: Preventing crime and disorder on public transport*. London: Routledge.

Smith, N. (1984). *Uneven development*. Oxford: Blackwell.

Thrift, N. (1996). *Spatial formations*. London: Sage.

Townsley, M., & Sidebottom, A. (2010). All offenders are equal, but some are more equal than others: Variation in journeys to crime between offenders. *Criminology, 48*(3), 897–917.

Tönnies, F. (1887). *Gemeinschaft und Gesellschaft*. Leipzig: Fues's Verlag. (Translated, 1957 by Charles Price Loomis as *Community and society*, East Lansing, MI: Michigan State University Press.)

United Nations – UN. (1997). Report of the economic and social council for 1997. A/52/3, General Assembly, 52nd Session. New York: United Nations Department of Economic and Social Affairs.

United Nations – UN. (2013). Creating safe public spaces. Retrieved April 9, 2015, from www.unwomen.org/en/what-we-do/ending-violence-against-women/creating-safe-public-spaces.

UN Women. (2014). Safe cities global initiatives. UN, 2. Retrieved April 9, 2014, from www.unwomen.org.

van Leeuwen, E. S. (2010). *Urban–rural interactions towns as focus points in rural development*. Heidelberg/Dordrecht/London/New York: Springer-Verlag.

Warr, M. (2000). Fear of crime in the United States: Avenues for research and policy. *Criminal Justice and Behavior, 4*, 451–489.

Websdale, N., & Johnson, B. (1998). An ethnostatistical comparison of the forms and levels of woman battering in urban and rural areas of Kentucky. *Criminal Justice Review, 23*, 161–196.

Weisheit, R. A., & Donnermeyer, J. F. (2000). Changes and continuity in crime in rural America. In G. LaFree (Ed.), *Criminal justice 2000: The nature of crime, continuity and change* (pp. 309–357). Washington, DC: US Department of Justice.

Weisheit, R. A., Falcone, D. N., & Wells, L. E. (2006). *Crime and policing in rural and small-town rural America.* Prospect Heights, IL: Waveland Press.

Weisheit, R. A., Wells, L. E., & Falcone, D. N. (1994). Community policing in small town and rural America. *Crime and Delinquency, 40*(4), 549–567.

White, R. C. (1932). The relation of felonies to environmental factors in Indianapolis. *Social Forces, 10*(4), 498–509.

Wiebe, D. J., Richmond, T. S., Poster, J., Guo, W., Allison, P. D., & Branas, C. C. (2014). Adolescents' fears of violence in transit environments during daily activities. *Security Journal, 27*(2), 226–241.

Wikström, P.-O., Ceccato, V., Hardie, B., & Treiber, K. (2010). Activity fields and the dynamics of crime. *Journal of Quantitative Criminology, 26*(1), 55–87.

Wiles, P., & Costello, A. (2000). The "road to nowhere": The evidence for travelling criminals (p. 207). London: Home Office Research Study.

Woods, M. (2005). Defining the rural. In *Rural geography* (pp. 3–16). London: Sage.

Woods, M. (2011). *Rural.* London/New York: Routledge.

Wyant, B. R. (2008). Multilevel impacts of perceived incivilities and perceptions of crime risk on fear of crime: Isolating endogenous impacts. *Journal of Research in Crime and Delinquency, 45*(1), 39–64.

Yarwood, R. (2015) Lost and hound: The more-than-human networks of rural policing. *Journal of Rural Studies* (in press).

Yarwood, R., & Edwards, B. (1995). Voluntary action in rural areas: The case of neighbourhood watch. *Journal of Rural Studies, 11*(4), 447–459.

Young, J. (2011). *The criminological imagination.* Cambridge: Polity Press.

Part II
Trends and patterns of crime

4   Rural–urban crime trends in international perspective

Since the mid-1990s, many countries have witnessed substantial and widespread drops in crime. Major decreases in crime were first observed in the United States, where violent crime including homicide fell 40 percent during the 1990s and attracted much international attention (Blumstein, 2000; Blumstein & Rosenfeld, 2008; Farrell, Tilley, Tseloni, & Mailley, 2010; LaFree, 1999; Levitt, 2004). Though there is little consensus on the reasons for this decline, the trend has been confirmed in many countries using data from the International Crime Victims Survey, with declines in all types of crime except burglary (Tseloni, Mailley, Farrell, & Tilley, 2010). Some claim some sort of "universality of the crime drop" (Levitt, 2004), as supposedly the decrease in crime affected all geographic areas and demographic groups. However, there have been efforts to question this "universal nature of the crime drop" that focus on broad explanations for such crime reduction (Parker, 2008). Still, most of this literature is based on cross-national studies or focused on urban centers only (see e.g., Tseloni et al., 2010). Most studies do not regard urban–rural differences in the decrease as a relevant issue in its own right (but see e.g., Levitt, 2004).

This chapter starts by comparing crime rates in Sweden with those in the United States and the United Kingdom. In all three countries, urban crime rates are higher than rural ones, regardless of definitions of crime types and how rural areas are conceptualized. An alternative to relying solely on official police statistics is to complement them, as much as possible, with data from national crime victim surveys, as it is done in this chapter. Despite the limitations of these sources of data, they are the most reliable data available for representing the geographic distribution of crime in Sweden and elsewhere. First, trends in crime rates and prevalence are compared in a selection of countries as background for the Swedish case. This chapter discusses evidence about the so-called "convergence hypothesis" of urban and rural crime rates. Then, the analysis focuses on specific types of violent and property crimes in rural areas, drawing conclusions for rural areas across countries whenever possible. The chapter also discusses crime variation by groups of individuals (including repeat victimization), but the focus is on crime variations over time in selected rural communities. The concept of population at risk using both resident population and floating population (by vehicle traffic) is also discussed. What the chapter does not do is to speculate about possible reasons for these trends, as it would not be wise to assume general explanations for the drop and completely immature to pose specific causes for urban–rural crime trends at the national level. Yet, this is an important new territory for future research that is beyond the scope of this book. The chapter concludes with a summary of the urban–rural trends in crime in Sweden and internationally and a request for better understanding of these trends that, at least in some places, are making rural areas more similar to urban ones.

Urban–rural crime trends

Are rural areas becoming more criminogenic? Crime victimization disproportionately affects more urban than rural residents, regardless of crime trends, country, or differences in rural–urban contexts. Although some would claim that crime is eminently an urban phenomenon, recent changes in rural–urban relationships have affected regional criminogenic landscapes; apparently this process is making individuals who live in some rural areas more exposed to crime than in the past. It is suggested that this trend goes undetected often because changes do not affect homogeneously rural areas. Victimization may also be selective and unequal across social groups and environments. Evidence on how these changes affect criminogenic conditions is difficult to ascertain because, as we will discuss in this chapter, it may be hidden under general "decreasing" or "stable" trends. By standardizing crime by population (not considering crime levels or prevalence only), this chapter later attempts to systematically look at concentration of victimization. This is relevant because, if rural crime increases, it could be either because there are more rural victims or the same number of victims who are victimized more often (repeat victimization).

In the United Kingdom, crime is decreasing regardless of area or data source (Home Office, 2011). In Sweden (Table 4.1) and, to some extent, in the United States (Levitt, 2004), the trend is patchier but still decreasing. In Sweden, some rural areas are more criminogenic now than they were previously. Police records over 15 years show that urban and accessible rural areas are at higher risk of crime than the most remote ones but that the increases converge toward the year 2014. Although the trends diverge somewhat in urban and rural areas, the short-term directions of change seem to track one another quite closely up to 2014, when rates dropped to levels similar to those found in 2002 (Figure 4.1). The biggest increases are in violence, criminal damage, and some types of property crime. Crime victim surveys in Sweden, although covering only five years, show a more stable picture, indicating a declining trend in crime.

In the United States, total crime rates for urban counties have declined, whilst crime rates in rural counties have increased, particularly for violent crime (Deller & Deller, 2010; Weisheit, Wells, & Falcone, 1994). As Fischer (2011) suggests, from the 1970s through the 1990s, the equation "big city equals violent crime" was often taken for granted. During the past 20 years, there have been signs in the United States that rural and urban crime rates are converging (Deller &

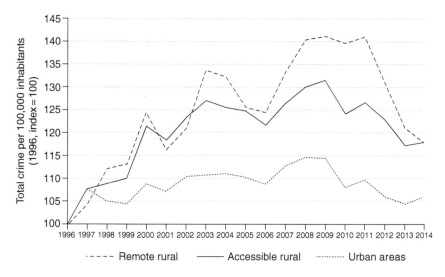

Figure 4.1 Increase in offending rates in Sweden per area, 2002–2010 (total crime per 10,000 inhabitants, 2002/2003 = 100) (source: Ceccato & Dolmen, 2013, p. 97).

Deller, 2010). Fischer (2011) suggests that the view of the 1970s and 1980s that associated big cities with "danger" may be fading away.

Kneebone and Raphael (2011) provide evidence of this convergence. In a study covering 5,400 communities located within the 100 largest US metropolitan areas, both violent and property crime were found to have declined significantly between 1990 and 2008, with the largest decreases occurring in cities. The Kneebone–Raphael analysis divided suburban communities into four types: "dense inner suburbs," "mature suburbs," "emerging suburbs," and rural "exurbs." On average, the inner suburbs experienced major declines in rates of violent crime, although not as great as the core cities. But the more outlying suburbs experienced little change or even increases in rates of violent crime. Violent crime rates dropped by almost 30 percent in cities, while property crime fell by 46 percent. Though city crime rates remain considerably higher than rates in the suburbs, smaller decreases in suburban violent and property crime rates over this time period narrowed the gap. In 90 of the 100 largest metropolitan areas, the gap between city and suburban property crime rates narrowed between 1990 and 2008. Cities and high-density suburbs saw violent crime rates decline, but predominantly rural communities experienced slight increases that are not explained by their changing demographics.

Carrington (2007) also suggests that rates for violent crime and property offenses have been growing at faster rates in rural Australia, where crime, particularly violent crimes, is not a predominantly urban phenomenon. In Sweden, as in the United States and, to some extent, the United Kingdom, a convergent pattern between urban and rural areas is found more often in crime rates from police statistics than in data from crime victim surveys (Table 4.1).

Table 4.1 Trends in violent and property crimes from police records and crime victimization surveys in Sweden, the United States, and United Kingdom, by areas

		Police records		Victimization surveys	
		Property	*Violent*	*Property*	*Violent*
Sweden[i]	Rural	Increase* (1996–2010)[1]	Increase (1996–2010)	Slight decrease/stable (2006–2010)[2]	Stable** (2006–2010)
	Urban	Decrease (1996–2010)	Increase (1996–2010)	Slight decrease/stable (2006–2010)	Stable (2006–2010)
	Total	Decrease (1996–2010)	Increase (1996–2010)	Decrease (2006–2010)	Stable (2006–2010)
USA	Rural	Decrease (1990–2008)[3ii]	Slight increases (1990–2008)	Decrease (1993–2005)[4iii]	Decrease (1993–2005)
	Urban	Decrease (1990–2008)	Decrease (1990–2008)	Decrease (1993–2005)	Decrease (1993–2005)
	Total	Decrease (1990–2008)	Decrease (1990–2008)	Decrease (1993–2005)	Decrease (1993–2005)
England/UK[iv]	Rural	Decrease (2002–2010)[5]	Decrease*** (2002–20108)	Decrease[6] Stable since 2001[7] (2001–2010)	Decrease[6] (2001–2010) Stable since 2001[7]
	Urban	Decrease (2002–2010)	Decrease (2002–2010)	Decrease[6] Decrease[7] (2001–2010)	Decrease[6] (2001–2010) Stable but a peak in 2005[7]
	Total	Decrease (2002–2010)	Decrease (2002–2010)	Decrease[6] Decrease[7] (2001–2010)	Decrease[6]**** (2001–2010) Stable but a peak in 2005[7]

Sources

1 The Swedish National Council for Crime Prevention (BRÅ), police-recorded data.
2 The Swedish National Council for Crime Prevention (BRÅ), crime victimization surveys.
3 Kneebone and Raphael (2011), based on FBI and census data.
4 US Department of Justice (2011) based on crime victimization surveys.
5 Higgins et al. (2010) based on police-recorded data.
6 Higgins et al. (2010) based on BCS – British crime and victimization survey data.
7 Higgins et al. (2010) based on BCS – Community Safety Partnership.

Notes

* Burglary, car-related theft, robbery, and vandalism.
** But increased serious assault in small towns and rural areas.
*** Stable for sexual violence across areas, increase for drug offenses for all areas.
**** But similar trends for both rural and urban, reduction for all areas.
i Remote rural (RR) areas are more than 45 minutes by car from the nearest urban neighborhood with more than 3,000 inhabitants, whilst Accessible Rural (AR) areas are 5–45 minutes by car from urban locations with more than 3,000 inhabitants. Municipalities with more than 3,000 inhabitants and reachable within 5 minutes by car are regarded as Urban Areas (UA).
ii Divided areas into "core cities" and suburban communities of four types: dense inner suburbs, "mature suburbs," "emerging suburbs," and the still rural "exurbs."
iii Large cities have a population of 100,000 or more, while small cities have a population of less than 100,000.
iv *Predominantly rural areas* are those classified as rural districts with at least 80% of their population in rural settlements and larger market towns. They also include rural districts with at least 50% but less than 80% of their population in rural settlements and larger market towns. *Significant rural areas* are those classified as dis-tricts with more than 37,000 people or more than 26% of their population in rural settlements and larger market towns. *Predominantly urban areas* are those classi-fied as major urban districts with either 100,000 people or 50% of their population in urban areas with a population of more than 750,000 but also large urban districts with either 50,000 people or 50% of their population in one of 17 urban areas with a population between 250,000 and 750,000. *Other urban* includes dis-tricts with fewer than 37,000 people or less than 26% of their population in rural settlements and larger market towns (Home Office, 2012, pp. 41–42).

In England, for burglary and offenses against vehicles there is some evidence of a narrowing of the disparity in crime rates between urban and rural areas (Higgins, Robb, & Britton, 2010). However, overall police-recorded crime figures for England in 2009/2010 show that crime rates in areas classified as predominantly urban were higher than in areas predominantly rural. Trends in levels of police-recorded crime were similar between 2002 and 2010 (Figure 4.2). A similar trend is found when looking at rates from crime victim surveys in England and Wales. The risk of being a victim of crime was 23 percent in urban areas and 16 percent in rural areas. The risk that a household was victimized was also higher in urban areas than in rural areas (18 percent compared to 12 percent). Trends in household crime incident rates have been broadly similar in urban and rural areas in England and Wales. Levels of household crime decreased 30 percent in urban areas and 26 percent in rural areas between the 2001/2002 and 2009/2010 surveys. Burglary, vehicle-related theft, and vandalism showed similar trends in both urban and rural areas, with decreases in all three crime types (Higgins et al., 2010).

Keeping in mind that violent crime and property crime might be defined differently in the penal code of each country, the next section discusses differences in the trends in these offenses.

Property crimes

Urban areas are often more criminogenic than rural areas not because they concentrate lots of people per area (and some degree of social control) but because

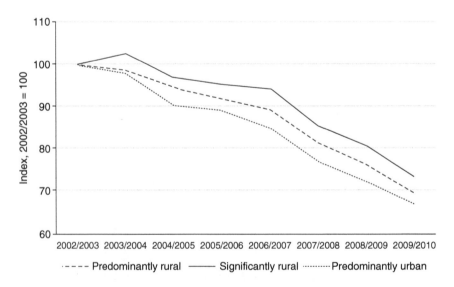

Figure 4.2   Increase in offending rates in England per area, 2002–2010 (total crime per 10,000 inhabitants, 2002/2003 = 100) (source: Home Office, 2011).

urban areas offer more opportunities for crime (that is, stock of goods) than rural ones do. This assumption is particularly true for property crimes.

Overall property crime rates are decreasing, but there are exceptions in all selected countries. In the United States, in 2005 the rates of burglary, motor vehicle theft, and household theft were the highest for households located in urban areas. However, rates of burglary were somewhat higher for rural households than for suburban households, but lower than for urban households. Suburban households were victims of motor vehicle theft and household theft at rates higher than those of rural households. Households in every region of the country experienced declines in property crime, and the trend is similar for all areas: 51 percent of inhabitants who experienced a decrease in property crime rates from 1993 to 2005 were living in urban areas, whilst suburban areas had declines of 54 percent and 49 percent for rural areas (US Department of Justice, 2011) (Table 4.2).

In the United Kingdom, crime statistics show that rural areas experience lower levels of robbery and theft of motor vehicles than in urban areas. However, crimes such as theft from a motor vehicle appear to be a disproportionate problem for rural residents (Marshall & Johnson, 2005, p. 26). Aust and Simmons (2002) noted that the incidence of property crimes increases as population density increases. Robbery seems to be a particularly urban phenomenon. Dodd, Nicholas, Povey, and Walker (2004) reported that more than half of all recorded robberies take place in just three police force districts: the Metropolitan, Greater Manchester, and West Midlands, which comprise 24 percent of the population. The Metropolitan police force alone is responsible for recording 40 percent of all robberies in England and Wales. Similar proportions were found in 2009/2010 by Higgins et al. (2010).

In Sweden, a drop in property crime rates was observed in the same period based on police statistics. Data from crime victim surveys also shows a declining trend for nearly all property crimes in Sweden compared to other EU countries. The prevalence rate for car thefts, car vandalism, burglary, shoplifting, and theft of bicycles is decreasing, following a declining trend also experienced in countries that took part in the International Crime Victimization Surveys (ICVS) between 1992 and 2004–2005. The exceptions are fraud and robbery in small towns (Tables 4.4 and 4.6). Going against the figures recorded in most ICVS countries (Van Dijk, van Kesteren, & Smit, 2007), the prevalence of fraud and robbery in small towns has increased in Sweden. With the advance of ICT and sales over the Internet and through telemarketing, people living in remote areas of Sweden may run a risk of becoming a victim of crime similar to people living in the Swedish capital. This fact per se requires new ways of understanding crime dynamics and crime prevention that go beyond existing administrative police boundaries.

Robbery, regarded as a violent offense, seems to follow the trend for violent crimes more than the trend for property offenses. Both police statistics and national victim surveys show that households in urban areas are more vulnerable to property crime (residential burglary, car theft, theft from cars,

Table 4.2 Property crime rates by selected household characteristics, 1993–2005 in the United States (number of property crimes per 1,000 households)

Location of residence	1993	1994	1995	1996	1997	1998	1999	2000	2001	2002	2003	2004	2005	% change 1993–2005
Urban	404.8	384.7	358.3	335.8	311.1	274.2	256.3	222.1	212.8	215.3	216.3	214.7	200.0	−50.6*
Suburban	305.1	297.2	280.6	252.6	238.0	204.5	181.4	163.7	156.7	145.3	144.8	143.2	141.4	−53.7*
Rural	246.4	245.2	228.4	206.4	191.7	173.5	159.8	152.6	131.9	118.3	136.6	134.4	125.1	−49.2*

Source: US Department of Justice (2011, p. 7).

Note
* Burglary, car-related theft, robbery, and vandalism.

bicycle theft) than households in rural areas. The pattern is similar in terms of car theft and theft of or from vehicles. For overall property crimes, there has been a decrease of about 30 percent (Table 4.3), mostly in car-related thefts. Note that the prevalence of burglary in small towns and rural areas has been unchanged since 2006 while for urban areas a decline of about one-quarter has been recorded.

Police statistics show that this pattern is not spatially homogeneous, as it varies by crime type and is particularly concentrated in urban areas. Whilst rural areas record increases in burglary, car theft, and robbery, urban areas have experienced a decrease in almost all types of theft. For instance, the number of "hot spots" in urban municipalities (municipalities with high theft rates close together) dropped, whilst in remote rural areas the number was nearly constant in the same period, and in some accessible rural areas the number of hot spots increased, particularly in southern Sweden. The difference in levels of theft by area was tested using one-way Anova with a post doc Scheffe test for 2007 (Table 4.4). The average of thefts by area significantly dropped from 16.46 in the urban areas to 13.90 in the accessible rural. Remote rural had a slightly higher average in 2007. Municipalities showing concentrations of total thefts increased in number in 2007, and compared with 1996 the pattern has become more polarized. In the most recent decade, the core of hot spots shifted, from Stockholm to Skåne County. In the next chapter, these geographical shifts will be discussed in more detail as well as possible explanations for such spatial variation in property crime rates.

Violent crimes

Kowalski and Duffield (1990) find that in rural areas the potential for violence decreases as individualism is reduced and cohesion is strengthened. Residents of a small community are more likely to know one another socially than in a larger city, and this informal guardianship leads to lower rates of crime in rural settings (Freudenburg, 1986). Still, rural areas are not free from violence, though in rural areas most violence happens among acquaintances. Capsambelis (2009) suggests that attention should be paid to domestic violence and neighborhood dispute calls in rural areas, because over time they may escalate into assault or even homicide.

Although isolation is a criminogenic characteristic of rural areas, there is an assumption that urbanity means higher anonymity among people (especially neighbors), which leads to lower social control, and thus the likelihood of successful completion of crime (Kaylen, 2011). The positive association between urbanity and crime rates does not always hold for all locations. When testing hypotheses in multiple European countries, Entorf and Spengler (2002) find that the proportion of the workforce that is agricultural (in other words, rural labor force) has a significant negative impact on homicide in Denmark and positive impact on homicide in Spain and Finland. Furthermore, it had a significant negative correlation with serious assault in Denmark, Germany, and the Netherlands

Table 4.3 Victims of fraud, burglary, and total property crime in Sweden (% of each group in the population)

		2005	2006	2007	2008	2009	2010	2011	2012	% change
	Metropolitan city	3.7	3.3	3.0	3.8	3.5	3.4	4.2	3.5	−5.4
Fraud	Large city	2.2	2.1	2.3	2.6	2.8	2.8	3.1	2.8	27.3
	Small town and rural area	2.3	2.0	1.8	2.0	2.4	2.6	2.7	2.5	8.7
	Metropolitan city	–	1.4	0.9	1.1	1.3	1.2	1.4	1.2	−14.3
Burglary	Large city	–	0.9	0.9	0.8	1.0	0.9	1.1	0.7	−22.2
	Small town and rural area	–	0.7	0.7	0.9	0.7	0.7	0.8	0.7	0
	Metropolitan city	–	14	12.1	11.9	12.4	11.1	11.7	10.2	−27.1
Total property	Large city	–	12.9	12.5	12.2	11.3	11.3	11.0	9.7	−24.8
	Small town and rural area	–	10.2	10.2	9	8.7	6.8	7.7	7.0	−31.4

Source: National Crime Victims Survey (BRÅ, 2013).

Table 4.4 Differences in theft in urban areas, accessible rural, and remote rural

Areas	Theft mean	F-test	Scheffe
Urban areas (1)	16.46	14.23*	(1) and (2)
Accessible rural (2)	13.90		(1) and (3)
Remote rural (3)	14.58		

Source: Dolmén (2010).

Note
* Significant at 95% level and above.

and a significant positive correlation in Spain. After an extensive review of literature on rural homicide in Europe, Kaylen (2011) concludes that "much of our knowledge about rural homicide comes from studies of rural violence or homicide more generally that briefly suggest explanations for rural homicide ... theoretical tests of crime and violence in rural Europe are scarce."

This lack of knowledge about differences in the nature of violence in urban and rural areas is revealed by an analysis of decreasing crime rates comparing urban and rural areas in the United States. Levitt (2004, p. 167) presents the percentage decline in homicide, violent crime, and property crime from 1991 to 2001 by region in the United States, urban–rural, and city size. He indicates that "in each of these subgroups and for all crime categories, the trend has been downward. Crime declines in the Northeast outpaced the rest of the country, whereas the Midwest was a laggard." The greatest reduction in crime occurred within metropolitan statistical areas and especially in large cities with 250,000 or more inhabitants. As regards violent crime in particular but also property offenses, rural areas showed much smaller declines in both absolute terms and percentages. For instance, Levitt (2004) shows that the homicide rate per 100,000 inhabitants in large cities fell 12.9 per 100,000 (from 26.2 to 13.3), while the drop in homicide rates for cities with populations less than 50,000 was only 1.5 (from 4.3 to 2.8). This fact certainly indicates potential differences in the nature of homicide between urban and rural areas in the United States during this time period.

In the United States, Kneebone and Raphael (2011) point out that violence in non-urban areas is less related to the demographics of these areas nowadays than it has been in the past. They suggest that violence in rural and some suburban areas has increased on average, whilst the inner suburbs experienced major declines in rates of violent crime, although not as great as the core cities. The inner regions of metropolitan areas have shown major declines (Figure 4.3). However, this trend does not hold if trends in homicide are taken into account, which possibly means that in suburban areas violence has increased but, for various reasons, has become less lethal. Statistics on homicide also show that trends have been similar for more than three decades for urban areas in the United States but not for all types of rural areas (Figure 4.4). Although urban homicide rates varied, from 8.9 to 2.5 per 100,000 inhabitants in 2008 (with the

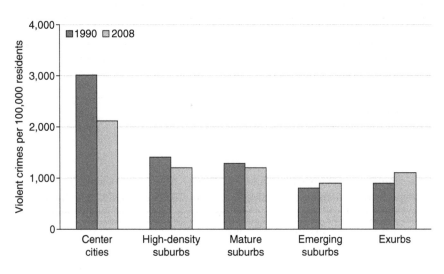

Figure 4.3 United States violent crimes per 100,000 residents, 1990 and 2008 (100 largest
metropolitan areas) (source: adapted from Kneebone & Raphael, 2011, p. 10).

percentage increase converging in 2005), in rural areas the rate has been less
than 2.0 since the early 1990s. Baharom, Muzafar, and Royfaizal (2008) also
show signs of a divergent trend using state-based statistics: crime rates in the
overwhelming majority of states are diverging from the national average (in only
eight cases are crime rates converging). The US Department of Justice (2011)
shows, for instance, that homicides in which the offender was known to be an
intimate (spouses, ex-spouses, boyfriends, girlfriends, and same-sex partners)
have declined in cities of all sizes and types. However, since the mid-1980s, the
percentage of homicides committed by an intimate has been larger in rural areas
than in suburban or urban areas. See Chapter 10 for more details on violence
against women in the United States.

In Sweden, violence also seems to be increasing in rural areas, according to
police records. Statistics show that more violent offenses occurred in 1990s and
2000s in rural areas than if they had followed the national trend. The trend is the
same when violent acts are standardized by resident population. Despite being
available since 2005, the national crime victim survey does not confirm such an
increase in violence rates but actually shows a decrease. For all types of violent
crimes, people living in urban areas tend to be more exposed to crime than those
living in smaller cities or rural areas – but there are exceptions. Robbery has shown
an increase in small towns and rural areas since 2005. There was no significant difference in the prevalence of assault between urban and rural areas (Table 4.5), or
harassment (a crime often committed by someone the victim knows).

In the United Kingdom, Aust and Simmons (2002) note that violent crime
was specifically concentrated in areas of the highest population density, with

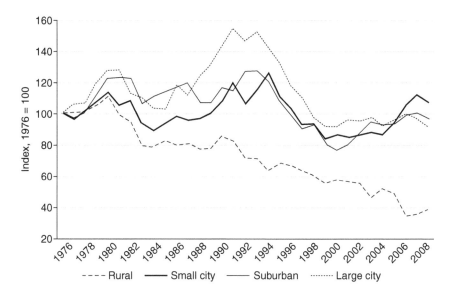

Figure 4.4 Homicide rates in the United States per area, 1976–2008 (total crimes per 100,000 inhabitants, 2002/2003 = 100) (source: Bureau of Justice Statistics, 2011).

roughly equivalent risks evident for the other types of area. This was later confirmed by Marshall and Johnson (2005), who indicate that the risk of becoming the victim of a violent crime in rural areas and urban areas, excluding cities, was actually similar. In 2009/2010, 54 percent of the total of selected serious offenses involving a knife were recorded in rural police forces. In more urban police forces, knives were involved in a greater proportion of recorded serious offenses than was the case in more rural forces (Higgins et al., 2010). Kaylen and Pridemore (2013) find that indicators of social disorganization are not a good explanation of the variation in rural crime rates. They suggest that previous links between rural violence and social change, lifestyles, alcohol consumption, and specifically rural concerns demand new empirical testing.

For homicide, for instance, Granath et al. (2011) show that although rates are low in Sweden, urban areas tend to have higher rates than rural areas. Compared with its neighboring country Finland, Sweden shows relatively low homicide rates. Drunken brawl-related homicides between unemployed alcoholic men cause most of the difference in the structure and rate of homicidal crime between Finland and Sweden (Granath et al., 2011, p. 93). In both countries, some rural areas are also in the upper top range of homicides. In the north, although there are few cases, they produce high rates in relation to the total resident population. For more details, see Chapter 5.

There are places where violence is prevalent in rural areas. Rural areas in Australia show a higher rate of violent crimes than property crimes. Carcach (2000) finds that in rural Australia violent crime outdoors was particularly

Table 4.5 Victims of assault, robbery, and violence (total) in Sweden (% of each group in the population)

Metropolitan city	*2005*	*2006*	*2007*	*2008*	*2009*	*2010*	*2011*	*1012*	*% change*
	2.6	2.8	3	2.5	2.8	2.4	2.4	2.1	-19.2
Assault									
Large city	2.9	2.4	3	2.6	2.1	2.5	2.8	1.7	-41.3
Small town and rural area	2.6	2.2	2.6	2.1	2.3	2.2	2.2	1.9	-27.0
Metropolitan city	1.6	1.7	1	1.5	1.2	1.6	1.6	1.3	-18.7
Robbery									
Large city	0.8	0.8	0.7	0.8	0.6	0.8	0.9	0.5	-37.5
Small town and rural area	0.4	0.5	0.6	0.5	0.4	0.5	0.6	0.6	49.9
Metropolitan city	15.0	14.0	13.6	12.9	13.7	13.0	12.7	13.2	-12.0
Violence									
Large city	12.9	11.5	11.7	11.3	10.8	11.1	11.3	10.5	-18.6
Small town and rural area	10.7	10.6	10.0	9.9	9.1	9.5	10.2	9.9	-7.5

Source: National Crime Victim Survey (2013).

prevalent in some remote rural regions. Rural areas also showed a higher crime rate for malicious damage, breaking and entering, assault, sexual assault, and drug offenses. Carrington (2007) suggests that family violence, domestic assault, assault, and sexual assault are growing at a faster rate in regional Australia and are consistently higher in some rural localities than state averages.

Honor- and revenge-related crimes are also part of the rural culture of violence in some parts of the world. For instance, İçli (1994) discusses the phenomenon of homicide related to revenge between families in rural Turkey, known as blood feuds. Disputes over land, resources, and matters of honor are often the root of conflicts that continue over generations. Honor killing[1] is not rare in rural areas of South Asia, in countries like Pakistan and India, and also occurs in Turkey and other countries in the Middle East.

Dramatic changes resulting from industrialization, the transition from a planned to a market economy, population shifts, and political instability have had different effects on rural violence. In some rural areas in the transition states of Estonia, Latvia, and Lithuania, violent crimes, including homicide and assault, were prevalent despite the fact that urbanity was still a key factor explaining regional differences in crime rates (Ceccato, 2007; Ceccato & Haining, 2008; Kerry, Goovaerts, Haining, & Ceccato, 2010). According to Kaylen (2011), the collapse of the Soviet Union has been shown to affect rates of violence in rural communities in Russia, Belarus, and Lithuania. In countries such as Estonia (Salla, Ceccato, & Ahven, 2011), the link between alcohol and violence has also been established for rural areas, particularly areas with a high proportion of ethnic minorities.

The hypothesis of convergence of rural–urban crime trends

Although rural areas traditionally experience lower levels of crime than urban areas do, international evidence shows signs of convergence of crime trends between rural and urban areas in some countries but not for all, and not for all types of crimes (e.g., Carcach, 2000; Marshall & Johnson, 2005; Osgood & Chambers, 2003). The key issue for criminologists is perhaps not to check whether the convergence is happening but rather whether it can be checked in different country contexts. It is the view here that testing the hypothesis of rural–urban crime convergence is a challenge for a number of reasons.

The first challenge is methodological, as it relates to changing proportions in the demographics of each area (e.g., because of migration) and areal categories (e.g., changes in boundaries over time) that affect both numerator (number of crimes and victims) as well as denominator (population at risk). It is important to note the value of population at risk. When it decreases in an area whilst crime remains stable, it might be assumed that crime increased in the area while actually the mechanisms associated with the change were related to emigration and not to the criminogenic features of the area. Moreover, biased victim samples can boost victimization incidence, for instance, urban victimization versus rural victimization (see e.g., the case of Eastern European samples discussed in Tseloni et al., 2010).

The second challenge is related to repeat crimes against the same victim (Davis, Weisburd, & Taylor, 2008; Tseloni et al., 2010). Of course, this is particularly important when the basis for analysis is crime victim survey data, because repeat incidents impact international crime reduction. Assumptions about trends in crimes with high repeat victimization should therefore be interpreted with some caution (for instance, violence against women or harassment) (BRÅ, 2014b). Tseloni et al. (2010) found, for instance, that a decline in personal theft to a large extent was associated with a decline in repeat incidents against the same victims. Osborn and Tseloni (1998) investigate factors that differ in repeat victimization from those that explain an isolated crime experience. They highlight the need to consider what they call "risk heterogeneity," which refers to the fact that some individuals or targets are more attractive than others and may remain so over time, leading to repeat victimization. In Sweden, this "risk heterogeneity" is often discussed under the discourse of "victimization-related inequality." Victimization-related inequality is often associated with the notion that a group of individuals is targeted more often than other groups in society rather than an individual is repeatedly victimized, although it may mean the same thing.

In Sweden, for instance, Nilsson and Estrada (2006) suggest that the reason behind the overall stability in victimization rates in relation to police records is that these rates hide an increasing polarization between different groups of society. For richer groups, the exposure to violence has stabilized since the mid-1980s, whilst the proportion of those victimized has become significantly greater among the poor. Overall, the National Council for Crime Prevention warns researchers to be careful in drawing conclusions based on data from crime victims' surveys by small geographic areas or within groups (BRÅ, 2014a).

Another challenge that makes the hypothesis of crime convergence hard to test is the difficulty of untangling differences in "unexplained heterogeneity" (Osborn & Tseloni, 1998) in crime targets in urban and rural areas. For instance, "[t]wo households can face risks which are systematically different from each other even when these households have identical measured characteristics" (Osborn & Tseloni, 1998, p. 308). The greater the level of unexplained heterogeneity, the poorer the predictability of crime risks (Tseloni et al., 2010). This issue concerns the dynamics of crime and their context in rural areas, for instance, how farms are differently embedded and exposed to local and regional routine activities. In Sweden, crime follows a north–south divide. Southern rural municipalities tend to be more criminogenic, because they are often accessible communities and more exposed to local and regional flows of people and goods than northern rural municipalities are (Ceccato & Dolmén, 2011). When violence rates are considered, there is a need to distinguish between violence caused by strangers (often in public places or outdoors) and that initiated by people who know each other and, not rarely, are intimates (often in the domestic sphere). The first type of violence is typical of urban environments (street robbery, assault) while domestic violence and violence among acquaintances is overrepresented in rural statistics of violent encounters.

Differences within rural areas and how they affect crime and its nature should also be noted in this context. One example is how the economic base in rural areas generates crime. An economic breakdown of the local economy, associated with high unemployment and demographic decay, may lead to anomic conditions and then more crime in certain areas. On the other hand, the convergence may also be happening in rural areas that are exposed to a temporary or continuous influx of population, that is, individuals bringing in themselves as well as goods (potential targets). Thus, an increase in crime here is associated with healthy rural economies. Rural touristic municipalities in Sweden tend to experience seasonal variations in crime rates, often dependent on visitor inflows. These municipalities also tend to have several service sectors (restaurants, hotels) that are not found in municipalities with a more "traditional" economic structure (mining, forestry), which may produce extra social interactions that could be criminogenic.

Repeat and inequality in victimization

A high percentage of crimes against individuals are committed against a small portion of the population. In the United Kingdom, the risk of being a victim of any household crime was higher for households living in the most deprived areas than for those in the least deprived areas in England. For burglary, for instance, while there have been sharp declines in burglary rates in the most deprived areas since 2001/2002, rates have remained broadly flat in the least deprived areas (Higgins et al., 2010). In some countries, such as Australia, unequal victimization has an ethnic-demographic dimension (Cunneen, 2007) and, in the United States, also a health dimension linked to an increase in cases of violence related to climate change (Mares, 2013).

In Sweden, as in other countries, victimization is unequal as previously noticed by Nilsson and Estrada (2006). Limited by data/sampling limitations, inequality in victimization cannot be tested by areas, because socioeconomic data from crime victims' surveys is not appropriate for meaningful analysis. Hypothetically, what could be done is to divide data by group and area over time as was done by Parker (2008) in the United States. She shows that homicide trends for distinct groups (blacks, whites, black males, black females, white females, and white males) varied greatly when compared to total homicide rates in an area. The decline in homicide rates involving whites started as early as 1980, whereas the overall decline in homicide rates began in the early 1990s. Also, racial disparities in homicide rates varied considerably over time: larger in the 1980s, narrowing in the 2000s. This does not mean that this is not an important issue. On the contrary, decreases in crime rates have been revealed thanks to crime prevention initiatives that target specific groups of victims to avoid repeat victimization.

Recent figures (BRÅ, 2013) show that more than half of crimes against persons (abuse, threats, sexual offenses, robberies, fraud, and harassment) were against a small group in the population (1.6 percent of the population, representing 14 percent of the people exposed to crime). Less common is repeated exposure to crime against property: about 3 percent of crimes against property are reported to have been committed against the few who have suffered four or more offenses in the same period in 2011. Repeated victimization is not randomly distributed in a population in Sweden. For instance, it is mainly young people who are victims of violence (four times or more), most commonly in the 20–24 age group. Women are slightly more common as repeat victims than men are, lone households and households with a single parent, and people with pre-secondary education or less. People who are foreign-born are overrepresented among those who are victimized on four or more occasions compared to those who are native Swedes (BRÅ, 2013). These statistics cannot easily be split by geographical area without compromising their quality. However, there are indirect indicators that point to greater repeat victimization in larger urban centers, as youth and foreign-born tend to be concentrated in large cities. Differences between counties are quite small (BRÅ, 2013), but Västmanland, Örebro, Stockholm, and Skåne generally rank somewhat higher than the other counties, which is largely expected and in line with the results of previous measurements.

Table 4.6 shows that repeat victimization is more accentuated in metropolitan areas, but for those who are victimized four times or more there are no major differences between urban and rural areas. Note that for violence, the percentage is the same for those who are victimized four times or more (violence against women or violence among people who know each other are certainly feeding the number of repeat victimization). Fraud might also be affecting the numbers of repeat victimization in rural areas, as this type of crime has increased in municipalities outside the metropolitan areas (Table 4.3). See also Lantbrukarnas-Riksförbund (2012).

These findings on repeat victimization in Sweden hold both research and policy implications. Previous research (e.g., Tseloni et al., 2010) indicates that repeat incidents influence crime rates. Thus, interventions that aim at reducing crime rates must support known victims to decrease their future risk of being victimized again. A recent review performed by BRÅ (2012a) based on 31 studies (no reference to urban–rural differences) suggests that repeat victimization can be tackled and be effective in preventing crime. The impact on crime varies with

Table 4.6 Repeat victimization, Sweden, 2012, by crime type and area (%)

	Metropolitan city	Victim	Once	2–3 times	4 or more
		13.2	8.8	2.8	1.5
Violence	Large city	10.5	7.1	2.1	1.2
	Small town and rural area	9.9	6.3	2.0	1.5
	Metropolitan city	10.2	8.5	1.6	0.0
Property	Large city	9.7	7.5	2.2	0.1
	Small town and rural area	7.0	5.9	0.9	0.1

Source: National Crime Victim Survey (2013).

the effectiveness of prevention interventions and the way they are put into practice (note that the studies were based on burglary, domestic violence, and sexual
victimization). BRÅ (2012a) indicates that information and education for victims
are not as effective as those tailored to specific situational crime interventions.

Future analysis of repeat victimization in rural areas should therefore be more
sensitive to the types of crime that affect those who live there. This issue is discussed in detail below. The analysis of repeat victimization should aim to do the
following:

1 *Consider the sparse and remote populations.* Although repeated crime
   victim data is useful, it is collected in a way that gives little attention to the
   specificities of certain types of crime that often lead to repeat victimization.
   For instance, violence caused by a known offender tends to happen more
   than once to the same victim. Knowledge on this type of crime is limited
   based on aggregated analysis from crime victim surveys. Such surveys do
   not allow disaggregation by small geographical units or by different socio-
   demographic groups because of limited sampling procedures. Similarly,
   little can be said for the whole of Sweden about fraud over the Internet that
   focuses on rural victims.

2 *Be specific to rural crime.* Repeat crimes against the same victim are a phenomenon typical among certain farmers. The Farmers' Safety Survey (Lantbrukarnas Riksförbund, 2012) shows that half of those who have been
   victims of crime were victimized twice or more times in the preceding two
   years. Farmers in southern Sweden more often than the national average
   suffer repeat victimization. In this case, their properties are more often the
   target than they themselves are, but being a victim of fraud is still the second
   most common type of crime they suffer, after theft of fuel and farm equipment and other products. At present, support to these victims is limited to a
   few specific areas and associations (for instance, Sweden CrimeStoppers) as
   crimes against farmers are not considered as a priority in local crime prevention councils (for more details, see Chapter 12). Knowledge about their
   protection practices and what works is not available at the national level
   despite the Farmers' Safety Survey and National Crime Victim Surveys.

3 *Include a wide spectrum of crimes as well as harm.* Some events in rural areas
   may happen during a certain time, several times, until they are detected, or if
   ever detected. Crimes against wildlife and nature are typical examples of such
   events. Since offenders are often corporations (not individuals), the prevention
   for this type of repeat victimization imposes challenges. Moreover, the victim
   plays a different role from a person whose car is stolen, for example. A mining
   company is certainly only one of the actors that may be in court if a case of
   repeated water contamination has been detected by environmental inspectors
   (see Chapters 8 and 12 for more details). The complexity of these types of
   crimes calls for a more holistic perspective on repeat crimes against the same
   victim. Some of these include temporal aspects of victimization that are discussed in detail in the next section.

Monthly and seasonal patterns of crime

Crime variations over time can be relevant when comparing crime profiles across areas. Crime opportunities are neither uniformly nor randomly organized in space and time (Ratcliffe, 2010, p. 5), but they do follow rhythmic patterns of human activity. What determines these patterns? Some relate these temporal differences to the influence of weather on behavior, such as aggression (Anderson, Anderson, Dorr, DeNeve, & Flanagan, 2000), whilst others associate to the indirect effects that seasonal variations in the weather have on people's routine activities, namely vacation during summer or else structured activities (Brantingham & Branting-ham, 1984; Cohen & Felson, 1979). In practice it is not always easy to untangle these factors into "weather-behavior" or "weather-routine activity-behavior." Although no causal relationship has been claimed, links between weather and crime are fairly well established. One of the earliest studies was the work of Quetelet ([1842] 1969) who indicated that the greatest number of crimes against a person is committed during summer and the fewest during winter.

Studies in the United Kingdom reported in Field (1992) find strong evidence in England and Wales that temperature was positively related to most types of property and violent crime, whilst Tennenbaum and Fink (1994) find an overall rise in murders across the United States in the summer months. In the United Kingdom, maximum temperature and hours of sunshine both had a statistically significant positive relationship with the number of sexual assaults committed in a day (McLean, 2007). For a comprehensive review see Cohn (1990) and also Cohn (1993); Cohn and Rotton (2000); Harries, Stadler, and Zdorkwski (1984); Horrocks and Menclova (2011); McDowall and Curtis (2014). Ceccato (2005) evaluates the influence of weather and temporal variations on violent behavior in Sao Paulo, Brazil, one of few studies of this type on a tropical country. Overall, the results show that temporal variables (variations in people's routines) are far more powerful than weather covariates in explaining levels of homicide for the Brazilian case. Despite a well-developed body of research, these studies make no reference to possible temporal variations in crime in rural areas.

Figure 4.5 shows variations in total crime in two rural touristic municipalities. Although crime varies seasonally, these variations reflect more population inflow during high season (potentially more targets and violent encounters) and changes in people's routine activities in these municipalities (from structured to leisure activities) than the claimed effect of weather per se (such as temperature or humidity) on crime. These patterns have a number of implications.

Note that while crime increases during the summer on the island of Gotland, when relative high temperatures occur, the crime peak in Åre, the ski resort, is in the cold months of the year. This inverse crime pattern summer/winter indicates the impact of changes in routine activities on crime for people either living in or visiting these municipalities. For instance, short-term visitors – young people especially – would be tempted to engage in activities such as excessive drinking or public disturbance that they would not otherwise do in their home muni-cipality because of the lack of anonymity. As Figure 4.5 illustrates, population

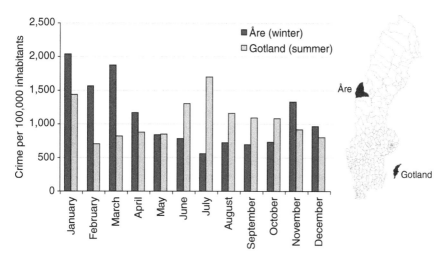

Figure 4.5 Crime rates in two touristic municipalities, Gotland (an island) and Åre, summer and winter respectively (data source: police records, BRÅ, 2012b).

inflow may be periodical, as it is in touristic places, but still has the potential to affect crime records.

Although crime rates seem to increase during high season (summer on Gotland and winter in Åre), this rise may be just an artifact of a "poor" denominator, that does not take the population inflow into account. Crime rates shown in Figure 4.5 take only resident population into account. This is important, because the debate surrounding investment in the tourist industry in rural communities often includes assumptions that these activities may attract or stimulate disorder and crime. As suggested by previous studies (Park & Stokowski, 2009; Stokowski, 1996), this development is often expected to lead to social disruption and impoverish social control, but evidence shows mixed and sometimes contradictory results.

An alternative to resident population as denominator for crime rates is some indicator for population inflow. In a study by Stokowski (1996), vehicle traffic was compared with resident population to standardize crime levels. The study aimed to compare crime before, during, and after the initiation of gaming in three rural Colorado towns. The results show that while crime has increased in some offense categories, it was not proportional to the numbers of tourists visiting. To check crime in relation to population inflow, vehicle traffic data from the Swedish Transport Administration was used for a number of examples of tourist municipalities in Sweden. The data measures incoming traffic on one major road on Gotland as a proxy for tourist population inflow. Gotland is a good example because it is an island, with limited connections to the continent beyond boats and airplanes, certainly capturing most of the "real" vehicle traffic of the area.

Figure 4.6 illustrates crime in 2012 in relation to vehicle flow from January to December. As vehicle traffic flow increases, so does crime. This indicates that if crime is standardized by vehicle traffic (instead of resident population), a better measure of risk can be derived. The likelihood of an individual being a crime victim on Gotland as a whole is stable and perhaps decreases in certain months, because the tourist population rises more than the number of crimes. In this case, the pattern of risk of victimization is fairly constant from January to December. Of course, this is a rough measure of risk, and the number of arrests could perhaps be used as a reference for a complementary picture of crime risk over time. Again, the risk of victimization is unequal among population groups (youth run a higher risk than the elderly for street crime and violence) and geographically. Visby concentrates more of the tourist population during the high season (June–August) than the rest of the island and suffers disproportionately from seasonal problems (see Figure 4.6). Not all types of crime increase. Heavy drinking, aggression, social disturbances, and other types of violent encounters dominate the police records. The type of population that increases during the high season is also relevant to whether or not crime increases. In areas that attract families with children, population inflow may have little effect on crime, compared to attractions that receive groups that are more prone to get involved in fights.

Although the risk of crime may be fairly constant over the year, there are "community costs" (Stokowski, 1996) associated with intense population inflow during the high season. Of course, some of these costs are compensated by economic gains, and overall the risk of being a victim of crime is relatively low. One of the tangible costs is new demands on local government (police officers,

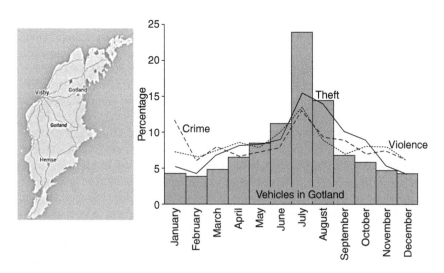

Figure 4.6 Crime (%) on Gotland (summer tourism) in relation to the vehicle flow, 2012 (data sources: Swedish Transport Administration (Trafikverket) (2012) Vehicle flow, Trafikverkets databas; BRÅ, 2012b).

healthcare). Gotland, for instance, receives police reinforcements from the Stockholm area for specific events that attract many visitors. Moreover, local perceptions of violence and social disturbance in the streets and public places may lead to community fear and also has costs. Cases of violence are currently reported by media, which may also affect the attitudes of future tourists that would consider visiting. They may also be averse to visiting a place where reports show that the community is out of control and perceptions of crime have increased.

Figure 4.7 shows two other Swedish municipalities, Åre and Malung-Sälen, with crime and indicators of population inflow, January to December. Both municipalities have winter attractions, and the high season is December to April. In Sälen, traffic flow data captures population inflow and an increase in crime, but Åre shows a patchier pattern over the year. A potential reason for this mismatch could be that Åre has several attractions that attract visitors in summer, while in Sälen winter attractions dominate. It may also be that traffic flow data does not estimate the real population inflow in the winter (note that the data is

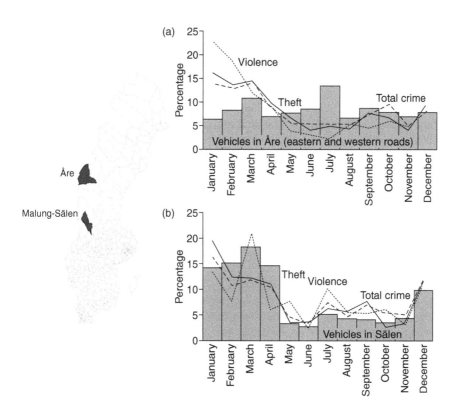

Figure 4.7 Crime (%) in relation to the flow of vehicles passing into or out of two municipalities that are dependent on winter tourism: (a) Åre and (b) Malung-Sälen (sources: Swedish Transport Administration, 2012; BRÅ, 2012).

based on two major roads only), partially because the vehicle traffic is not composed of passenger cars but trucks and other freight vehicles. Another reason for this mismatch is that the datasets are not from the same year: vehicle traffic flow data is from 2008, while crime data is from 2012.

The presence of a floating population – seasonal workers, tourists, and daily commuters – may change the dynamics of the communities where they spend time in different ways. For locals, social control may not be as effective as usual because of the relative inflow of population. Those who belong to the temporary population may be engaged in offenses, become victims, or act as guardians (Bucher, Manasse, & Tarasawa, 2010). Even when they stay in the country for months as temporary workers, they compose a heterogeneous group. Depending on their conditions in the country, some would keep a low profile and would not report the offence to the police even if they were victimized. Also, this group shows little motivation to intervene if anything happens (Ceccato & Haining, 2004; Reynald, 2010), as they are in transit or temporarily linked to that particular place. As an example, Chapter 6 illustrates the challenges of those who come to Sweden as temporary labor (for berry picking) in the summer in some rural municipalities.

Concluding remarks

This chapter shows that, not surprisingly, rural areas traditionally experience lower levels of crime than urban areas, but a comparative inspection of the international data sources for selected countries shows mixed, often declining, trends. This is the big picture. The "exceptions to the rule" are actually the most interesting part of the analysis, because they provide clues to further understanding what happens in both rural and urban municipalities. Thus, this chapter ends by indicating several crimes that need more attention in the Swedish rural context. These offenses are discussed in detail in Chapter 5 as well as in Chapters 8–10 and 12–14.

In the United States and the United Kingdom, a decrease in crime for all types of areas has characterized trends from both police statistics and victim surveys, but in Sweden police statistics show a slightly upward trend since the mid-1990s for a number of crimes. The tendency is toward convergence when crime increases are shown side by side for urban and rural areas since 2010. A more stable picture of victimization is found when looking at the past seven years of overall prevalence rates from national victims' surveys. However, even there exceptions are found in victimization for certain crime types and areas. The prevalence of residential burglary and assault are stable across urban and rural areas. A key issue for future research in this context is to understand the causes of changes in crime rates in rural areas and how they relate to specific rural conditions for each area. Although crime in rural areas may not always be specifically rural, its nature fails to be fully understood by the current urban-based theories.

Are rural and urban crime rates converging? It is difficult to say. If it is happening, evidence cannot be based on official statistics as they are collected nowadays. Rural–urban convergence of crime rates may also be hidden under general crime trends that disregard unequal victimization in rural areas or differentiated levels of crime-reporting practices. The challenges in dealing with the issues of crime trends over space are not limited to methodology or data quality. Crime trends have to be considered against a background of what is happening in these areas: changes in their economic base, each population's socioeconomic and demographic challenges, and people's routine activities – just to name a few issues. These conditions affect levels and processes of social control in these areas and, consequently, crime.

The concept of population at risk, using both resident population and floating population (by vehicle traffic), is discussed in high and low seasons. The chapter also highlights the need for and more nuanced evaluations of whether crime affects rural municipalities, as much of the debate on the impact of temporary population on local communities is often based on perceptions of increased crime.

Inequality in victimization by groups is still a major challenge when crime trends are compared between areas. Most of the groups that are overrepresented in repeat victimization against the same victims are found in urban areas, but for certain crimes and for frequent victimization the differences between those living in urban and rural areas are low or nonexistent. As it has been discussed in this chapter, the analysis of inequality in victimization demands an approach that is informed by crime, group, area, and time. The next chapter takes the first step toward a more nuanced picture of crime in rural areas by illustrating the cases of property and violent crimes in rural Sweden.

Note

1 Defined as the homicide of young women by their family members, because the perpetrators believe the victim has brought dishonor upon the family or community.

References

Anderson, C. A., Anderson, K. B., Dorr, N., DeNeve, K. M., & Flanagan, M. (2000). Temperature and aggression. *Advances in Experimental Social Psychology, 32,* 63–133.
Aust, R., & Simmons, J. (2002). Rural crime: England and Wales. London: Home Office.
Baharom, A. H., Muzafar, S. H., & Royfaizal, R. C. (2008). Convergence of violent crime in the United States: Time series test of nonlinear. *MPRA Paper, 12,* 59.
Blumstein, A. (2000). *The crime drop in America.* New York: Cambridge University Press.
Blumstein, A., & Rosenfeld, R. (2008). Factors contributing to U.S. crime trends. In A. S. Goldberger and R. Rosenfeld (Eds.), *Understanding crime trends: Workshop report* (pp. 13–43). Washington, DC: National Academic Press.
Brantingham, P., & Brantingham, P. (1984). *Patterns in crime.* New York: Macmillan.
Brottsförebyggande rådet – BRÅ (National Council of Crime Prevention). (2012a). Preventing repeat victimization: A systematic review (p. 48). Stockholm: BRÅ.
Brottsförebyggande rådet – BRÅ (National Council of Crime Prevention). (2012b). Crime statistics. Retrieved April 11, 2015, from www.bra.se/bra/brott--statistik.html.
Brottsförebyggande rådet – BRÅ (National Council of Crime Prevention). (2013). The national victims survey. Stockholm: BRÅ.

Brottsförebyggande rådet – BRÅ (National Council of Crime Prevention). (2014a). Brottsstatistik och resultat från NTU i URBAN15-områden (p. 14). Stockholm: BRÅ.

Brottsförebyggande rådet – BRÅ (National Council of Crime Prevention). (2014b). Nationella trygghetsundersökningen 2006–2013. Stockholm: BRÅ.

Bucher, J., Manasse, M., & Tarasawa, B. (2010). Undocumented victims: An examination of crimes against undocumented male migrant workers. *Southwest Journal of Criminal Justice, 7*(2), 159–137.

Bureau of Justice Statistics (2011). Homicide trends in the United States, 1980–2008. US Department of Justice. Retrieved April 11, 2015, from www.ojp.gov.

Capsambelis, C. (2009). *Policing in rural America: A handbook for the rural law enforcement officer.* Durham, NC: Carolina Academic Press.

Carcach, C. (2000). Size, accessibility and crime in regional Australia. *Trends and issues in crime and criminal justice* (Vol. 175). Canberra: Australian Institute of Criminology.

Carrington, K. (2007). Crime in rural and regional areas. In J. F. D. E. Barclay, J. Scott, and R. Hogg (Eds.), *Crime in rural Australia* (pp. 27–43). Sydney: Federation Press.

Ceccato, V. (2005). Homicide in São Paulo, Brazil: Assessing spatial-temporal and weather variations. *Journal of Environmental Psychology, 25*(3), 307–321.

Ceccato, V. (2007). Crime dynamics at Lithuanian borders. *European Journal of Criminology, 4*(2), 131–160.

Ceccato, V., & Dolmén, L. (2011). Crime in rural Sweden. *Applied Geography, 31*(1), 119–135.

Ceccato, V., & Dolmén, L. (2013). Crime prevention in rural Sweden. *European Journal of Criminology, 10*, 89–112.

Ceccato, V., & Haining, R. (2004). Crime in border regions: The Scandinavian case of Öresund, 1998–2001. *Annals of the Association of American Geographers, 94*, 807–826.

Ceccato, V., & Haining, R. (2008). Short and medium term dynamics and their influence on acquisitive crime rates in the transition states of Estonia, Latvia and Lithuania. *Applied Spatial Analysis and Policy, 1*(3), 215–244.

Cohen, L. E., & Felson, M. (1979). Social change and crime rate trends: A routine activity approach. *American Sociological Review, 44*, 588–608.

Cohn, E. (1993). The prediction of police calls for service: The influence of weather and temporal variables on rape and domestic violence. *Journal of Environmental Psychology, 13*, 71–83.

Cohn, E. G. (1990). Weather and crime. *British Journal of Criminology, 30*(1), 51–64.

Cohn, E. G., & Rotton, J. (2000). Weather, seasonal trends and property crimes in Minneapolis, 1987–1988: A moderator-variable time-series analysis of routine activities. *Journal of Environmental Psychology, 20*(3), 257–272.

Cunneen, C. (2007). Crime, justice and indigenous people. In E. Barclay, J. Donnermeyer, J. Scott, & R. Hogg (Eds.), *Crime in rural Australia* (pp. 142–154). Sydney: Federation Press.

Davis, R., Weisburd, D., & Taylor, B. (2008). Effects of second responder programs on repeat incidents of family abuse: A systematic review. Washington, DC: US Department of Justice.

Deller, S. C., & Deller, M. A. (2010). Rural crime and social capital. *Growth and Change, 41*(2), 221–275.

Dodd, T., Nicholas, S., Povey, D., & Walker, A. (2004). Crime in England and Wales 2003/2004 (Vol. 10/4, p. 159). London: Home Office.

Dolmén, L. (2010) Social uthållighet i den svenska glesbygden brott, upplev oro för brott och brottsförebyggande i glesbygdssamhällen. FORMAS seminar on rural research in Jönköping.

Entorf, H., & Spengler, H. (2002). *Crime in Europe: Causes and consequences*. Berlin: Springer.

Farrell, G., Tilley, N., Tseloni, A., & Mailley, J. (2010). Explaining and sustaining the crime drop: Clarifying the role of opportunity-related theories. *Crime Prevention and Community Safety, 12*(1), 24–41.

Field, S. (1992). The effect of temperature on crime. *British Journal of Criminology, 32*(3), 340–351.

Fischer, C. (2011). City crime, country crime. Retrieved April 11, 2015, from http://blogs.berkeley.edu/2011/06/15/city-crime-country-crime/.

Freudenburg, W. R. (1986). The density of acquaintanceship: An overlooked variable in community research? *American Journal of Sociology, 92*(1), 27–63.

Granath, S., Hagstedt, J., Kivivuori, J., Lehti, M., Ganpat, S., Liem, M., & Nieuwbeerta, P. (2011). Homicide in Finland, the Netherlands and Sweden: A first study on the European homicide monitor data (Vol. 15). Swedish National Council for Crime Prevention, the National Research Institute of Legal Policy, and the Institute for Criminal Law and Criminology at Leiden University.

Harries, K., Stadler, S., & Zdorkwski, R. (1984). Seasonality and assault: Explorations in inter-neighbourhood variation, Dallas 1980. *Annals of the Association of American Geographers, 74*, 590–604.

Higgins, N., Robb, P., & Britton, A. (Eds.). (2010). *Geographic patterns of crime* (Vol. 12/10). London: Home Office.

Home Office. (2011). Crime in England and Wales 2010/11 (p. 110). London: Home Office.

Horrocks, J., & Menclova, A. K. (2011). The effects of weather on crime. *New Zealand Economic Papers, 45*(3), 231–254.

İçli, T. G. (1994). Blood feud in Turkey: A sociological analysis. *British Journal of Criminology, 34*(1), 69–74.

Kaylen, M. T. (2011). Rural homicide in Europe: A review of the literature. *Handbook of European homicide research: Patterns, explanations and country studies*. New York/Dordrecht/Heildelberg/London: Springer.

Kaylen, M. T., & Pridemore, W. A. (2013). Social disorganization and crime in rural communities: The first direct test of the systemic model. *British Journal of Criminology, 53*(5), 905–923.

Kerry, R., Goovaerts, P., Haining, R. P., & Ceccato, V. (2010). Applying geostatistical analysis to crime data: Car-related thefts in the Baltic states. *Geographical Analysis, 42*(1), 53–77.

Kneebone, E., & Raphael, S. (2011). City and suburban crime trends in metropolitan America. In *Metropolitan opportunity press* (p. 22). Washington, DC: Brookings.

Kowalski, G. S., & Duffield, D. (1990). The impact of the rural population component on homicide rates in the United States: A county-level analysis. *Rural Sociology, 55*(1), 76–90.

LaFree, G. (1999). Declining violent crime rates in the 1990s: Predicting crime booms and busts. *Annual Review of Sociology, 25*, 145–168.

Lantbrukarnas Riksförbund (2012). Brott på landet: En undersökning bland lantbrukare (J. Johansson, Ed., p. 40). Stockholm: Sveriges Lantbruk.

Levitt, S. D. (2004). Understanding why crime fell in the 1990s: Four factors that explain the decline and six that do not. *Journal of Economic Perspectives, 18*(1), 163–190.

McDowall, D., & Curtis, K. M. (2014). Seasonal variation in homicide and assault across large U.S. cities. *Homicide Studies*. doi: 10.1177/1088767914536985.

McLean, I. (2007). Climatic effects on incidence of sexual assault. *Journal of Forensic and Legal Medicine, 14*(1), 16–19.

Mares, D. (2013). Climate change and levels of violence in socially disadvantaged neighborhood groups. *Journal of Urban Health, 90*(4), 768–783.

Marshall, B., & Johnson, S. (2005). Crime in rural areas: A review of the literature for the rural evidence research centre. Jill Dando Institute of Crime Science, University College, London.

Nilsson, A., & Estrada, F. (2006). The inequality of victimization: Trends in exposure to crime among rich and poor. *European Journal of Criminology, 3*(4), 387–412.

Osborn, D., & Tseloni, A. (1998). The distribution of household property crimes. *Journal of Quantitative Criminology, 14*(3), 307–330.

Osgood, D. W., & Chambers, J. M. (2003). Community correlates of rural youth violence. *Juvenile Justice Bulletin,* May, 12.

Park, M., & Stokowski, P. A. (2009). Social disruption theory and crime in rural communities: Comparisons across three levels of tourism growth. *Tourism Management, 30*(6), 905–915.

Parker, K. F. (2008). *Unequal crime decline: Theorizing race, urban inequality, and criminal violence.* New York/London: New York University Press.

Quetelet, A. J. ([1842] 1969). *A treatise on man and the development of his faculties.* Gainsville, FL: Scholar's Facsimiles and Reprints.

Ratcliffe, J. (2010). Crime mapping: Spatial and temporal challenges. In A. R. Piquero & D. Weisburd (Eds.), *Handbook of quantitative criminology* (pp. 5–24). New York: Springer.

Reynald, D. M. (2010). Guardians on guardianship: Factors affecting the willingness to supervise, the ability to detect potential offenders, and the willingness to intervene. *Journal of Research in Crime and Delinquency, 47*(3), 358–390.

Salla, J., Ceccato, V., & Ahven, A. (2011). Homicide in Estonia. In M. C. A. Liem & W. A. Pridemore (Eds.), *Handbook of European homicide research: Patterns, explanations, and country* (pp. 421–437). New York/Dordrecht/Heidelberg/London: Springer.

Stokowski, P. A. (1996). Crime patterns and gaming development in rural Colorado. *Journal of Travel Research, 34*(3), 63–69.

Tennenbaum, A., & Fink, E. (1994). Temporal regularities in homicide: Cycles, seasons, and autoregression. *Journal of Quantitative Criminology, 10*(4), 317–342.

Tseloni, A., Mailley, J., Farrell, G., & Tilley, N. (2010). Exploring the international decline in crime rates. *European Journal of Criminology, 7*(5), 375–394.

US Department of Justice. (2011). National crime victimization survey (NCVS). Washington, DC: Bureau of Justice Statistics.

Van Dijk, J., van Kesteren, J., & Smit, P. (2007). Criminal victimisation in international perspective, keyfindings from the 2004–2005 ICVS and EU ICS. The Hague: WODC.

Weisheit, R. A., Wells, L. E., & Falcone, D. N. (1994). Community policing in small town and rural America. *Crime and Delinquency, 40*(4), 549–567.

5   The geography of property and violent crimes in Sweden

Chapter 5 starts showing the changing rates and geography of a selected group of offenses by municipalities in Sweden. Police records are used as the main source of the analysis but reference is also made as much as possible to the National Crime Victim Surveys. This chapter aims at improving the knowledge base regarding the rates and spatial distribution of crimes in Sweden. Focus is given to shifts in geography between rural (remote and accessible) and to urban municipalities (especially Stockholm, Gothenburg, and Malmö), and vice versa. Geographical information systems (GIS) and spatial statistics techniques are used to assess concentration of thefts and violence. There is an inequality in victimization that is worth highlighting as trends in crime may impress different geographies in space.

Which are the main factors behind the geography of crime in Sweden? Are these factors in urban areas different from the ones found in rural municipalities? Following the main strand of theories in environmental criminology, the second section of this chapter searches for factors that can explain the spatial arrangement of crime. Crime rates are modeled cross-sectionally as a function of the municipalities' structural indicators, such as demography, socioeconomic conditions, and lifestyles. Note that this chapter is based on previous work published by the author with the criminologist Lars Dolmén in 2011[1] but it makes an effort to take distance from the previous study by expanding the analysis, including detailed analysis of property crime and updating the violence section with new statistics. The chapter ends with a discussion of unanswered questions about the geography of crime in Sweden and the methodological challenges of analysing the regional distribution of crime using police recorded data at municipal level. Finally, a relevant issue that is also discussed in the final section of this chapter is the adequacy of current criminological theory in supporting the analysis of crime dynamics that go beyond the urban and/or neighborhood contexts.

Property crimes

Both property and violent crimes are concentrated in urban areas, but across the country the pattern is patchy. Municipalities with either high or low property crime rates are found located close to each other. Confirming this clustering pattern, a global measure of spatial autocorrelation, Moran's I^2 shows that property crimes show more concentrations than would happen by chance in the country as a whole ($I=0.2131$, $p=0.00$, $I=0.3042$, $p=0.00$ in 2007). Again, this is not a big surprise since according to Tobler (1970), "everything is related to everything else, but near things are more related than distant things." Crime, as a social phenomenon, is no different: it reflects the organization of human activities in space.

A significant clustering pattern of crime, as indicated by Moran's I statistics, is informative because it indicates that crime does not happen at random. However, this indicator does not allow checking where these crime concentrations are. More helpful would be a test that identifies the location, magnitude, and significance of clusters of crime across the country. A Local Indicator of Spatial Association (LISA)[3] can provide just that: it reveals the municipalities with either high or low concentrations of crime (cold and hot spots, respectively). Figure 5.1 illustrates the location of clusters of total thefts, thefts from cars and residential burglary in the mid-1990s and 2000s based on police recorded data. Skåne County but also Stockholm and Gothenburg metropolitan areas as the most urbanized regions are constant hot spots of property crime.

As illustrated in Chapter 4, the number of police-reported property crimes have dropped since the mid-1990s which was also indicated by the data from the National Crime Victim Surveys. The National Crime Victim Surveys also show that victimization varies somewhat between different counties. Skåne County has the highest and significant proportion of victims both for crimes against property and against persons, while some counties in the north had the lowest proportion at risk. The differences between the Swedish counties are not dramatic, but some differences are significant. Most counties show victimization levels close to the national average (BRÅ, 2007c).

Not surprisingly, the largest cluster of thefts (mostly composed of Stockholm County's municipalities) shrank from 1996 to 2007 (Figure 5.1a, b). Less than half of municipalities belonging to the core hot spots of residential burglary were located in the south of the country in the mid-1990s whilst in 2007, they compose near 80 percent of the hot spots core (Figure 5.1e, f). Despite a less concentrated pattern, still a number of municipalities around Stockholm show high rates of residential burglary (high-high areas). Note that the low-low clusters for theft are pretty much constant over time, in some cases, such as theft from cars and to some extent burglary, have increased since the mid-1990s, for instance central-north municipalities.

Although the shift from Stockholm to Skåne County is less pronounced for thefts from cars (Figure 5.1c, d) than for residential burglary, changes in the geography of thefts from cars have occurred which are important to highlight. The number of municipalities with high crime property crimes classified as "urban" dropped from 32 in 1996 to 23 municipalities in 2007, whilst some accessible rural municipalities have become the core of these clusters, particularly in southwestern parts of the country (close to Malmö, Helsingborg, and Gothenburg). The change in the geography of property crimes from Stockholm to southern urbanized areas can be associated with a couple of factors; here two are discussed in detail.

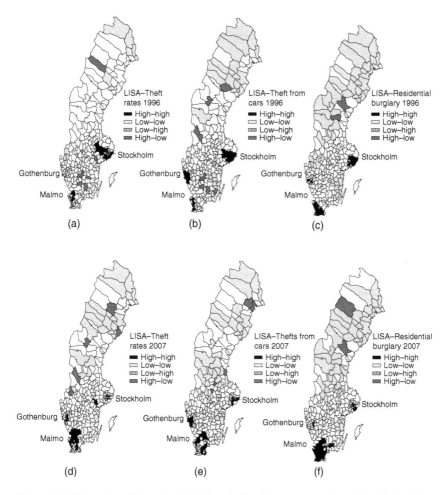

Figure 5.1 Hot and cold spots of thefts, thefts from cars, and residential burglary, 1996–2007 (Clusters significant at 1% level or less) (data source: Police recorded data, Swedish National Council for Crime Prevention).

1   *Inequality in the distribution of economic resources.* The concentration of property crimes in the region can also be related to old and new crimino-genic conditions in the area. Pre-existent but also new demographic and socioeconomic conditions in the region should be considered as an important factor behind the regional increase in acquisitive crime rate, such as the increase in segregation levels in Malmö region (Persson, 2008) and the rise of organized crime (Bengtsson & Imsirovic, 2010). Drug addicts may get involved in residential burglary (Wiles & Costello, 2000) and thefts in order to obtain quick money to buy drugs. Explanations for the geography of crime may be related to socioeconomic and demographic changes of the

areas, sometimes for short time. For instance, some rural touristic municipalities tend to experience seasonal variations of crime rates, often dependent
on visitor inflows (Ceccato & Dolmén, 2013 and examples from Chapter 4).

2   *Changes in the dynamic of the borders.* One important fact that took place
between 1996 and 2007 was the completion of a bridge linking Copenhagen
and Malmö in July 2000, the Öresund bridge (previously the flow of people
and goods was carried out by boats and other vessels). Goods transportation
is now facilitated by the bridge as a natural channel to the continent before
driven by ferry boats only. This physical link has been accompanied by
large-scale, long-term infrastructural and business investments in southern
Sweden as well as in northern Denmark. Such changes have had both a
direct and an indirect effect on crime patterns by creating a new site for
offending and victimization. With the bridge, easier movement of people
and goods impose new challenges to detection of criminal activities in the
urban areas concerned and particularly for the border patrol. Border crime,
such as smuggling, may affect other types of crime. Some of these crimes
are committed by short-time visitors in both sides of the bridge.

Already four years after the bridge was inaugurated, Ceccato and Haining
(2004) indicated that the category of offense that had increased most in
number in the Swedish Öresund region was theft of different types, particularly from cars and bicycles but also drug-related crimes. It is possible that
the bridge increased the car stock in these areas and, consequently, the
number of targets for possible vehicle theft and theft from vehicles. In the
cities, parking lots are targeted by thieves as individuals leave vehicles for a
relatively long time to take the train to Denmark, and then to the airport.

There are also criminogenic conditions that are intensified with the bridge,
especially those related to organized crime groups (within the triangle Malmö–
Gothenburg–Stockholm) with international links. These activities include
smuggling of alcohol, drugs, weapons, and people. About a decade ago,
Ceccato and Haining (2004, p. 810) reported that "the drug trade between
Denmark and Sweden was a consequence of drugs in Denmark being cheaper,
of better quality, and easier to buy than in Sweden." In addition, there is a
more liberal attitude toward drugs in Denmark than in Sweden. Since then, the
situation has not changed much. The result is that local and decentralized
criminal organizations take advantage of these conditions to repeatedly
smuggle small quantities of narcotics by train. This intense but localized
smuggling is known in the region as *Myrtafiken* (ants' traffic) and may involve
also other products, such as loads of alcohol that will attend more than people's own consumption. This has been intensified since the mid-1990s when
Sweden became part of the European Union, when alcohol smuggling has
been facilitated by liberal importing rules (Korsell, 2008; Weding, 2007).

These regional patterns in crime records and victimization raise a number of
questions about possible explanations for these differences, and similarities
between them. Which are the factors that underlie the regional geography of

crime? Is there something special with the regional arrangement of these localities that triggers crime? For instance, to what extent is the regional variation due to local factors affecting the scope and character of the conditions of crime?

There have been an increasing number of studies that attempt to associate local and regional differences in crime with structural indicators of communities, such as the population's demography, employment levels, and daily commuting patterns (e.g., Ceccato & Dolmén, 2011; Kaylen & Pridemore, 2011, 2013; Kerry, Goovaerts, Haining, & Ceccato, 2010; Kim & Pridemore, 2005). Some of the crime underlying factors relate to make up of these populations. International literature often indicates links between crime and (un)employment (Sampson & Laub, 1993; Uggen & Thompson, 2003), others between crime and poverty in rural areas (Higgins, Robb, & Britton, 2010; Petee & Kowalski, 1993). Little evidence is found for instance that the decentralization of poverty contributes to higher crime in distant suburbs (but see Kneebone & Raphael, 2011). In the US, as crime rates fell and communities diversified relationships between crime and community demographic characteristics weakened significantly, especially in rural areas. In Sweden, although there is no empirical evidence linking rural poverty and victimization, Johansson, Westlund, and Eliasson (2009) suggest that inequality in rural areas is increasing. In England and Wales, for instance, households living in the most deprived areas are more often victimized by crime compared with those in the least deprived areas in England (19 percent compared with 14 percent).

Other factors may be more related to the dynamics that characterize individuals' movement in space (e.g., the commuting flows, or in other words, people's routine activity patterns), than the statistic characteristics of the areas. Large commuting distances between place of residence and workplace may expose individuals at a higher risk of becoming a crime victim. Population inflow might be periodical but still has the potential to affect crime records (e.g., in touristic places). In everyday life, only a small portion of individuals would consider committing crime. More interesting is to investigate why some individuals would consider crossing the borders of a municipality or country to commit crime. Lack of employment opportunities are suggested as one of the motivations but it is not the only one. Ceccato (2007) suggests, for instance, that for tobacco smuggling in Lithuania cigarettes are often transported by young people or residents of border zones, who are usually unemployed. However, without a regional European market, businesses would not be profitable. There is evidence (Eisenberg & Von Lampe, 2005) that larger shipments pass undetected in East European countries, reaching other destinations through large-scale smuggling schemes. Regional patterns of crime may indicate processes orchestrated over large areas, and some characterizing a chronic "culture of violence" (Messner & Rosenfeld, 1999). In Italy, for instance, regional patterns of crime cannot be assessed without looking at the geography of organized crime: a distinct pattern of violent crime is found between northern and southern parts of the country (Cracolici & Uberti, 2009). Entorf and Spengler (2000) identify a similar geographical divide was also between West and East Germany as well as (Baller,

Anselin, Messner, Deane, & Hawkins, 2001) in the United States. They found a north–south divide in homicide patterns, with a clear diffusion process in the south throughout a period of three decades (Baller, Anselin, Messner, Deane, & Hawkins, 2001).

The penultimate section of the chapter presents the findings of the hypotheses' testing of links between crime rates and structural indicators at municipality level in Sweden. Before that, a complementary picture of the geography of crime is next portrayed, now focusing on violent offenses.

Violent crimes

The categories of offenses that have increased most in number in Sweden since the mid-1990s are drug offenses, followed by violence and criminal damage. Drug offenses are highly sensitive to police practices, so such an increase may be related, at least partially, to programs directed to substance abuse and dealing, but also to changes in the way the offense is recorded. For criminal damage, although there has been an increase, the expected number for both rural and urban regions is smaller than the national trend. For violence, there is a controversy around its increase.

On a national level, reported crimes of violence have increased since the mid-1990s while other sources (e.g., National Crime Survey, health statistics) show a more stable picture over time of violence. The National Council of Crime Prevention (BRÅ) suggests that lethal violence, for instance, is decreasing while the vulnerability to crimes against the person, especially assault in public places since the mid-2000s, has recently decreased after a continuous large increases since the 1970s (BRÅ, 2014).

What explains the rise in police records of violence? The view is that the increase can be interpreted in the light of an increasing tendency among the population to report violence (Estrada, 2005), as a consequence of society's increased sensitivity to such behavior, and national political focus to violent crimes, without mentioning international trends of crime reduction (BRÅ, 2014). This is also backed up by figures from the National Crime Victim Survey that shows that the percentage of respondents who declare that they reported assault to the police has increased overall during the period 2007–2012 from 27 to 38 percent (BRÅ, 2014). Still, the view is that a drastic increase in reported violence such as this may also reflect a genuine rise in levels of violence at least in some parts of the country, and for some types of violence as suggested by BRÅ (2007b), Andersson and Mellgren (2007) and Ceccato and Dolmén (2011). These authors suggest that overlapping societal processes such as increasing segregation, economic deprivation, and, most importantly, increasing alcohol consumption are also the causes of the rise of violence records, particularly in urban areas.

Regardless of the controversy about trends in violence, a more interesting issue is whether patterns of victimization vary over space and time. Just by looking at crime levels, one notices that in 2007, more violent offenses occurred in rural areas than if they had followed the national trend; more recorded cases than the expected in remote rural and more cases in accessible rural. This trend varies by crime type and regions (Ceccato & Dolmén, 2011).

The trend is the same when violent acts are standardized by resident population. An increase from an average of 45 to 83 per 10,000 inhabitants from 1996 to 2007 was detected. From 1996 to 2013, rural municipalities have had increase of more than 100 percent in the rates (e.g., Storuman in the north, 29 to 75 per 10,000 inhabitants; Aneby in the south, from 22 to 82 per 10,000 inhabitants). As in the case for property crimes, violence also shows a clustering pattern since the mid-1990s (Table 5.1), with a significant and larger Moran's I in 2013.

Despite the widespread increase in violence rates, cluster techniques show that the core clusters of violence remain fairly constant (Figure 5.2). LISA statistics were applied to check the geographical distribution of areas with both high and low crime rates. Hot spots of violence (municipalities with high violence rates close together) were found mostly in Stockholm County and surrounding areas, while municipalities with low violence rates close by, the so-called cold spots, were concentrated in northern Sweden.

Ceccato and Dolmén (2011) suggest that although there is evidence that this rise reflects an increase in population propensity to report violence, the view is that such an increase also reflects a genuine rise in levels of violence, related to a rise in socioeconomic polarization and alcohol consumption. In other words, the reasons behind such a development are difficult to establish, but there seem to be demographic and structural socioeconomic changes that are affecting rural and urban areas differently. The authors looked specifically at the issue of proximity to urban centres as it relates to rural violence. They found increases in crime in both remote rural and accessible rural areas over the last decade. For more detail, see the next section.

Lethal violence has been fairly constant over time but still shows ecological patterns in space. Granath et al. (2011) suggest, for instance, that the presence of a criminal milieu and the frequency and characteristics of alcohol consumption associated with marginalization are factors that have a large impact on lethal violence levels. The study by Granath et al. (2011) shows that increases are not restricted to large urban areas. Besides Stockholm, the southeast had higher than average homicide rates, while southwestern and central regions had the lowest crime levels. According to BRÅ (2007a) for homicides in large urban areas the victim is often not acquainted with the offender, and homicides are often related to criminal motives and associated with the use of firearms. In rural areas, mental health problems are often the cause of homicides.

Table 5.1 Violence rates – global measure of spatial autocorrelation (Moran's I)

	1996	*2007*	*2013*
Violence rates (log)	0.1819*	0.0941*	0.512*

Source: Police recorded data, Swedish National Council for Crime Prevention.

Note

* $p = 0.00$.

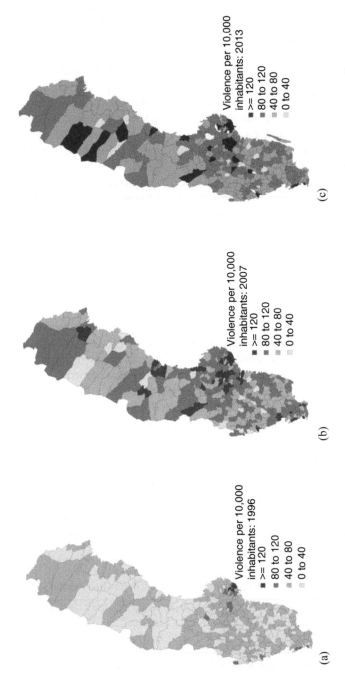

Figure 5.2 (a), (b), and (c) Violence rates per 10,000 inhabitants, 1996, 2007, and 2013 (data source: police recorded data, Swedish National Council for Crime Prevention).

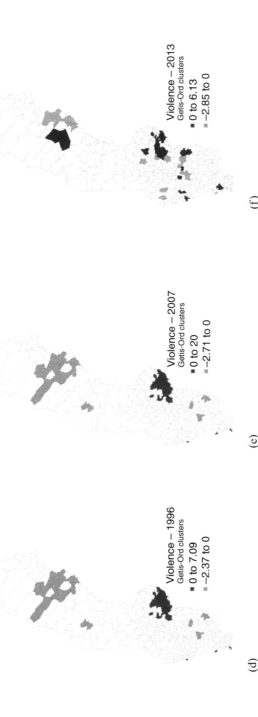

(d)

(e)

(f)

Figure 5.2 (d), (e), and (f) Clusters of violence rates, 1996, 2007, and 2013 (data source: police recorded data, Swedish National Council for Crime Prevention).

Note
Dark gray areas are hot spots, light gray areas are cold spots (Getis-Ord values significant at 1% level or less).

Domestic violence, particularly violence against women, shows an increasing trend that is confirmed both by police records as well as hospital admissions. Chapter 10 illustrates in detail the nature, levels, and geography of gendered violence in Sweden.

The geography of property and violent crime: theory and hypotheses

The international literature has a long tradition of searching for links between socioeconomic structural conditions and crime. This section reviews a set of theories that flag for potential links between crime and structural conditions as a background for the modeling of crime rates presented in the next section.

Durkheim (1897) was the first to argue that social change creates anomie, which can have a negative impact on society and may lead to crime. In the same line of thought, Merton (1938) proposed that crime rates can be explained by examining the cultural and social structure of society. He was particularly interested in explaining the relatively high rates of crime present in the United States. The research by Messner and Rosenfeld in the 1990s (1994, 1999) attempted to explain high crime rates as a function of society's structural conditions in the United States. These authors expanded Merton's theory of structural anomie to include the relationships among the various social institutions in society, which is now known as institutional anomie theory. They suggested that in a dominant capitalist society, social institutions tend to be devalued in comparison to economic institutions and lose their power to positively influence crime rates. Since its introduction, several researchers have attempted to partially test these theoretical assumptions using aggregated level data (e.g., Ceccato & Haining, 2008; Chamlin & Cochran, 2007; Kerry et al., 2010; Maume & Lee, 2003; Messner & Rosenfeld, 1997). Kim and Pridemore (2005) as well as Maume and Lee (2003) drew on Messner and Rosenfeld's (1997) institutional anomie theory to argue that societal negative effects are mitigated where pro-social institutions are strong (e.g., family, welfare, and polity). In countries in which the welfare state is strong, such as in Sweden, it could be expected that these anomic conditions are mitigated by social institutions since they moderate the negative effects of rapid social changes, for instance, crime.

For the Swedish case, these assumptions can be helpful to interpret social changes from the mid-1990s to the late 2000s. This period of time is relevant because Sweden has overcome a number of structural changes, particularly after its entrance to the European Community in 1995. In line with these changes, regional policies have shifted focus from being a welfare project, run by the need to care for "the whole of the nation" throughout the 1950s to 1980s, toward the "regions' dynamic growth" (Westholm, 2008). In practice, this development has led to a greater regional differentiation. Regions have differed in the way they invest in welfare, promote socially oriented institutions, and, to a certain extent, decide on how to support vulnerable social groups. There are indications that municipalities have become more market-oriented, privatizing and rationalizing many basic services. Those areas characterized by historical population decrease and relatively high unemployment rates are expected to have been affected the most by these changes. There are reasons to believe that changes like these would have a direct effect on both crime levels and geography. For instance, during the second half of the 1990s more than 200 of the 290 municipalities had a population decline. The main causes of this rural population decline are low birth rates and out-migration, particularly of young people; in other words, population is aging. The percentage of the population aged 65 and above is higher than the national average in most remote rural and accessible rural areas, whilst relatively few people aged 20–29 live in these areas (Amcoff & Westholm, 2007; Karlsson, 2012). This development is not geographically homogeneous. The city regions and their hinterlands grew quickly while rural and peripheral areas were generally worse off. It is expected that municipalities that struggle with socioeconomic and demographic changes (e.g., anomic conditions, unemployment, and population changes) show higher crime levels.

Individuals are more prone to crime within a social context where there is an unequal distribution of material resources and where there is an absence of pro-social-oriented institutions (Messner & Rosenfeld, 1997). The theory has suggested the importance of social institutions in moderating the negative effects of economic-structural problems in a society that might otherwise be associated with higher rates of offending (Chamlin & Cochran, 2007; Sampson, 1986). Evidence suggests that crime levels would be lower in areas with high expenditure in social care, despite negative socioeconomic development (e.g., high unemployment rate). There are reasons to believe that in Sweden, crime levels are moderated by "collectivistic" approaches to supplying public resources (e.g., investments in democracy and social cohesion as well as police resources per municipality).

Another important theory that relates structural characteristics and crime is social disorganization theory (Kornhauser, 1978; Shaw & McKay, 1942). The theory was developed to explain urban crime patterns and has been tested primarily in urban areas. However, recent theoretical and empirical work in this area has extended to rural communities (Kaylen & Pridemore, 2011). Traditionally, the social disorganization theory suggests that communities with high rates of poverty, residential instability, family disruption, and ethnic heterogeneity are poorly integrated and thus less able to exert informal social control, socialize youth, and solve shared problems. Social disorganization theory suggests that structural disadvantage breeds crime and suggests that offending occurs where impaired social bonds are insufficient to encourage or enforce legitimate behavior and discourage deviant behavior (Bottoms and Wiles, 2002). Social control in socially disorganized communities tends to be weak given among other things, intense housing mobility. As a result, these communities have higher rates of crime.

In this context, family structure is suggested as a predictor for offending (Ceccato, 2007; Sampson, 1986). In American and British literature, one of the mechanisms that links broken families with offending is the increase in poverty (Corcoran & Chaudry, 1997) but in Scandinavia it is related to psychological challenges that lead to higher mortality, morbidity, and crime. The divorce rate was constant in Sweden between 1996 and 2007 (from 2.4 to 2.3 divorces per 1,000 persons) and at similar rates to other Scandinavian countries (Eurostat, 2008). More recent investigations suggest that socioeconomic polarization combined with the loss of collective efficacy have an effect on crime levels (Sampson, Raudenbush, & Earls, 1997), although not for rural areas. Despite such potential, current research suggests a lack of support for the generalizability of these theories to rural communities (see e.g., Kaylen & Pridemore, 2013). According to these authors, these studies are limited because they missed the intervening social organization factors that may operate to influence crime.

Crimes also depend on how individuals move around in space and to what extent this movement leads to opportunities to crime. The convergence in space and time of motivated offenders, suitable targets, and absence of capable guardians, as suggested by routine activity theory (Cohen & Felson, 1979). At the regional level, day/night population density, location at the border, order of center in an urban hierarchy, and transportation lines and nodes are often used as indicative of people's movement flows (Ceccato, 2007). Large urban centers tend to show indications of social disorganization, therefore it is expected that the geography of crime follows a distance-decay pattern from larger urban centers in Sweden.

Conditions for property crimes are impacted by population shifts. In the case of Sweden, often when the population within a community grows, this may be followed by an increase in housing construction, recreational, and other facilities, which offer more crime opportunities and, at least in the short term, weaker social control. Particularly in accessible rural areas single family houses might constitute potential targets for crime since they are not equally equipped with security devices as in typical single family neighborhoods in urban areas. Changes in residence also mean that people's daily routine activity is altered putting them hypothetically at a higher risk of becoming a crime victim than they may have been previously. Offenders may also take advantage of people's routine activity and mobility during the day or summer, when properties are unattended. The example below exemplifies the flexibility of thieves in farms across the county in southern Sweden and the availability of a number of crime targets:

> Burglaries have increased drastically in two months, they happen every night in homes, barns, sheds and garages, around the county. Thieves gather large amounts of chainsaws and later, transport them out of the country. The police believe that they are active at night time, use often rural and minor roads.[4]

Population inflow might be periodical (e.g., in touristic places) but still has the potential to affect crime records, such as in the example above. Other aspects that affect people's routine activity are location (e.g., south, north) and geography (e.g., being at a border) (Ceccato, 2007; Ceccato & Haining, 2004). For instance, the close location to Denmark and therefore transport corridors of rural municipalities located in southern areas of Sweden, could potentially be more criminogenic than relatively isolated northern rural municipalities. Southern municipalities, particularly those within the urbanized triangle of Stockholm–Malmö–Gothenburg (the three largest urban areas in Sweden), are expected to be more exposed to local and regional flows of people and goods than the northern municipalities and therefore are more criminogenic than elsewhere in the country. For more details of the conceptual framework of this analysis, see Ceccato and Dolmén (2011, p. 122).

Modeling geographical variation in property and violent crime rates

Using ordinary least square regression, the geography of offense patterns in Swedish rural areas was tested by fitting models for the whole of Sweden that contrast 1996 and 2007 data. Based on the last section of this chapter, the following indicators were chosen:

1   *Socioeconomic, welfare and lifestyle indicators*
    Proportions of:
    Young male population (13–25 years) "YoungMale"
    Divorced population "Divorce"
    Foreign population "Foreigner"
    Total unemployed population "Unemp"
    Population increase "PopIncrease"
    Average income "Income"
    Voter turnout "Voterturnout"
    Resources earmarked for democratic issues (1/0) "Demo"
    Employed in the police by municipality "Police"
    Alcohol-serving licenses per 10,000 inhabitants "AlcoServ"
    Alcohol purchase per inhabitants "AlcoPurch"
    Population density "PopDens"
    Southern municipalities, particularly those within the urbanized triangle of Stockholm–Malmö–Gothenburg (the three largest urban areas in Sweden), should be more exposed to local and regional flows of people and goods than the northern municipalities (the dummy triangle was significant in all models) and affect crime rates.
2   *Land use indicators (population dynamics)*
    Dummy for border regions "Border"
    Dummy for Stockholm–Malmö–Gothenburg triangle "Triangle"
    Dummy for urban areas ("UA"), remote rural ("RR"), and accessible rural ("AR")

Main results

Models predicting both violence and property crimes do not show any special dimension that is typical "rural": the ones that strike the most are similar for both urban and rural municipalities. However, the predicting variables in these models are not exactly the same (Tables 5.2, 5.3, and 5.4). Young male population and divorce rate were the most important covariates based on social

Table 5.2 Regression results for crimes rates in 1996 and 2007, Sweden with dummies UA, AR and RR ($N = 287$, backward approach)

Log transf.	1996			2007		
	R2% (LIK)	Significant variables	Diagnostic tests	R2% (LIK)	Significant variables	Diagnostic tests
Theft	OLS 58.48 (−4.71)	3.48Constant 0.15YoungMale*** 0.006AlcoholSer*** 0.18Divorce*** 0.2Police** 0.15Triangle***	VIF no. ≤1.20 Jarque-Bera 6.13 Prob 0.05 Koenker-Basset 4.91 Prob 0.46 Moran's I 2.02 Prob 0.04[1]	OLS 41.12 (−22.12)	3.55 Constant 0.14YoungMale*** 0.004AlcoholSer*** 0.12Divorce*** 0.006PopIncrease*** 0.21Triangle*** 0.18UA* Demo***	VIF no. ≤1.23 Jarque-Bera 3.50 Prob 0.17 Koenker-Basset 12.37 Prob 0.05 Moran's I 7.12 Prob 0.00[1]
Car theft	OLS 54.42 (−130.81)	58.82Constant 0.31YoungMale*** 0.24AlcoPur*** 0.21Divorce*** −0.05Foreign*** 0.27AccessRural*** 0.18Triangle*** 0.05UA* Divorce***	VIF no. ≤7.60 Jarque-Bera 796.16 Prob 0.00 Koenker-Basset 10.81 Prob 0.15 Moran's I 2.73 Prob 0.01[1]	OLS 48.81 (−98.36)	1.78Constant 0.14YoungMale*** 0.10Divorce*** −0.02Foreign*** 0.10Police*** 0.32AccessRural*** 0.24Triangle*** 0.23UA* Unemployment*** −0.08UA* Police***	VIF no. ≤5.23 Jarque-Bera 669.53 Prob 0.00 Koenker-Basset 8.87 Prob 0.35 Moran's I 4.80 Prob 0.00[1]
Theft from cars	OLS 52.73 (−127.40)	1.14Constant 0.25YoungMale*** 0.17Divorce*** 0.28Triangle*** 0.12Border**	VIF no. ≤1.21 Jarque-Bera 7.45 Prob 0.02 Koenker-Basset 9.55 Prob 0.05 Moran's I 2.23 Prob 0.03[1]	OLS 26.01 (−131.51)	3.18Constant 0.10Divorce*** 0.36Triangle*** 0.31UA* Demo***	VIF no. ≤1.0 Jarque-Bera 1.93 Prob 0.38 Koenker-Basset 6.68 Prob 0.10 Moran's I 5.65 Prob 0.00[1]

	OLS		VIF / diagnostics	OLS	VIF / diagnostics
Robbery	52.23 (−183.19)	−0.67Constant 0.18Divorce*** 0.21Border*** 0.24Triangle*** −2.28UA** 0.09UA* Foreign*** 0.02UA* Voter*	VIF no. ≤12.27 Jarque-Bera 0.06 Prob 0.96 Koenker-Bassett 13.56 Prob 0.03 Moran's I 0.74 Prob 0.55	49.92 (−233.49) −0.75Constant 0.16Divorce*** 0.13Border* 0.39Triangle*** 0.0001PopIncrease** 0.06Police*** 0.11UA* Foreign*** 0.02UA* AlcoholSer**	VIF no. ≤2.70 Jarque-Bera 11.51 Prob 0.00 Koenker-Bassett 6.25 Prob 0.51 Moran's I 2.73 Prob 0.01[1]
Residential burglary	40.92 (−200.26)	0.56Constant 0.24Divorce*** −0.04Police*** 0.58Triangle***	VIF no. ≤1.16 Jarque-Bera 83.44 Prob 0.00 Koenker-Bassett 3.29 Prob 3.44 Moran's I 3.70 Prob 0.00[1]	39.91 (−315.74) −2.72Constant 0.25Divorce*** 0.25YoungMale*** *0.48AccessRural**** −0.19Border** −0.02AlcoSer*** −0.06UA* AlcoSer***	VIF no. ≤2.92 Jarque-Bera 1.51 Prob 0.47 Koenker-Bassett 12.44 Prob 0.05 Moran's I 5.08 Prob 0.00[1]
Shoplifting	38.54 (−271.11)	1.03Constant 0.24Divorce*** 0.58AlcoPur*** 0.09Police*** 0.26Triangle***	VIF no. ≤1.17 Jarque-Bera 6.82 Prob 0.03 Koenker-Bassett 17.47 Prob 0.00 Moran's I 0.36 Prob 0.71	43.29 (−252.68) 1.65Constant 0.001PopIncrease*** 0.14Unemployment*** 0.11Police*** 0.38AlcoPur*** 0.26Triangle*** *0.93AccessRural**** 0.88UA*** 0.97UA* AlcoPur**	VIF no. ≤7.25 Jarque-Bera 16.65 Prob 0.02 Koenker-Bassett 11.74 Prob 0.11 Moran's I 1.92 Prob 0.05[1]

Notes

1 Spatial lag or spatial error model was tested here but although autocorrelation on residuals was solved in some cases, the model performed poorer than OLS model.

* 10% significance level

** 5% significance level

*** 1% significance level

Table 5.3 Regression results for crimes rates in 1996 and 2007, Sweden with dummies UA, AR and RR ($N=287$, backward approach)

Log transf.	1996			2007		
	R2% (LIK)	*Significant variables*	*Diagnostic tests*	*R2% (LIK)*	*Significant variables*	*Diagnostic tests*
Violence	OLS 47.46 (−120.81)	3.48Constant 0.006AlcoholSer** 0.21Divorce*** 0.08Police** 0.17Triangle*** −0.06UA* Police*** 0.37UA* AlcoPur***	VIF no. ≤5.05 Jarque-Bera 150.43 Prob 0.00 Koenker-Basset 12.78 Prob 0.05 Moran's I 1.44 Prob 0.50	OLS 46.93 (−55.53)	3.48Constant 0.20YoungMale*** 0.08Unemployment*** 0.21Divorce*** 0.15Triangle***	VIF no. ≤1.31 Jarque-Bera 54.72 Prob 0.00 Koenker-Basset 7.52 Prob 0.11 Moran's I 1.40 Prob 0.16
Violence women indoors	OLS 36.66 (−171.01)	2.63Constant 0.19Divorce*** 0.005AveIncome** −0.03VoterTurn*** 0.03Police**	VIF no. ≤1.60 Jarque-Bera 340.59 Prob 0.00 Koenker-Basset 7.53 Prob 0.11 Moran's I 0.66 Prob 0.51	OLS 42.31 (−100.39)	−0.18Constant 0.17YoungMale*** 0.18Divorce*** 0.9Police** −0.01UA* Police*** 0.10UA* Unemployment***	VIF no. ≤5.04 Jarque-Bera 73.56 Prob 0.00 Koenker-Basset 15.25 Prob 0.01 Moran's I 2.13 Prob 0.03
Violence outdoors	OLS 36.45 (−245.34)	−2.27Constant 0.25YoungMale*** 0.01AlcoholSer*** 0.39AlcoPur*** 0.22Divorce*** 0.04Police** 0.03Unemployment** 0.22Triangle***	VIF no. ≤1.40 Jarque-Bera 41.07 Prob 0.00 Koenker-Basset 18.51 Prob 0.01 Moran's I 1.46 Prob 0.14	OLS 28.15 (−251.08)	−0.84Constant 0.25YoungMale*** 0.01AlcoholSer*** 0.22Divorce*** 0.09Police*** 0.27Triangle***	VIF no. ≤1.17 Jarque-Bera 493.85 Prob 0.00 Koenker-Basset 13.94 Prob 0.01 Moran's I 1.64 Prob 0.11

Note
1 Spatial lag model was tested here but although autocorrelation on residuals was solved, the model performed poorer than OLS model.
 * 10% significance level
 ** 5% significance level
 *** 1% significance level

Table 5.4 Regression results for crimes rates in 1996 and 2007, rural areas only (N=176, backward approach)

Log transf.	1996			2007		
	R2% (LIK)	Significant variables	Diagnostic tests	R2% (LIK)	Significant variables	Diagnostic tests
Violence	OLS 29.51 (−94.19)	1.90Constant 0.007AlcoholSer** 0.22Divorce*** 0.07Police*** 0.24Triangle***	VIF no. ≤1.09 Jarque-Bera 83.82 Prob 0.00 Koenker-Basset 6.89 Prob 0.14 Moran's I 0.96 Prob 0.34	OLS 30.29 (−40.96)	1.48Constant 0.14YoungMale*** 0.16Divorce*** 0.10Police*** 0.10Demo*	VIF no. ≤1.18 Jarque-Bera 30.27 Prob 0.00 Koenker-Basset 3.76 Prob 0.44 Moran's I 0.06 Prob 0.95
Violence women indoors	OLS 15.27 (−126.49)	3.71Constant 0.17Divorce*** −0.03VoterTurn**	VIF no. ≤1.08 Jarque-Bera 132.14 Prob 0.00 Koenker-Basset 5.09 Prob 0.10 Moran's I 0.26 Prob 0.79	OLS 17.93 (−84.27)	−0.50Constant 0.23YoungMale*** 0.18Divorce***	VIF no. ≤1.13 Jarque-Bera 55.65 Prob 0.00 Koenker-Basset 2.29 Prob 0.32 Moran's I 0.80 Prob 0.42
Violence outdoors	OLS 26.56 (−158.67)	−0.46Constant 0.02AlcoholSer*** 0.12Divorce*** 0.11Police** 0.07Unemployment** 0.55AccessRural*** 0.30Triangle***	VIF no. ≤0.98 Jarque-Bera 8.76 Prob 0.02 Koenker-Basset 7.62 Prob 0.26 Moran's I 2.56 Prob 0.01	OLS 29.31 (−166.70)	−1.48Constant 0.22YoungMale** 0.01AlcoholSer*** 0.13Divorce** 0.16Police*** 0.007PopInc*** 0.63AccessRural***	VIF no. ≤1.27 Jarque-Bera 164.52 Prob 0.00 Koenker-Basset 13.38 Prob 0.04 Moran's I 0.51 Prob 0.60

Notes
* 10% significance level
** 5% significance level
*** 1% significance level

disorganization that account for the variation of both violence and theft. Among the routine activity covariates, the dummy that flags for differences in urbanization between north and south Sweden and alcohol serving licenses per inhabitants emerged significant for both 1996 and 2007 for most crimes, including violence.

These results shed light on the importance of taking into account the diversity of rural localities and avoid generalized models that may not apply for rural areas. However this is not the same as saying that the hypotheses' testing was able to fully test principles of social disorganization theory, routine activity, or institutional anomie. This analysis, together with others found in the international literature faced a number of challenges when applied to rural areas. The incapacity to fully test the models and the dependence on police records (which imply problems of data quality) for this type of analysis constitute serious limitation (Kaylen & Pridemore, 2011).

The reasons behind the link between divorce rates and victimization are difficult to ascertain at this aggregated level but may be related to other factors beyond economic hardship as suggested by Fröjd, Marttunen, Pelkonen, von der Pahlen, and Kaltiala-Heino (2006) and Weitoft, Hjern, Haglund, and Rosén (2003). An alternative interpretation for the effect of divorce on crime is through the parent–child relationship. Social control theory suggests that ineffective socialization processes or weak parental attachment (in this case, following a divorce) may lead to a breakdown in social conformity, as manifested, for example, in law breaking. Other forms of instability, such as economic ones (e.g., triggered by long-term unemployment), are less consistent and only in a few cases associated with crime rates. For more details see Ceccato and Dolmén (2011).

As hypothesized, municipalities that experienced population increase since 1996 show higher rates of thefts and robbery. Shoplifting rates are also greater in municipalities with higher unemployment rates. Contrary to what was initially suggested, no moderating effect was found for social institutions on crime in these models. The variables (e.g., earmarked resources for democracy) did not function as expected. Instead, they behave as proxies for urbanity or have an impact that is not geographically homogeneous, which is not captured by the model employed here. The only exception was found for theft in urban areas.

The variable for police resources did not function as an indicator for the moderating factor of social institutions on crime. Proportion of police resources (police employees) has an unexpected impact (a rise) on rates of violence and thefts in Sweden. Neither were variables voter turnouts and resources earmarked for democratic issues. An explanation for this is that the welfare state in Sweden shifted its focus toward a more market-oriented system, public resources have shrunk, which certainly affect formal social control in rural communities (fewer police) and less support for bottom-up initiatives, and, consequently, crime would increase. Another explanation for this finding is the fact that police resources do partially reflect the municipalities' population sizes (the larger the population, the greater the number of police officers and related administration) and therefore it is actually unsurprising that it showed positively in relation to offense rates. Furthermore, high crime rates relate to more police in models for both 1996 and in 2007, which indicates that the distribution of police resources has not altered much in the last decade despite changes in the welfare system and regional policy.

The impact of the border on crime in each region was assessed by including in the model a dummy variable for municipalities located at the border (both for land and sea). Interestingly, findings show that being located at the border has no effect on crime, the only exception being theft in rural municipalities in 2007. Outliers for a diversity of offenses were found for some municipalities at the border such as Strömstad, at the border with Norway, but were not strong enough to affect modeling results.

As expected, findings indicate that the criminogenic conditions in Sweden follow a north–south divide, having southern rural municipalities being more criminogenic because they are often composed of accessible rural municipalities, and more exposed to local and regional flows of people and goods than northern rural municipalities (see the significance of variable: triangle, Stockholm–Gothenburg–Malmö).

Property crimes

Chapter 4 shows evidence of a drop in property crime rates in Sweden which is confirmed both by police recorded statistics and victim crime surveys. Such trend is not however homogeneous over the country and varies by crime type. The analysis focuses first on geographical differences of property crime between urban areas, accessible rural areas, and remote rural areas. For property crimes, an important change in the regional geography of crime between 1996 and 2007 is the shift of clusters of high rates of theft and residential burglary from Stockholm County to Skandia region. The number of urban areas comprising the core hot spots dropped, whilst some accessible rural municipalities instead became part of the new cores. In line with these shifts, there has been a decrease in the number of cold spots of theft between 1996 and 2007. Modeling results show links between spatial variation of property crime rates and regions' demography, socioeconomic and locational characteristics both in 1996 and 2007.

Property crimes is a phenomenon typical of urban or densely populated municipalities, the largest concentrations are found at and close to Stockholm, Gothenburg, and Malmö. They are the economically leading regions, where both positive and negative sides of a successful economy are experienced: investments create new jobs and the supply of goods (targets) but also exacerbate income disparities through wage differentials and selective unemployment, also affecting the pool of motivated offenders.

However, crime might be an urban phenomenon but it does not mean that offenses are concentrated only in urban areas. Among the rural municipalities, the accessible rural are extra vulnerable to offenders committing burglaries, thefts, robbery, since there are more targets to steal than the remote rural areas.

The effect of being an accessible rural area is higher on crime in 2007 than in 1996, particularly for car theft, residential burglary, and shoplifting, which indicate a rise in the vulnerability of these municipalities to some types of crimes.

Violent crimes

As for property crimes, characteristics of family structure (divorce rate) and proportion of young male population are significantly linked to high rates of violence at municipal level both in the mid-1990s and mid-2000s (Tables 5.3 and 5.4). For rural municipalities only, being accessible rural areas put them at higher risk for violence than remote rural ones. Moreover, there was no moderating effect of prosocial institutions on violence. The variables (e.g., earmarked resources for democracy) did not function as expected. Instead, they behave as proxies for urbanity.

The link between alcohol consumption and outdoor life and violence outdoors is indicated by the significance of the variable alcohol-serving licenses per inhabitants and, to a lesser extent, alcohol purchase. Note that according to the Swedish National Council for Crime Prevention violence records in public places are often composed of offenses committed by young people directed against other young people.

> A common scenario of street violence often involves young people, most often two youngsters who know each other from before and enter in conflict with each other during a late weekend night in a public place. The conflict results in minor injuries.
>
> (BRÅ, 2012)

The modeling findings indicate that outdoor violence is more related to differences in patterns of routine activity (e.g., violent encounters after work hours, weekends, outside home) than alcohol consumption alone. When people are often away from home, there is a greater risk of victimization (especially when the perpetrator is unknown to the victim). "Being on the move" means that there is a greater chance that potential victims or targets (e.g., a car) are in the same place at the same time as motivated offenders.

Violence may strike seasonally. Some of the rural municipalities that show relatively high rates of premises selling alcohol per inhabitant are often touristic places. Crime takes place when changes in routine activities in these communities are imposed by the inflow of large numbers of an external population at particular times of the year. As previously shown in Chapter 4, ski resorts in the winter and summer destinations as well as municipalities in the "cottage belt" around Stockholm, are examples of this dynamic.

Concluding remarks

Results from the regression models indicate that accessible rural municipalities were more criminogenic in the late 2000s than they were in the 1990s, particularly those located in southern Sweden (these findings are of course bound to the previously discussed limitations of police recorded data). Changes in routine activities associated with existent and new risky factors are pointed as potential causes of increased vulnerability of accessible rural areas in the last decade. These results show increasing links of dependence between the city and the countryside with regard not only to the population's demographic and socioeconomic characteristics but also lifestyle and criminogenic conditions. Crime rates are higher where urban criminogenic conditions emerge, not necessarily in urban areas but in settings that have strong links with urban centers.

Some evidence of anomic conditions is found when population increase does affect crime rates. However, as in other similar studies, it still unclear whether pro-social institutions moderate or mediate the negative effects of the economy on the rate of crime. The effect is not confirmed either for property or violent crimes. As it is suggested by Bjerregaard and Cochran (2008) this fact may be due to the complex nature of this institutional anomie theory and the lack of systematically collected data that properly operationalize its key dimensions, as it may have occurred also in this study.

The search for more adequate dependent variables as well as covariates should be part of future studies of this type. Kaylen and Pridemore (2013) suggest the use of data from national crime victim surveys as better measures of victimization than police recorded data, as was used in this study. However, the problem is that the sampling of respondents in rural areas in many countries (including in Sweden) is relatively small compared with urban areas which impose a number of methodological problems, even after data aggregation. In terms of covariates, Kaylen and Pridemore (2013, p. 905) broke down variables into two groups (the exogenous sources of social disorganization and intervening measures of community organization) which are claimed to allow "the first test of the full social disorganization model."

In a more technical account, future studies should also consider more appropriate models that suit the case of small counts (Osgood & Chambers, 2003), particularly where some counts are zero as here in the case of rural areas (for instance, the negative binomial model). Data permitting, future research should attempt to include indicators of social change rather than the ones (rates cross-sectionally) used in this analysis. Moreover, the model specification needs the inclusion of both change and cross-sectional rates variables in order to capture both short- and long-term social dynamics that affect crime. Moreover, future studies should also test the importance of differences in regions' functionality (e.g., if they contain capital cities, holiday resorts, or industrial towns) since they affect human interactions and, as a consequence, crime. The inclusion of variables that function as good indicators of social institutions as moderators of poor socioeconomic conditions on crime is an example. An important area of study that has not been covered by this chapter is the effect of organized crime on local crime dynamics. This may, for instance, explain crime clusters in some border regions, such as between Sweden and Denmark or Sweden and the Baltic countries. It would be useful to identify potential links between international/regional organized crime and crimes that take place within national territories. To approach the question of the mechanisms underlying such a relationship, it would be beneficial in future analysis to integrate individual level data, such as data on offense, victim, and offender. A key issue here is to investigate the nature of crimes in rural areas.

Findings from this chapter raise questions of whether there is a need for criminological theories (or new theoretical frameworks) that can regard large-scale crime patterns. The call for new ways of theoretically dealing with crime in this fluid framework of human interactions is not new (see e.g., Bottoms & Wiles, 2002). As it is now, most environmental criminology theories fit at their best the analysis of intra-urban underlying forces of crime but do a poor job in identifying criminogenic conditions that extend over large geographical areas, particularly beyond state borders. This is particularly true for areas that are sparsely populated, rural, and covering large areas of the country, and where human interactions happen in nodes in space. The question of scale (micro=individual, meso=neighborhood, macro=region/country/global) is fundamental here: (1) What makes an individual commit a crime is certainly determined by similar processes either in urban or rural areas (it is argued here that there are not necessarily special mechanisms when an individual breaks the law in rural areas than if he does in the city). (2) Rural areas (and its environment) promote particular types of crimes that may not happen elsewhere. (3) Yet a crime attractor (a train station for instance) does not necessarily change just because it is in a rural area, it is still a place where people converge, at least at certain times of the day. (4) The same areas/dynamics that facilitate crime because of their socioeconomic and cultural contexts are also expected to be similar in nature in both urban and rural areas. (5) Crimes that happen in rural areas may be generated by processes that are far from the conditions that they are created. However, it is submitted here the mechanisms that explain why crimes occur in points 1–5 are not enough to provide clues behind the location and spatial context in which large concentration of crimes occur. Some of the potential candidates to help explain large-scale patterns of crime (for instance, group of municipalities, across borders) require systemic thinking (e.g., von Bertalanffy, 1974) that links individuals in settings, these nested in areas, and they, in their turn, in larger contexts that sometimes go beyond national borders; but often, not necessarily in this particular order.

The need for new criminological theories that can support the interpretation of large-scale processes of crime must accommodate the notion of "space of flows" (Castells, 1989, p. 146), with the current extensive use of modern modes of transportation as well as telecommunications technology. This concept of space is based on human action and interaction occurring in real time and sometimes orchestrated remotely, over cyberspace. Needless to point out the potential usefulness this type of framework may have to interpret organized crime, but certainly its potential can also shed light on trivial local crime problems. One important question to be analyzed in rural areas is whether thefts are committed by local offenders or whether they are actions by outsiders coming from neighboring communities or both. Traditionally, outsiders are often blamed for certain types of crimes. Of course this is an empirical question that can be checked looking at how the flow of information from the targets reaches potential offenders, supposedly living outside the community. It is crucial to analyze the potential travel to crime for different types of offences/targets. As these examples show, challenges of interpreting crime in space requires paradoxically less attention to spatial boundaries (perhaps leaving behind the thought of crime following the tyranny imposed by police administrative districts), and more focus on multi-scale temporal factors that affect individuals, settings, areas, countries – in a systemic way.

Notes

1 Ceccato and Dolmén, 2011.
2 Spatial autocorrelation is characterized by a correlation in a signal among nearby locations in space, this means for example that a positive sign shows that areas with similar values of violence rates tend to be clustered together in space, either high or low (+1). A random arrangement of values would give Moran's I a value that is close to zero and a completely dispersed pattern of rates would produce a negative Moran's I (–1). Moran's I was calculated in GeoDa 0.9.5–1 (Anselin, 2003), with row-standardized binary weight matrix, queen criterion, first order neighbours. Moran's I statistic summarizes the spatial pattern for the whole study area. Swedish islands in the weight matrix were manually linked to the mainland by replacing the zero values to a known neighbour (Öland was linked to Kalmar, and Gotland to Oskarshamn and Nynäshamn) but they do not belong to any cluster, and are excluded from Figures 5.1 and 5.2.
3 LISA analysis allows us to identify where are the areas of high values of a variable that are surrounded by high values on the neighboring areas, namely high-high clusters (black). The low-low clusters are also identified from this analysis (gray), which are the areas with low values surrounded by low values. High-low clusters are areas with high values neighboured by low values (hashed) while low-high are areas with low values neighbored by high values (spots).
4 Press release, County Police authority, 2012.

References

Amcoff, J., & Westholm, E. (2007). Understanding rural change: Demography as a key to the future. *Futures, 39*(4), 363–379.

Andersson, F., & Mellgren, C. (2007). Våldsbrottsligheten är ökande, minskande eller konstant? *FOU-rapport.* Malmo: Hälsa och samhälle.

Anselin, L. (2003). GeoDa™ 0.9 user's guide. Urbana, IL: Center for Spatially Integrated Social Science, University of Illinois. Retrieved April 11, 2015, from www.csiss.org/.

Baller, R. D., Anselin, L. U. C., Messner, S. F., Deane, G., & Hawkins, D. F. (2001). Structural covariates of U.S. county homicides rates: Incorporating spatial effects. *Criminology, 39*(3), 561–588.

Bengtsson, R., & Imsirovic, H. (2010). *Ungdomsbrottslighet: En komparativ undersökning av två av Malmös stadsdelar.* Malmö: Malmö högskola.

Bjerregaard, B., & Cochran, J. K. (2008). A cross-national test of institutional anomie theory: Do the strength of other social institutions mediate or moderate the effects of the economy on the rate of crime? *Western Criminology Review, 9*(1), 31–48.

Bottoms, A. E., & Wiles, P. (2002). Environmental criminology. In R. M. M. Maguire, & R. Reine (Eds.), *The Oxford handbook of criminology* (pp. 620–656). Oxford: Oxford University Press.

Brottsförebyggande rådet – BRÅ (National Council of Crime Prevention). (2007a). Brottsutveckling i Sverige fram till år 2007. Stockholm: BRÅ.

Brottsförebyggande rådet – BRÅ (National Council of Crime Prevention). (2007b). Det grova våldet i sjukvårdsdata: En metodstudie (E. Kühlhorn, Ed.). Stockholm: BRÅ.

Brottsförebyggande rådet – BRÅ (National Council of Crime Prevention). (2007c). Utsattheten för brott varierar i landet. *Apropå, 4.* Retrieved April 11, 2015, from www.bra.se/bra/nytt-fran-bra/arkiv/apropa/2007-12-01-utsattheten-for-brott-varierar-i-landet.html.

Brottsförebyggande rådet – BRÅ (National Council of Crime Prevention). (2012). Rättsväsendets hantering av ungdomsärenden. Stockholm: BRÅ.

Brottsförebyggande rådet – BRÅ (National Council of Crime Prevention). (2014). Brottsutvecklingen för vissa brott mot person fram till 2013 (p. 41). Stockholm: BRÅ.

Castells, M. (1989). *The informational city: Information technology, economic restructuring, and the urban-regional process.* Oxford: Basil Blackwell.

Ceccato, V. (2007). Crime dynamics at Lithuanian borders. *European Journal of Criminology, 4*(2), 131–160.

Ceccato, V., & Dolmén, L. (2011). Crime in rural Sweden. *Applied Geography, 31*(1), 119–135.

Ceccato, V., & Dolmén, L. (2013). Crime prevention in rural Sweden. *European Journal of Criminology, 10,* 89–112.

Ceccato, V., & Haining, R. (2004). Crime in border regions: The Scandinavian case of Öresund, 1998–2001. *Annals of the Association of American Geographers, 94,* 807–826.

Ceccato, V., & Haining, R. (2008). Short and medium term dynamics and their influence on acquisitive crime rates in the transition states of Estonia, Latvia and Lithuania. *Applied Spatial Analysis and Policy, 1*(3), 215–244.

Chamlin, M. B., & Cochran, J. K. (2007). An evaluation of the assumptions that underlie institutional anomie theory. *Theoretical Criminology, 11*(1), 39–61.

Cohen, L. E., & Felson, M. (1979). Social change and crime rate trends: A routine activity approach. *American Sociological Review, 44,* 588–608.

Corcoran, M. E., & Chaudry, A. (1997). The dynamics of childhood poverty. *Future of Children, 7,* 40–54.

Cracolici, M., & Uberti, T. (2009). Geographical distribution of crime in Italian provinces: A spatial econometric analysis. *Jahrbuch für Regionalwissenschaft, 29*(1), 1–28.

Durkheim, E. (1897). *Suicide: A study in sociology.* New York: Free Press.

Eisenberg, U., & Von Lampe, K. (2005). Provisional situation report on trafficking in contraband cigarettes. *Assessing Organized Crime project* – excerpts published in *Trends in Organized Crime, 9,* 8–15.

Entorf, H., & Spengler, H. (2000). Socioeconomic and demographic factors of crime in Germany: Evidence from panel data of the German states. *International Review of Law and Economics, 20*(1), 75–106.

Estrada, F. (2005). *Våldsutvecklingen i Sverige e en presentation och analys av sjukvårdsdata* (Vol. 4). Stockholm: Institutet för framtidsstudier.

Eurostat. (2008). Demographic statistics: Divorce. Retrieved April 11, 2015, from: http://epp.eurostat.ec.europa.eu/.

Fröjd, S., Marttunen, M., Pelkonen, M., von der Pahlen, B., & Kaltiala-Heino, R. (2006). Perceived financial difficulties and maladjustment outcomes in adolescence. *European Journal of Public Health, 16*(5), 542–548.

Granath, S., Hagstedt, J., Kivivuori, J., Lehti, M., Ganpat, S., Liem, M., & Nieuwbeerta, P. (2011). Homicide in Finland, the Netherlands and Sweden: A first study on the European homicide monitor data (Vol. 15). Swedish National Council for Crime Prevention, the National Research Institute of Legal Policy, and the Institute for Criminal Law and Criminology at Leiden University.

Higgins, N., Robb, P., & Britton, A. (Eds.). (2010). *Geographic patterns of crime* (Vol. 12/10). London: Home Office.

Johansson, M., Westlund, H., & Eliasson, K. (2009). The "new rurality" and entrepreneurship: Attributes influencing enterprise propensity in rural Sweden. Paper presented at the *Congress of Regional Science Association International*, Lodz, Poland.

Karlsson, A. (2012). Unga bor i storstan: äldre i glesbygd. *Välfärd, 25*. Retrieved, April 11, 2015, from www.scb.se/sv_/Hitta-statistik/Artiklar/Unga-bor-i-storstan–aldre-i-glesbygd/.

Kaylen, M. T., & Pridemore, W. A. (2011). A reassessment of the association between social disorganization and youth violence in rural areas. *Social Science Quarterly, 92*(4), 978–1001.

Kaylen, M. T., & Pridemore, W. A. (2013). Social disorganization and crime in rural communities: The first direct test of the systemic model. *British Journal of Criminology, 53*(5), 905–923.

Kerry, R., Goovaerts, P., Haining, R. P., & Ceccato, V. (2010). Applying geostatistical analysis to crime data: Car-related thefts in the Baltic states. *Geographical Analysis, 42*(1), 53–77.

Kim, S.-W., & Pridemore, W. A. (2005). Social change, institutional anomie and serious property crime in transitional Russia. *British Journal of Criminology, 45*(1), 81–97.

Kneebone, E., & Raphael, S. (2011). City and suburban crime trends in metropolitan America. In *Metropolitan Opportunity Series* (p. 22). Washington, DC: Brookings.

Kornhauser, R. (1978). *Social sources of delinquency*. Chicago, IL: University of Chicago Press.

Korsell, L. (Ed.). (2008). *Hur organiserad är den organiserade brottsligheten?* Stockholm: BRÅ.

Maume, M. O., & Lee, M. R. (2003). Social institutions and violence: A sub-national test of institutional anomie theory. *Criminology, 41*(4), 1137–1172.

Merton, R. (1938). Social structure and anomie. *American Sociological Review, 3*, 672–682.

Messner, S., & Rosenfeld, R. (1994). *Crime and the American cream*. Belmont, CA: Wadsworth.

Messner, S. F., & Rosenfeld, R. (1997). Political restraint of the market and levels of criminal homicide: A cross-national application of institutional anomie theory. *Social Forces, 75*, 1393–1416.

Messner, S., & Rosenfeld, R. (Eds.). (1999). *Social structure and homicide: Theory and research* (Vols. 27–34). London: Sage.

Osgood, D. W., & Chambers, J. M. (2003). Community correlates of rural youth violence. *Juvenile Justice Bulletin*, May, 12.

Persson, R. (2008). Segregation, education and space: A case study of Malmö. Luleå: University Faculty of Engineering.

Petee, T. A., & Kowalski, G. S. (1993). Modeling rural violent crime rates: A test of social disorganization theory. *Sociological Focus, 26*(1), 87–89.

Sampson, R. J. (1986). Crime in cities: The effects of formal and informal social control. *Crime and Justice, 8*, 271–311.

Sampson, R. J., & Laub, J. H. (1993). *Crime in the making: Pathways and turning points through life*. Cambridge, MA: Harvard University Press.

Sampson, R. J., Raudenbush, S. W., & Earls, F. (1997). Neighborhoods and violent crime: A multilevel study of collective efficacy. *Science, 277*(5328), 918–924.

Shaw, C. R., & McKay, H. D. (1942). *Juvenile delinquency and urban areas*. Chicago, IL: University of Chicago Press.

Tobler, W. (1970). A computer movie simulating urban growth in the Detroit region. *Economic Geography, 46*(2), 234–240.

Uggen, C., & Thompson, M. (2003). The socio-economic determinants of ill-gotten gains: Within person changes in drug use and personal earnings. *American Journal of Sociology, 109*(1), 146–185.

von Bertalanffy, L. (1974). *General system theory: Foundations, development, applications*. New York: George Braziller.

Weding, L. (2007). Organisationsmönster för storskalig alkoholsmuggling och distribution: En pilotstudie (Master's degree, Stockholm University, Stockholm).

Weitoft, G. R., Hjern, A., Haglund, B., & Rosén, M. (2003). Mortality, severe morbidity, and injury in children living with single parents in Sweden: A population-based study. *Lancet, 361*(9354), 289–295.

Westholm, E. (2008). Vad menas egentligen med landsbygd? Ska hela Sverige leva? *Ska hela Sverige leva?* (pp. 49–58). Stockholm: Formas.

Wiles, P., & Costello, A. (2000). The "road to nowhere": The evidence for travelling criminals (p. 207). London: Home Office Research Study.

Part III

Perceived safety in rural areas

6   The nature of perceived safety in rural areas

Imagine that some farmers declare they are worried about having their livestock stolen. Should this be enough to influence crime prevention efforts by the local police force? Or consider the case of a woman who is in fear because of constant threats from her violent partner. Should her fear be taken seriously by workers in social services or the police to avoid something more serious happening?

Fear of crime is not typically considered a conventional policing matter and seems to be even less of an issue in rural communities. One reason for this neglect is that the police, as well as those who devote their time to crime prevention, often work reactively, requiring an offense to be committed before any action can be taken. Another problem is that fear (of crime) may be triggered by the trauma of victimization, though that is not its only source. Anxieties are fed by multi-scale factors. This chapter examines how the multifaceted nature of fear makes perceived safety a difficult issue to tackle. Instead of denying such complexity, this chapter attempts to provide examples of how such anxieties form and are associated with the fear of crime in rural environments in Sweden. "Perceived safety" is a general concept used in this chapter to characterize both fear of crime and other overall anxieties, often measured by safety and crime victims' surveys.

Lack of perceived safety – or, more specifically, fear of crime – has been the subject of interdisciplinary research for many decades, but the results are far from unproblematic. Crime victims' surveys and interviews are often the basis of this type of research, which has been criticized for offering a shallow picture of what fear is actually is. This chapter examines fear as an informative resource that may improve quality of life for those living in rural communities. If fear is a reflection of everyday life experiences, what are those experiences in rural communities?

The nature of perceived safety in rural areas

Rural areas are regarded worldwide as relatively safer environments than urban areas (Barclay, Scott, Hogg, & Donnermeyer, 2007; Bradford & Myhill, 2015; BRÅ, 2011; Ceccato & Dolmén, 2013; Donnermeyer & Kreps, 1986; Maxfield, 1984; Shappland & Vagg, 1985). Despite this widespread belief, research has also found that this apparently homogeneous pattern of safety in rural areas does not hold up to scrutiny. Fear and other types of anxiety are as much an issue in rural areas as they are in big cities or, at least, are for some groups of individuals at particular times (Panelli, Little, & Kraack, 2004). The literature suggests that people in rural towns are not actually fearful of crime itself but are concerned with what they perceive as a threat to their rural idyll (Marshall & Johnson, 2005). Power relationships in the community may trigger fear, at least for some by some (Hunter, Krannich, & Smith, 2002; Scott, Carrington, & McIntosh, 2012; Yarwood & Gardner, 2000). Thus, the nature of perceived safety (or the lack thereof – fear) is a phenomenon affected by multi-scale factors (Day, 2009; Los, 2002; Wyant, 2008). Some factors are local and tangible, whilst others may be more difficult to assess but still affect individuals' anxieties at the local level. Fear can be multidimensional, as an individual can fear for oneself (personal fear) and fear for others (e.g., children, spouses, friends) whose safety the person values.

Fear is, according to Warr (2000, p. 453), "an emotion, a feeling of alarm or dread caused by awareness or expectation of danger." If one concentrates on looking at "fear of crime" only, Ferraro (1995, p. 8) defines it as "an emotional reaction of dread or anxiety to crime or symbols that a person associates with crime." Thus, an increase in crime would hypothetically affect perceived safety. However, this simplistic causal relationship is rarely confirmed by empirical studies, as the fear of crime refers to the *fear* of being a victim of crime as opposed to the *actual probability* of being a victim of crime, that is, the actual risk (Hale, 1996). As Pain (2009) suggests, the concept of fear of crime has less significance than is widely expected. Yet, its construct, as it is argued here, can be informative in the context of perceived safety in rural context.

Furstenberg (1971) was one of the first researchers who recognized the difficulty in distinguishing between concern about and fear of crime. Concern about crime, the author suggests, is an estimation of the seriousness of crime as a public issue, while fear of crime is the perceived risk of victimization. The author found that concern and fear of crime were not significantly related to each other: concern with crime was associated with resentment to social change, while fear of crime was not related to attitudes toward social change, and therefore these were not interchangeable concepts. Later, Lotz (1979) has suggested that concern about crime is related to a variety of individuals' politically conservative attitudes. Still, not everyone agrees with these explanations and the conceptual differences.

Previous research has shown that an individual's fears depend on his/her individual characteristics, such as physical abilities, age, gender, socioeconomic status, and ethnic background (Box, Hale, & Andrews, 1988; Garofalo & Laub, 1979; Pain & Smith, 2008). Individual factors play an important role in defining perceptions of risk and safety. Gender and age are perhaps the strongest ones.

The individual dimension of fear is often related to the vulnerability hypothesis, in which those perceiving themselves as vulnerable are likely to be more fearful.

Gender

Traditionally, women are portrayed as being more fearful than men about their personal safety (Box et al., 1988; Koskela, 1999; Loukaitou-Sideris, 2004). This degree of fear by women is higher in public places than in domestic settings. One of the reasons for these unbalanced levels of fear is that women and men are victimized in different places. Regardless of which part of a city a woman lives in, her home tends to be more dangerous than any outdoor environment. For example, although the majority of rapes are committed indoors by someone the victim knows (e.g., a partner or parent), the international literature on sexual violence indicates that rape in public places is the one that feeds the idea of public places as dangerous places (Canter & Larkin, 1993; Ceccato, 2014; Pyle, 1974). It has also been suggested that women are more fearful because of their physical and social vulnerabilities (Furstenberg, 1971; Gray & O'Connor, 1990; Jackson & E. Gray, 2010; Skogan & Maxfield, 1981).

In one of the seminal studies in this area, Valentine (1990) finds that women anticipate being at risk in several specific public settings (e.g., bus stops, open spaces, alleys, underground passages) than in the domestic arena. Gender differences in stated personal safety may also be related to the fact that women and men are traveling in different ways or spending time in different places (Kunieda & Gauthier, 2007). However, gender is not the only factor that affects perceived safety. For instance, Bromley and Nelson (2002) find significant gender differences in the perceived safety of boys and girls in the city center environment (e.g., where many transportation nodes are located) but no difference in perceived safety in their home areas.

Age

Research also finds that feelings of insecurity typically increase with age, partly because of the inevitable increase in individuals' physical and/or mental vulnerability. Previous research has shown that while young people are statistically more at risk of being victimized, older and/or disabled individuals tend to be more fearful (Furstenberg, 1971; Lagrange & Ferraro, 1989). Sweden is not an exception (Hayman, 2011). Those who feel that they have one or more disabilities experience more anxiety and fear of being a victim to crime and avoid going out (City of Stockholm, 2011). In Sweden, although the elderly represent only 18 percent of the population, more than two-thirds of all fatal accidents occur among them; more than half of these accidents take place around their homes (Torstensson, Forslund, & Tegnell, 2011). Many people stop using public transportation when they get older, even in small municipalities. Wretstrand and Svensson (2008) show that 46 percent of elderly people interviewed refrain from taking the bus because they are afraid of traveling alone.

Vulnerability interacts with other factors to determine an individual's perceived safety. For example, new evidence shows perceived vulnerability to be the strongest predictor and mediator of the relationship between perceived disorder in a place and perceived safety (Acuña-Rivera, Brown, & Uzzell, 2014). The authors indicate that the more disordered a place is perceived to be, the more a person relies on the perception of risk to estimate how safe she/he might be. A relevant question here is, safety for whom? Homeless people temporarily parked in a central station may be perceived as threats by the local inhabitants, while the itinerants themselves are frightened by the lack of familiarity and the anonymity of transients. Overall, factors in the local social environment were found to be more important as drivers of fear of crime (including values, social networks, and familiarity) than the physical environment in a qualitative study by Lorenc et al. (2013).

Previous victimization

Among the individual factors, prior victimization (or awareness of others' victimization) is often considered a determinant of a person's fear. Current perceived safety in both urban and rural areas may be affected by the experience of having been a victim of a crime, for example, having been robbed, subjected to intimidation, or assaulted. Experiencing or witnessing other people's victimization (particularly someone close, family, or friends) may also affect an individual's level of personal safety (for a review, see e.g., Skogan, 1987). However, previous studies show ambiguous links between victimization and fear of crime (Cates, Dian, & Schnepf, 2003; Garofalo & Laub, 1979), as its effect on people's behavior and attitudes may be moderated by other factors. At the community level, rural communities with relatively little crime may express high levels of fear because of occasional serious crimes, such as homicide. These "rare events" can disproportionately affect rural residents' fear of crime. Physical isolation may also lead to a disproportionately high declared fear of crime because of individuals' relative vulnerability. For example, rural farm residents are more sensitive to risk than are their counterparts living elsewhere (Bankston, Jenkins, Thayer-Doyle, & Thompson, 1987).

Physical environment

Fear (of crime) is a reflection of what one sees and perceives with one's senses. Fear is a function of an individual's emotional reactions to a place and memories and associations that a place brings to the surface. In rural contexts, forests, parking lots, and service stations along roads and other desolated areas in a rural village may generate fear among visitors to a small village but may be just the place that young people treasure the most, as they can gather and spend time free from adult supervision. In other words, fear is a feeling produced by the social constructs of a physical space. Skår (2010), for instance, illustrates how feelings of a forest (in Norway) are dynamic in terms of gender and explores how men and women experience – and respond to – feelings of fear and anxiety in nature.

Signs of disorder and crime

Lack of clearly defined private–public spaces is said to affect perceived safety (Newman, 1972). At the same time, barriers and the construction of fortresses around buildings can create, at least in urban areas, geographical disruption and generate suspicion and fear (Landman, 2012). Thus fear of crime goes beyond buildings and streets. It is sometimes regarded as a reflection of the state of the community, and the meaning attached to an environment at a particular time.

Social interactions that occur at certain places may also lead to lack of perceived safety, around bars or transport nodes, for instance. The mechanisms linking visible deterioration to a fear of a place can be likened to the Wilson and Kelling's broken window syndrome (Wilson & Kelling, 1982), which suggests that unrepaired damage to property encourages further vandalism and other types of crimes. They indicate that acts of vandalism and public disorder function as symbols of the extent to which an area is in decline. Signs of physical deterioration are also thought to be more important determinants of fear of crime than the actual crime itself. Signs that nobody has control – abandoned buildings, litter, vandalism, and loitering – are thought to trigger fear of crime (Lewis & Maxfield, 1980) and are indicators of more serious crimes. As Skogan (1996) suggests, this is not only because signs of physical deterioration are often visible but also because they are able to capture a much broader range of problems and are therefore more informative to residents than official crime statistics. Public perceptions of disorder have also been linked to implicit stereotypes about race and deprivation (Sampson & Raudenbush, 2004) and, at least in urban areas, they help perpetuate segregation and suspicion among groups. Rural areas are not as immune to physical deterioration as the literature would suggest (LaGrange, Ferraro, & Supancic, 1992), quite the opposite, signs of disorder and crime often translates into a differentiated rural housing market (Wilhelmsson & Ceccato, 2015).

Mobility patterns

Fear can be affected by the way people travel and the environments to which they are exposed. The simple decision one takes to leave home implies a change in one's safety status (increase or decrease), depending on how and when one moves (Ceccato, 2013). People's fears and risk perceptions are determinants for the kinds of risk they can accept to be exposed to (Fyhri & Backer-Grøndahl, 2012). In rural areas, particularly in the most remote ones, long distances separate people's homes from their work and basic services. Recent changes in the Swedish regional market have imposed more frequent and longer commutes. These are often onerous for individuals: men still travel further to work than women, but both spend a similar amount of time commuting, which has implications for gender equality (Bergström, 2008; Gil Sola, 2010).

Familiarity

Newcomers may feel unsafe if they do not know an area. Valentine (1990) suggests that, in the absence of prior experience or familiarity with a particular place, judgment is likely to be based on preconceived ideas about similar settings and their occupants. This familiarity can also be linked to the individual's social context and norms. Rural residents moving to large urban centers may feel unsafe, at least for some time, by the fact that such places offer anonymity that may be perceived as a threat. Milgram (1974, p. 46) suggests that anonymity can vary, from total anonymity, to full acquaintance, and that the various degrees of anonymity may influence how individuals feel in cities and towns. For example, "conditions of full acquaintance offer security and familiarity but they may be stifling because an individual may be caught in a web of established relationships" and expected behaviors, sometimes unknown to the outsider. Panelli et al. (2004) also contest constructions of the rural community as an emotionally harmonious, safe, and peaceful space by exposing women's experiences of fear in various rural communities in New Zealand.

Social cohesion and collective efficacy

Perceived safety relates to the social environment an individual may encounter. Places characterized by strong social ties and cooperative behavior (social cohesion) are often associated with high perceived safety. Social relationships in rural communities are traditionally thought to be based on networks of personal ties that perpetuate over time, while in urban areas social networks are thought to be less stable. This echoes the popular cultural oppositions between the city as the site of an artificially imposed order and the country as a naturally ordered, bonded, and cohesive community. The dichotomy between *gemeinschaft* and *gesellschaft* (Tönnies, 1887) provides a framework for potential urban/rural differences in terms of social ties and cooperative behavior. In certain cases, this active engagement leads to collective efficacy (Sampson, Morenoff, & Felton, 1999). Cancino (2005) shows evidence that the differential ability of residents to realize mutual trust and solidarity (i.e., social cohesion) is a major source of variation in citizens' perceived safety in a non-metropolitan area in Michigan. Safety is a reflection of patterns of assistance and protection within groups regardless of whether the members reside in rural or in urban areas (Hofferth & Iceland, 1998; Milgram, 1974). In practice, criticisms of the effect of strong ties in communities suggest that strong social networks strengthen communities but may also have the unintended effect of "enabling" exclusion and other types of harmful behavior (DeKeseredy & Schwartz, 2008).

Othering

Fear (and other anxieties) may also result from the overall sense of change that a place is undergoing. Rapid changes in the economy, especially with population inflow, are argued to have an impact on residents' quality of life. Because of the nature of rural areas, even a relatively small population inflow has the potential to affect the dynamics of a village. Other changes are more tangible, such as the construction of encapsulated rural gated communities (Spocter, 2013). Differences between residents and incomers can be maximized by both groups, giving expression to *us–them* feelings (as part of *othering* or the process of transforming a difference into *otherness*). Fear of others is often one cause of the animosity between newcomers and locals, previously identified by Sandercock (2005) as an expression of the fear of the unknown.

Fear of "stranger danger" in public spaces has been much more engrained from childhood in women than in men. Therefore it is not odd that surveys show women declare feeling more unsafe than men do when on the move (Ceccato, 2013; Whitzman, 2007). Sandercock (2005) argues that expressions of fear are expressions of fear of difference. Sandercock (2000) claims that there is something about us that is in conflict with the stranger: "The stranger threatens to bring chaos into the known world.... *We* must secure our centrality, and *they* who upset our homely space must be pushed out from the center. They are not *like us* and therefore they are threatening" (p. 205).

Many examples are found in the international literature. For example, Ruddell and Ortiz (2015) report how locals express concerns about reductions in quality of life (due to anti-social behavior, drug use, and aggressive, impaired, or dangerous driving) that the residents regard as a result of a large inflow of population into a Canadian rural town. In the United States, Hunter et al. (2002) assess the fear of crime across three categories of community residents with different migration histories in three rural boom municipalities: lifetime residents, migrants who joined the boomtown community during its period of rapid growth, and post-boom migrants. The authors find that boom migrants express greater fear of crime than longer-term residents or post-boom migrants. In a rapidly growing rural area in the United States, Crank, Giacomazzi, and Heck (2003) find that perceptions of drug and gang problems are associated with a wide variety of police order and crime problems. Fear of crime seems to incorporate what residents regard as cultural threats to their dominant constructions of rurality (Yarwood & Gardner, 2000), which sometimes reveal hidden layers of intolerance and racism (Garland & Chakraborti, 2006; Hubbard, 2005; Palmer, 1996). Norris and Reeves (2013) assess whether fear of crime represents itself differently according to the social environment in which it is experienced. They find that more authoritarian residents in a rural area are concerned about offenders traveling into their community to offend ("the danger is out there" feeling), whereas there were no differences among urban dwellers.

A homeless person is exposed to an increased risk of victimization and fear. Gaetz (2004) shows, for instance, that in Canada the conditions that place street youth at risk and cause fear are connected to such youths' experiences of social exclusion in terms of restricted access to housing, employment, and public spaces. Similarly, Gypsies and travelers in rural England face similar challenges in rural communities (Greenfields, 2014); such people are regarded as a constant source of anxiety for the locals but themselves feel a burden of exclusion. Targeted by the police when public order issues arise, travelers in the United

Kingdom live with permanent feelings of fear from feeling out of place (Halfa-cree, 2011).

In England and Wales, exclusion of ethnic minorities from the life of rural communities is not the result of a *monolithic entity* (as described by Robinson and Gardner, 2012, p. 85) and takes different shapes, generating anxieties experienced on a daily basis (Robinson & Gardner, 2012). In Australia, Scott et al. (2012) reveal how *crime talk* in a mining town is a result of specific social constructions and the relative ability of groups to act as a cohesive network, used in the power relations between locals and newcomers. In Sweden and Finland, Jensen (2012) illustrates how economic change in rural areas, dissatisfaction, and anxieties create fertile ground for the proliferation of xenophobic ideas, expressed by the advance of extreme-right-wing political parties in recent elections. Similar expressions of discrimination are reported among the young Sami population, a group that has historically been a minority in Scandinavia. For more details, see the next section of this chapter.

Macro-societal changes

Some contemporary anxieties are generated by a sense of loss of personal security imposed by changes that go far beyond the local community. The transition from "modernity" to "late modernity" (Giddens, 1991, pp. 70–88) or by the preeminence of the risk society (Beck, 2000) is said to cause major changes in our sense of safety. This is an ongoing process that occurs worldwide yet also produces local effects. These transformations, according to Bottoms and Wiles (2002), have had a direct effect on crime and fear of crime. In "late modernity," the moment in time that most characterizes what we are undergoing now, globalization is creating potential risks that concern all types of people. According to Beck (2000), "these dangers" cannot be socially delimited in either space or time. Thus, the potential threat eludes the control of institutions of society and cause feelings of anxiety about who is at risk or who is responsible for what. The challenge of catching international networks of organized crime is just one example of the challenges faced by authorities when trying to control the flow of people and money in a quasi-borderless Europe. Perhaps it is irrelevant, though, to attempt to quantify individuals' fear as an everyday life experience. More important to one's perceived safety is perhaps "fear attractors" that are quite mundane, daily life experiences or facts that make one anxious or worried but do not affect the individual directly (e.g., mass-media coverage of violence), and "fear generators," such as being victimized by a crime or seeing someone else become a victim of crime.

Victimization is an important fear generator, but anxieties may also be fed by an individual's uncertainties and frustrations in everyday life, such as being unemployed or having a sense of the gap between the individual's limited resources and society's overall unlimited opportunities for consumption (anomic conditions). As Hope and Sparks (2000, p. 5) suggest, fear of crime may "intersect with the larger consequences of modernity." Thus, as suggested by

Hummelsheim, Hirtenlehner, Jackson, and Oberwittler (2010, p. 5), "if fear of crime can be both a specific concern about crime and a more general projection of a range of connected social anxieties, then fear of crime should be closely connected with feelings of social insecurity." The authors find evidence that European countries with high levels of social protection display low levels of fear whilst low levels of social protection show high levels of insecurity feelings, supporting the expected negative association between the extent of social protection and fear of crime.

Current anxieties are said to be generated by a lack of individuals' embedded biography with a plurality of social worlds, beliefs, and diversification of lifestyles that can be accessed by mass media via ICT. Some of these feelings relate to a lack of an individual's sense of order and continuity in regard to one's experiences in life (Giddens, 1991), being experienced as threats that can take different shapes. The perceived collective danger is a social construct fed by the attention put on its existence, either real or not. The increasing commodification of security (by proliferation of a market for personal security products and services), for instance, indicates that fear of crime is one of these contemporary perceived "dangers." Mass media coverage has an important role to play in this context, where the notion of "stimulus similarity" is suggested as important in explaining the reaction of fear (Winkel & Vrij, 1990). When an individual reads a newspaper and identifies with the described victim or feels that his/her own community is similar to the one described in the news, then the image of risk may be taken up, personalized, and translated into personal safety concerns.

Commodification of security

Security as a public good in today's society is now delivered by a set of actors no longer limited to the police forces and relies on a broader project that depends on the interplay of different actors (some public, other private or neither) (Loader, 2000). Differential access to protection affects how risks are distributed among individuals, social groups, and places. In practice, this "materialization of fear does not only change the landscape for all, it reflects also a sharp unequal distribution of fear, privilege and risk" (Pain, 2009). As with any other commodity, the "safe feeling" cannot be purchased by all. Wilhelmsson and Ceccato (2015) show that house buyers in a rural municipality, as in large cities, are willing to pay more for dwellings that are less targeted by crime and disorder than for those located in criminogenic parts of a village. In extreme cases, the market for safety leads to the development of gated communities, even in rural areas (Macari, 2009; Spocter, 2013). As suggested by Goold, Loader, and Thumala (2010), although gated communities might be considered a *failed good* in Western Europe, the security industry in general is growing (Zedner, 2009). In countries such as South Africa and Brazil, the proliferation of rural gated developments has been linked to a market for consumers able to pay for exclusivity in an idyllic rural setting. These housing developments often offer other commodities that allow easy transport to urban centers, resembling the traditional features of garden cities. Thus, these housing projects are the product of wider processes of change in rural areas related to counter-urbanization and extraction of amenity value from the rural landscape (Macari, 2009; Spocter, 2013).

Concluding remarks

Are individuals living in the countryside less worried about crime than those living in urban areas? They might be, but in this chapter attempts were made to illustrate that the safety perceived by people living in rural areas is a more complex phenomenon than the one reflected in overall expressions of fear of crime.

Poor perceived safety may be triggered by previous victimization. Thefts of livestock from neighboring farms may mobilize local farmers to be proactive out of the fear that something will happen with their own livestock. Foreign women brought to rural Sweden may live in fear because they do not know their rights, whether they can seek help and assistance if isolated in remote areas.

Given the multifaceted nature of perceived safety and the complexity of fear of crime, a relevant question is: how can fear be informative to those living and working with safety issues in rural communities?

At an individual level, it is important to differentiate between a dysfunctional worry about crime that erodes quality of life and a functional worry that motivates vigilance and routine precaution (Jackson & Gray, 2010). In Jackson and Gray's study, around one-quarter of research participants who said they were worried about crime and took precautions that made them feel safer also said they did not experience a reduction in quality of life as a result of their worry or cautionary activity. Adopting measures that aim at reducing both risk and worry about victimization by different groups of society seems to be central.

Crime prevention measures are traditionally used to reduce crime risk and consequently fear of crime. For instance, tackling crime through the situational conditions of crime in some cases has had a proven impact on perceived safety combined with long-term social crime prevention. Actions to improve safety have to be inclusive and avoid stigmatizing those who are already in a disadvantaged position in society. For this to happen, actors must be aware of their roles and the challenges involved when working with specific safety issues embedded in particular contexts. They should strive to work toward practices that are inclusive and fair (different target groups but also based on a coalition of different actors) and, as much as possible, to work within participatory frameworks. The process of discussing local fears and sources of anxiety demands an open and communicative process, involving negotiation and mediation to work through these fears with those directly affected.

In a neutral world, both crime and protection from victimization would be evenly distributed in society. With the commodification of security, preventing crime implies costs for the individual and society in general. As with any other commodity, security is not evenly obtained by all, which inevitably generates inequalities in victimization and perceived safety. Perceived safety as an individual right entails a dimension of reflexivity, which means that it depends on those who observe and produce it. Not all people would agree that the problem is worthy of attention, and most may disagree that particular action is needed, but the process of bringing people together can itself make parties talk through their concerns. Such an approach requires communicative skills among those who take part in the process, a process that, in the best of worlds, should be sensitive to gendered fear as well as a cross-cultural understanding of the fears. Thus, the main task for those working to improve perceived safety is perhaps to identify the sources of anxiety and mediate possible alternatives for action that can make those involved feel informed and, finally, safer.

The implication of this is that there is no such thing as a remedy that can solve the problems of crime and perceived safety, let alone a single actor (such as the police) that can tackle problems. It is submitted here that perceived safety is a collective project that requires constant assessment by those who produce it: those who are in fear, the community itself, stakeholders. Perceived safety is both the cause and the product of people's everyday life practices and experiences, embedded in a context that is not politically neutral, or limited to the village, rural areas, or individual nations. At the same time, there is no doubt that some tangible attributes of perceived safety stem from local rural conditions, where daily anxieties arise from victimization, discrimination, economic change, and many other root causes of fear.

The approach that would seem to make sense, given the discussion in the previous section, is for local communities to organize themselves around problems of perceived safety that cause them concern. These actions can enhance existing models of participation to develop culture- and gender-informed governance structures that give voice to those who feel unsafe. The definition of priorities to be dealt with must adhere to limits that take into account realistic goals. An isolated and remote location can be an advantage and a motivation for rural communities in searching for more appropriate solutions to local problems, such as the sources of fear. Fear is not a problem to be solved or that can be solved in the same way as crime. Given the multifaceted nature of fear, some sources of anxiety cannot be tackled at the level of those who fear. Some declared fears or anxieties are a tiny fraction of the old and new challenges faced by groups in the community and by those who may spend some time there, as in the case of temporary workers. Signs of relatively poor mobility among certain groups, as shown in this chapter, can be used as a reference that could guide future efforts to tackle the structural causes of fear and other anxieties.

References

Acuña-Rivera, M., Brown, J., & Uzzell, D. (2014). Risk perception as mediator in perceptions of neighbourhood disorder and safety about victimisation. *Journal of Environmental Psychology, 40*(0), 64–75.

Bankston, W. B., Jenkins, Q. A., Thayer-Doyle, C. L., & Thompson, C. Y. (1987). Fear of criminal victimization and residential location: The influence of perceived risk. *Rural Sociology, 52*(1), 98–107.

Barclay, E., Scott, J., Hogg, R., & Donnermeyer, J. (Eds.). (2007). *Crime in rural Australia*. Sydney: Federation Press.

Beck, U. (2000). The cosmopolitan perspective: Sociology of the second age of modernity. *British Journal of Sociology, 51*(1), 79–105.

Bergström, G. (2008). Ett könsperspektiv på resor i arbetet. *Arbetsmarknad & Arbetsliv, 4*(2), 29–50.

Bottoms, A. E., & Wiles, P. (2002). Environmental criminology. In R. M. M. Maguire, & R. Reine (Eds.), *The Oxford handbook of criminology* (pp. 620–656). Oxford: Oxford University Press.

Box, S., Hale, C., & Andrews, G. (1988). Explaining fear of crime. *British Journal of Criminology, 28*, 340–356.

Bradford, B., & Myhill, A. (2015). Triggers of change to public confidence in the police and criminal justice system: Findings from the Crime Survey for England and Wales panel experiment. *Criminology and Criminal Justice, 15*(1) 23–43.

Bromley, R. D. F., & Nelson, A. L. (2002). Alcohol related crime and disorder across urban space and time: Evidence from a British city. *Geoforum, 33*, 239–254.

Brottsförebyggande rådet – BRÅ (National Council of Crime Prevention). (2011). The national victims survey. Stockholm: BRÅ.

Cancino, J. M. (2005). the utility of social capital and collective efficacy: Social control policy in nonmetropolitan settings. *Criminal Justice Policy Review, 16*(3), 287–318.

Canter, D., & Larkin, P. (1993). The environmental range of serial rapists. *Journal of Environmental Psychology, 13*, 63–69.

Cates, J. A., Dian, D. A., & Schnepf, G. W. (2003). Use of protection motivation theory to assess fear of crime in rural areas. *Psychology, Crime and Law, 9*(3), 225–236.

Ceccato, V. (2013). *Moving safely: Crime and perceived safety in Stockholm's subway stations*. Plymouth: Lexington.

Ceccato, V. (2014). The nature of rape places. *Journal of Environmental Psychology, 40*, 97–107.

Ceccato, V., & Dolmén, L. (2013). Crime prevention in rural Sweden. *European Journal of Criminology, 10*, 89–112.

City of Stockholm (2011). Trygg i Stockholm? 2011 En stadsövergripande trygghetsmätning. Stockholm: City of Stockholm, Social care.

Crank, J. P., Giacomazzi, A., & Heck, C. (2003). Fear of crime in a nonurban setting. *Journal of Criminal Justice, 31*(3), 249–263.

Day, K. (2009). Being feared: Masculinity and race in public space. In M. L. S. Farrall (Ed.), *Fear of crime: Critical voices in an age of anxiety* (pp. 82–107). New York: Routledge-Cavendish.

DeKeseredy, W. S., & Schwartz, M. D. (2008). Separation/divorce sexual assault in rural Ohio: Survivors' perceptions. *Journal of Prevention and Intervention in the Community, 36*(1), 105–119.

Donnermeyer, J., & Kreps, G. M. (1986). The benefits of crime prevention: A comparative analysis. Columbus, OH: National Rural Crime Prevention Center.

Ferraro, K. F. (1995). *Fear of crime: Interpreting victimization risk.* Albany, NY: State University of New York Press.

Furstenberg, J. F. F. (1971). Public reaction to crime in the streets. *American Scholar, 40*(40), 601–610.

Fyhri, A., & Backer-Grøndahl, A. (2012). Personality and risk perception in transport. *Accident Analysis and Prevention, 49,* 470–475.

Gaetz, S. (2004). Safe streets for whom? Homeless youth, social exclusion, and criminal victimization. *Canadian Journal of Criminology and Criminal Justice/La Revue canadienne de criminologie et de justice pénale, 46*(4), 423–456.

Garland, J., & Chakraborti, N. (2006). "Race", space and place: Examining identity and cultures of exclusion in rural England. *Ethnicities, 6*(2), 159–177.

Garofalo, J., & Laub, J. (1979). Fear of crime: Broadening our perspective. *Victomology, 3,* 242–253.

Giddens, A. (1991). *Modernity and self-identity: Self and society in the late modern age.* Cambridge: Polity Press.

Gil Sola, A. (2010). Regionförstoring innebär längre restider för både kvinnor och män. *Plan, 2,* 13–17.

Goold, B., Loader, I., & Thumala, A. (2010). Consuming security? Tools for a sociology of security consumption. *Theoretical Criminology, 14*(1), 3–30.

Gray, D. E., & O'Connor, M. (1990). Concern about and fear of crime in an Australian rural community. *Australian and New Zealand Journal of Criminology, 23,* 284–298.

Greenfields, M. (2014). Gypsies and travellers in modern rural England. In G. Bosworth & P. Somerville (Eds.), *Interpreting rurality: Multidisciplinary approaches* (pp. 219–234). London/New York: Routledge.

Hale, C. (1996). Fear of crime: A review of the literature. *International Review of Victimology, 4,* 79–150.

Halfacree, K. (2011). Still "Out of place in the country"? Travellers and the post-productivist rural. In R. I. Mawby & R. Yarwood (Eds.), *Rural policing and policing the rural: A constable countryside?* (pp. 124–135). Farnham: Ashgate.

Hayman, S. (2011). Older people in Canada: Their victimization and fear of crime. *Canadian Journal on Aging/La Revue canadienne du vieillissement, 30*(3), 423–436.

Hofferth, S. L., & Iceland, J. (1998). Social capital in rural and urban communities. *Rural Sociology, 63*(4), 574–598.

Hope, T., & Sparks, R. (2000). *Crime, risk, and insecurity: Law and order in everyday life and political discourse.* London: Routledge.

Hubbard, P. (2005). "Inappropriate and incongruous": Opposition to asylum centres in the English countryside. *Journal of Rural Studies, 21*(1), 3–17.

Hummelsheim, D., Hirtenlehner, H., Jackson, J., & Oberwittler, D. (2010). Social insecurities and fear of crime: A cross-national study on the impact of welfare state policies on crime-related anxieties. *European Sociological Review, 27*(3), 327–345.

Hunter, L. M., Krannich, R. S., & Smith, M. D. (2002). Rural migration, rapid growth, and fear of crime. *Rural Sociology, 67*(1), 71–89.

Jackson, J., & Gray, E. (2010). Functional fear and public insecurities about crime. *British Journal of Criminology, 50*(1), 1–22.

Jensen, M. (2012). Rasism, missnöje och "fertile grounds" Östergötland Sverige jämförs med Birkaland Finland: Sverigedemokraterna vs Sannfinländarna (Master's degree, Linköping University, Linköping).

Koskela, H. (1999). Fear, control and space: Geographies of gender, fear of violence, and video surveillance (PhD, University of Helsinki, Helsinki).

Kunieda, M., & Gauthier, A. (2007). Gender and urban transport: Fashionable and affordable. Sustainable transport: A sourcebook for police makers in developing cities. Eschborn: GTZ.

Lagrange, R. L., & Ferraro, K. F. (1989). Assessing age and gender diferences in perceived risk and fear of crime. *Criminology, 27*(4), 697–720.

LaGrange, R. L., Ferraro, K. F., & Supancic, M. (1992). Perceived risk and fear of crime: Role of social and physical incivilities. *Journal of Research in Crime and Delinquency, 29*(3), 311–334.

Landman, K. (2012). Reconsidering crime and urban fortification in South Africa. In V. Ceccato (Ed.), *The urban fabric of crime and fear* (pp. 239–264). Dordrecht: Springer.

Lewis, D. A., & Maxfield, M. G. (1980). Fear in the neighborhoods: An investigation of the impact of crime. *Journal of Research in Crime and Delinquency, 17*(2), 160–189.

Loader, I. (2000). Plural policing and democratic governance. *Social and Legal Studies, 9*(3), 323–345.

Lorenc, T., Petticrew, M., Whitehead, M., Neary, D., Clayton, S., Wright, K., Thomson, H., Cummins, S., Sowden, A., & Renton, A. (2013). Fear of crime and the environment: Systematic review of UK qualitative evidence. *BMC Public Health, 24*(13), 496.

Los, M. (2002). Post-communist fear of crime and the commercialization of security. *Theoretical Criminology, 6*(2), 165–188.

Lotz, R. (1979). Public anxiety about crime. *Pacific Sociological Review, 22*(2), 241–254.

Loukaitou-Sideris, A. (2004). Is it safe to walk here? Paper presented at the Conference Proceedings *Research on Women's Issues in Transportation*. Chicago, IL.

Macari, A. C. (2009). Condominios fechados em areas rurais: O caso de Rancho Queimado na Região Metropolitana de Florianópolis (Master's degree, Universidade de Florianopolis, Florianopolis, Brazil).

Marshall, B., & Johnson, S. (2005). Crime in rural areas: A review of the literature for the rural evidence research centre. Jill Dando Institute of Crime Science, University College, London.

Maxfield, M. G. (1984). Fear of crime in England and Wales. London: Home Office, Research and Planning Unit.

Milgram, S. (1974). The experience of living in cities. In C. M. Loo (Ed.), *Crowding and behavior* (pp. 41–54). New York: MSS Information Cooperation.

Newman, O. (1972). *Defensible space: Crime prevention through urban design.* New York: Collier Books.

Norris, G., & Reeves, H. (2013). Fear of crime and authoritarianism: A comparison of rural and urban attitudes. *Crime Prevention and Community Safety, 15*(2), 134–150.

Pain, R. (2009). Critical geopolitics and everyday fears. In M. Lee & S. Farrall (Eds.), *Fear of crime: Critical voices in an age of anxiety* (pp. 45–58). New York: Routledge-Cavendish.

Pain, R., & Smith, S. J. (2008). Fear: Critical geopolitics and everyday life. In R. Pain & S. J. Smith (Eds.), *Fear: Critical geopolitics and everyday life* (pp. 1–24). Aldershot: Ashgate.

Palmer, D. L. (1996). Determinants of Canadian attitudes toward immigration: More than just racism? *Canadian Journal of Behavioural Science/Revue canadienne des sciences du comportement, 28*(3), 180–192.

Panelli, R., Little, J. O., & Kraack, A. (2004). A community issue? Rural women's feelings of safety and fear in New Zealand. *Gender, Place and Culture, 11*(3), 445–467.

Pyle, G. (1974). *The spatial dynamic of crime.* Chicago, IL: Department of Geography, University of Chicago.

Robinson, V., & Gardner, G. (2012). Unravelling a stereotype: The lived experience of black and minority ethnic in rural Wales. In N. Chakraborti & J. Garland (Eds.), *Rural racism* (pp. 85–107). Abingdon/New York: Routledge.

Ruddell, R., & Ortiz, N. (2015). Boomtown blues: Long-term community perceptions of crime and disorder. *American Journal of Criminal Justice, 40*, 129–146.

Sampson, R. J., Morenoff, J. D., & Felton, E. (1999). Beyond social capital: Spatial dynamics of collective efficacy for children. *American Sociological Review, 64*(5), 633–660.

Sampson, R. J., & Raudenbush, S. W. (2004). Seeing disorder: Neighborhood stigma and the social construction of "broken windows". *Social Psychology Quarterly, 67*(4), 319–342.

Sandercock, L. (2000). When strangers become neighbours: Managing cities of difference. *Planning Theory and Practice, 1*(1), 13–30.

Sandercock, R. J. (Ed.). (2005). *Difference, fear and habitus: A political economy of urban fear.* Aldershot: Ashgate.

Scott, J., Carrington, K., & McIntosh, A. (2012). Established-outsider relations and fear of crime in mining towns. *Sociologia Ruralis, 52*(2), 147–169.

Shappland, J., & Vagg, J. (1985). Social control and policing in rural and urban areas. Oxford: Centre for Criminological Research, University of Oxford.

Skogan, W. G. (1987). The impact of victimization on fear. *Crime and Delinquency, 33*(1), 135–154.

Skogan, W. G. (1996). The police and public opinion in Britain. *American Behavioral Scientist, 39*(4), 421–432.

Skogan, W. G., & Maxfield, M. G. (1981). *Coping with crime: Individual and neighborhood reactions.* Thousand Oak, CA: Sage.

Skår, M. (2010). Forest dear and forest fear: Dwellers' relationships to their neighbourhood forest. *Landscape and Urban Planning, 98*(2), 110–116.

Spocter, M. (2013). Rural gated developments as a contributor to post-productivism in the Western Cape. *South African Geographical Journal, 95*(2), 165–186.

Torstensson, G., Forslund, M., & Tegnell, A. (2011). Förslag till nationell handlingsplan för säkerhetsfrämjande arbete för äldre personer (Vol. 12, p. 48). Stockholm: Socialstyrelsen.

Tönnies, F. (1887). *Gemeinschaft und Gesellschaft.* Leipzig: Fues's Verlag. (Translated, 1957 by Charles Price Loomis as *Community and society*, East Lansing, MI: Michigan State University Press.)

Valentine, G. (1990). Women's fear and the design of public space. *Built Environment, 16*(4), 288–303.

Warr, M. (2000). Fear of crime in the United States: Avenues for research and policy. *Criminal Justice and Behavior, 4*, 451–489.

Whitzman, C. (2007). Stuck at the front door: Gender, fear of crime and the challenge of creating safer space. *Environment and Planning A, 39*(11), 2715–2732.

Wilhelmsson, M., & Ceccato, V. (2015). Challenging the idyll: Does crime affect property prices in Swedish rural areas? *Journal of Rural Studies, 39* (in press).

Wilson, J. Q., & Kelling, G. L. (1982). Broken windows. *Atlantic Monthly, 249*, 29–38.

Winkel, F. V., & Vrij, A. (1990). Fear of crime and mass media crime reports testing similarity hypotheses. *International Review of Victimology, 1*(3), 251–265.

Wretstrand, A., & Svensson, H. (2008). Resmöjligheter i medelstora städer: närhet avgörande för mobilitet På rätt spår? – om tillgängliga resor för äldre och funktionshindrade. Lund: Teknik och Samhälle.

Wyant, B. R. (2008). Multilevel impacts of perceived incivilities and perceptions of crime risk on fear of crime: Isolating endogenous impacts. *Journal of Research in Crime and Delinquency, 45*(1), 39–64.

Yarwood, R., & Gardner, G. (2000). Fear of crime, cultural threat and the countryside. *Area, 32*(4), 403–411.

Zedner, L. (2009). *Security*. London: Routledge.

7 Perceived safety in Swedish rural areas

People fear crime less in rural areas than they do in urban areas. It is submitted that this fact represents a partial picture of perceived safety, because people can fear greatly even if they perceive a slim likelihood of crime actually occurring. In this chapter, instead of reducing the issue of perceived safety to risk of victimization, the discussion is placed in a broader context with particular attention to rural areas in Sweden. As previously stated, "perceived safety" is a general concept used in this book to characterize both fear of crime and other overall anxieties captured by different indicators of fear and anxiety. The chapter looks beyond actual statistics of perceived safety between rural and urban areas in order to shed light on the nature of fear among people living in rural areas. The chapter includes critical analysis of two examples of expression of fear in relation to the process of *othering* in the Swedish country side: Sami youth (the old other), followed by the berry pickers (the new other). In order to illustrate in more detail patterns of perceived safety, two non-metropolitan municipalities: Jönköping and Söderköping are discussed in this chapter. The chapter closes with suggestions for possible further research on fear of crime in rural contexts.

Rural perceptions of safety and fear of crime

Traditionally, fear of crime is an urban phenomenon and is claimed to be a function of community size: greater fear in larger towns and cities, less fear in smaller towns and rural areas (Carcach, 2000; Ceccato & Dolmén, 2013; Christie, Andenaes, & Skirkbeckk, 1965; Hough, 1995). Higher rates of victimization in large cities are likely the core explanation of lower perceptions of safety (BRÅ, 2011; Donnermeyer & Kreps, 1986; Skogan, 1990). However, looking more closely at this pattern, it is patchier than expected, heterogeneous across space and time and among groups.

Chapter 6 reviews a vast number of studies indicating that measures of fear of crime often capture other worries and anxieties than fear of crime itself. One reason is that both rural and urban areas are in constant change and in some cases converging, as new lifestyles are imposed by commuting patterns and wider access to ICT, for instance. Some of these changes imply new risks to individuals, producing new dynamics of fear and anxiety. Researchers have speculated that differences in declared perceived safety in certain rural and urban areas may not be that great (e.g., Ceccato & Dolmén, 2013; Lawtley & Deane, 2000; Pain, 2000).

In Sweden, if two individuals, one residing in Stockholm, the capital city, and another in the most remote area of the country, chosen at random are asked whether they have felt worry during the preceding 12 months, the chance of selecting an individual who declares feelings of worry is surprisingly similar in both places (Figure 7.1a). The same can be said about those who worry about their family's finances (Figure 7.1b).

However, where one lives seems to shape one's worry about crime. This is confirmed by different sources: Living conditions survey and Crime victims survey (Figure 7.1c and 7.1d). The chances of selecting an individual who will declare that he/she avoids going out in his/her own neighborhood because of a

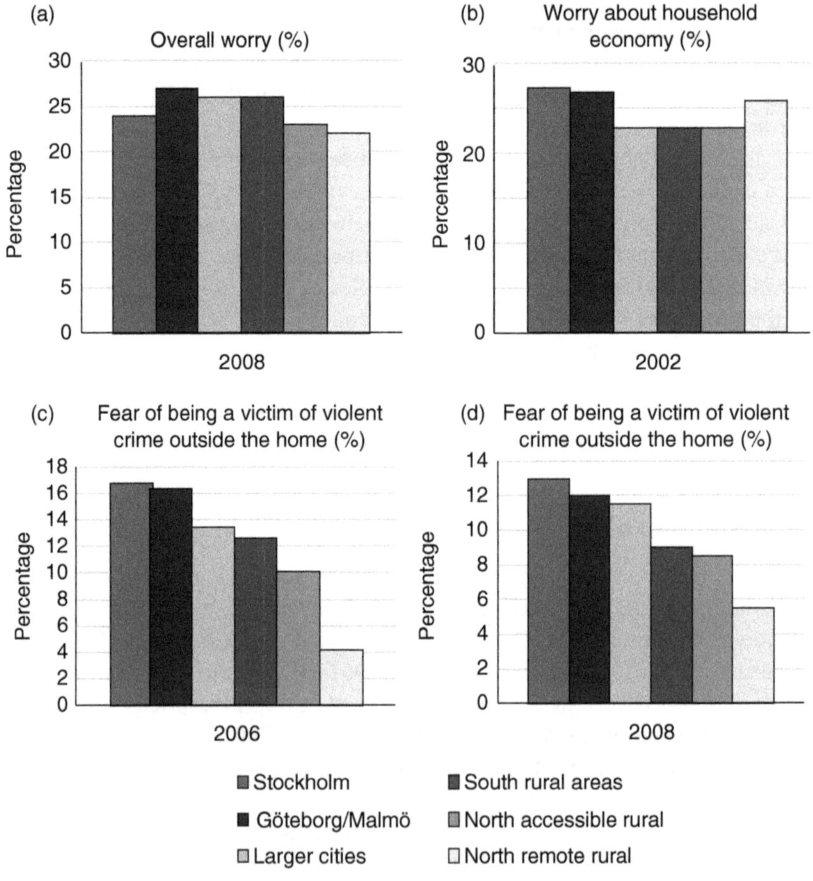

Figure 7.1 Indicators of overall worry/fear of crime in Sweden (data sources: (a) Living conditions survey, Statistics Sweden; (b) Victimization survey, Swedish National Council for Crime Prevention; (c) Living conditions survey, Statistics Sweden; (d) Victimization survey, Swedish National Council for Crime Prevention).

fear of becoming a victim of crime is at least four times greater in Stockholm than in most remote rural areas of Sweden.

Why does overall anxiety not vary widely across the country though fear of becoming a victim of crime does? This mismatch between overall fear and fear of crime flags a number of unanswered questions.

1 *Does perceived safety go beyond a deterministic link between fear and victimization?*

In the Swedish case, overall worry seems to encompass more than a declared fear of crime as the pattern is quite uniform across the country (Figures 7.1a and 7.1b) and shows notably marginal differences between metropolitan and rural areas.

This pattern is not unique for Sweden. It reflects "a condensation of broader concerns about crime, stability and social change" (Gray, Jackson, & Farrall, 2008, p. 377) found in many other studies elsewhere. For instance, Furstenberg (1971) has long suggested that these constructs were not significantly related to each other, that overall worry was more often associated with resentment and attitudes to social change that a place might be undergoing.

Interestingly, rural Sweden has become more criminogenic now than it was 10 years ago, and although crime rates remain lower in rural areas, the gap has narrowed slightly: accessible rural areas are nowadays in many respects similar to urban areas when police records are compared (Ceccato and Dolmén 2011). Yet, declared overall worry is similar in remote rural areas and metropolitan areas. Social changes are expected to affect lifestyles through access to information technology that creates opportunities as well as new risks. More-over, the homogeneous pattern of declared overall worry may also be related to the fact that asking individuals about overall worry leads them to represent future-oriented anxiety rather than a summary of past episodes or current feel-ings of fear, as suggested by previous research (Sacco, 2005; Warr, 2000). The mechanisms that are at work in this case are, however, not clear.

2 *Do patterns of declared overall anxiety follow the ecology of household/ family financial insecurity?*

At first sight, Figures 7.1a and 7.1b are similar, which reinforces the idea that the ecology of overall worry has to do with patterns of individuals' con-cerns about their finances and perhaps future employment. Still, this is spec-ulative as this potential link is based on an aggregated cross-sectional data set. The data does not provide hints about individual mechanisms linking current economic conditions and worry. For instance, concerns about one's health could also be part of the declared "overall fear" (Figure 7.1a).

Even more interesting, there is no significant difference between indi-viduals living in the most remote rural areas in Sweden and individuals in the Swedish metropolitan areas with regards to worry about their household finances (Figure 7.1b). One possible explanation for this could be that *overall fear* is fed to a large extent by *fear of crime* in large cities, while in rural areas *overall fear* is mostly determined by concerns about individuals' and households' economic conditions – but both are expressed as "overall worry" as shown in Figure 7.1a. An alternative interpretation is that *overall worry* in large cities is composed of a mix of concerns but mostly expressed as *fear of crime*, as that is widely seen as a significant "social problem" (Gray et al., 2008, p. 377) shared by all people who live in big cities. In rural areas, *overall worry* is rather a result of unstable and limited employment opportunities and thus the vulnerability of the household economy.

Inequality in victimization may also explain this pattern. The poor are victims of crime more often and reveal more anxieties than wealthier groups in Sweden (Estrada, Nilsson, Jerre, & Wikman, 2010). The poor are over-represented in some large Swedish cities, such as Stockholm, Malmö, and Gothenburg, which would explain the urban–rural pattern in fear of crime illustrated in Figures 7.1c and 7.1d. Educational level and ethnic background are also related to unequal victimization and thus fear. The 2013 Swedish Crime Survey (BRÅ, 2014b, p. 92) reports that people born in Sweden with both parents born abroad are somewhat more concerned that relatives will be victimized by crime (28 percent) than those with at least one native-born parent (23 percent) and those who are foreign-born respondents (24 percent). Respondents with secondary education or higher state that they are concerned about relatives more often than those with no more than lower secondary education. Altruist fear is at work when couples with children are more worried than corresponding groups without children. In addition people living in rural areas are less worried about their family becoming victims of crime than those living in larger cities and metropolitan areas.

All the same, we cannot discard the possibility that *overall worry* is homogeneously distributed over the country, because that may reflect the a-spatial dynamics of victimization, such as through cybercrime. As suggested in Chapter 6, imposed daily commuting patterns from rural areas to larger cities may also dilute the sources of worry, as fear can be affected by the environments to which people are exposed.

3   *Do patterns of declared fear of crime follow the hierarchy of the urban structure?*

The answer is certainly affirmative to this question if Figures 7.1c and 7.1d are taken as reference. Also, the 2013 Swedish Crime Survey (BRÅ, 2014b) reveals differences in insecurity among respondents living in metropolitan regions (17 percent), those living in other major cities (14 percent), and people residing in small towns or rural areas (11 percent). Moreover, respondents from metropolitan regions indicate that fear has a greater impact on their behavior and quality of life than residents of other rural areas. The pattern is largely the same as in previous years.

Previous research indicates that high crime rates promote fear (Skogan, 1990) but that the physical and social environment affects levels of fear of crime (Wilson & Kelling, 1982). Thus, it is not a surprise that respondents living in apartments believe that fear has a greater influence on their behavior and quality of life than those living in single-family homes (BRÅ, 2014b). Urban areas provide a number of settings that trigger fear, some of which are crime attractors or generators (Brantingham & Brantingham, 1995; Ceccato, 2013; Ceccato & Hanson, 2013). Moreover, larger urban areas concentrate signs of physical deterioration, which is thought to be a more important determinant of fear of crime than actual crime is (Lewis & Maxfield, 1980). As previously stated in Chapter 6, social interactions that take place at certain places may also lead to lack of perceived safety. Rural residents moving to large urban centers, for instance, may feel unsafe because the environment offers anonymity that may initially be perceived as a threat. Lack of familiarity, assistance, and protection (Hofferth & Iceland, 1998; Milgram, 1974) may trigger fear. In urban settings, fear of the unknown or of others (Sandercock, 2005) can, more often than in rural areas, take various forms including a declared fear of crime.

Alternatively, urban areas concentrate groups of individuals who may be more fearful because of the conditions they are exposed to and, consequently, the risks they suffer (Box, Hale, & Andrews, 1988; Jackson & Gray, 2010). If there is an unequal risk of victimization (Estrada et al., 2010), and people who live in big cities are more at risk, then it is not surprising that people in big cities declare being more fearful about crime than those living in smaller and rural areas. This calls for a more detailed analysis of patterns of perceived safety by area and group. The next section explores some of these unanswered issues.

The experience of crime according to Swedish National Crime Surveys

In Sweden, the National Crime Surveys have been conducted since 2006 and have shown an overall stable victimization structure. The proportion of people who are very concerned about crime in the community has decreased, from 29 percent in 2006, to 19 percent in 2013. From 2006 to 2013, the tendency is clear: large cities – particularly those in the metropolitan counties of Stockholm, Skåne, and Västra Götaland – have a higher proportion of victims, more respondents declare feeling unsafe (for themselves or for their families), and more respondents have less confidence in the criminal justice system than respondents in the country as a whole. For 2013, the Swedish Crime Survey reports that respondents in metropolitan regions indicate vulnerability as victims of crime to a greater extent (4.9 percent) than those living in smaller cities or rural areas (3.6–3.9 percent).

More interestingly, the proportion of respondents living in Stockholm County who are concerned about crime has fallen steadily, from 30 percent in 2006, to 17 percent in 2013, while in the southern county of Skåne, the share of those worried about crime has remained relatively stable since the mid-2000s. These southern parts of the country also show a higher proportion of respondents who agree that fear affects their quality of life (BRÅ, 2014a).

Figure 7.2 illustrates differences in perceived safety by type of municipality. Figure 7.2 matches at first glance the patterns shown in Figures 7.1c and 7.1d. As expected, fear tends to be higher in urban areas (χ^2=57.1, df=4, p<0.00) (Figure 7.2), where most people are victimized (χ^2=40.9, df=2, p<0.00), often younger people (16–24 years old). Half of the respondents to the Swedish Crime Victim Survey (2007–2008) living in urban municipalities declare being more fearful in their own neighborhood than those living in rural and accessible rural areas (the relationship is significant: χ^2 (4)=79.63, p<0.00). However, some patterns in Figure 7.2 suggest a number of interesting possibilities.

1   Although measures of *fear of crime* and *declared unsafety in the neighborhood* are on the decline, the proportion of respondents *avoiding going out because of fear* is fairly constant over time (Figure 7.2a). This is an indication that there is always a group that is going to declare themselves to be more fearful and that the fear will affect their mobility patterns and quality of life regardless of their overall risk and society's perceptions. This group is composed of those who are less mobile and feel more vulnerable if victimized (the elderly, the disabled).

2   The graphs illustrating *fear of crime* and *avoiding going out because of fear* indicate that respondents living in large cities and towns declare slightly higher levels of fear than those in metropolitan areas (Stockholm, Gothenburg, and Malmö). A possible explanation for this is that cities and large towns have become more criminogenic than urban neighborhoods in the metropolitan areas in recent decades (Ceccato & Dolmén, 2011). Another possible explanation is that whilst most *fear measures* are declining, the proportion of respondents declaring *fear of residential burglary* has been fairly constant since 2006 (Figure 7.2b), perhaps a reflection of the percentage of households reporting burglary (0.9 percent of vulnerable households in the country) and police statistics for burglary (see for instance, BRÅ, 2014b, pp. 58–59). Some of these municipalities have had population inflows (at least temporarily) which can affect crime risk and perceived safety of residents.

3   *Fear of becoming a victim of a car-related theft has decreased since 2006 for all types of municipality.* The proportion of households reporting having been exposed to car-related theft has declined, from 0.9 percent in 2006, to 0.4 percent in 2012. A significant reduction can also be observed in the register-based statistics of reported car thefts during the same period: from approximately 27,000, to 12,000 between 2006 and 2012 (BRÅ, 2014b). According to Ceccato and Dolmén (2011), technologies implemented in new cars after the mid-1990s make these vehicles more difficult targets to steal from or to be stolen (e.g., use of immobilizers). People are reporting fewer car-related thefts also because insurance companies have increased their deductible amounts. If the value of stolen goods does not exceed the minimum value at which reimbursement can be claimed, there is a strong chance that a victim of crime will not bother to report the offense to the police. Finally, there may have been a displacement from more traditional types of crimes (such as car thefts), to

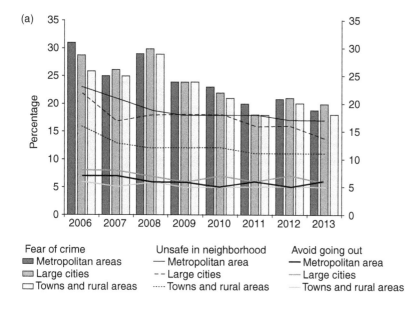

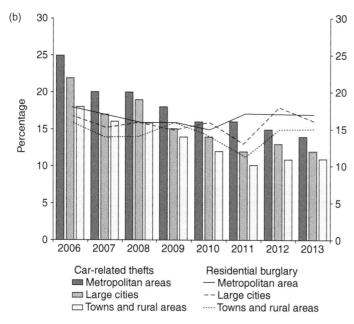

Figure 7.2 (a) Percentage of respondents on perceived safety by type of municipality and (b) fear of being victimized, car-related thefts, and residential burglary (%) (data source: BRÅ, 2014b, pp. 106, 108, 110).

other types of offense, such as fraud. Still, this explains lower reporting rates but not exactly lower declared fear levels for car-theft victimization.

Respondents living in small towns or rural areas worry that they will become the victim of assault to a lesser degree than residents of urban areas do (7 percent and 10–13 percent, respectively). The differences in concern about crime between urban and rural areas mainly relate to assault and burglary when the effects of other factors such as age, gender, family, and type of housing are controlled for.

Note that figures from the Swedish Crime Victim Survey show that *overall worry* does differ in remote rural and urban areas (Figure 7.2) – a difference not much pronounced in Figure 7.1a, based on a national living conditions survey. Even greater differences are apparent between urban and remote rural areas concerning the *fear of being a victim of crime in the neighborhood*, as previously noted. Methodological differences and types of aggregation could also explain differences in the patterns seen in Figure 7.1a and Figure 7.2.

The proportion of those feeling unsafe walking alone after dark in the neighborhood is close to 7 percent of respondents in accessible rural areas and 2 percent in remote rural, compared to 12 percent in urban areas. Similar figures are found by the British Crime Survey, reported by Marshall and Johnson (2005), namely 8 percent for rural areas and 13 percent for urban areas (for the inner city in urban areas, one-quarter of respondents declare feeling unsafe).

Following the findings of international research on fear, gender, and victimization (see Chapter 6), in Sweden previous victimization (of oneself or a family member) strongly correlates with declared fear, different measures of fear, and the experience of witnessing violence (BRÅ, 2014b). Unequal victimization and fear appear when only rural areas are assessed. In rural areas, a strong correlation was found between those who were victimized (or someone from the family was victimized or witnessed violence) and those who feel unsafe where they live or often avoid activities outdoors because of fear of being victimized (around $r=0.90$–0.97 significant at 0.01 level, based on data for 2006–2008). Females tend to be more fearful than men regardless of where they live, but those living in urban areas in the south declare themselves to be more fearful than those living elsewhere in the country.

Corroborating the hypothesis of fear and social change, the Swedish data shows that half of respondents living in urban municipalities or in accessible rural areas that have had a positive population increase state more frequent worries about crime than those living in rural municipalities (The relationship is significant: $\chi^2 (4)=71.86, p<0.00$.)

Fear of crime and the perceived seriousness of offenses

Fear induced by different crimes depends not only on the perceived risk but also on the perceived seriousness. In reality, the relationship between the seriousness of crime and fear is not well understood. Homicide ranked low on the list of fears, while residential burglary outranked all other offenses. To generate strong fear, Warr (2000, p. 458) suggests, an offense must be perceived as both serious and likely to occur. The author exemplifies by reporting empirical evidence from Seattle, WA. Residential burglary is the most feared crime in the United States because it is viewed as both relatively serious and rather likely. Murder, on the other hand, is perceived to be very serious but unlikely to occur (for a review, see Warr, 2000).

In Sweden, similar trends are found for property and violent crimes, at least in the 2013 National Crime Survey. For violence, the proportion anxious about becoming a victim of assault decreased, from 15 percent in 2006, to 10 percent in 2013, while for residential burglary the fear levels remained relatively stable throughout the survey period, around 16 percent. Perceptions of crime seem also to follow crime trends. The rate of exposure to residential burglary has remained relatively unchanged since 2006, while the proportion who stated that they had been the victim of assault declined gradually, from 2.7 percent in 2006, to 1.9 percent in 2012 (BRÅ, 2014c).

In the United Kingdom, there seems to be little difference between the proportion of those worried about becoming the victim of violence or theft. For instance, in the mid-2000s 15 percent of respondents declared they were worried about becoming a victim of either physical attack or residential burglary if they lived in urban areas. However, if they lived in rural areas, about 10 percent of respondents declared they were worried about becoming a victim of assault or property crime (Marshall & Johnson, 2005). In the 2010/2011 British Crime Survey, 10 percent of adults were worried about burglary and car crime, and 13 percent of adults were worried about violent crime – a measure for the whole country. These proportions were the lowest recorded since the questions were introduced in the 1990s (Chaplin, Flatley, & Smith, 2011).

Safety from the perspective of farmers, the elderly, and minorities

Victimization and perceived safety among Swedish farmers

As much as 57 percent of farmers in Sweden feel at least a bit worried about becoming a victim of crime and 25 percent are worried about the future (Figure 7.3), according to the Farmers' Safety Survey (Lantbrukarnas Riksförbund, 2012).

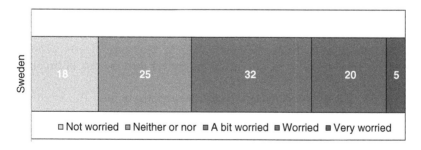

Figure 7.3 Do you worry that you and/or your farm will be victimized? (%) (data source: Farmers' Safety Survey (*N*=527), 2012).

2012). Although only three out of 10 farmers have been victims of crime in the past two years, seven out of 10 farmers know at least one other person who has been victimized. SAS is a postal questionnaire sent to 1,000 farmers who operate agricultural properties with more than 10 hectares of field. In 2012, the survey had a 62 percent response rate, considered enough to represent the group.

Victimization is more concentrated in the south than the rest of the country. In southern Sweden, the proportion is larger (eight out of 10), especially among those respondents who own farms with more than 50 hectares (they are often more victimized than the rest). Thefts tend to dominate the victimization statistics for farmers. Thefts of fuel and building equipment are common, but also fraud by telephone and Internet as well as payment of false invoices. Farmers are also victims of theft of livestock, burglary in the house or other farm property, as well as vandalism (residential, on the property, and on roads). Half of those who have been victims of crime were targeted two or more times. There is a clear lack of confidence in local police forces to solve these crimes. One in four respondents had had a case dismissed by the police. The same proportion of farmers was worried that their properties or their family would be victimized in the future. Those in northern Sweden feel less anxious than the national average about the prospect of being victimized by crime, whether themselves, their family, or their property. Chapter 8 discusses victimization and perceived safety among farmers in more detail.

Victimization, fear, and the elderly

In Sweden, approximately 19 percent of the current population is older than 65 years of age, and by 2020 one-quarter of the population will be older than 65 (Schyllander & Rosenberg, 2010). A substantial portion of the elderly live in smaller urban and rural areas, and the proportion of the elderly living in rural and many smaller urban areas in much of the country is higher than the national average (Karlsson, 2012). Those who want to have some degree of independence are vulnerable to the way indoor and outdoor environment is built. Although many elderly are afraid to go out because of possibly becoming a victim of crime, they run a low risk of victimization. The biggest threat to their safety is the risk of falling. The most dominant cause of elderly people falling in Sweden is slipping, tripping, and stumbling, often at home or nearby – and not crime (Bamzar & Ceccato, 2015). There is reason to believe that the fear of being outdoors declared by many elderly people reflects other types of risk (e.g., fear of falling) rather than the risk of becoming a victim of crime.

Nationwide, victimization among the elderly is relatively low. The Swedish Crime Survey shows that elderly victimization through assault, threats, sexual offenses, robberies, fraud, and harassment has decreased during the past five years, from 7 to 4.4 percent. For the oldest group, 75–79 years old, victimization varied between 3.7 and 4.7 percent. The most common type of crime against the elderly is theft, usually theft from the residence without a break-in. The results of the national public health survey also show that older people declare being victims of physical violence, threats, and other types of violence. In contrast, three of every four women in all age groups declare that they refrain from going out alone for fear of being attacked or robbed. There are probably many unre-ported cases of domestic violence (Torstensson, Forslund, & Tegnell, 2011). In 2013, the lowest percentage of victimization was in the age groups 65–74 years (0.3 percent) and 75–79 years (0.2 percent). As expected, the low risk of victimi-zation does not translate into high perceived safety. According to BRÅ (2014b), it is mainly older people who say they feel unsafe outdoors. From 2006 to 2013, women aged 75–79 years were the group that felt least safe late at night out-doors, especially those living in urban areas (26 percent, compared to 19 percent in the youngest group).

In Jönköping, the town used as an example in this chapter, elderly people do not express themselves as fearful beings, quite the opposite. Contrary to what is commonly found in the international literature, in Jönköping the elderly (65 years and older) are not necessarily more anxious about their safety than other respondents. They feel safer in relation to their risk of being victimized ($\chi^2(2, N=454)=13.0$, $p=0.00$) and have not been victimized in the 12 months preced-ing the survey ($\chi^2(2, N=452)=3.38$, $p=0.06$). Together with mothers on mater-nity leave and part-time employees, they show indications of having better knowledge about what happens in the area. This group is more sensitive to litter-ing and vandalism ($\chi^2(2, N=433)=3.60$, $p=0.06$) and more critical about the adequacy of the outdoor environment for young people ($\chi^2(2, N=453)=6.57$, $p=0.01$) than other groups of respondents are. The elderly also seem to be less suspicious about people ($\chi^2(2, N=455)=9.81$, $p=0.00$) and think they can trust them more than other respondents do ($\chi^2(2, N=455)=3.57$, $p=0.06$). Previous studies in urban areas highlighted the proportion of elderly as an indication of strong social control. For instance, drawing on the work of Felson and Cohen (1980), LaGrange (1999) points out that residents are likely to be absent from their homes more frequently, so guardianship may be substantially reduced. Spending time in the area improves individuals' knowledge of it, making them feel safer. This is true for the elderly and people with no full-time job.

Ethnic minorities and expressions of fear

Feeling unsafe is more common for foreign-born individuals than for those who were born in Sweden (23 percent and 13 percent). In addition foreign-born indi-viduals are more likely to declare that low perceived safety affects their quality of life than are people born in Sweden (14 and 8 percent, respectively). Lower per-ceived safety among ethnic minorities is linked to greater victimization. According to BRÅ (2014b), foreign-born individuals (2.7 percent) are victims of assault more often than residents with two parents born abroad (2.2 percent) or one parent born abroad (1.7 percent). There are no significant differences in exposure to violence based on where one lives (urban or rural areas), except for serious assault. People living in big cities experience a slightly higher exposure to serious assault (0.6

percent) than those living in other major cities, small towns, or rural areas (0.3–0.4 percent). Foreign-born individuals are also over-represented among victims of threat, robbery, and fraud, particularly those with a secondary education. For harassment, foreign-born individuals living in urban areas state that their vulnerability to harassment is slightly higher than people living in large cities or in rural areas.

At a local level, the pattern is the same. In Jönköping, for example, residents born outside the Nordic countries tend to be overrepresented among those who fear most their neighborhood ($\chi^2(2,\ N=445)=3.78,\ p=0.05$)). A total of 11 percent of respondents feel that there are people in their neighborhood who are threatening, and 10 percent of respondents feel fear due to their ethnic affinity, either Swedish or non-Swedish. Ceccato and Wilhelmsson (2014) also show that the perception of discrimination where one lives has a direct effect on how attractive an area is valued in the housing market.

Minorities and discrimination: fear of the *other* in rural areas

This section takes two Swedish examples to illustrate fear of *others*, considering the issue through the eyes of those who have a contradictory position: sometimes viewed as suffering a number of anxieties themselves for not being the *norm*, and sometimes as being the source of the local fears. Two groups were selected: young Sami people living in northern areas of Sweden who have historically suffered discrimination (the *old others*), and berry pickers who come temporarily to Sweden in the summer to work (the *new others*). The Sami and berry pickers were also chosen because they contrast with the current representations of Swedish modernity. The nomadic Sami culture or underdeveloped berry picker industry survive in parallel and contrast with, as indicated by Pred (2000), the Swedish market image of a progressive, liberal, and modern society free from racism, sexism, and other inequalities.

The Sami youth

Fear is an expression of the exclusion long experienced by young Sami. Sami are the indigenous people (an estimated 40,000 inhabitants) of Sweden who have a long history of discrimination, racism, and conflict that, according to Omma (2013), has had a significant impact on Sami self-esteem and on their health, especially mental health. They are not a homogeneous group and, in Sweden, they are geographically spread from central Sweden to the north. Sami in Sweden are traditionally engaged in reindeer husbandry, woodworking, hunting, and fishing (Skielta, 2014). As Omma (2013) reports, poor health is one of the symptoms expressed by this group of young people. She shows that unfair treatment because of their ethnic background was declared to be frequent among young adult Sami (about half of all respondents reported this experience, and 70 percent of reindeer herders).

Young people continually develop their own understandings of their culture in order to interpret their own lives. Omma (2013) suggests that feeling safe is fundamental to developing a sense of feeling at home for the Sami. The author reports that a majority of young adult Sami have declared themselves proud to be Sami and expressed a wish to preserve their culture. However, the lack of knowledge in mainstream society makes the Sami feels they must constantly explain and defend the Sami way of life. Both young adult Sami and a reference group of young Swedes from the same geographical area reported having suicidal thoughts to a high degree, but it was more common among Sami. Sami reindeer herders and those poorly treated because of their ethnicity reported a higher degree of suicide attempts compared to Sami without this experience (Omma, 2013).

Discrimination against *old minorities* in rural contexts is not an exclusively Swedish phenomenon, of course, but is well documented in Australia (e.g., Babacan, 2012; Cunneen, 2007; Forrest & Dunn, 2013; Scott et al., 2012), Canada (Jain, Singh, & Agocs, 2000), and the United States (Hartshorn, Whitbeck, & Hoyt, 2012), to name a few. Young people in these groups are often unable to participate as equals and benefit from the opportunities available to other citizens. In Swedish society, this gives rise to long-term anxieties that hamper young people's opportunities in life. For society as a whole, these findings have a number of implications. One is that the denial of racism can send a message that racist behavior is allowed and not punished. Another implication is that the situation requires in-depth knowledge about minorities in rural contexts, their right to full citizenship, and the construction of fear.

Temporary summer workers: berry pickers

Every summer, the Swedish media is populated by articles reporting travelers' whereabouts and temporary workers in rural areas. Most report the work and living conditions of this temporary labor force. Fear and feelings of insecurity characterize accounts of conflicts between the temporary workers and locals.

In times of intense mobility (Urry, 2002), the movement of temporary labor in European countries is still regarded as problematic. An example of this is the case of berry pickers. This flow of low-wage labor is characterized by a number of fears, unsafe working conditions, and racism in a high-profit industry. Sweden and Finland are the largest bilberry exporters among the Nordic countries (Eriksson & Tollefsen, 2013). Communities that host these temporary workers show cases of poor tolerance for nomadic labor. These workers are perceived with suspicion and fear. Since 2010, the number of work permits granted for berry pickers in Sweden has increased (Figure 7.4). After accusations of abusive working conditions, rules for employing berry pickers were recently tightened (Axelsson, 2014), reducing their inflow in 2014.

The author also reports that all berry pickers came to Sweden voluntarily from Bulgaria and other Eastern European countries, as the previous years' good berry crop had fueled rumors that it was possible to make money on berries in Sweden. This specific case refers to the inflow of about 500 berry pickers in 2012, mainly from Bulgaria, into Mehedeby, a community in northern Sweden

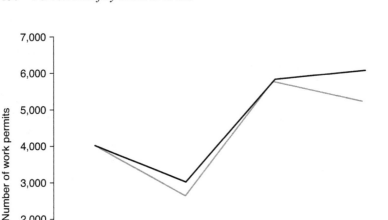

Figure 7.4 Work permits for berry pickers, 2010–2013 (source: Axelsson, 2014).

with 450 inhabitants, as reported by Leander (2012). The mood in the camp seemed friendly, but many workers wanted to talk about their living conditions, as they did not have access to drinking water or toilets. They had to collect water from a service station a few miles away. Still, a resident expressed concerns about the "incomers."

> They must be removed. We cannot have 600–700 people here ... many thefts have been committed since they arrived here.... They go into the plots and look for food in the garbage.
>
> (Leander, 2012)

Hollway and Jefferson (1997) indicate how the narrative of locals informs an order in which some behaviors are perceived as extreme threats to the social order and others are ignored or dismissed. This partial view is exemplified by the case above, where workers' living conditions are ignored in the discourse of the local resident.

Although nomadic populations and travelers have long been associated with crime and problems of social order in the media (e.g., Jansson, 2011), Halfacree (2011, p. 124) points out how these groups in the United Kingdom "are routinely constructed as a key public order problem (real or imagined)." As suggested by Scott et al. (2012), concerns are rarely a reflection of objective risk that *the new* impose, but are bound up in a wider context of meaning and significance, involving the use of metaphors and narratives about social change, as illustrated by the following narrative. In the Swedish case, Leander (2012) reports the mismatch between villagers' perceptions of incomers and actual signs of crime and disorder as indicated by the local police chief:

> The fear among the residents (of the village) is great, but we have not seen any major increase in crime.

The case of berry pickers in Mehedeby exemplifies the challenges that rural communities face when receiving a large number of foreign temporary workers in the Swedish countryside. The police feel local pressure to keep an extra eye on the temporary workers living in the forests. Still, Halfacree (2011) notes that an important question is *why* this particular group of workers requires extra attention from residents, the police, and all other local actors involved in policing work. "Who are the offenders?" is also a relevant question, as alleged cases of slavery and human trafficking have been associated with this temporary labor force. The berry industry across Europe is pointed out by the media as failing to provide basic satisfactory conditions for work, particularly to those workers coming from outside the European Union: "The food industry today announces stricter demands on wholesalers to improve conditions for berry pickers. 'Control is inadequate,' according to the national coordinator against human trafficking in Sweden" (Fagerlind, 2013).

A better understanding of the role and the impact of these temporary workers on the rural community is necessary, hopefully associated with a more extensive debate on the need to improve their living and working conditions in the countryside up to the level that a modern society, such as Sweden, is expected to have.

Perceived safety in the rural

Using Chapter 6 as a reference, this section reports perceived safety through the eyes of those who live far from the metropolitan regions of Stockholm, Gothenburg, and Malmö. This section focuses primarily on an analysis of safety surveys of Jönköping. As much as possible, findings from Jönköping are compared with perceived safety in the town of Söderköping, 170 km away from Jönköping and 170 km away from Stockholm.

The experience of crime according to the Jönköping crime survey

Jönköping is located in central-southern Sweden, a three-hour drive from Stockholm (320 km). Jönköping has a population of about 130,000, which makes it Sweden's ninth largest city. The urban area is a result of the conurbation process of two localities: Jönköping and Huskvarna. The city unofficially has two "centers" around Lake Vättern: Jönköping to the west and Huskvarna to the east. Jönköping Municipality has shown a slight increase in total population, while several small towns in the same county have experienced a decrease (Länstyrelsen, 2012). The average net income for families in Jönköping is less than for the nation as a whole. So-called "vulnerable residential areas" are dominated by apartment buildings and a population with high unemployment and low education levels. In these areas, dependence on social allowance is high compared to the city as a whole. These areas often have a large proportion of foreign-born persons (Jönköping city office, 2009) and are located on the outskirts of the municipality.

It is no surprise that Jönköping is perceived by its inhabitants as a safe place. According to the 2013 victimization survey,[1] a large majority feels safe at home and in the neighborhood where they live, more often in daytime (80 percent) than nighttime (78 percent). Among those who do not feel safe all the time, it is often in the dark hours of the day that they feel less safe (note that in winter in Stockholm, the hours of daylight may be as few as six hours a day while in north Sweden, the hours of daylight may be less than three hours a day). They are concerned about loved ones, family, and friends if they are out (16 percent). Some declare being suspicious about those they meet, or taking other roads than usual when they are out at these times, or avoiding going out during these times (7 percent). A similar pattern of perceived safety is found in Söderköping, a town smaller than Jönköping. There, 90 percent declare feeling safe or very safe (Lundin, 2006).[2] Table 7.1 summarizes some of the key indicators of perceived safety in Jönköping and Söderköping.

In Jönköping as in Söderköping, the perception of safety is not evenly distributed across groups and space (Figure 7.5). On the maps in Figure 7.4, those who declare being fearful may run a slim risk of becoming a victim of crime, either violent crime or residential burglary (Figure 7.5a and 7.5b, respectively). Fear of being victimized by crime may be inversely correlated to average income in other Swedish cities (City of Stockholm, 2011), but in Jönköping the pattern is patchy (Figure 7.5c). Although personal victimization is a significant differentiator between those who are fearful and those who are not, such a relationship is difficult to identify for the whole sample ($\chi^2(2, N=454)=34.7, p=0.00$) on the map (Figure 7.5d).

These findings of perceived safety in Jönköping do follow the patterns found in international studies (see Chapter 6). For instance, the group that tends to declare feeling more worried about places and people are those that have already been a victim of crime or are unemployed ($\chi^2(2, N=456)=7,63, p=0.01$). Immigrants also tend to feel more vulnerable to crime as victims than native

Table 7.1 Victimization and safety in two Swedish towns

In the last 12 months (%)	Jönköping N = 462	Söderköping N = 300
Victimization of crime	6	15 (urban core) 8 outside
Feel safe (or very safe)	80	90
Avoid going out because of fear	7	16
Fear for others	16	11

Data sources: Ceccato and Wilhelmsson (2013): Lundin (2006).

Figure 7.5 Fear of being victimized by crime in relation to rates of (a) violence, (b) residential burglary, (c) average income, and (d) personal victimization (data source: Jönköping Safety Survey, 2013).

inhabitants do ($\chi^2(2, N=444)=9.10, p=0.01$). Interestingly, those who live alone are more fearful than those living in a household with two or more residents ($\chi^2(2, N=451)=3.51, p=0.06$).

In Jönköping, no significant gender differences are apparent for declared fear, as was found in Söderköping (Lundin, 2006). However, in Jönköping women more often than men avoid going out at certain times of the day ($\chi^2(2, N=456)=6.01, p=0.01$). In Jönköping, women's avoidance behaviors do not seem to be triggered by the physical or social environment where they live (bad illumination, dark tunnels or forests, the neighborhood layout, people asking for money, drunkards/ drug addicts in public places, or disturbing neighbors). However, women are more sensitive to neighbors and other individuals, such as peepers (*fönstertittare*) ($\chi^2(2, N=436)=2.76, p=0.09$). Still, women are used to chatting and exchanging favors with neighbors more often than men are (about two-thirds of women).

There are signs that altruistic fear is at work here, too. From those who declare worry (sometimes or often), one-quarter are concerned for themselves, their family, and friends. As suggested in Chapter 6, declared fear in the neighborhood is also triggered by the conditions of physical and social environment. Respondents complain about poor illumination (30 percent) and littering (26 percent). Half of respondents were able to indicate one or more places in their neighborhood that trigger "unsafety," such as tunnels, bus stops, parks, and parking lots. Signs of physical deterioration in these areas seem to indicate that something else is happening. For instance, these areas are also indicated as having problems with graffiti and vandalism (28 percent) and theft (16 percent). One participant in the survey highlights the need for both formal and informal social control in the area:

> Burglary is not uncommon ... we need more police and to keep an eye on what happens here.
>
> (Survey participant, 2013)

More interesting is that 45 percent of the interviewed population declares being a *bit worried* or worried about being victimized by crime in their own home, in their neighborhood, or in Jönköping as a whole, even if they have never been a victim of crime. Wilhelmsson and Ceccato (2015) indicate that the number of police-reported crimes per 1,000 inhabitants in Jönköping is lower than the national average. This applies to both violence and thefts, but since early 2000, rates of reported violence have increased faster than for the national as a whole (about 33 percent in Jönköping and 28 percent in Sweden). For theft, Jönköping follows the national trend of 30 percent reduction since 2000. In Söderköping, for instance, the perception of future victimization is similar to the one illustrated above for Jönköping. However, it depends on type of crime (40 percent for violence, 52 percent for residential burglary, 32 percent for theft, 23 percent for vandalism, and 18 percent for robbery).

Street violence and vandalism happen mostly in the inner-city areas, which impacts on people's perceived safety regardless of where they live. The center of Jönköping (50 percent) and, to a lesser extent, the center of Huskvarna (20 percent) were perceived as less safe than respondents' own neighborhoods, even when most respondents are familiar with central areas, going there at least twice a week. This fact corroborates the theory that inner-city areas, even in small towns such as Jönköping, have features that negatively affect the perceived safety of residents. The following two participants highlighted features of inner city areas that, according to them, decrease the safety of the area:

> Our safety is compromised by what happens during the night. Close down the strip club. It's 50 meters from a secondary school and 20 meters from an elderly-care home!
>
> (Survey participant, 2013)

> They turn off the lights at 11:00 p.m. here. We need better illumination especially along pathways and in tunnels and parks.
>
> (Survey participant, 2013)

Residents declare they feel safer in places they are more familiar with and where they spend more time, except for inner city areas. For instance, most think their neighborhood is safer than any other neighborhood ($\chi^2(2, N=450)=7.53$, $p=0.06$). However, 44 percent of respondents still feel some concern about becoming a victim of crime in their own dwelling or nearby places (bus stop, stairwell, basement, laundry room, convenience store).

The quality of the physical environment does contribute to poor perceived safety: 60 percent of respondents think that pedestrian tunnels are the most dangerous places, 55 percent think that Jönköping's downtown area is dangerous, while parks are selected by 30 percent of respondents, followed by bus stops, 22 percent. Better illumination is also associated with the quality of walking and cycling routes; 15 percent believe these places are unsafe.

Perhaps it is not only the time spent in one place that matters to safety but also what one does. Overall 65 percent believe that their neighborhood is safer than any other place in Jönköping when they know people locally ($\chi^2(2, N=451)=16.7, p=0.00)$). Half of those who were interviewed rely on neighbors to keep an eye on their property when they are away. The criminology literature has long suggested the importance of social environment to safety. Bursik (1999) suggests that much focus has been put on the effect of "supervisory" capacity of communities to limit crime and contribute to safety. Yet within neighborhoods, the ability of residents to exchange favors and develop mutual trust differs, which results in variation in residents' perceived safety, according to Cancino (2005). Some respondents expressed willingness to act for the "common good" as a sign of the collective efficacy of the group (Sampson, Raudenbush, & Earls, 1997), such as by working on neighborhood watch schemes. As expected, those who own their home ($\chi^2(2, N=449)=24.0, p=0.00$) declare feeling safer than those who rent. Owners also believe that the environment they live in is good for their children ($\chi^2(2, N=459)=25.1, p=0.00$), have often lived there for more than five years, and have established contacts with neighbors.

But not everybody feels safe "at home." Most of those who are fearful feel unsettled where they live now ($\chi^2(2, N=458)=30.2, p=0.00)$). According to Jönköping's safety survey, more than one-quarter of respondents are worried about crime, either for themselves or close family members, which makes them extra vigilant (9 percent), avoid going out at certain times (7 percent), choose taxis (6 percent), and avoid talking to people they do not know (5 percent). Foreign-born respondents are more fearful than natives where they live ($\chi^2(2, N=445)=3.78$, $p=0.05)$). Some of these areas have a high proportion of rental units. As previously suggested, these areas tend to have a less-permanent resident population than well-established owner-occupied housing tracts. In the former areas, residents may be unable or unwilling to participate in the social life of the area. It is important to note that dynamics linking perceived safety to housing tenancy, social cohesion, and ethnicity are intertwined in the case of Jönköping and thus cannot be assessed in isolation, because of the small sample and the way the survey was conducted. The next section touches on the issue of fear of crime as it relates to the housing market in a small town.

Perceived safety and the housing market in Jönköping

Most international evidence shows that crime and/or the fear of crime negatively affect the quality of life of residents. As a consequence, housing prices
are discounted to compensate for the lack of safety. All other things being
equal, buyers are willing to pay more for a house that is located in a safe area.
The international literature is populated by examples of the effect of crime on
housing prices (Thaler, 1978; Buck, Hakim, & Spiegel, 1991; Bowes & Ihlanfeldt, 2001; Lynch & Rasmussen, 2001; Gibbons, 2004; Tita, Petras, & Greenbaum, 2006; Munroe, 2007; Troy & Grove, 2008; Hwang & Thill, 2009;
Ceccato & Wilhelmsson, 2011, 2012). However, little has been published
about the effect of crime and perceived safety on property prices in small
towns and rural areas.

Two recent studies in a relatively small housing market but large enough to
allow the analysis (Jönköping) assess whether crime and fear of crime impact
property prices (Ceccato & Wilhelmsson, 2014; Wilhelmsson & Ceccato,
2015). Findings show that residential burglaries decrease house prices but
such an effect is slightly more significant for more expensive types of homes
than for cheaper ones. The authors also recognize the need to test the potential
effect of perceived safety in property prices. They show that low perceived
safety decreases property prices after controlling for attributes of the property
and neighborhood characteristics, including residential burglary. Also, prices
are discounted in areas where people, despite never having been victims of
crime, believe that their ethnic background makes them more vulnerable to
crime in the neighborhood.

Crime risk may be a driving force of housing security measures such as locks,
alarms, security doors, dogs, CCTVs, and many other measures. Studies elsewhere
have found that fear of crime led to increased adoption of housing security measures (Hirschfield, Bowers, & Johnson, 2004), while others have found no relationship (May, Rader, & Goodrum, 2010). Lewakowski (2012), studying the adoption
of household security measures in Stockholm, finds that adoption of measures
increases with the perception of crime and altruistic fear but not with victimization. In the case of Jönköping, one-quarter of all respondents had invested in
housing security measures, such as safety locks (22 percent) and housing alarms
(17 percent) in the preceding 12 months, either by themselves or through their
homeowners' association. No significant difference was found between groups.

These results mean that, at least in the Swedish context, the mechanisms of
buyers' willingness to pay in relatively small housing markets are similar to
the ones found in metropolitan areas, evidence that was so far lacking in the
international literature. This also means that investing in safety (either on
crime-reduction measures or perceived safety) is worthwhile if the goal is to
keep prices at current housing market levels, as poor safety is unquestionably
a factor that reduces housing prices. This is true even in relatively small municipalities, as was the case here. The analysis does not take into account the
rental market and assumes that individuals have the same willingness to pay

for a commodity, which is not realistic, of course. Housing is a commodity that is not evenly attained, and so is safety, measured either as crime or perceived safety.

Concluding remarks

This chapter reports on the perception of safety in Sweden focusing on the urban–rural divide and drawing on the theoretical basis discussed in detail in Chapter 6. According to the National Crime Victims survey, there are indications that measures of poor perceived safety have decreased in Sweden since 2006. Regardless of this trend, one group of individuals declares themselves to be more fearful than others. For them, poor perceived safety affects their mobility patterns and quality of life. This group may be composed of those who are more vulnerable to crime in the first place, for a number of reasons, and therefore more fearful. There is no clear urban–rural divide for this group.

As elsewhere in the international literature, fear of victimization in rural Sweden does not only reflect the severity of the crime. Instead, findings show that fear of crime reflects reductions in perceived crime risk, that is, changes in the situational conditions for crime, especially for car-related crime. For example, modern security systems have made it much more difficult to burgle a car, so the fear of becoming a victim of this offense has also dropped. This supports what Warr (2000) once suggested, that the subjective probability of victimization is a proximate cause of fear – not fear itself.

Regardless of this improvement in perceived safety, the trend is not homogeneously distributed geographically or among groups of individuals. In the Swedish case, overall worry seems to encompass more than a declared fear of crime and risk of victimization, as the pattern is quite uniform across the country and shows notable differences between metropolitan and rural areas. This reflects concerns about crime, stability, and social change. One possible explanation for this pattern could be that to a large extent overall fear is fed by fear of crime in large cities, while in rural areas overall fear is mostly determined by concerns about individuals' and households' economic conditions, though both are expressed as "overall worry." Inequality in victimization may also explain this pattern. The poor are victims of crime more often and reveal more anxieties than wealthier groups in Sweden. The poor are overrepresented in some large Swedish cities, such as Stockholm, Malmö, and Gothenburg, which would explain the urban–rural pattern in fear of crime.

Perceived safety varies by group of individual and has an impact on the quality of life of people. Among farmers in Sweden, almost 60 percent feel at least a bit worried about becoming a victim of crime. They tend to be located in the south and have little confidence that, if something happens, they can rely on the police. Although only one-third of farmers have been victims of crime in the past two years, two-thirds know at least one other person who has been victimized. Farmers worry about their properties and about their families. As expected, feeling unsafe is more common for foreign-born individuals than for those who were born in Sweden. The same applies to the elderly and ethnic minorities. Alienation, poverty, and poor assistance or protection of human rights is also a fear generator, particularly among the itinerant population. See the case of Sami population and berry pickers. However, there are exceptions. Young women declare, to some extent as elderly women do, a fear of becoming the victim of sexual assault. In the case of Jönköping municipality, the elderly do not feel more worried than the rest of the population, perhaps because they seem to be deeply involved in the local life and social control of their neighborhood.

Crime and fear impact housing markets in small towns and rural areas as they do in urban areas. Again drawing on evidence from Jönköping, crime (residential burglary) and fear of crime had a significant negative effect on housing prices. In the same municipality, "fear of other people" has also shown a direct impact on how attractive an area is valued in the housing market.

Several lessons may be learned from these patterns of perceived safety in Sweden. If crime would cease to exist tomorrow, fear of crime and other anxieties would still be around. This indicates that perceived safety is fed by factors other than perceived risk of victimization. Another lesson is that urban–rural divides in perceived safety (with more people being fearful in urban environments than in rural) represent a rough picture of reality, because there is inequality in both victimization and perceived safety by groups. Some of the factors affecting perceived safety are associated with individual, group, and/or area characteristics. Moreover, some processes triggered by fear seem to have the same impact on people's lives regardless of where they take place. Note the case of the impact of fear on housing prices, for instance.

Another lesson for policy is that it is dangerous to ignore indications of fear. If individuals feel completely safe, they might fail to take the necessary precautions for their own safety, the protection of their property, or the safety of others, and thus increase the risk of victimization. In this case, fear is a positive reaction because it leads to prevention. In another extreme, choosing to boost feelings of fear and other anxieties is an equally poor decision to being taken, as individuals may engage in needless precautions that may be costly without knowing whether there are risks, and if they exist, to know their nature. Individuals' perceived safety may be the tip of the iceberg for a number of triggers that go beyond individual and area-level features. As illustrated in Chapters 6 and 7, perceived safety entails a dimension of reflexivity, which means that it depends on those who observe and produce it, as well as on particular time and space contexts.

What is the role of the police in the reduction of fear in rural areas? The nature and extent of proactive policing measures by police forces in rural communities can help reduce fear. Such measures might include visibility, patrolling, and constant checks. An important question to be answered is safety for whom? As the next few chapters show, neither crime nor perceived safety is the responsibility of a single actor in community policing. Some crime types require efforts of other actors than the police both in crime prevention and/or fear reduction; see Chapters 12 to 14 for examples.

Notes

1 The perceived safety variables are derived from the 2013 Safety Survey applied to a stratified sample over urban districts of the municipality of Jönköping. The questionnaire was distributed in spring 2013, with a response rate of 50 percent out of 992 questionnaires (excluding old or incorrect addresses). The questionnaire is composed of 34 questions about victimization, perceived safety in the home, proximity to one's home (neighborhood), and city overall, as well as questions about the respondent's background (e.g., age, gender, income, and education). Respondents were: 57 percent women, 43 percent men; 20 percent primary school education only, 40 percent university degree or equivalent; 28 percent single, 40 percent living in a household with two people; 44 percent rent their home; 22 percent have children at home under 18 years old; 22 percent have household income less than SEK20,000 after taxes, 40 percent SEK21,000–35,000, 28 percent above SEK35,000, and 10 percent did not state their income; 12 percent were born outside the Nordic countries; 51 percent are employed, 3 percent seeking employment, 33 percent retired, 9 percent at home (maternity leave, retired, or seeking employment); 50 percent have lived in the same place more than five years, 80 percent previously lived elsewhere in Jönköping Municipality; 50 percent would be willing to move, but only 2.4 percentage points of those because of insecurity.
2 Söderköping, population approximately 7,000, is 170km from Stockholm, half way to Stockholm from Jönköping. The survey team contacted 880 households for telephone interviews in the municipality in 2005. A total of 300 people were interviewed, 220 in the urban area and 80 in the outer areas of the municipality. The response rate was 38 percent in Söderköping and 27 percent outside the main urban area (see details in Lundin, 2006).

References

Axelsson, C. (2014). Färre åker till Sverige för att plocka bär. *Dagens Nyheter*. Retrieved July 3, 2014 from www.dn.se/ekonomi/farre-aker-till-sverige-for-att-plocka-bar/.
Babacan, H. (2012). Racism denial in Australia: The power of silence. *Australian Mosaic, 32*, 1–3.
Bamzar, R., & Ceccato, V. (2015). The nature and the geography of elderly injuries in Sweden. *GeoJournal, 80*(2), 279–299.
Bowes, D. R., & Ihlanfeldt, K. R. (2001). Identifying the impacts of rail transit stations on residential property values. *Journal of Urban Economics, 50*(1), 1–25.
Box, S., Hale, C., & Andrews, G. (1988). Explaining fear of crime. *British Journal of Criminology, 28*, 340–356.
Brantingham, P., & Brantingham, P. (1995). Criminality of place: Crime generators and crime attractors. *European Journal on Criminal Policy and Research, 3*, 1–26.
Brottsförebyggande rådet – BRÅ (National Council of Crime Prevention). (2011). The national victims survey. Stockholm: BRÅ.
Brottsförebyggande rådet – BRÅ (National Council of Crime Prevention). (2014a). Nationella trygghetsundersökningen 2006–2013. Stockholm: BRÅ.
Brottsförebyggande rådet – BRÅ (National Council of Crime Prevention). (2014b). NTU 2013: Om utsatthet, otrygghet och förtroende (p. 172). Stockholm: BRÅ.
Brottsförebyggande rådet – BRÅ (National Council of Crime Prevention). (2014c). The Swedish Crime Survey 2013: Concerning exposure to crime, insecurity and confidence (p. 12). Stockholm: BRÅ.
Buck, A. J., Hakim, S., & Spiegel, U. (1991). Casinos, crime, and real estate values: Do they relate? *Journal of Research in Crime and Delinquency, 28*(3), 288–303.
Bursik, R. J. (1988). Social disorganisation and theories of crime delinquency: Problems and prospects. *Criminology, 26*(4), 519–551.

Bursik, R. J. (1999). The informal control of crime through neighborhood networks. *Sociological Focus, 32*(1), 85–97.

Cancino, J. M. (2005). The utility of social capital and collective efficacy: Social control policy in nonmetropolitan settings. *Criminal Justice Policy Review, 16*(3), 287–318.

Carcach, C. (2000). Size, accessibility and crime in regional Australia. *Trends and issues in crime and criminal justice* (Vol. 175). Canberra: Australian Institute of Criminology.

Ceccato, V. (2013). *Moving safely: Crime and perceived safety in Stockholm's subway stations*. Plymouth: Lexington.

Ceccato, V., & Dolmén, L. (2011). Crime in rural Sweden. *Applied Geography, 31*(1), 119–135.

Ceccato, V., & Dolmén, L. (2013). Crime prevention in rural Sweden. *European Journal of Criminology, 10*, 89–112.

Ceccato, V., & Hanson, M. (2013). Experiences from assessing safety in Vingis Park, Vilnius, Lithuania. *Review of European Studies, 5*(5), 1–16.

Ceccato, V., & Wilhelmsson, M. (2011). The impact of crime on apartment prices: Evidence from Stockholm, Sweden. *Geografiska Annaler: Series B, Human Geography, 93*(1), 81–103.

Ceccato, V., & Wilhelmsson, M. (2012) Acts of vandalism and fear in neighbourhoods: Do they affect housing prices? In V. Ceccato (Ed.), *The urban fabric of crime and fear* (pp. 191–212). New York/London: Springer.

Ceccato, V., & Wilhelmsson, M. (2013). Jönköping safety survey [Database]. Stockholm: CEFIN-KTH.

Ceccato, V., & Wilhelmsson, M. (2014). The impact of safety on a small town's housing market. Paper presented at the *ENHR Conference*, Edinburgh.

Chaplin, R., Flatley, J., & Smith, K. (2011). Crime in England and Wales 2010/11. *Home Office Statistical Bulletin*. London: Home Office.

Christie, N., Andenaes, J., & Skirkbeckk, S. (1965). Study of self-reported crime. *Scandinavian Studies in Criminology, I*, 86–116.

City of Stockholm (2011). Trygg i Stockholm? 2011 En stadsövergripande trygghetsmätning. Stockholm: City of Stockholm, Social care.

Cunneen, C. (2007). Crime, justice and indigenous people. In E. Barclay, J. Donnermeyer, J. Scott, & R. Hogg (Eds.), *Crime in rural Australia* (pp. 142–154). Sydney: Federation Press.

Donnermeyer, J., & Kreps, G. M. (1986). The benefits of crime prevention: A comparative analysis. Columbus, OH: National Rural Crime Prevention Center.

Eriksson, E., & Tollefsen, A. (2013). Of berries and seasonal work. In M. Geiger & A. Pécoud (Eds.), *Disciplining the transnational mobility of people* (pp. 185–205). Basingstoke: Palgrave Macmillan.

Estrada, F., Nilsson, A., Jerre, K., & Wikman, S. (2010). Violence at work: The emergence of a social problem. *Journal of Scandinavian Studies in Criminology and Crime Prevention, 11*(1), 46–65.

Fagerlind, A. L. (2013). Högre krav på bärplockarnas arbetsvillkor. *Dagens Nyheter*. Retrieved April 11, 2015, from www.dn.se/ekonomi/hogre-krav-pa-barplockarnas-arbetsvillkor/.

Forrest, J., & Dunn, K. (2013). Cultural diversity, racialisation and the experience of racism in rural Australia: The South Australian case. *Journal of Rural Studies, 30*, 1–9.

Furstenberg, J. F. F. (1971). Public reaction to crime in the streets. *American Scholar, 40*(40), 601–610.

Gibbons, S. (2004). The costs of urban property crime. *Economic Journal, 114*(499), 441–463.

Gray, E., Jackson, J., & Farrall, S. (2008). Reassessing the fear of crime. *European Journal of Criminology, 5*(3), 363–380.

Halfacree, K. (2011). Still "Out of place in the country"? Travellers and the post-productivist rural. In R. I. Mawby & R. Yarwood (Eds.), *Rural policing and policing the rural: A constable countryside?* (pp. 124–135). Farnham: Ashgate.

Hartshorn, K. J. S., Whitbeck, L. B., & Hoyt, D. R. (2012). Exploring the relationships of perceived discrimination, anger, and aggression among North American indigenous adolescents. *Society and Mental Health, 2*(1), 53–67.

Hirschfield, A., Bowers, K. J., & Johnson, S. D. (2004). Inter-relationships between perceptions of safety, anti-social behaviour and security measures in disadvantaged areas. *Security Journal, 17*(1), 9–19.

Hofferth, S. L., & Iceland, J. (1998). Social capital in rural and urban communities 1. *Rural Sociology, 63*(4), 574–598.

Hollway, W., & Jefferson, T. (1997). The risk society in an age of anxiety: Situating fear of crime. *British Journal of Sociology, 48*(2), 255–266.

Hough, M. (1995). Anxiety about crime: Findings from the 1994 British Crime Survey (Vol. 147). London: Home Office, Home Office Research.

Hwang, S., & Thill, J.-C. (2009). Delineating urban housing submarkets with fuzzy clustering. *Environment and Planning B: Planning and Design, 36*(5), 865–882.

Jackson, J., & Gray, E. (2010). Functional fear and public insecurities about crime. *British Journal of Criminology, 50*(1), 1–21.

Jain, H. C., Singh, P., & Agocs, C. (2000). Recruitment, selection and promotion of visible-minority and aboriginal police officers in selected Canadian police services. *Canadian Public Administration, 43*(1), 46–74.

Jansson, L. (2011). Romerna – Det criminella kolletivt: En diskursanalys av svensk medias skildring av romer och kriminalitet (Master's degree, Mid Sweden University, Sundsvall).

Jönköping city office. (2009). Statistiskt faktablad om Jönköping. Jönköping: Jönköping kommun. Retrieved April 12, 2015 from www.jonkoping.se/.

Karlsson, A. (2012). Unga bor i storstan: äldre i glesbygd. *Välfärd, 25*. Retrieved April 11, 2015, from www.scb.se/sv_/Hitta-statistik/Artiklar/Unga-bor-i-storstan-aldre-i-glesbygd.

Lagrange, T. C. (1999). The impact of neighborhoods, schools, and malls on the spatial distribution of property damage. *Journal of Research in Crime and Delinquency, 36*(4), 393–422.

Länstyrelsen. (2012). Analys av situationen på bostadsmarknaden 2012. (Vol. 17). Jönköping: Länstyrelsen i Jönköpings län.

Lantbrukarnas Riksförbund (2012). Brott på landet: En undersökning bland lantbrukare. (J. Johansson, Ed., p. 40). Stockholm: Sveriges Lantbruk.

Lawtley, A., & Deane, M. (2000). Community safety in rural areas. London: NACRO.

Leander, P. (2012). Bärplockare lever i misär i Sverige. *Expressen*. Retrieved April 11, 2015, from www.expressen.se/nyheter/barplockare-lever-i-misar-i-sverige/.

Lewakowski, B. (2012). Half locked? Assessing the distribution of household safety protection in Stockholm (Master's thesis, Royal Institute of Technology, Stockholm).

Lewis, D. A., & Maxfield, M. G. (1980). Fear in the neighborhoods: An investigation of the impact of crime. *Journal of Research in Crime and Delinquency, 17*(2), 160–189.

162   *Perceived safety in rural areas*

Lundin, T. (2006). Safety survey in Söderköping (p. 53). Söderköping: Söderköpings kommun.
Lynch, A. K., & Rasmussen, D. W. (2001). Measuring the impact of crime on house prices. *Applied Economics, 33*(15), 1981–1989.
Marshall, B., & Johnson, S. (2005). Crime in rural areas: A review of the literature for the rural evidence research centre. Jill Dando Institute of Crime Science, University College, London.
May, D. C., Rader, N. E., & Goodrum, S. (2010). A gendered assessment of the "threat of victimization": Examining gender differences in fear of crime, perceived risk, avoidance, and defensive behaviors. *Criminal Justice Review, 35*(2), 159–182.
Milgram, S. (1974). The experience of living in cities. In C. M. Loo (Ed.), *Crowding and behavior* (pp. 41–54). New York: MSS Information Cooperation
Munroe, E. D. K. (2007). Exploring the determinants of spatial pattern in residential land markets: Amenities and disamenities in Charlotte, NC, USA. *Environment and Planning B: Planning and Design, 34*(2), 336–354.
Omma, L. (2013). *Ung same i Sverige: Livsvillkor, självvärdering och hälsa.* Umeå: Umeå University.
Pain, R. (2000). Place, social relations and the fear of crime: A review. *Progress in Human Geography, 24*(3), 365–387.
Pred, A. (2000). *Even in Sweden: Racisms, racialized spaces, and the popular geographical imagination.* Berkeley, LA/London: University of California Press.
Sacco, V. (2005). *When crime waves.* London: Sage.
Sampson, R. J., Raudenbush, S. W., & Earls, F. (1997). Neighborhoods and violent crime: A multilevel study of collective efficacy. *Science, 277*(5328), 918–924.
Sandercock, R. J. (Ed.). (2005). *Difference, fear and habitus: A political economy of urban fear.* Aldershot: Ashgate.
Schyllander, J., & Rosenberg, T. (2010). Skador bland äldre i Sverige. Stockholm: Myndigheten för samhällsskydd och beredskap (MSB). Retrieved April 12, 2015, from www.msb.se/RibData/Filer/pdf/25570.pdf.
Scott, J., Carrington, K., & McIntosh, A. (2012). Established-outsider relations and fear of crime in mining towns. *Sociologia Ruralis, 52*(2), 147–169.
Skielta, A. (2014). Sapmi. Retrieved July, 7, 2014, from www.samer.se.
Skogan, W. G. (1990). *Disorder and decline: Crime and the spiral of decay in American neighborhoods.* New York: Free Press.
Thaler, R. (1978). A note on the value of crime control: Evidence from the property market. *Journal of Urban Economics, 5*(1), 137–145.
Tita, G., Petras, T., & Greenbaum, R. (2006). Crime and residential choice: A neighborhood level analysis of the impact of crime on housing prices. *Journal of Quantitative Criminology, 22*(4), 299–317.
Torstensson, G., Forslund, M., & Tegnell, A. (2011). Förslag till nationell handlingsplan för säkerhetsfrämjande arbete för äldre personer (Vol. 12, p. 48). Stockholm: Socialstyrelsen.
Troy, A., & Grove, J. M. (2008). Property values, parks, and crime: A hedonic analysis in Baltimore, MD. *Landscape and Urban Planning, 87*(3), 233–245.
Urry, J. (2002). Mobility and proximity. *Sociology, 36*(2), 255–274.
Warr, M. (2000). Fear of crime in the United States: Avenues for research and policy. *Criminal Justice and Behavior, 4*, 451–489.
Wilhelmsson, M., & Ceccato, V. (2015). Challenging the idyll: Does crime affect property prices in Swedish rural areas? *Journal of Rural Studies, 39* (in press).
Wilson, J. Q., & Kelling, G. L. (1982). Broken windows. *Atlantic Monthly, 249*, 29–38.

Part IV

Crime in a rural context

8 Farm crimes and environmental and wildlife offenses

This chapter deals with two topics that are relatively neglected areas of research in the criminological literature: farm crime, and environmental and wildlife crime. The chapter has two sections, and both place Sweden in an international context. These offenses involve from diesel theft to drug manufacture, but also cases of crimes and harm against nature, such as illegal hunting. They present trends over time using Swedish police statistics and, data permitting, alternative data sources. Finally, geographical patterns of environmental and wildlife crimes (EWC) are discussed focusing mostly on urban–rural differences.

Farm crime: framing Sweden in an international perspective

No book on crime in rural areas would be complete without a section that discusses farm crime (Barclay, Donnermeyer, Doyle, & Talary, 2001). But, why should one care about farm crime? One important reason is that although such crimes may not be numerous compared to the types of crime that happen in urban areas, they may have an impact that goes beyond the locality where they occur. Barclay et al. (2001) point out that at the local level farmers are affected by loss in cases of theft, loss of work time, and higher insurance premiums. When a crime happens, it creates a feeling of suspicion, some of which is directed at neighbors. Thus, farm crime has the potential to undermine the cohesiveness of rural communities. At the national level, crime jeopardizes international trade in rural labeled products; for example, when a farmer's cattle are stolen, the guarantee of quality attached to the product's origin is lost.

There is no common definition of what farm crime is. Intuitively, farm crime would be ordinary crimes that take place in rural contexts, such as theft of livestock or tractors. Donnermeyer, Barclay, and Mears (2011, p. 193) define two broad categories for crimes taking place on farms: " 'Ordinary crimes' ... such as the theft of livestock, machinery and farm supplies, vandalism, rubbish dumping, and damage from trespassers and hunters ... 'extraordinary' for their potential impacts ... organized drug production, such as marijuana and methamphetamines."

In the Swedish context, some extraordinary types of crime are classified as crimes against nature, such as dumping garbage or illegal hunting, but these would also include theft of certain chemicals (e.g., fertilizers) that can be used in the preparation of explosives or drugs. In Australia, Barclay and Donnermeyer (2007, p. 57) suggest that crime on farms includes

> theft of livestock and other farm produce, tools and machinery, chemicals and fertilizers as well as vandalism, arson, trespassing and illegal hunting ... also environmental crimes such as illegal dumping of rubbish and waste, theft of water and timber or the growing of cannabis or other drug production on farmland.

It is as if farm crimes are defined to include all crimes that happen in outdoor places or on private property but exclude interpersonal violence, particularly what happens in the private sphere, committed by people who know each other. It may also involve violence, but in the European context, it is against nature and wildlife, which may not be the case in other countries (e.g., in Brazil and South Africa, robbery followed by lethal violence are not unusual events on farms, see e.g., Rede Hoje, 2013; Kumwenda, 2012). This book considers EWC as any offense that is more complex in nature and thus is discussed separately in the second section of this chapter. Farm crimes have a more strict definition, involving a combination of property offenses and some less serious crimes.

Nevertheless farm crime is a relatively neglected area of research in the criminological literature. Exceptions are the research done in the United States and in Australia, in the United Kingdom (Donnermeyer et al., 2011; Jones & Phipps, 2012; Marshall & Johnson, 2005) and to a much lesser extent in Scandinavian countries (e.g., Ceccato & Dolmén, 2013).

Donnermeyer et al. (2011) suggest that there have been two waves of farm crime studies: the first was a small cluster of victimization studies in the United States, and the second wave was more international, including research reports from Australia and the United Kingdom. Some of the most important studies are discussed below in detail, but for a short review, see Donnermeyer et al. (2011, pp. 193–195).

As with most other crimes, farm crimes depend on the situational conditions. Particularly important here are the notions of opportunity, guardianship, and accessibility. Donnermeyer et al. (2011) suggest that if a farm is situated in close proximity to main routes and/or urban centers, the result is an increased likelihood of becoming a victim of crime. Studies by Barclay and Donnermeyer (2007) and Mears, Scott, and Bhati (2007) provide evidence of these hypotheses. An analysis of garbage dumping in a rural Swedish county corroborates the idea that accessibility to a place makes it easy to dump cars and garbage but also makes it easier for transients to detect and report these crimes (Ceccato & Uittenbogaard, 2013).

Donnermeyer et al. (2011) also suggest that farms tend to experience higher rates of theft when equipment and machinery are stored at isolated locations, where there are few people, and some distance to the main operations. The authors also point out that these conditions may vary by type of crime. For instance, those farms that were situated near a public road but were relatively remote from urban settlements were more likely to experience trespassing, vandalism, and illegal dumping. They also suggest that farms encompassing difficult terrain, such as in mountainous areas, were most likely to suffer trespassing, poaching, and livestock theft, as reported by Barclay and Donnermeyer (2002). Anecdotes are found in the media about farms at the end of roads being especially targeted (with the same effect as cul-de-sacs), particularly during vacation periods.

Situational conditions of farm crime are affected by time. The winter season, when fewer people are working on farms, may provide better opportunities for theft than summer, when many people are needed to work. In other parts of the country, garbage dumping by roads and on farms may become a problem in municipalities with much tourism. As the temporary population does not establish long-term social ties to the permanent population, these rural communities may become more at risk for these farm crimes. In Australia, Barclay et al. (2001) suggest the number of transient people is increasing in some rural communities, mostly composed of workers. The temporary inflow, the authors indicate, means that local residents are no longer assured that they know everyone in the community, which impacts their ability to exercise social control. Keeping an eye on what happens in the community becomes crucial in rural areas, as people may live further apart, and local law enforcement has limited resources to effectively cover large areas.

Victimization is widespread in rural areas. Barclay et al. (2001) find that 69 percent of farmers declared that they had been a victim of crime in the preceding two years, using a victimization survey sent to 1,100 farmers in one rural region in Australia. The most common types of crime were illegal trespassers and shooters and thefts of tools and equipment, livestock, and fuel. These findings were confirmed by numbers from the Australia Crime Victims Survey in 2006.

Drug cultivation or production of synthetic drugs is often detected far from large urban areas and often regarded as farm crime. As early as 2001, a report in Australia indicated that 6 percent of the farms in that study had cannabis growing illegally on their land according to the farmers interviewed. Also in Australia, authors report that cannabis is cultivated in national parks. Due to isolation, some rural areas are also the site of amphetamine production (Barclay et al., 2001). About the same time, in the United States, synthetic drug production facilities were also commonly found at sites in isolated areas. These drugs include methamphetamines, crack cocaine, and cannabis (Weisheit & Donnermeyer, 2000). Cannabis is nowadays the most widespread illegal drug worldwide. Decorte, Potter, and Bouchard (2011) report on examples from different countries regarding demand, cultivation, and control of cannabis in Australia, Belgium, the Caribbean, Denmark, Finland, Morocco, and the Netherlands, to name a few. While drug production may be a rural phenomenon, consumption among the young in Europe, for instance, is significantly more concentrated in metropolitan areas than in non-metropolitan ones (United Nations, 2013).

Drug production leads to other types of offenses. Drug-related thefts, that is, theft of ingredients for the production of narcotics, have also being reported in Australia, the United States, and the United Kingdom. Also, Nutt, King, and Phillips (2010) suggest that the use and production of a drug causes environmental damage locally, such as through toxic waste from amphetamine factories and needles discarded by users.

Patterns of farm crime in Sweden: from diesel theft to drug manufacture

As many as three of 10 farmers have been victims of crime themselves, or their properties have been, in the preceding two years, with an aggregated loss value of approximately SEK200 million. In each case, the value of the loss for a victim can range from a few hundred to several hundred thousand Swedish crowns. This was one finding from the Swedish Farmers' postal survey, sent to 1,000 farmers in 2012 and commissioned by the Farmers' Association (Lantbrukarnas Riksförbund, 2012). The survey was sent to farmers who operate agricultural properties with more than 10 hectares of cropland. In 2012, 61 percent of farmers responded to the questionnaire, which contained questions about crime victimization and prevention, among other things.

Interestingly, half of those who have been victims of crimes have been targeted two or more times, indicating that criminals may come back to steal what was left the first time. Although relatively little is known about the types of offenders that target farms in Sweden, there seems to be specialization: some specialize in stealing vehicles and tools, others focus on diesel or other fuel, while others target building sites for building materials. It is estimated that the costs of diesel theft was around SEK200 million in Sweden in 2013, while theft in the construction business reached SEK1.5 billion, including machinery, tools, and built material (CrimeStoppers, 2014).

Not very different from research results elsewhere (Barclay et al., 2001; Donnermeyer et al., 2011) findings from the Farmers' Safety Survey (Lantbrukarnas Riksförbund, 2012) show that fuel, machinery, equipment, and other farm property are common targets of theft on farms. Farmers in southern Sweden are exposed to crime two or more times as much as the national average amongst those who responded to the survey, but there are differences in certain types of crime; for example, theft of fuel is slightly higher in the north than in the south. This north–south pattern in victimization is confirmed by police records as well as by data from Crimestoppers (see Figure 8.3 later in the chapter). As much as seven out of 10 farmers in Sweden know one person (or more) who has been the victim of a crime in the preceding two years. This figure is slightly higher in the south, in the woodlands in Götaland (eight of 10). Higher victimization among farmers in the south follows the overall pattern of victimization in Sweden discussed by Ceccato and Dolmén (2011). The authors suggest that location (e.g., the south or north) and geography (e.g., closer to the European continent) are relevant to determining an area's vulnerability to crime, because of its differentiated pattern of routine activity (Ceccato & Haining, 2004). For instance, rural municipalities located in southern areas of Sweden tend to be more criminogenic than relatively isolated northern rural municipalities. They show higher population density than elsewhere in the country. In southern Sweden, regardless of size, municipalities are affected by their proximity to Denmark (potential inflow of people), transport corridors from Sweden to the continent (and vice versa), and consequently strong daily commuting flows. On top of that, southern areas are relatively easy for law enforcement to cover because of the relatively high population density, whilst in the north some of the police regions are extensive.

The survey also shows that younger farmers with properties containing more than 50 hectares of cropland and who live in accessible rural areas are more likely to know someone who has been a victim of crime than the average respondent is. They might have been a victim themselves or know someone in the community. As pointed out by previous research (Ceccato & Dolmén, 2011; Donnermeyer et al., 2011; Jones & Phipps, 2012), the geography of farm crime greatly reflects opportunities for crime, accessibility to targets, and poor guardianship. Larger properties are more certain attractors as they often have more locations to steal from and, if they are fairly accessible, they make good targets if no one is around.

One in four farmers is worried that their properties or their family will become victimized in the future. Those in northern Sweden feel less anxious than the national average about the prospect of becoming a victim of a crime, whether themselves, their family, or their property. Interestingly, as in the case of Australia, half of the farmers believe that a police report has no effect or somewhat or very little effect. One in five had no opinion. There is no significant difference in the answers from farmers across the country, except that in northern Sweden farmers answered "No opinion" more often than farmers elsewhere in Sweden. The problem is that by not reporting crime, farmers are contributing to a lack of knowledge about these crimes and their offenders, and therefore compromising the work of the police.

The numbers of frauds that reach those living in rural areas through the Internet and by telephone is increasing nationwide (BRÅ, 2011). Among farmers interviewed, one-quarter had been victimized by a false invoice or, more often, by Internet or telephone fraud, especially those living in southern Sweden (Figure 8.1b). Crime has become less dependent on space. An individual living in Stockholm, capital of Sweden, may run the same risk of being victimized by computer fraud as someone living in the remote rural areas of Sweden (Ceccato, 2013). At the same time, new types of computer-based communication, for instance "chat rooms," may become facilitators for traditional crime as can be seen in the physical world (e.g., drug production and dealing, purchase of illegal medicine, dangerous products, or engendered animals).

The Internet also plays an increasingly important role in the manufacture and distribution of narcotics. Information on manufacturing, new types of drugs, ways to abuse, way to take drugs, for the exchange of knowledge, are examples of how Internet-based communication is used in the drug context. The next section presents the geography of police recorded data of drug production.

Drug production in the countryside

Compared with other crimes reported to the police, drug production shows relatively low levels, around 1 percent of all crimes (BRÅ, 2012). In Sweden, records of drug production tend to be more concentrated in rural areas (Figure 8.1). In reality, not much is documented about drug production in the countryside, excepting recent media interest on the subject (e.g., Sveriges Radio, 2010).

Illegal drug production occurs to a lesser extent in Sweden than in many Western European countries and when they are disclosed, they are relatively in

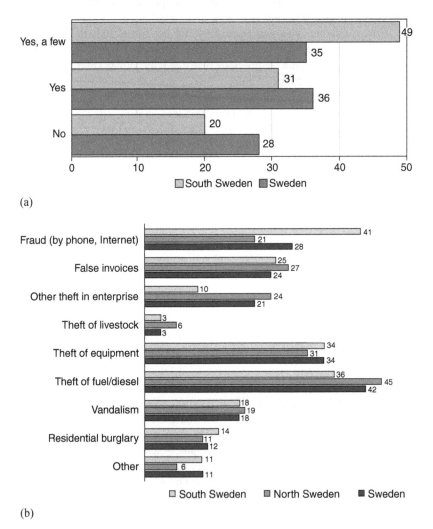

(a)

(b)

Figure 8.1 (a) Do you know anyone in the countryside near where you live who has been the subject of some form of crime, either as a citizen or a business owner in the past two years? (b) Farmers' victimization by type and region (data source: Swedish Farmers' postal survey (*N*=527), 2012).

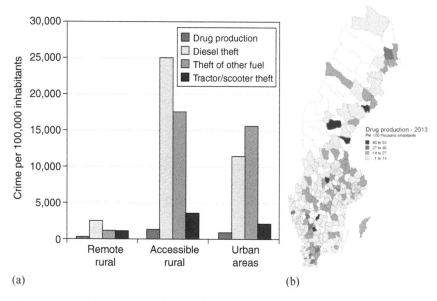

Figure 8.2 (a) Crime rates per 100,000 inhabitants by municipality type, 2013, (b) drug production rates per municipality in Sweden, 2013 (data source: BRÅ, 2013).

limited to quantities. Most illegal laboratories found by the police were manufacturing amphetamine, but other synthetic drugs, such as methamphetamine. The most common way to reveal an illegal laboratory is following a tip to police indicating that there is an ongoing production. The source of such tips may vary. They can be criminals, who are often themselves addicts. Tips can also come from police or customs. Another source is the legal manufacturers or distributors of chemicals (Rikspolisstyrelsen, 2007).

Recently, suspicion of production of synthetic cannabis has been reported by the media in northern Sweden. The demand for acetone has increased for the production of "Spice," or synthetic cannabis. This drug has spread locally among young people, and local stores have noticed increased demand among young people. To prevent young people from accessing the product, supermarkets drastically raised the price of the product or put the bottles behind the counter in many places in the country (Sveriges Radio, 2013):

> There have been teenagers who came in and bought a few bottles [of acetone] … but when they come in a week later to buy again, you start to react.
>> (Manager, local store A, northern municipality)

> Many young addicts purchased pure acetone. In the end, we raised the price from SEK16.90 to SEK50 and put the bottles at the checkout.
>> (Manager, local store C, northern municipality)

Drug production may lead to an increase in theft, either to get access to the ingredients to produce the drug, as illustrated below, or to get "fast cash" to purchase the drug in the market:

> We have not noticed any increase in sales. However, we noticed that very many of [the products] disappeared. Since the thefts, we moved acetone bottles from the shelf to the checkout counter.
>
> (Manager, local store B, northern municipality)

Theft of diesel and other fuels

Accessible rural municipalities are often targeted by thieves looking for diesel and other types of fuels, such as gasoline (petrol). Figure 8.3 shows that, though police statistics show the largest rates of diesel theft scattered around the country (such as Vingåker, Arjeplog, Ockelbo, Markaryd, Ljusnarsberg, Laholm), the 2012 Swedish Farmers' postal survey and Crimestoppers (2013) show a concentration in central and northern municipalities. In northern Sweden alone, the cost of diesel theft is estimated at SEK7 million per year (roughly US$1 million) (Figure 8.3a).

A possible explanation for this mismatch between police statistics and victim surveys is that not all thefts are reported to the police. An expert who works on preventing these crimes on a daily basis believes that the shadow figure of non-reported crime is much larger. He believes that those cases that are registered with the police are the ones that the value of theft reaches the basic insurance premium, while minor ones are never reported.

> If the theft is not up to the deductible, insurance companies will not cover the loss (50–200 liters today). Some insurance companies do not accept diesel thefts at all. I estimate that we may have an additional cost for diesel theft of SEK3–6 million for the whole country.... And we have not figured out all the costs of vandalism, sabotage and theft of tools, etc., at each burglary, that often goes along with diesel theft.
>
> (Security network representative, northern Sweden)

Table 8.1 Thefts of diesel – estimates for northern Sweden

Northern Sweden	Time	Volume	Costs
Jämtland	January 2012 to May 2012	76 m³	
Västernorrland	2011	52 m³	
Gävleborg	May 2012	40 m³	
Västerbotten	Autumn 2011	112 m³	
Norrbotten	2011	110 m³	
Dalarna	May 2012	70 m³	
Northern Sweden	2011–2012	460 m³	SEK6,900,000

Data source: CrimeStoppers (2013).

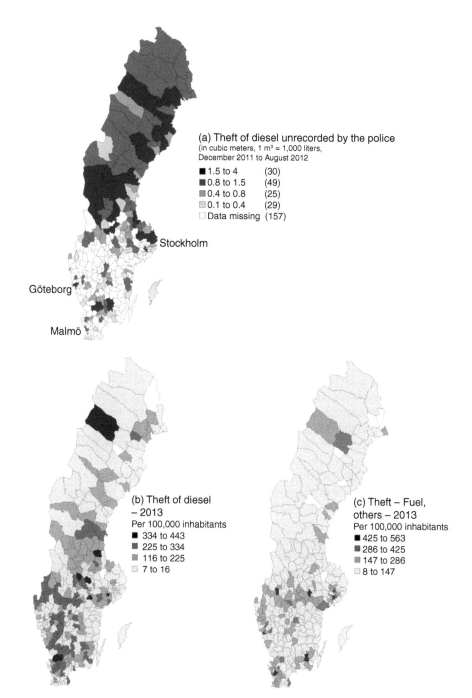

Figure 8.3 (a) Crimestoppers' estimate of theft of diesel in cubic meters; (b) Theft of diesel; and (c) 2012 Theft of other fuels (data sources: BRÅ, 2013; CrimeStoppers, 2013).

It is not unusual for theft of diesel to happen in connection with vandalism or sabotage of machinery. It is estimated that each diesel theft can cost a farmer on average SEK15,000. Some thefts also involve the theft of machinery or tools, costs that may reach SEK100,000 (CrimeStoppers, 2014). According to the Swedish Farmers' postal survey in 2012, an affected farmer may lose on average SEK47,000 in a two-year period. These findings were compared with previous surveys, and according to the Farmers' Association the number of victims of crime in rural areas has increased, despite several efforts by farmers and the police.

Environmental and wildlife crimes

This section first frames environmental and wildlife crime (EWC) in Sweden in an international perspective. Then it presents EWC trends over a period of 11 years using police-recorded statistics and media archives. Finally, geographical patterns of EWC are discussed, focusing mostly on urban areas in comparison to accessible rural and remote rural areas by type of EWC. This section makes use of findings from Ceccato and Uittenbogaard (2013) and sheds light on new issues that came up recently in the public debate and were covered by the national media in Sweden.

Environmental and wildlife crime: Sweden in international context

EWC is defined in different ways. Some researchers use a strict legal definition of environmental crime, such that crime only exists when it is regulated by law. Others adopt the concept of environmental harm, in which environmental crime happens as soon as harm is caused to nature (White, 2014, p. 448).

Sweden follows a more strict definition of environmental crime by law, and therefore based less on the concept of environmental harm. Swedish environmental legislation consists mainly of the Environmental Code, which came into force in 1999. The role of the Swedish authorities is to monitor and ensure that the law is followed. Municipalities are the main framers of the tasks of the environmental inspector whose job is to give notice of cases that do not follow the law and environmental requirements, though the county administration and other state authorities may also be involved. Thus the crimes are detected mainly through the control and supervision of the authorities, which means that increased control by these authorities directly impacts the crime statistics.

EWCs can also be classified as *primary crimes* as they directly result from the destruction and degradation of the Earth's resources, through human actions, such as pollution of air, water, or soil. Other, *secondary crimes*, may arise from the flouting of rules that seek to regulate environmental disasters, for example, organized crimes and dumping of toxic waste (White, 2008). In Sweden, EWCs involve both primary and secondary offenses, from illegal hunting of animals, to pollution by emissions. An environmental crime can be said to be any activity that involves air, soil, or water pollution or otherwise affects the environment such that the health of animals, plants, or humans is damaged (BRÅ, 2014)

EWCs are often regarded as victimless, as they do not always produce a consequence (at least not a visible one). The harm may be diffused or go undetected for a long period of time. The motivation behind EWC also varies, particularly by type of offense. There are various types of environmental crimes where the aim is economic profit, whilst others are due to negligence or lack of knowledge in dealing with waste. In rural areas, littering and dumping waste reach the news and are often related to actions of local residents, not companies. In rural Australia, for example, Barclay and Donnermeyer (2007) found that other farmers were commonly pointed out as offenders in cases of theft of water from river systems and dams, the pollution of water and wetlands, irrigated pastures or grazing livestock, the illegal damming of waterways which causes flooding or reduced water access to neighboring farms, spray drift through aerial spraying of chemicals, and the illegal clearing of native vegetation. A recent study by Barclay (2015) confirms these results. The author examined incidents that occur on farms where individual farmers are victims using data from a nationwide survey in Australia. Using three cases the author assessed the social construction of environmental crime by investigating the way farmers defined environmental harms as "crime." While participants found some harms difficult to associate with criminal intent, the infestation of weeds and pest animals due to mismanagement on neighboring properties was defined by participants as environmental crime. Interestingly, all actions leading to harm were considered criminal if intentional, while accidental acts were not. Negligence was also used to define some actions as environmental crimes.

EWC statistics are often underestimated, either because the crimes may go undetected or because these offenses fall between the responsibilities of different authorities and are not reported. Even when detected, cases are dismissed because of lack of evidence. In Australia, for example, Barclay and Donnermeyer (2007) suggest that less than half of all declared crimes have been reported to police. The reasons for this were that many farmers believed reporting thefts were a waste of time because it was difficult to convict offenders. Other reasons to avoid going to the police were that they were unsure when the crime occurred or they preferred to deal with the problem themselves. In Sweden and Canada, companies and private groups are often overrepresented among suspects and/or offenders (BRÅ, 2006; Skinnider, 2011).

Crimes may not get reported because the environmental damage may actually have been legal in the past (at least during a certain period of time) and now, although an offense, it takes place with the consent of society just because it may not be regarded as a "big problem." Barclay and Donnermeyer (2007) also indicate that in certain cases conflicts between neighbors generate a code of conduct and blaming. Some victims were declared to deserve being victims of crime because they were not good managers, for instance. There was also a common acceptance of a certain level of crime in rural communities, as part of daily business. The authors conclude that these attitudes toward crime impacted on the commission of the offense itself and consequently on reporting rates.

Records of harm against nature depend on a legal basis that sometimes conflicts with other relevant interests and local traditional rural practices. This tolerance of these harming activities creates a lag in action, fed by a local culture of acceptance or by economic interests that are equally important for the long-term social sustainability of the area.

The question is: Why do certain activities become intolerable and are criminalized? Pendleton (1997) suggests that a number of violations and thresholds have to be broken before criminalization and criminal sanctions take place. A relevant issue is whether criminal sanctions enforce compliance. Research shows evidence that criminal sanctions deter environmental crimes, which shows the importance of environmental legislation (Almer & Goeschl, 2010). The issues above exemplify the growing complexity and multidimensionality of this subject area. As White (2003, p. 503) suggests, criminologists need to be able to unravel "layers of ambiguity and contestation," which often characterize cases of EWC. Different interests play an important role in keeping environmental harm unnoticed or breaking through the acceptance and making it public as a criminal offense.

The processes of finding out, recording, investigating, prosecuting, and sentencing for EWCs are selective in Sweden, presumably as in other countries. According to a survey conducted by the Swedish newspaper *Svenska Dagbladet* (2012), there were 74 environmental inspectors in the police authority in Sweden. The Prosecutor-General in Sweden reveals that environmental inspectors do not have time to investigate all crimes. The investigation of most crimes is the responsibility of prosecutors, who send out reminders to authorities and investigators, which does not always advance the case. Of these inspectors, only 29 were working exclusively on environmental crime. Considering the 290 municipalities, environmental inspectors may face an excessive workload if each is responsible for 10 municipalities.

Norinder and Karlsson (2013) show that there is a relationship between the number of environmental inspectors and reported EWC in Sweden, in other words, that the number of environmental inspectors has a positive and significant impact on the number of EWCs reported. Interestingly, it is not only the inspectors who play a role in the detection of EWC.

Ceccato and Uittenbogaard (2013) found that more EWC complaints and more media attention to EWC are found in municipalities with larger populations. Similar results were obtained when testing rural municipalities only. However, no correlation was found between the size of municipality (area) and the number of reports and media articles.

In practice, the police play a minor role in EWC, which essentially consists of investigating crimes that have already been discovered and reported by the environmental inspectors. BRÅ (2006) shows that police officers do not always know what environmental crime is. In Sweden, environmental crimes are punishable by fines or imprisonment not exceeding two years, depending on whether they are carried out with intent or by negligence. According to the government penal database, serious environmental crimes refer to actions that cause or may cause serious long-term environmental damage by pollution of air, water, soil or subsoil, or storage or disposal of waste or similar substances (Regeringskansliet, 2012).

Environmental inspectors have a key role to play in EWC detection. In Sweden, the people who first detect EWCs are the individuals who cause the damage, such as in cases of accidents. Next is the local environmental office, chemical inspectors, the coast guard, the public, the police, the customs service, and, last, general physicians. Environmental inspectors have a dual role, both to be service-oriented and to report crimes. In practice, not all crimes are reported, sometimes because the inspector "knows" from experience that their complaints rarely lead to prosecution. There is also a tendency for the investigation to only move forward in the cases where it is easier and less time-consuming to prove the crime. Since no authority is actively looking for environmental crimes to any appreciable extent, only the most obvious and visible ones come to the attention of the authorities.

Checking for EWC is primarily performed by the supervisory authorities, local environmental agencies and county governments. Lack of skills among those involved is also an obstacle to investigating EWC. For instance, a prosecutor has to have a good scientific background to be able to prove in court the damage the offense has caused to the environment or what could have happened. EWCs that are committed by organized crime or are more difficult to investigate are often rejected by the prosecutor on the grounds that the offense cannot be proved. When combined with other types of crimes, such as tax evasion or fraud, they may be redirected to other prosecutors and are no longer classified as EWCs.

Crime against wildlife is often related to hunting and other illegal acts that harm species and less on illegal trafficking. The term "poaching" describes a number of illegal actions that directly harm animals and threaten the sustainability of their populations, including killing and trapping animals (Fyfe & Reeves, 2011). In the media, poaching is often associated with illegal hunting in Africa (e.g., Lemieux, 2011), South America (e.g., Wright et al., 2001), and Asia (e.g., Loeffler, 2013), but this violence against nature can be found anywhere in the world: in Europe (e.g., Caniglia, Fabbri, Greco, Galaverni, & Randi, 2010), Australia (e.g., Davis, Russ, Williamson, & Evans, 2004), and North America (e.g., Saumure, Herman, & Titman, 2007). In Sweden, Korsell and Hagstedt (2008) report that the country imports and, to a lesser extent, exports animals and plants. As an importing country, endangered species most trafficked from other parts of the world are used as pets, in collections, or in the form of tourist objects, and as ingredients for health foods. As an exporting country, there are cases of poaching large predators. It is very difficult to obtain precise figures about wildlife crimes, and Sweden is no exception. In Scotland, Fyfe and Reeves (2011) report claims that in 2006 more than 600 calls were made about wildlife crime, mostly poisoning incidents, one of the worst years so far in terms of records.

EWCs do not often make the news as they tend to be regarded as less important. A low media interest in covering EWCs leads to public misunder-standing and ignorance of such crimes (Jarell, 2009; Marsh, 1991). Activism and the environmental movement often help to shed light on cases of EWC (Almer

& Goeschl, 2010; Sazdovska, 2009). When crimes show up in the media, they tend to give a distorted or partial picture of reality (Burns, 2009; Burns & Orrick, 2002; Jarell, 2009; Lynch, Stretesky, & Hammond, 2000; Marsh, 1991). Marsh (1991) notes that the source is often cited as being the police, who clearly have a voice in what information comes out and thereby regulate what is published in the media. Jarell (2009) suggests that enterprises apply positive marketing to the media, thereby influencing public perception of the problem. Furthermore, the media often covers EWC cases in a narrow timeframe, with the discovery of the crime often receiving the most attention (Burns & Orrick, 2002). Despite these limitations, media coverage is of interest for EWC research because it represents a data source independent of police records and victimization surveys.

Types and trends in EWC in Sweden

Each year there are about 5,000 EWCs reported to the police in Sweden. These include the dumping of oil or other chemicals on land or in bodies of water, illegal hunting and fishing, air pollution, illegal construction, deforestation, and some petty crimes, such as the burning of furniture, noise from sawmills, and littering. In an interview in a national newspaper (*Svenska Dagbladet*, 2012), the Prosecutor-General notes that there has been an increase in the number of reported environmental crimes in recent years, mainly discharge and improper handling of hazardous substances. This increase seems to reflect better cooperation between regulators, police, and prosecutors.

To investigate the nature, trends, and geography of EWC, two data sources were used: 11 years of police records and newspaper articles (printed media archives). The number of EWC for the 290 Swedish municipalities was retrieved from the homepage of the Swedish National Council for Crime Prevention (BRÅ) for the period 2000–2011. For this study, crimes in the 8000 series (codes 8001–8019) have been selected, as they represent all crimes against the environment and wildlife. A total of 2,026 newspaper articles on crimes against environment and wildlife were found in the Swedish national media archive. These articles were accessed through the National Library of Sweden in Stockholm for the period January 1, 2000 to May 12, 2012. A total of 1,332 articles remained after 694 articles were excluded because they were not related to the subject or were duplicates. For more details about the methodology employed in this study, see Ceccato and Uittenbogaard (2013).

Serious EWCs are composed of intentional actions that cause serious environmental damage through the pollution of the air, water, soil or subsoil, or the storage or disposal of waste or similar substances. *Chemical environmental crimes* constitute unlawful handling of chemicals, disruption of control, and disregard of regulations and permits of use, while *crimes related to nature and wildlife* refer to all crimes against the protection of nature, animal abuse, and illegal animal possession as well as disregard of protected species. *Minor and other EWCs* are composed of all minor EWC such as dumping of garbage or illegal waste transportation.

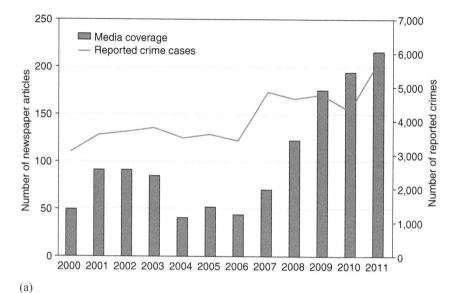

(a)

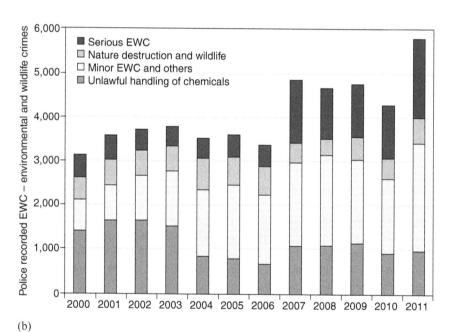

(b)

Figure 8.4 (a) Environmental and wildlife crimes in Sweden, according to police records and newspaper articles (counts between 2000 and 2011), (b) environmental and wildlife crimes recorded by the police by type (source: Ceccato and Uittenbogaard, 2013).

The two data sources indicate similar increasing trends. EWCs have increasingly reached the media in the past 10 years in Sweden, with a 330 percent increase between 2000 and 2011. One important reason for this increase is that prior to 2007 data reported to the police involved only reported crimes in which there was a reasonable suspect. From 2007 onwards, this restriction was eliminated, and cases without a suspect have been recorded in police statistics.

Although EWC police records are problematic (as there are crimes that are never reported) and a comparison with all newspaper articles is not feasible, it is interesting to note that they follow a similar upward trend (Figure 8.4). After 2007, crimes that did not have a suspect were also reported, which explains some of this increase. This rise in records may also reflect a real rise in EWC, as more offenses of this type have reached the police statistics as a result of, for example, new practices. The increase may also be a result of the public's greater willingness to report such crimes due to improved environmental awareness from increased media coverage of EWCs.

In Sweden, the municipalities and county councils have an obligation to report an infraction against nature as a crime, for instance during a control check. If these authorities have been more active or have been targeting certain areas, that could also have influenced the levels and patterns of EWC as well as the media coverage. For instance, since February 2007 the European Union (EU) has applied an EU-wide policy directing its member states to implement minimum legal sanctions for environmental crimes, possibly increasing the number of cases going to trial. Moreover, after the mid-2000s changes in national and European laws meant that the criminal justice system had improved possibilities to prosecute EWC. At the national level, the strict requirement to prove that an injury or threat was caused by EWC was alleviated; thus, more cases can potentially be prosecuted.

Compared with other countries, in Sweden an issue that may have an impact on EWC levels is the "right of public access" (*allemansrätt*) to nature. *Allemansrätt* is the right everyone has to use others' property, land, and water, mainly by traveling across them on foot or by residing there for a short time. This right is limited and also implies that the public must respect rights that affect one's domestic peace and/or economic interests. The law is violated when a person unlawfully intrudes or remains where another person has his residence (*hemfridsbrott*), or when a person accesses places using motorized vehicles. It is forbidden to drive vehicles on bare ground or on private roads (Naturvårdsverket, 2011). Although *hemfridsbrott* is not an EWC, it indicates the uncertainties of interpreting an individual's right to use private property as a public good, including its natural resources.

Spatial patterns of EWC in Sweden

Some parts of the country report more EWCs than others, and the types of EWC differ from place to place within municipalities. Although the majority of recorded crimes took place outside the largest Swedish urban areas, a large proportion of those crimes was registered in municipalities classified as accessible rural. Different types of EWCs show different geographies (Figure 8.5).

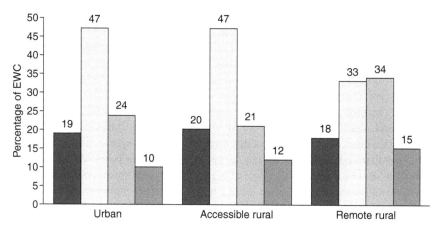

Figure 8.5 Percentage of EWCs in Sweden by type of municipality, 2000–2011 (data source: police records, 2000–2011).

EWCs registered by the police increased when media coverage increased, or vice versa. In fact, the focus of media coverage in certain cases led to thorough investigations by the police. Municipalities with high-profile media coverage of EWC have a medium to high level of police cases. Although the media rarely help detection of EWCs, it still plays an important role in general public awareness of the potential problem. In Sweden, the media focuses on describing the early stages of crime detection (whether or not a crime has occurred) and on the outcome (amount of fines). Little is reported by the media during the investigation and trial. It is unknown whether certain cases never reach court because of external pressure that those involved may be exposed to when investigating EWC.

Serious EWCs are often found in accessible rural municipalities within the urban triangle of Malmö–Gothenburg–Stockholm and in larger municipalities in the north, while minor EWCs are recorded in smaller rural municipalities, mainly in the central and northern regions of Sweden. This serious-to-minor EWC geographical pattern is reflected, to some extent, in the print media. Media coverage of wildlife crimes occurs only in rural areas, which is understandable considering the type of crime, the greater possibility for hunting and accessing nature, and local public interest in their immediate, natural surroundings. Details of the geography of EWC are discussed later in this chapter.

The nature of EWCs covered by media and of EWCs reported to the police is slightly different but reflects the same scenario. The category that has increased the most in police records since 2000 is serious EWCs. Although official police statistics of serious EWCs cannot be broken down by type (air, water, and soil pollution), newspaper articles show a larger proportion of and increase in water pollution cases compared to soil and air pollution cases. Newspaper articles dealing with water pollution are normally related to oil spills from ships in harbors or from factories close to rivers or lakes, as well as intentional dumping of materials, such as oil or other chemicals. Articles on soil pollution are related to soil being polluted by leakage of chemicals or biohazardous materials. According to the Naturvårdsverket (2014), more than 1,000 areas in the country have the highest environmental risk, including old factories, abandoned industrial sites, and chemical cleaners.

Crimes against wildlife also involve trade in endangered species. Endangered animals and plants are in demand for all sorts of purposes, both alive and dead. Korsell and Hagstedt (2008) suggest that there are also local species that are endangered and therefore protected by law. Such species include bears and all orchid species and can be a target of this type of crime. Endangered species are sometimes sold by legal businesses, and often those who buy them are not aware of the legal protection of the species. Korsell and Hagstedt note that this type of crime is not only about smuggling but also generates a number of collateral crimes and risks, including animal cruelty, contamination, and invasive species that pose a threat to Swedish animals and plants. The report also shows that this type of crime continues unnoticed, because agencies are not doing enough to detect these crimes. For instance, in 2006, police and customs in Sweden carried out 38 seizures of endangered species, compared to 163,000 seizures in the United Kingdom. The authors also suggest that behind every case of illegal trade in endangered animals, there is a hunting offense. For instance, there is great demand for bear bile and, to some extent, lynx fur, two species found in Sweden. Such demand may give rise to illegal hunting, though most hunting offenses, found in official records, are committed by an individual infringing hunting quotas.

In Sweden, as in the United Kingdom (e.g., Marshall & Johnson, 2005), some animals have been hunted for centuries. In Sweden, the risk of overpopulation of certain species makes hunting not only acceptable but also encouraged. These animals include moose, certain types of foxes, hares, rabbits, beavers, magpies, and other types of birds, such as geese and crows. Although a large majority of hunters in Sweden are affiliated with the Swedish Association for Hunting and Wildlife Management, which defines hunting standards (e.g., methods, territory, weapons, proficiency, and hunting season), crime against wildlife does happen. For example, the start and duration of the season for a particular species varies geographically; moose hunting in southern and central Sweden is allowed for two months, while in certain small geographic areas it is only allowed for a few days. According to statistics from the National Crime Prevention Council reported in a monthly journal for forestry and agriculture (*Skogsaktuellt*, 2012), 612 violations of the Hunting Act were recorded in 2012, compared with 473 reported crimes in 2007, when environmental legislation was amended. The strongest growth was witnessed in Södermanland and Skåne counties, but violations decreased in northern Sweden, such as in Norrbotten County. The percentage of solved crimes during the same period was relatively stable at around 10 percent. The low risk of detection is the main cause of this development, according to the National Police Board.

Littering and other minor EWCs account for the second largest share of offenses in the police statistics and media coverage. This category is dominated by disposal of garbage in forests and on the outskirts of main urban areas; these offenses tend to be registered close to roads, too. In police records, the category "waste dumping and other minor crimes" includes burning of materials and dumping of materials (e.g., batteries), waste, and old cars. As examples, Figure 8.6 shows the geography of waste and garbage dumping in Västernorrland County, and Figure 8.7a shows vehicles abandoned in a forest, one destroyed by fire.

Levels of littering and garbage dumping are potentially associated with garbage collection fees. Nationwide, the difference in garbage collection fees among municipalities is SEK25,003 per year, according to the Swedish Home-owners Association's 2012 survey. Thus, it could be that individuals living in municipalities with high fees for garbage collection would be more motivated to burn furniture and dump waste than individuals living where garbage collection is cheap. The difference between the cheapest municipal fee and the fee paid by homeowners in the rural county of Västernorrland, for example, is about SEK800, whereas the fee in Västernorrland is one-third less than the fee charged in the most expensive Swedish municipalities (Swedish Homeowners Association, 2012).

However, Ceccato and Uittenbogaard (2013) find no significant correlation between high fees for garbage collection and high levels of waste dumping either

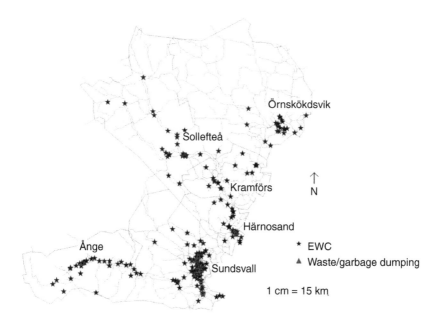

Figure 8.6 Types of environmental and wildlife crimes in Västernorrland County, Sweden (data source: police records 2005–2008).

(a)

(b)

Figure 8.7 (a) Cars dumped in forest, (b) oil leak from an industrial area, (c) heavy metal contamination, and (d) illegal hunting (photographs: Sundin, 2011; Eklund, 2014; Björkland, 2013; APU, 2012).

(c)

(d)

Figure 8.7 Continued.

for the whole of Sweden or for the rural municipalities. This relationship is more complex than expected: a bit more than one-third of rural municipalities show high levels of waste dumping (including serious cases) and expensive garbage fees. They are mainly in the south and on the west coast of the Skåne region and on the east coast close to Stockholm, with some located in central Sweden. Those municipalities that show low garbage collection fees and low waste dumping are often in smaller southern rural municipalities, with short commuting distances between them. Coastal municipalities, especially those that receive many summer tourists, tend to show high levels of waste dumping despite having low garbage collection fees. At the same time, small municipalities in northern Sweden tend to have high waste collection fees, though the fees do not appear to influence the level of waste dumping or at least it is not detected.

The increase of vehicle dumping in nearby forests is said to be associated with the lack of incentive for car owners to take their cars to a junkyard. Instead, many vehicles end up in the woods or even out on the street. The government incentive expired in the 2010s. In a case of abandonment, the owner is informed about the car and is invited to collect it, but they rarely do. Taxpayers currently cover the cost of vehicle salvage, and local authorities have to spend resources to administer the process. For example, in Sollefteå municipality alone, the police take care of 30 to 40 cars a year, according to the local newspaper (Sundin, 2011).

People's routine activities and spatial awareness of their environment are important to EWC detection in rural areas. The detection of these crimes depends on the accessibility of the area by road or river or through an urbanized area. Figure 8.6 shows that in Västernorrland county 75 percent of police-recorded environmental and wildlife offenses were located less than 2 km away from a road. Garbage dumping is particularly noticeable due to its visibility from roads and in the outskirts of urban areas, as indicated by triangles in Figure 8.6. According to BRÅ (2006), it is often the general public or individual citizens who detect crimes that are visible in nature, such as garbage dumping, old vehicles, waste found in nature, or oil spills in water areas. Recorded cases depend on detection, and detection is based on what people witness as they go about their daily activities.

EWC records of unlawful handling of chemicals present a concentrated pattern in rural areas spread out over the country that often include a medium-size city, which indicates some relation to factories and/or industries working with chemicals. The Coast Guard Authority has invested substantial resources in detecting the discharge of oil, which could also lead to improved crime detection and an increase in the number of police records. However, rarely does a complaint lead to indictment and prosecution. The data from 2004 shows that, out of 3,509 reported crimes, only 267 resulted in indictments, 177 reached trial, and 107 resulted in a final judgment. Of these cases, no one went to prison; all sentences were suspended or fines imposed (BRÅ, 2006).

During recent decades, new environmental laws have stipulated action against crimes against nature that are contrary to the way natural resources have traditionally been exploited in certain areas. At the same time, as Jarell (2009) suggests, EWCs are often put aside as a "cost of doing business." Some cases may even be covered up or minimally reported to defend the local economy. However, in daily practice the dilemma of choosing between economic and environmental sustainability of these areas makes the situation more difficult to judge. For example, the economies of many municipalities in northern Sweden depend on mining, an activity that has long been in conflict with other traditional economic activities. Mining in particular affects the environment in two ways: directly, when chemicals are spilled into the environment above the limits allowed, and indirectly, when grazing land for reindeer, for instance, is restricted by the expansion of mining activities. Current conflicts in northern Sweden between locals and mining companies have reached the national news (Blume, 2013), revealing a fragile protection of wildlife and of traditional reindeer grazing activities in this part of the country. For certain groups, reindeer husbandry has been practiced for generations and is regarded as part of the social, economic, and environmental sustainability of these municipalities.

In northern Sweden, the mining companies challenge the boundaries of environmental crime laws and take advantage of a faulty criminal system that does not provide evidence of EWC at early stages of the process. In Västerbotten County, for example, for some time environmentally hazardous emissions by the majority of Swedish mining companies have been higher than permitted, reported often by the media (Figure 8.7c). In several cases, the levels are far above the limit deemed acutely harmful to animals and plants. Experts interviewed by Swedish broadcasting (SVT Västerbotten, quoted by Klefbom, 2010) provide several examples that the companies continue doing business as usual.

A mining company in Västerbotten dumped 1,700 kg of zinc in rivers in 2010, three times more than allowed. Another mining company was charged with high dust emissions in 2004 but was acquitted in the Court of Appeal. The contract is too vague to have legal substance and win convictions.

In Maurliden outside Skellefteå, police reported a discharge in 2002, but the investigation was closed because the police did not investigate it properly. Another mine contaminated a pond near Gällivare, but the prosecutor found no entity responsible for the spill.

Some municipalities try to deal with the problem as part of their daily challenges but in a long-term perspective, as suggested by a representative of a crime prevention group.

What we have here are "old sins." We are fighting with an old paper mill [here] but also with "old sins" at the harbor that we are trying to solve. We had a huge flood here almost 10 years ago, and that is something everybody remembers.

(Politician, Southern Sweden)

Newspaper articles similarly focus on unlawful handling of chemicals in soil and water.

> In May 2008, employees leaked 200 liters of a solution with organic compounds into the wild. The chemical spill could be detected and sanitized. Only a small amount has reached outside the factory area, and no significant damage was found.
>
> (Local newspaper, northern Sweden, 2010)

Sweden has a long coast and many rivers and lakes. Environmental crimes related to illegal construction and water-resource management close to these bodies of water have been registered (see example in Figure 8.7b). Media reports show that both individuals and construction companies are common offenders. Some are multiple offenders, as in the case below.

> In 2009, a man was convicted when contaminated water from a construction site was pumped into a lake which is a source of drinking water. He has done it again. He built his house by the lake without planning permission. His punishment was limited to a fine of SEK90,000.
>
> (Local newspaper, central Sweden, 2012)

According to BRÅ's report, this is a common problem that causes serious damage to Sweden's coastal ecosystem (BRÅ, 2006, pp. 32–34). It is unclear how municipalities deal with their double role, as they have a monopoly over the decision to approve building permits for new construction at the same time that they also constitute the most important authority in detecting EWC.

Another important issue identified when evaluating media articles on EWC was the lack of skills among those involved in collecting and assessing evidence during the investigation of environmental damage. This turns out to be an obstacle to conviction. Lack of evidence at late stages of the process often lead to the acquittal of the offender or, as described in the case below, to a conviction on a minor offense.

> An entrepreneur in X municipality was convicted of littering. His company entered bankruptcy not long after the municipal environmental authorities discovered the trash.... The accused entrepreneur was not convicted of environmental crime, instead, he was convicted of littering, and his punishment was limited to a fine of 80 *dagsböter*.[1]
>
> (Local newspaper, northern Sweden, 2010)

This is also the case of Swedish mining companies that exceed their emission limits but are not sentenced for environmental crimes. According to an investigation carried out in Västerbotten County and reported by Klefbom (2010), the evidence is not sufficient to win a conviction. Swedish Television in Västerbotten has examined legal cases of emissions from Swedish mining companies in the past decade. Since 2010, the Swedish Environmental Protection Agency (Naturvårdsverket) has worked with the environmental courts to tighten conditions so that it is easier to bring these cases to trial.

Yet, mining companies are still freed from the charges. As late as June 2013, a mining company was accused of having discharged far more heavy metals than allowed by law. At its peak, the company discharged 18 times more arsenic than the state allows, and zinc and nickel concentrations have been about 10 times higher than the allowed quantities (see Björkland, 2013). Unfortunately, one month later, the same newspaper reported that the mining company was acquitted by a court of the suspected environmental crimes. According to the prosecutor, the damage would go far beyond the mining area. However, the district court upheld that the discharge went to a clarification pond that belongs to the mining concession area. The prosecutor asked the company to pay a corporate fine, but the district court did not agree that mine employees were guilty of environmental offenses and the company went free.

Concluding remarks

There is an overall lack of interest in the criminological literature for both farm crime and crimes against the environment and wildlife as criminal offenses. There are numerous reasons for this disinterest. Although they might have an impact that affects society as a whole, these crimes are often considered minor or lacking a victim (such as in a case of harm against nature). As they happen far from metropolitan areas and large cities, they do not usually interest the mainstream media or, if they do, they are often considered less important than big city crimes, such as violent offenses. The academic disinterest in this topic is partially related to the lack of systematic data and availability of knowledge on these offenses from official sources. For instance, police records on thefts or narcotics cannot be broken down by type. For environmental crime, the situation is even more complicated. Even when they are detected, those responsible are rarely prosecuted. This chapter has shown that there are major difficulties in detecting and prosecuting these offenses. Farm crimes and crimes against nature are important aspects of safety in rural communities and require further attention from academics as well as from rural policy makers and practitioners devoted to rural development.

As many as three out of 10 farmers or their properties have been victims of crime in the past two years. Farmers have been victimized mostly by theft of diesel and other fuels, machinery, and tools as well as by different types of fraud. Half of those who have been victims of crime were targeted two or more times, indicating that in the case of theft, criminals may come back to steal what was left. Farmers in the south have been exposed to crime two or more times more than the national average, but there are differences by type of crime. According to several sources, theft of fuel is slightly higher in northern Sweden than in the south. Some of these crimes are never reported. Therefore in the future, victimization surveys should incorporate questions that are more appropriate for rural areas, with samples that allow meaningful analysis across rural municipalities and regions.

As with most crimes, farm crimes depend on the circumstances. The geography of farm crime greatly reflects the opportunities for crime, accessibility to targets, and poor guardianship. Larger properties are more certain attractors than smaller ones, as they often have more locations to steal from, and if they are fairly accessible they make the right target if nobody is around, such as in remote areas and accessible rural areas. A remaining question for future research is the assessment of how seasons regulate the flow of people, activities, and consequently crime. Hypothetically rural areas at border regions would be more exposed to crime than elsewhere because of in- and outflow of people and goods. The relative location of the municipalities in relation to big roads or railways is expected to have an effect in farm and EWC crime.

International evidence based on urban environments suggests that the majority of offenders commit a crime close to where they live (for a review see Ceccato and Dolmén, 2011), which could for most crime types be an area smaller than municipal boundaries. There has been a myth in rural areas that most crimes are committed by individuals that do not live locally (the idea that "naughty kids come always from neighboring communities" or media articles showing plenty of examples when foreign temporary workers are blamed by acts of crime). Future research should make use a combination of data on the location of offenses, offenders, and victims (or targets) to assess whether farm crime is committed by people living locally or by those traveling to such municipalities for the purpose of crime or staying there temporarily.

Findings also show that despite community efforts to deal with farm crime, victimization has not decreased. A systematic analysis of interventions targeting crime in rural areas should allow identification of actions, technologies, and preventive programs that work. The use of technology, such as CCTV cameras should be properly assessed, as well as the implementation of programs that can use social media to prevent these crimes. Chapter 12 will illustrate such interventions in Swedish rural areas.

Compared with the United States or Australia, in Sweden drug production attracts less attention than farm crime does. According to police records, drug production in Sweden tends to be concentrated in rural areas. Media articles report cases of cannabis cultivation in apartments and cellars but also on farms in southern Sweden. Production of synthetic cannabis has also been reported in northern Sweden. However it is unclear how these reports relate to levels of drug addiction, and much less is known about the type of users and potential dealers in the rural context. Future studies should investigate the existence of a demand for drugs in rural contexts among youth that seem to be both producers and users of popular synthetic drugs. The relationship between alcohol and drug consumption should be further investigated in a broad social and cultural context of rural communities. There are reasons to believe that, in certain rural contexts, there is an acceptance of both alcohol and narcotic use.

The Swedish case reveals that regardless of long distances, ICT surmounts the physical barriers of communication and increases the risk for crime, at least for some types of crime. Fraud over the Internet and telephone are common types of crimes that farmers often fall as victims. Further investigation based on the profile of victims of fraud in rural areas may shed light on why farmers often become vulnerable to this type of crime. Note that many Swedish rural communities have an overrepresentation of elderly, a group that are often targeted by telephone calls from strangers, some leading to fraud.

This chapter also provides a glimpse of EWC in Sweden. Police records and newspaper articles indicate an increase in EWC recorded by the police as well as by media coverage in the past decade. It is important to note that before 2007 only crimes with a suspect were recorded by the police. This explains in part the rise between 2006 and 2007, for example. Although crimes against the environment and wildlife are rural phenomena, the geography of EWC varies by crime type. The proportion of serious EWC, unlawful use of chemicals, and crimes related to nature and wildlife is similar in both urban and accessible rural municipalities. Urban and accessible rural municipalities also show high numbers of minor EWC reported, such as littering, garbage dumping, and illegal waste transportation. Remote rural municipalities have a significantly high percentage of chemical environmental crimes, comprising unlawful handling of chemicals, disruption of control, and disregard of regulations and permits for the use of chemical components. A slightly higher percentage of crimes against the protection of nature and wildlife (animal abuse and illegal animal possession as well as disregard of protected species) is also recorded in remote rural municipalities than in accessible and urban municipalities. It is essential to investigate how much each municipality, county, and state authority spends on detecting EWC. Previous research has shown that the number of inspectors plays an important role in EWC detection. Environmental inspectors are a factor of interest, because they are the main actors in the detection of the crime. Future studies should also assess how inspectors' professional profiles, skills, and experience in the field impact EWC detection.

This chapter shows only what has happened within national boundaries. There seems to be consensus that future research should focus on cross-border trafficking of waste as well as of endangered species of plants and animals, an apparently lucrative business. As previously mentioned, this type of crime continues unnoticed, because agencies are not doing enough to detect the crime. Environmental inspectors are overloaded by domestic cases. Little is known about their nature and whether they may generate a number of other crimes and risks, including animal cruelty, or pose a threat to native animals and plants. There is little empirical evidence on this from Sweden or elsewhere in the literature. What exists is still based on received knowledge and anecdotes in the media that do not hold up under the scrutiny of a systematic analysis. Thus, more research is needed.

192 Crime in a rural context

Note

1 *Dagsböter* is a fine based on the income of a person found guilty of a crime. The fine is expressed as a particular number of days, depending on the penalty for the crime, based on severity or culpability, and an estimate of the person's daily income. Thus two people can be convicted of the same crime and be fined for the same number of "days" but pay different fines because they have different incomes. *Dagsböter* differs from fines of a fixed monetary amount. The number of depends on the severity of the crime, from a low of 30, to a maximum of 150 *dagsböter*. These fines are common in countries such as Sweden, Finland, Denmark, and Germany (Wikipedia, 2014).

References

Almer, C., & Goeschl, T. (2010). Environmental crime and punishment: Empirical evidence from the German penal code. *Land Economics, 86*, 707–726.

Anti Poaching Unit – APU. (2012). Anmälan om jaktbrott upprättad. Retrieved May 1, 2014, from http://antipoachingunit.org/arkiv2012.html.

Barclay, E. (2015). Defining environmental crime: The perspective of farmers. *Journal of Rural Studies, 39* (in press).

Barclay, E., & Donnermeyer, J. F. (2002). Property crime and crime prevention on farms in Australia. *Crime Prevention of Community Safety, 4*(4), 47–61.

Barclay, E., & Donnermeyer, J. F. (2007). Farm victimisation: The quintessential rural crime. In E. Barclay, J. F. Donnermeyer, J. Scott, & R. Hogg (Eds.), *Crime in rural Australia* (pp. 57–68). Sydney: Federation Press.

Barclay, E., Donnermeyer, J. F., Doyle, B. D., & Talary, D. (2001). Property crime victimisation and crime prevention on farms. Report to the NSW A.-G. C. P. Division (Ed.), Institute for Rural Futures, University of New England.

Björkland, S. (2013, 12 June). Gruva riskerar stora böter för miljöbrott. *Västerbottens Kuriren.* Retrieved April 14, 2015, from www.vk.se/892133/gruva-riskerar-stora-boter-for-miljobrott-2.

Blume, E. (2013). Protesterna mot gruvan har bara börjat. *Dagens Nyheter.* Retrieved April 14, 2015, from www.dn.se/ekonomi/protesterna-mot-gruvan-har-bara-borjat/.

Brottsförebyggande rådet – BRÅ (National Council of Crime Prevention). (2006). Är vi bra på miljöbrott? En snabbanalys *Webrapport 2006.*

Brottsförebyggande rådet – BRÅ (National Council of Crime Prevention). (2011). The national victims survey. Stockholm: BRÅ.

Brottsförebyggande rådet – BRÅ (National Council of Crime Prevention). (2012). Brottsutvecklingen i sverige år 2008–2011, Narkotikabrott (pp. 211–231).

Brottsförebyggande rådet – BRÅ (National Council of Crime Prevention). (2013). Police recorded statistics [Database]. Stockholm: BRÅ. Retrieved December 12, 2014, from www.bra.se/bra/brott-och-statistik/statistik.html.

Brottsförebyggande rådet – BRÅ (National Council of Crime Prevention). (2014). Miljöbrott. Retrieved May 1, 2014, from http://bra.se/bra/brott-och-statistik/miljobrott.html.

Burns, R. G. (2009). Environmental crime. In J. Miller (Ed.), *21st Century criminology: A reference handbook* (pp. 481–489). Thousand Oaks, CA: Sage.

Burns, R. G., & Orrick, L. (2002). Assessing newspaper coverage of corporate violence: The dance hall fire in Goteborg, Sweden. *Critical Criminology, 11*, 137–150.

Caniglia, R., Fabbri, E., Greco, C., Galaverni, M., & Randi, E. (2010). Forensic DNA against wildlife poaching: Identification of a serial wolf killing in Italy. *Forensic Science International: Genetics, 4*(5), 334–338.

Ceccato, V. (2013). Integrating geographical information into urban safety research and planning. *Proceedings of the ICE – Urban Design and Planning, 166*, 15–23.

Ceccato, V., & Dolmén, L. (2011). Crime in rural Sweden. *Applied Geography, 31*(1), 119–135.

Ceccato, V., & Dolmén, L. (2013). Crime prevention in rural Sweden. *European Journal of Criminology, 10*, 89–112.

Ceccato, V., & Haining, R. (2004). Crime in border regions: The Scandinavian case of Öresund, 1998–2001. *Annals of the Association of American Geographers, 94*, 807–826.

Ceccato, V., & Uittenbogaard, A. C. (2013). Environmental and wildlife crime in Sweden. *International Journal of Rural Criminology, 2*(1), 23–50.

CrimeStoppers. (2013). Estimate of theft of diesel [Database]. Retrieved January 1, 2014, from www.crimestoppers.se/.

CrimeStoppers. (2014). Allt fler drabbas av kostsamma dieselstölder, vad kan man göra åt detta? Retrieved May 3, 2014, from www.crimestoppers.se/2014/03/08/forebygg-pa-ratt-satt/.

Davis, K. L. F., Russ, G. R., Williamson, D. H., & Evans, R. D. (2004). Surveillance and poaching on inshore reefs of the Great Barrier Reef Marine Park. *Coastal Management, 32*(4), 373–387.

Decorte, T., Potter, G. W., & Bouchard, M. (Eds.). (2011). *World wide weed: Global trends in cannabis cultivation and its control.* Farnham: Ashgate.

Donnermeyer, J. F., Barclay, E. M., & Mears, D. P. (2011). Policing agricultural crime. In R. I. Mawby & R. Yarwood (Eds.), *Rural policing and policing the rural: A constable countryside* (pp. 193–204). Farnham: Ashgate.

Eklund, B. (2014). Läckan i Selångerån kan polisanmälas. Retrieved April 28, 2015, from www.dagbladet.se/medelpad/sundsvall/lackan-i-selangeran-kan-polisanmalas.

Fyfe, N. R., & Reeves, A. D. (2011). The thin green line? Police perceptions of challenges of policing wildlife crime in Scotland. In R. Mawby & R. Yarwood (Eds.), *Rural policing and policing the rural: A constable countryside?* (pp. 169–182). Farnham: Ashgate.

Jarell, M. L. (2009). Environmental crime and injustice: Media coverage of a landmark environmental crime case. *Southwest Journal of Criminal Justice, 6*, 25–44.

Jones, J., & Phipps, J. (2012). Policing farm crime in England and Wales. Paper presented at the *Papers from the British Criminology Conference, 12*, 3–24.

Klefbom, E. (2010, December 7). Gruvor fälls inte för miljöbrott. *Milijöaktuellt.* Retrieved April 14, 2015, from http://miljoaktuellt.idg.se/2.1845/1.357821/gruvor-falls-inte-for-miljobrott.

Korsell, L., & Hagstedt, J. (2008). *Illegal handel med hotade djur- och växtarter: En förstudie* (Vol. 14). Stockholm: BRÅ.

Kumwenda, O. (2012). Farm murders highlight apartheid's toxic legacy in South Africa. *Reuters.* Retrieved April 14, 2015, from www.reuters.com/article/2012/11/29/us-safrica-farming-crime-idUSBRE8AS02120121129.

Lantbrukarnas Riksförbund. (2012). Brott på landet: En undersökning bland lantbrukare. (J. Johansson, Ed., p. 40). Stockholm: Sveriges Lantbruk.

Lemieux, A. M. (2011). Policing poaching and protecting pachyderms: Lessons learned from Africa's elephants. In R. Mawby & R. Yarwood (Eds.), *Rural policing and policing the rural: A constable countryside?* (pp. 183–192). Farnham: Ashgate.

Loeffler, K. (2013). Breeding wildlife to extinction in China. *Journal of Applied Animal Welfare Science, 16*(4), 387–387.

Lynch, M. J., Stretesky, P., & Hammond, P. (2000). Media coverage of chemical crimes, Hillsborough County, Florida, 1987–97. *British Journal of Criminology, 40*(1), 112–126.

Marsh, H. L. (1991). A comparative analysis of crime coverage in newspapers in the United States and other countries from 1960–1989: A review of the literature. *Journal of Criminal Justice, 19*, 67–79.

Marshall, B., & Johnson, S. (2005). Crime in rural areas: A review of the literature for the rural evidence research centre. Jill Dando Institute of Crime Science, University College, London.

Mears, D. P., Scott, M. L., & Bhati, A. S. (2007). A process and outcome evaluation of an agricultural crime prevention initiative. *Criminal Justice Policy Review, 18*(1), 51–80.

Naturvårdsverket. (2014). Riskbedömning av förorenade områden. Retrieved April 14, 2015, from www.naturvardsverket.se/Stod-i-miljoarbetet/Vagledningar/Fororenade-omraden/Riskbedomning-av-fororenade-omraden/.

Norinder, M., & Karlsson, J. (2013). Påverkas antalet anmälda miljöbrott i Sverige av antalet miljöinspektörer? (Master's thesis, University of Gothenburg, Gothenburg).

Nutt, D. J., King, L. A., & Phillips, L. D. (2010). Drug harms in the UK: A multicriteria decision analysis. *Lancet, 376*(9752), 1558–1565.

Pendleton, M. R. (1997). Beyond the threshold: The criminalization of logging. *Society and Natural Resources, 10*, 181–193.

Rede Hoje. (2013). Família é trancada em quarto durante assalto a fazenda no município de Guimarânia. Retrieved May 2, 2014, from www.patrociniohoje.com.br/index.php/noticias/patrocinio-hoje/4373-assassinato-a-facadas-em-irai-de-minas-assalto-a-fazenda-em-guimarania-e-mais-no-policia-hoje.

Regeringskansliet. (2012). Grovt miljöbrott. Regeringskansliets rättsdatabaser. Stockholm: Regeringskansliet. Retrieved June 13, 2014, from http://rkrattsbaser.gov.se/.

Naturvårdsverket (Swedish Environmental Protection Agency). (2014). Riskbedömning av förorenade områden. Stockholm: Naturvårdsverket. Retrieved April 14, 2015 from www.naturvardsverket.se/Stod-i-miljoarbetet/Vagledningar/Fororenade-omraden/Riskbedomning-av-fororenade-omraden/.

Swedish Homeowners Association (Villaägarnas Riksförbund). (2012). Avfallsavgifter för småhusägare per kommun 2011–2012. Solna: Villaägarnas Riksförbund.

Rikspolisstyrelsen (Swedish National Police Board). (2007). Narkotika och narkotika kemikaler: Samverkan mot olaglig hantering av narkotika och narkotikalika droger. Stockholm: Rikspolisstyrelsen/Läkemedelsverket.

Saumure, R. A., Herman, T. B., & Titman, R. D. (2007). Effects of haying and agricultural practices on a declining species: The North American wood turtle, Glyptemys insculpta. *Biological Conservation, 135*(4), 565–575.

Sazdovska, M. M. (2009). Elimination of ecological crime as a part of organized crime in the former Yugoslav Republic of Macedonia. *Review of International Affairs, 60*, 80–91.

Skinnider, E. (2011). *Victims of environmental crime: Mapping the issues*. Vancouver: International Centre for Criminal Law Reform and Criminal Justice Policy.

Skogsaktuellt. (2012). Antalet anmälda jaktbrott ökar. Retrieved April 14, 2015, from www.skogsaktuellt.se/?p=41490&pt=108&m=1422.

Sundin, J. (2011). Skrotbilar i naturen. Retrieved April 28, 2014, from http://allehanda.se/start/solleftea/1.2557754-skrotbilar-i-naturen?m=print.

Svenska Dagbladet. (2012). Miljöbrott kan få egen enhet Retrieved May 1, 2014, from www.svd.se/nyheter/inrikes/miljobrott-kan-fa-egen-enhet_7084035.svd.

Sveriges Radio. (2010). Större cannabisodling avslöjad. Retrieved May 3, 2014, from http://sverigesradio.se/sida/artikel.aspx?programid=128&artikel=4102382.

Sveriges Radio. (2013). Unga köper aceton för att tillverka narkotika. *P1*. Retrieved May 3, 2014, from http://sverigesradio.se/sida/artikel.aspx?programid=83&artikel=5474620.

Naturvårdsverket (Swedish Environmental Protection Agency). (2011). Utvärdering av tillsynen över verksamhetsutövarens egenkontroll. Stockholm: Naturvårdsverket.

United Nations – UN (2013). World drug report, 2013 (p. 115). Vienna: United Nations Office on Drugs and Crime.

Weisheit, R. A., & Donnermeyer, J. F. (2000). Changes and continuity in crime in rural America. In G. LaFree (Ed.), *Criminal justice 2000: The nature of crime of crime, continuity and change* (pp. 309–357). Washington, DC: US Department of Justice.

White, R. (2003). Environmental issues and the criminological imagination. *Theoretical Criminology, 7*, 483–506.

White, R. (2008). *Crimes against nature: Environmental criminology and ecological justice*. Portland, OR: Willan Publishing.

White, R. (2014). What is to be done about environmental crime? In B. Arrigo & H. Bersot (Eds.), *Handbook of international crime and justice studies* (pp. 445–466). Oxford: Routledge.

Wikipedia. (2014). Dagsböter Retrieved April 14, 2015, from http://sv.wikipedia.org/wiki/Dagsb%C3%B6ter.

Wright, T. F., Toft, C. A., Enkerlin-Hoeflich, E., Gonzalez-Elizondo, J., Albornoz, M., Rodríguez-Ferraro, A.,... Wiley, J. W. (2001). Nest poaching in neotropical parrots. *Conservation Biology, 15*(3), 710–720.

9 Youth in rural areas

Young people are vital for any type of society – but certainly more important for rural communities as their future depends on them. If young people cannot continue living in these communities, the demand for services and other types of consumption decreases, and consequently the community breaks down. Paradoxically, young people are far too often seen as a source of local problems. This chapter attempts to characterize both sides of this coin using available official statistics. It starts with demographic, socioeconomic, and lifestyle differences among young individuals in Sweden as background for understanding regional differences in offending and victimization among youth. This is followed by a discussion of factors associated with youth crime and victimization in rural areas; apparently they are similar to those in urban areas. As much as possible, the Swedish case is compared with the international literature, often from examples coming from British and North American research. The systemic nature of criminogenic conditions that is relevant for small municipalities in Sweden is exemplified here by two phenomena.

i   The south is home to domestic criminal motorcycle groups that have confirmed links to a number of criminal activities. The impact of these organizations and their networks of influence in rural areas opens up for controversy as younger members may belong to the community.
ii   Young people flow into Sweden after being recruited in their home towns, outside Sweden. The rural–urban link is illustrated by tracing individuals' journeys from regions in the Baltic countries to urban Sweden. Thus, young people become cross-border commodities and are often forced to engage in activities orchestrated by grounds that look like criminal networks.

The chapter concludes with a summary of the specificities of the Swedish case.

Youth in Swedish rural areas

In Sweden, the exodus of young people from rural areas to larger urban centers is nothing new, but after decades of relative population stability, the 1990s and particularly 2000s saw new waves of population concentration in Sweden. The country has the strongest trend of urbanization since 2005 in Europe, and young individuals have historically made up a significant share of this inflow to urban centers. Urbanization means that mid-sized and big cities are growing not primarily because people are coming from the countryside, but because the cities are receiving higher immigration from abroad and, for some, have a positive net birth rate (Örstadius, 2014). This development is not geographically homogeneous. Nowadays 141 of the 290 municipalities are experiencing a decline in population. The city regions and their hinterlands are growing, while rural and peripheral areas end up generally losing population (Amcoff & Westholm, 2007; Magnusson & Turner, 2000).

Youth concentrates in big cities: only 22 percent of the rural population is composed of children and adolescents (Karlsson, 2012). The population structure in municipalities outside Sweden's major cities can be described as fairly representative of the entire country. During the past 40 years, the proportion of children and adolescents has decreased, while the proportion aged 65 and over (especially women) has increased (Karlsson, 2012). If current trends persist, in the future several local rural municipalities will fail to offer citizens the vital services the community needs, including basic services.

Population shifts, particularly of young people, affect density of acquaintance-ship, that is, the degree to which members of the community know each other (Weisheit & Donnermeyer, 2000). If people move out, such social ties are broken and may generate socioeconomic instability and "normlessness" (e.g., Kaylen & Pridemore, 2011; Kim & Pridemore, 2005). Changes in residence also mean that young people's daily routines are altered (e.g., longer commutes between residence and workplace), hypothetically putting them at a higher risk of becoming a crime victim than they may have been previously. The situation becomes particularly problematic for young people living in rural areas that have long distances to major labor market areas. Without access to private motor vehicles, public transportation may also be a limiting factor, as buses or trains may not operate frequently on limited geographical routes (Ceccato & Dolmén, 2011).

Other effects on community life may occur when emigration is selective (age, gender, and education related), often leaving behind the poorly educated elderly – and males. In countries like Sweden and Australia, women more often are the ones that leave for study and work. Barclay, Hogg, and Scott (2007) suggest that instead of being a matter of choice, the decision to leave reflects limited economic and cultural opportunities available to young women in many rural communities. Nilsson (2013) shows that in 2012, 44 percent of people aged 24 years old started a college education, but there are large differences between urban and rural municipalities. More than three-quarters of youth in the metropolitan area go to university, while less than one-fifth does in the sparsely populated rural municipalities. There are also gender differences by type of municipality. The greatest difference between the sexes is found in rural municipalities: 21 percentage points between the proportion of men and women who go to university. In municipalities in sparsely populated regions and manufacturing municipalities, too, the differences are relatively large. The smallest difference between females and males that go to university is found in big cities, such as Stockholm and Gothenburg, with 13 percentage points. In the tourism-intensive municipalities close to major cities, the differences are also relatively small. Attainment of college education strongly correlates with the educational level of the parents and the likelihood of further study.

Not only women but young people in general may feel alienated from mainstream values in rural areas, undervalued and under supported (Barclay et al., 2007). In Sweden, not all young people want to move to the cities but many still "jump ship" for big cities. Knape and Strömbäck (2012) report young people's expectations about the future in Sweden. Using the text of 500 letters from secondary school students from north to south municipalities in Sweden, the material was later published by the Swedish Association of Local Authorities and Regions (SKL). The message is clear: many youngsters would prefer to stay where they live now. Knape and Strömbäck (2012) exemplify the motivation of a youngster in northern Sweden.

> Norrland is an obvious option for me because I would like to see children grow up without the stress in the South. They should have the forest and nature around the corner. The fantastic air in Norrland is not harmful to anyone.
>
> (Notes from a student from Arjeplog)

So why are so many leaving? Young people describe their lack of choices by raising a number of issues that flag for the root for the problems. Young people from rural municipalities were invited to point out what was needed for them to stay and, for those who had already left, to return to their home villages. Box 9.1 summarizes the list (Knape & Strömbäck, 2012).

Box 9.1 Youth's wish list for remaining in rural areas

1 **More jobs for young people.** A good job is the most common dream for the future.
2 **Housing that fills the needs of young people at reasonable rents.** This is important to those who have already moved away and face problems finding affordable housing in larger cities.
3 **Better schools.** Young people want a choice of secondary schools in their locality.
4 **Opportunity of living an environmentally friendly life.** These include convenient public transport, safe bike lanes, electric cars, local food, and alternative energy sources.
5 **Having an attractive community.** Creating features that can become a tourist attraction and that they can be proud of, such as a "cool building," sculptures, or a park.
6 **More meeting places for young people.** Creating a culture of acceptance of young people and their leisure needs.
7 **Good and accessible healthcare.**

This "wish list" contains an explicit call for the basics of a rural community (e.g., school, housing, healthcare) as well as an implicit request for better understanding of youth's needs and lifestyle (e.g., meeting places, environmentally friendly lifestyle, attractive landscape). In small municipalities, many services have already been closed down or merged with other community functions. As young people move out, schools may be obliged to close, too. In other cases, secondary education cannot be offered in the local community because there are too few students. Moreover, some mid-sized cities receive a net influx of young people, who may face a housing deficit or rental prices not affordable by the young because of high demand. Similar expectations are found elsewhere (Barclay et al., 2007; Donnermeyer, Jobes, & Barclay, 2006; Woods, 2011).

Meeting places, such as community centers or local youth associations for the young in rural areas may be the only adult-free zones in the community. When they are not open, or when social belonging is denied in certain places, the local pizzeria or gas station may become the gathering place. Harsh winters impose a number of limitations on "just hanging around" with friends in public places. Still, public places such as in interstitial spaces between commercial areas, parks, and school grounds are places where young people are visible. What is an inoffensive youth gathering to most locals can be a source of discontentment to others. In worse cases, they are labeled "the source of the problem" and a symbol of disorder in the local community. Barclay et al. (2007, p. 107) provide examples of when youth are considered trouble in rural Australia, as they may be noisy and have high visibility in public places. The authors point out that young people's visibility and behavior (running, yelling, skateboarding, or bicycling) make them an unwelcome group whether or not they break the law. This puts them in the spotlight but not always in a positive way. Many young people may feel they do not belong, as they are not supported and valued as a group. Youth may perceive safety walks and other safety interventions as intrusive (for details see Chapter 13).

Rye (2006) suggests that although young people's vocabulary for describing their rural environments (in Norway) echoes that of adults, the literature suggests that young people are less likely to subscribe to the idyllic version of rurality. In particular, they seem to emphasize the narrower range of opportunities in rural areas, particularly those related to the limited range of public and private services, especially with respect to leisure and entertainment. In Sweden, Pettersson (2013) indicates a "love–hate relationship" between youth and their rural community, even for those who have already left. The author shows examples of how rural areas can exert a pull effect on young people and, at the same time, how they push them away, lacking attractive qualities.

Life opportunities for those who remain in rural areas are shaped by overall societal contexts that, despite variation over time and space, still reproduce known patterns of choices for family and friends. For some, the prospect of not being able to break out of their parents' patterns is a motivation to leave the countryside. In an ethnographic study, Jonsson (2010) attempted to interpret the everyday lives of some young people and their notions about the future when the survival of rural communities is at risk as a result of the shift from a welfare model to a market-oriented one. The author found that despite differences such as gender and resources, in most cases, youth who remain tend to follow their parents' paths in terms of jobs and lifestyle. This is not to say that the values of young people in rural areas are not constantly changing, quite the opposite. Woods (2011) shows through examples that youth identify formation in rural areas is a complex process that involves in some cases behavior conformity but also testing the boundaries of expected behaviors.

Some changes in values favor rural living, while other changes challenge the rural community. With the emergence of information and communication technology (ICT), for instance, new ways of communication and socialization provide a range of new opportunities in jobs and leisure but at the same time impose challenges to the traditional schemes of social life in rural areas. Some examples are sports and leisure associations. Sandberg (2012) shows, for instance, how Swedish sports associations in rural areas are affected by recent changes in society and struggle to remain alive. Sports associations are experiencing severe problems in the recruitment of new members, volunteer trainers, and board members. According to the author, the shift in societal values has affected people's attitudes toward local associations, forcing the associations to become more market-oriented and adapt their activities to the short-term demands of certain target groups. The study also shows an ongoing conflict between urban and rural associations which in particular concerns the allocation of resources and other political priorities, where rural areas are often the losers.

Youth health and mortality in rural and urban areas

Children's and young people's health and socioeconomic conditions in Sweden are good, even compared to other welfare countries. Sweden – with the other Scandinavian countries and the Netherlands – is among the countries where economic vulnerability of families with children is least extensive (Biterman, 2013). In an era of remote communication, Swedish kids and teenagers have no problem accessing the Internet and the like regardless of where they reside in the country. How is Sweden doing in other dimensions of quality of life?

Sweden is not as much in the forefront in terms of the older kids as it is for children. Symptoms on reduced mental wellbeing are more common among Swedish 15-year-olds than in other European countries. Drug use is less common among Swedish youngsters, while alcohol consumption is at an average European level (Biterman, 2013). There are regional differences in consumption of alcohol, tobacco, and drugs, and trends in consumption vary also by drug type (CAN, 2013). There has been a decrease in youth offending and victimization in recent decades but not homogeneously across the country, and it is rarely related to poor socioeconomic conditions alone (Bäckman, Estrada, Nilsson, & Shannon, 2013).

Symptoms of worry and anxiety among young people have increased since the 1980s regardless of their origins, family circumstances, socioeconomic situation, employment, or social status. The larger the city, the higher the proportion of young people suffering from symptoms of anxiety and worry (Figure 9.1). Young women in rural areas have fewer psychological problems than those living in larger cities. However, for young people who live in small towns the risk of dying in a car accident is several times higher than the risk for young people who live in the three metropolitan areas of Stockholm, Gothenburg, or Malmö.

It is unknown whether mental health affects the mortality of young people in rural areas. What is known is that, between the ages of 15 and 24, young men are more than twice as likely to die as young women are. Although not broken down into rural and urban, data show that in 2011, 136 women and 316 men died aged 15–24 years. The reason for this was that accidents and suicides are more common among young men. Since the early 1990s, suicides have declined in all age groups except 15–24, where suicide has become somewhat more common. Death by alcohol consumption, which in this age usually involves acute alcohol poisoning, has been higher among young men in the 2000s than in the 1990s (Socialstyrelsen, 2013). International literature suggests that in many cases the suicide of a young adult living in a rural setting can be attributed to drug and alcohol use (see e.g., Barclay et al., 2007).

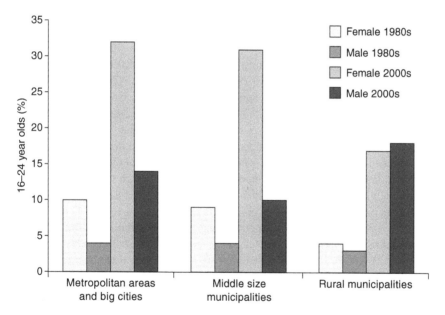

Figure 9.1 Percentage of people who reported mild or severe symptoms of anxiety or anxiety by gender, aged 16–24 (data source: Socialstyrelsen, 2009, p. 83).

Notes
Averages for the years 1988/1989 and 2004/2005. Metropolitan areas=big cities, suburban municipalities, larger cities, and commute municipalities; middle size municipalities=manufacturing municipalities and other municipalities, more than 25,000 inhabitants; rural municipalities=sparsely populated municipalities (less than 7 residents/km² and fewer than 20,000 inhabitants) and other smaller municipalities.

Youth jobs, unemployment, and "no-job-no-education"

Counties in Sweden with large portions of rural population tend to have a slightly larger share of youth without employment, education, or in training (around 13 percent) than those with large urban areas (around 9 percent), such as Stockholm. Sweden tends to have higher youth unemployment than the average for European countries among younger adolescents: the unemployment rate was 34.3 percent among persons aged 15–19, while it was 18.0 percent among 20–24 year olds. Note that unemployment rates include those in education or seeking jobs (Broman & Samuelsson, 2013).

A relatively large proportion of young people in the labor force commute to neighboring countries such as Denmark or Norway to work. Men commute more often than women, but up to 24 years, women make up the majority. In 10 years, the number of cross-border commuters from Sweden to Denmark and Norway more than doubled. Above all, Norway attracts young Swedes, and cross-border commuting is especially prevalent among young people aged 16–29 (Hanaeus & Wahlström, 2014). For many young people, this is an opportunity to have a break after high school studies and to earn money to travel abroad before pursuing higher education. In both Norway and Denmark, the wage levels are higher than in Sweden, which also attracts workers.

Youth leisure and ICT use in rural areas

Recreational activities play important functions in people's lives. This is particularly true for those who live in rural communities where activities are limited in comparison with urban areas. For young people, leisure and sport centers may be the only parent-free zones available to them. The local pub, news agent, and pizzeria as well as the local hotel or gas station are also meeting places for youth. Leisure in rural areas fills another important role. Leisure activities demand professionals in the local community, either paid employees or volunteers, such as sports coaches, trainers, temporary staff, and field workers. Although controversial, recreational activity centers are also said to have a preventative effect against crime.

In Sweden, leisure for young people is closely associated with various sports activities as well as the use of computers (e.g., playing games) and the Internet (e.g., social media). For young women, book reading is also a relatively common activity (SCB, 2009). Regional differences are apparent in recreational activities. Fishing and hunting are common leisure activities in rural Sweden, as would be expected. Recreational fishing is a distinctly male activity, and differences between men and women increase with exercise frequency. Among young women, the lower percentage of women fishing (19 percent) can partially be explained by factors related to family formation, which may also apply to many other recreational activities (SCB, 2009).

Regardless of location in the country, the Internet is the most important news source among young people, according to Findahl (2013). Based on a national Internet users' survey, the author also reports that one-third of young people's

Internet time is spent on social networks in Sweden. More people in the city than in the countryside use a tablet. Among the overall population, the city and the countryside show no significant difference when it comes to the use of the Internet (89 and 88 percent, respectively) and mobile phone (95 percent). On the other hand, more people have smartphones in cities (71 percent) than in rural areas (61 percent), and use it for a longer time (6.8 hours a week versus 5.7 hours). Most have access to broadband in both the city and countryside, but, as might be expected, more people are without broadband in rural than in urban areas: 6 and 4 percent, respectively.

In a study about young people's activities in two rural areas in Sweden, Berg and Holm (2004) found gender differences regarding computer game use, in particular, and in areas such as movies (thrillers for boys and comedies for girls) differences between boys and girls in the city and in the countryside. Young people at risk are extra vulnerable to media exposure in rural areas, as they may be isolated from mainstream community activities. As the authors suggest, the risk in excessive use of media is that it can encourage escapism or abnormal consumption of computer games, for example, and surfing the Internet. There are already groups for users addicted to computer/games and pornographic and sex webpages.

Young homeless in rural areas

Homeless youth can be found both in urban and rural areas and, as shown in the research below, they are often associated with big cities. Young homeless people face specific challenges in rural areas where basic support services may not be available to the same extent as in large cities. There are no generally accepted definitions of homelessness. Homeless youth are individuals who are not more than 21 years of age (often regarded as under 18) for whom it is not possible to live in a safe environment with a relative and who have no other safe alternative living arrangement. Implicit in this definition is the notion that homeless youth are not accompanied by a parent or guardian (Haber & Toro, 2004).

Regardless of country, the young homeless show numerous examples of victimization of different types before becoming homeless and later in their lives. In the United States, for instance, the histories of boys typically include physical abuse during childhood and physical assault on the street, while the experiences of girls are more often marked by sexual abuse during childhood and on the street (Cauce et al., 2000). In Sweden, boys and girls may express higher incidences of depression and various behavioral problems after the period of homelessness compared to people with fixed residences (Swärd, 2001, 2010). There are no good estimates of the number of juveniles or young adults who become homeless after being in jail. In the United States, Toro, Dworsky, and Fowler (2007) follow a number of cases. A shelter for homeless youth in New York City reported that approximately 30 percent of youth they serve have been detained or incarcerated. Interestingly, 49 percent also had a history of out-of-home care placement before incarceration.

In the United States, young homeless people are concentrated in urban areas, while rural areas have more unsheltered persons in families compared to urban areas. Few differences have been found when urban, suburban, and rural homeless youth have been compared (Cauce et al., 2000). Most reports indicate that people who are homeless in rural areas are somewhat younger than those in urban areas (Robertson, Harris, Frit, Noftsinger, & Fischer, 2007). Ethnic minorities are overrepresented among homeless regardless of age. In both rural and urban areas, the majority of people who are chronically homeless are unsheltered, which means living on the streets, in cars, abandoned buildings, and other places not meant for human habitation (Sermons & Henry, 2010). In the United States, about 50,000 youth sleep on the streets for six months or more. Urban areas have a higher total rate of homelessness than rural areas, approximately 29 homeless people per 10,000, while rural areas have a rate of 14 per 10,000, this figure including all ages. There are 13,000 who experience repeated incidences of homelessness (9 percent) and 15,000 who remain homeless over long periods of time (10 percent) (Nationa l Alliance to End Homelessness, 2014).

In Australia, it is estimated that there are 100,000 homeless, half are under 24 years old and 10,000 are children. The largest single cause of homelessness in Australia is domestic and family violence, which overwhelmingly affects women and children. Homelessness is also an issue for indigenous people living in both urban and remote environments. In 2003, indigenous people comprised 10 percent of clients in social services in urban areas, 21 percent in regional areas, and 71 percent in remote areas. For this group, eviction was a more common reason for accessing a service in urban and rural areas than those living in remote areas. The issue for indigenous people is simply that the existing housing stock does not have the capacity to house the indigenous population at reasonable household occupation levels (Australian Government, 2008).

The prevalence rates for homelessness among young people vary regionally in the United Kingdom. In England, Scotland, and Wales only "statutory homeless" people are entitled to housing. Most statistics are based on this group. The percentages are highest in Scotland, including Orkney and Shetland. Rural areas of Northern Ireland tend to mirror rural England, with lower numbers of young people being accepted as homeless. While this almost certainly reflects the wider definitions of prioritized need in Scotland, it may also reflect higher levels of need, though this cannot be established for certain. In England, authorities with the highest rates included 12 of the 32 London boroughs and several authorities in a few coastal towns; Wales, Swansea, Cardiff, much of the south coast were all prominent. The highest rates of homelessness in Northern Ireland were in Belfast and other regional centers. Lower rates of prevalence of homelessness among youth are found in the rural areas of the north of England and the southwest of England, for instance. Authorities in Scotland and Wales tended to report higher numbers of homeless young people than in England. Particularly in rural areas, homelessness can be associated with fracturing of young people's social networks, as they often have to move away from their previous home area to access housing and support services. Homeless people are unlikely to be from minority ethnic backgrounds in Scotland, Wales, or Northern Ireland but they make up the majority of homeless people in England, particularly in London (Quilgars, Johnsen, & Pleace, 2008).

In Sweden, headlines that youth homelessness is increasing have become frequent lately,[1] at least for the larger cities. Homeless rates in Stockholm, Gothenburg, and Malmö are slightly higher but do not differ much from the rates of other Nordic capitals (Benjaminsen & Dyb, 2008). Little is known about the phenomenon across the country. In Stockholm, young homeless constituted 17 percent of the total homeless (2,892) in 2010, but that number was on the rise. Youth homeless often consist of males who have some sort of psychiatric disorder and/or addiction problems, but there are young women, too. Some are temporarily homeless (Stockholms stad, 2010). The truth is that, for several reasons, it is difficult to get reliable data on children and young people 0–21 years living in unsafe housing conditions (Swärd, 2004, 2010). The picture of youth homelessness is patchy, composed of different types of statistics and qualitative accounts based on case studies, often focusing on big cities. What is known is that around 2,500 youngsters were affected by eviction notices between 2008 and 2010. That figure does not include rentals in the "black" market.

Another group overrepresented among the homeless in Sweden is composed of undocumented migrants, and those figures are particularly uncertain for children and youth. Estimates range between 10,000 and 50,000 people and between 2,000 and 3,000 children in this group. Another group of "potentials" are teenagers living in overcrowded conditions. Interviews by Andersson and Swärd (2008) with children in Sweden show that overcrowding was particularly stressful for the teenagers, who would consider living somewhere else as an alternative. Again, this was based on youth living in big Swedish cities.

Another report shows that about 11 percent of youth in secondary school who leave home prematurely do so to escape a parent or partner or because they are thrown out by a parent or partner. Threats of violence, mental and physical abuse and assault are a few crucial factors. Nearly half of young people were 15 or younger when they left home. The majority was girls and left home several times. The report also mentions a survey of Swedish municipalities in 2010, in which half indicated that they had a "roof-over-head guarantee" for individuals who were homeless. Many municipalities do their own surveys of the number of individuals living in homelessness, and every sixth municipality, or about 17 percent, reports an increase in the proportion of young people under 21 years old who are homeless. One-quarter of municipalities have also noticed an increase in families at risk of homelessness. They are both small and large municipalities spread all over the country (Stockholms stadsmission. 2011). These figures, despite being general, are indicators of the existence of youth homeless across the country, at least for some time. It is however unsure how this vulnerability put these young people at risk for addiction, offending, and victimization. What is known is those that are already homeless tend to have problems of addiction of alcohol and drugs (Stockholms stad, 2010).

Alcohol and drug abuse among youth

Youth living in the smallest communities are not immune from substance abuse problems (Edwards, 1995). In the United States, despite popular notions that substance abuse is essentially an urban phenomenon, recent data demonstrates that it is also a significant problem in rural America. Rural youth now abuse most substances, including alcohol and tobacco, at higher rates and at younger ages than their urban peers (Pruitt, 2009). Edwards (1995) finds that community risk for youth substance abuse is not simply a matter of population density or proximity to urban areas. Rural and urban youth differ in many ways, such as economic conditions, ethnic representation, and proximity to drug sources. Pruitt (2009) also suggests that limited social services and healthcare infrastructures undermine the efficacy of programs toward youth dependency of drugs and alcohol in rural areas. The engagement of school in young people's lives after school hours may be fundamental to keep them away from trouble. For instance, Shears, Edwards, and Stanley (2006) found a strong negative correlation between school bonding and substance use, no matter the level of rurality. Results also suggest that school bonding might act as a preventative to drunkenness and marijuana use in the most remote communities.

In the 1990s, Edwards (1995) compared substance use by youth by community size and found that there is little difference in the percentage of youth using alcohol by community size, but the use of alcohol causes more problems for rural youth than for youth living elsewhere. The author suggests that this may be in part because fewer alternative leisure activities are available to rural youth and drinking becomes one of the primary purposes for congregating, which may lead to more consumption at any given time. Less surprisingly, the author found a lower level of drug use among youth in very small, rural communities than among those in larger rural and metropolitan communities. In the 2000s, adolescent substance use in rural communities was equal to or greater than urban use for many substances. Rural teens abuse virtually all drugs at rates greater than their urban counterparts, whether cocaine (associated more with urban areas) or methamphetamine (associated more with rural areas). Differences are noticeable between different ethnic groups. Moreover, non-metropolitan youth and young adults are significantly more likely to engage in binge drinking. Rural youth also abuse hallucinogens at higher rates than their urban counterparts (Pruitt, 2009; Shears et al., 2006). The contrast between the rural communities illustrates that even communities similar in size and geographic location can have very different youth drug-use profiles.

In the United Kingdom, rates of illicit drug use among young people (15–16 years old) in England and Wales are high but have been decreasing since the 1990s. According to the European Monitoring Centre for Drugs and Drug Addiction (EMCDDA, 201220/13), two in five 15-year-olds in the United Kingdom have tried cannabis. This number is higher than anywhere else in Europe. Along with Spain, the United Kingdom also has the highest number of young cocaine users. The European School Survey Project on

Alcohol and Other Drugs (ESPAD, 2012) found that 26 percent of boys and 29 percent of girls in the United Kingdom had indulged in binge drinking at least three times in the previous month. As many as 42 percent of boys and 35 percent of girls admitted they had tried illegal drugs at least once. According to a report published by the Home Office (2012–2013), frequent drug users compose 3.1 percent of the total young population in urban areas and 1.8 percent in rural areas. However, statistics from British Crime Survey reveal the proportion of 16–24 year olds reporting use of drugs in the preceding year was practically the same in rural and urban areas, 23 percent and 22.4 percent, respectively (Hoare, 2009). Although "illegal drug use may not only be seen as part of many young people's lifestyles but, significantly, part of the lifestyles of young living in rural areas," little is known about drug use in rural areas (Barton, Storey, & Palmer, 2011, p. 149).

Compared with youth in other European countries, fewer Swedish adolescents consume alcohol, but those who drink do it in greater quantity. This is clear from the 2012 ESPAD survey. In Sweden, less than 40 percent of 15–16 year olds drank alcohol in the 30 days preceding the time of the survey, while in countries such as Denmark, Germany, and Greece more than 70 percent of 15–16 year olds consumed alcohol. Although alcohol consumption is on the decrease throughout Europe, the trend is clear in Sweden. The decrease in alcohol consumption has also been confirmed by Ring (2013) (Table 9.1).

The estimated average annual consumption of alcohol by ninth graders is almost 3 liters for boys and just less than 2 liters for girls (CAN, 2013). This compares with a total population average annual consumption of about 9 liters of pure alcohol. This downward trend in alcohol consumption among ninth graders has many different potential causes, and the fact that young people start to drink later in life is one. They start drinking when they are about 13 years old, and in 2012 one in three ninth graders had alcohol-related problems after consumption, including fights, accidents, injuries, relationship problems, financial loss or theft, poorer school performance, and unwanted or unprotected sex.

Young people in Swedish rural areas consume on average 1.6 liters less than youth living in large cities, Stockholm being the leader (Guttormsson, Andersson, & Hibell, 2004), but there are regional differences in consumption of alcohol. Urban counties and high-density counties such as Skåne, Stockholm, and Västra Götaland tend to have higher rates of consumption among youth than rural and more remote areas of northern Sweden. Southern Sweden reports high numbers for several related indicators of alcohol consumption, while Stockholm County is high in terms of experience with drugs and daily tobacco use.

The threat of the Internet as a source of drugs has been said to be overestimated, at least for young people. As many as 2 percent of girls and 3 percent of boys in ninth grade, and 2 percent of girls and 5 percent of boys in the second year of upper secondary school have used a drug bought over the Internet. Spice and its variants are the most common group of substances available. Friends or acquaintances are commonly the main source of the drug. A little more than 1 percent of young people have themselves bought a drug online (CAN, 2013).

Table 9.1 Usage patterns among Swedish students (year 9) who used drugs, 2000–2013 (%)

	N	Use of cannabis	Use of other narcotics only	Use of both	Use of narcotics in the previous 30 days	Use of narcotics 6 or more times	Debut in use of cannabis at age 14 or younger
2000	455	59.5	8.0	24.0	26.1	28.8	–
2001	503	53.1	10.0	30.4	27.2	34.3	41.8
2002	438	58.6	7.6	25.8	32.5	34.3	47.5
2003	376	61.6	9.9	20.9	26.2	33.9	55.4
2004	396	61.0	6.2	24.0	32.5	34.5	41.5
2005	376	57.0	9.2	25.9	31.1	34.6	41.7
2006	304	50.4	12.9	24.1	31.1	32.1	38.9
2007	299	49.9	11.7	33.2	25.5	35.1	33.2
2008	300	54.5	7.1	31.1	28.7	34.1	41.6
2009	415	56.1	8.2	28.3	28.3	38.3	42.4
2010	404	61.0	7.6	23.8	32.6	39.7	38.5
2011	385	50.4	9.6	29.7	22.1	41.5	46.0
2012	313	61.2	3.4	26.7	27.1	39.4	40.8
2012[1]	334	64.6	6.9	24.9	32.4	41.0	35.6
2013	322	66.2	5.3	21.9	32.1	43.8	41.9

Source: Gripe and Leifman (2013).

Note

1 From 2012, Spice is included as cannabis.

Table 9.2 Alcohol, narcotics, and tobacco among Swedish students (year 9), 2012–2013 (%)

Region	Use of alcohol in the previous 12 months	Smoke daily	Use sometimes narcotics
Stockholm County*	53	4	8
Skåne*	57	5	8
Västra Götlands County*	53	5	7
South Sweden (Kronoberg, Kalmar, Gotland, Blekinge, and Halland)	58	3	6
Central Sweden (Uppsala, Södermanland, Östergötland, Värmland, Örebro, Västmanland, Dalarna, and Gävleborg)	51	4	6
North Sweden (Västernorrland, Jämtland, Västerbotten, and Norrbotten)	49	3	4

Source: Gripe and Leifman (2013).

Note
* These counties contain the three metropolitan areas: Stockholm, Malmö, and Gothenburg, respectively.

Chapter 8 shows that drug production is at a relatively low level, around 1 percent of all crimes (BRÅ, 2012). It is unknown how much production affects use, but people who produce drugs are believed to be addicts themselves. In Sweden, most illegal laboratories found by the police in 2006 manufactured amphetamines, but other synthetic drugs, such as methamphetamine, were also produced (Rikspolisstyrelsen, 2007). Smuggling of drugs and alcohol contributes to overall consumption, but the statistics are not broken down by age. Local newspapers have also reported a few cases of the use of acetone by young people in rural areas for drug production. Karlsson (2013) indicates that only a few percent of the population use anabolic androgenic steroids and they are mostly young males (20–30 years old), individuals who have an interest in working out and competition, or members of criminal gangs, and use the drug to improve their performance.

Youth offending in rural areas

Poverty and deprivation alone are rarely the sole cause of youth-related problems in rural areas but are clearly important predictors of youth offending (Barton et al., 2011; Bäckman et al., 2013; Estrada & Nilsson, 2012; Ford, 2008; Osgood & Chambers, 2003). Many of the potential wellsprings of youth crime are similar in many ways to those in urban areas: socioeconomic deprivation, family breakdown, abuse and neglect, and drug and alcohol abuse (Barclay et al., 2007; Donnermeyer, 1995). Donnermeyer (1995) posed the following question: Why do rural young people commit crime? For the author, the answer relates to economic, social, and cultural forces. Institutions that reinforce law-abiding behavior have become weaker, while peer and other groups that encourage law-breaking behavior have gained in influence. These factors create conditions in which some rural communities are more likely to exhibit weaker social control and/or stronger influences from deviance-reinforcing peer and other groups. These are certainly the necessary conditions but still do not explain relationships between an individual's circumstances, addiction, and offending. Some of these young people receive little attention from society until they become "trouble" and attract disproportionate attention from the criminal justice system afterwards.

The truth is that young people grow and interact simultaneously in different social contexts in which family, school, peers, and the community are central. Many of the risk factors for addiction and/or crime may be at work in different ways depending on the environment in which they are exposed (e.g., Wikström, Ceccato, Hardie, & Treiber, 2010), either rural or urban. Barclay et al. (2007) mention studies that point out aspects of contemporary rural life that impose additional pressures on young people. For instance, small populations and the fact that everybody knows everybody in rural communities also mean that anything young people do, suffers more social control by the community than in big cities. In this section, a brief discussion of factors related to criminal involvement are discussed taking into account as much as possible the rural–urban differences in the United States, the United Kingdom, Australia, and Sweden.

The criminological literature has long shown that being male is by far the most common risk factor for offending. Crime-prone youth come from poor socioeconomic conditions, which affect family relationships and health, more often than others. Adolescents who come from a family with long-term social allowance assistance or who have a parent who was sentenced to prison are more likely than others to commit repeat offenses. Having a single parent also increases the chances of a child's criminal activity. School-related factors, such as grades, truancy, and dropping out, have been previously shown to have clear connections with juvenile delinquency. Ethnic minorities are often associated with greater engagement in youth offending, which has partly been explained by cultural differences, social exclusion, and the discriminatory exercise of authority by the police and judiciary (for a summary of these factors, see Bäckman et al., 2013; Payne & Welch, 2013). Do rural youth differ from those living in large urban areas in relation to offending risk factors?

Rural per capita rates of juvenile arrest for violent offenses are significantly and consistently associated with residential instability, ethnic diversity, and family disruption in non-metropolitan communities in Florida, Georgia, Nebraska, and South Carolina (Osgood & Chambers, 2003). Family disruption, in particular, appears to be a critical element of social disorganization in non-metropolitan communities. The study results diverged from the standard findings for urban areas in that they indicated no association between poverty and delinquency. These findings support Shaw and McKay's contention that it is not poverty per se but an association of poverty with other factors that weakens systems of social relationships in a community, thereby producing social disorganization (Osgood & Chambers, 2003).

Kaylen and Pridemore (2011) contest the degree of generalizability of social disorganization as an explanation of the distribution of youth violence to rural areas. The nature of social structure and its impact on social relations in rural communities may be different from that in urban communities. As examples, the authors refer to findings that collective efficacy (Sampson, Raudenbush, & Earls, 1997) or social capital (Bourdieu, 2000) moderates the effects of social structure on crime.

When social capital is put to the test, its effect on crime is not as neat as might be expected. Deller and Deller (2010) suggest that, although the impact of social capital on crime is significant (that certain elements of social capital have a strong negative association with rural crime rates), this effect is not the same for all types of crime. Moreover, while the results of this study suggest that higher levels of social capital have a dampening effect on rural crime, these findings are highly dependent on the measures used as "social capital."

On a small scale, social capital may have an effect on the wellbeing of young people living in rural areas or in isolated communities. Björnberg (2010) shows an example of children and young people living in communities waiting to be granted residency in Sweden. In a period of uncertainty for asylum seekers and other immigrant families, contact with relatives in their home country, friends, as well as persons in official contexts, the schools, and healthcare are all fundamental to wellbeing and future achievement.

Trends and geographical patterns of youth offending

Crime rates among young people declined between 1995 and 2011, but a recent study from the Swedish National Board of Health and Welfare shows that the group that engages in criminal activities as teenagers and young adults suffers consequences that may last their whole lives. The report shows that youngsters who have been convicted of crimes have significantly worse health in young adulthood compared to those without a criminal record, especially when it comes to alcohol and drug abuse. Young people who are prosecuted as teenagers or young adults are also at a significantly higher risk to remain outside the labor market in middle age (Bäckman et al., 2013). The good news is that, as previously mentioned, criminal involvement at young ages has decreased.

National surveys show that the proportion of students in ninth grade (15 years old) who report they committed any theft-related action, such as burglary, receiving stolen goods, shoplifting, or bicycle theft, has declined, from 66 to 45 percent, a decline evident throughout Sweden (Ring, 2013). Theft and criminal damage decreased most. The author suggests that attitudes toward committing crime have become less permissive. For example, the percentage of students indicating that they would think it was "okay" or "pretty okay" if their buddies shoplifted in a store decreased, from 27 percent in 1997, to 17 percent in 2011. Strong family ties and better social control by adults seem to be related to less crime involvement. Those who commit crime hang out with friends who are more often crime prone and they have overall a more permissive attitude toward crime.

The pattern of youth violent crime is more fragmented when assessed in three different cohorts (from 1965 to 1985). The proportion of young people prosecuted for assault increased for these cohorts, while there is no evidence that young people's use of violence and exposure to violence has increased, as victims and self-assessment studies show. For serious violence requiring medical attention or resulting in the victim's death, both hospital data and mortality statistics indicate levels have been stable in recent decades (Bäckman et al., 2013).

The decrease in offending among youth in Sweden is not geographically homogeneous. A report from BRÅ (2007) shows that for Skåne County, in south Sweden, for example, where the third largest city of the country is located (Malmö), levels are significantly higher for two of the three types of crime studied (vandalism and violent crime). Another source shows a similar trend in the arrest of minors. Skåne is also the county where young minors are most often put in jail in Sweden, followed by the Stockholm metropolitan areas. A police district in the municipality of Malmö alone accounts for two-thirds of nearly 600 arrests in 2011 (Bubenko, 2013). For Västmanland and Stockholm counties the situation is similar, whilst for the remote Västernorrland County and the inland county of Jönköping the situation is reversed. In the two latter counties, the proportion of adolescents who report involvement in crime is consistently low for all types of crime. Figures 9.2 and 9.3 illustrate the change in percentage of youth involvement in thefts and violence in

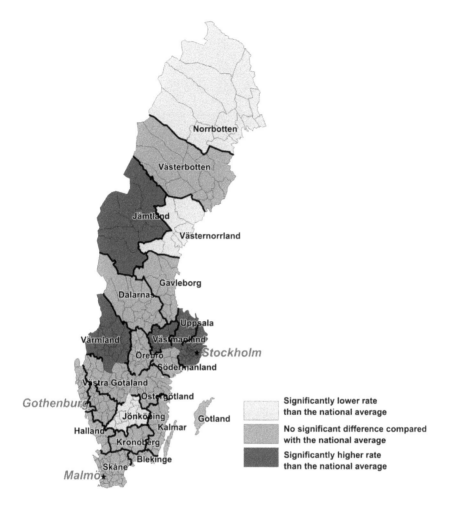

Figure 9.2 Change in percentage of youth (15 years old) who reported that they committed theft, 1995–2005 (source: BRÅ, 2007).

1995 and 2005. Violence clearly shows a more urban pattern than thefts do.
Note that all percentage changes are significantly higher in two metropolitan
areas: Stockholm and Malmö.

Despite this decrease in youth offending, Hellgren (2010) shows that all
metropolitan counties – Stockholm, Gothenburg, and Malmö – as well as
Sweden as a whole have experienced an increase since 2000 in the number of
15–20 year olds suspected of assault. The increase is said to be associated the
so-called "enforcement waves" targeting particular crimes. The author suggests that this is not an indicator that youth violence is increasing. Vulnerability to violence or the threat of young people has not increased during the

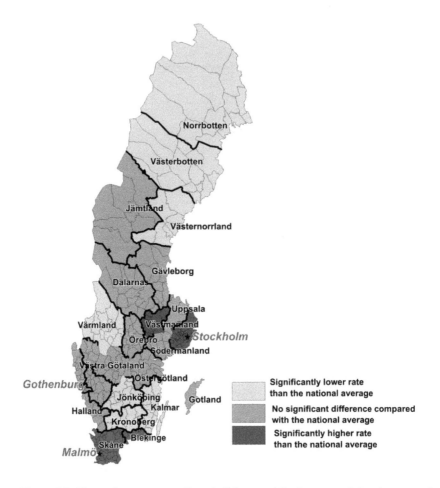

Figure 9.3 Change in percentage of youth (15 years old) who reported that they committed violence, 1995–2005 (source: BRÅ, 2007).

same period. Victimization surveys and life-conditions surveys as well as school surveys indicate no increase in victimization among 16–24 year olds and 16–19 year olds. In the worst case, levels can be interpreted as relatively stable, and in the best case we can speak of a slight decrease in the number of young people exposed to any violence or abuse. The link between alcohol consumption and violence is not clear among those under 18 years old. The amount of alcohol consumed by ninth graders has increased since 1995, but violence has not. These findings apply to all counties and for Sweden as a whole. The author suggests that it is possible that alcohol becomes more relevant and shows a clear correlation with violent crime when young people turn 18 and therefore become more mobile.

Youth and organized crime

Southern Sweden, particularly the Skåne region, is known for its organized crime. In a brief study of youth organized crime groups in Skåne, Cruce (2004) finds that they are composed of young members (15–17 years old) with an over-representation of foreign-born adolescents. About 90 percent of these criminal organizations are composed of boys. The gangs are mostly in large urban areas in western Skåne. These areas are disadvantaged, characterized by segregation and a high proportion of unemployed persons. The crimes committed by the groups are mainly theft and vandalism, violent crimes, and drug offenses. Some offenses are preceded by active planning, while others are spur of the moment. Working in crime prevention with these groups is a challenge, and at best only temporal effects are achieved as the group moves to another location. The author suggests that these organized criminal groups demand enhanced cooperation with society's other actors (more than the police) who have to work with a long-term form of intervention based on in-depth relationships with these youngsters.

Another type of organization criminals use is the motorcycle gang. These gangs recruit young people but are not seen as youngsters' organizations. The two most influential criminal motorcycle gangs (Hells Angels and Bandidos) were initially based in the southern cities of Malmö and Helsingborg and in Stockholm. After the mid-1990s, the number of these mobile criminal organizations expanded significantly, and, in the mid-2000s, they were represented in 24 municipalities in Sweden. Geographically, they are mainly in southern Sweden and have expanded into smaller rural communities.

The business of criminal motorcycle gangs includes financial crime, drugs, extortion, and theft crimes. The local police often know who the members are and focus on disrupting their activities in different ways. It is more difficult to intervene when members come from the local community. One way to obstruct them has been to prevent these groups from buying or renting premises in a community. Surveillance on certain points where they meet is said to have helped to hamper their business. Although raids against the club premises and members' homes are common, it is unclear how much these disturbances affect local crime in these communities. To answer this question, Hilldén (2006) examined whether municipalities' crime rates were affected by the existence of criminal motorcycle gangs. The author used a panel of municipal data for the years 1996–2003 as a basis for the analysis. Findings show that the number of reported crimes actually decreased as criminal motorcycle gangs were established in the municipality. Interestingly, Hilldén (2006) finds similar results in an examination of the long-term effects of these criminal organizations on crime reporting rates. The author suggests that this decrease may be the result of a deterrent effect developed because of gang presence and/or by intimidation and other methods used by the gangs that lead to fewer reported crimes.

In 2007, the Police in southeast Sweden (Östergötland County) started tackling the problem of criminal motorcycle gangs, and the effect on reported crime was the opposite. Nissle (2009) found an increase in reported crime from year to year for most categories of crime associated with organized crime (assault, extortion, drug trafficking, and financial crimes). This was also confirmed when the author broke down the statistics at the municipality level, where biker gangs have been active. Drug offenses are mostly driven by criminal motorcycle gangs. There was a fairly significant increase in drug reported offenses in Norrköping and Linköping when the police started targeting these criminal motorcycle gangs (as these crimes were more targeted by the police). In one of the municipalities, the motorcycle gang left and a declining trend in crime records was observed.

Youth as victims of crime: regional differences

The proportions of young people who say they are victims of violence have not increased in recent years. The proportion of victims of serious violence is about the same level as in the 1980s. Since the 1970s, around 15 individuals aged 10–24 years have died as a result of violence each year. Boys are more vulnerable to abuse than girls. Girls are in turn considerably more exposed to sexual violence than boys. Furthermore, there is a clear pattern in which young men are more often a victim of violence in public places, while violence against young women occurs more often indoors. BRÅ (2007) shows that between 1995 and 2005 an annual average of nearly one-third of ninth-grade pupils in Sweden were victimized by crime: theft of bicycles, wallets, or other valuable property in the 12 months preceding the survey. Rural counties, especially in northern Sweden, often have the lowest level of reported victimization by theft among young people: Västernorrland, Jämtland, Norrbotten, and Dalarna. Västmanland exhibits higher levels than the national average but not greater than Örebro County, in the center inland of the country, where 37 percent of youth have been victimized.

The urban–rural divide is clearer for declared victimization by violence among youth. The lowest proportions of adolescents (around 10–12 percent) who report exposure to or the threat of serious violence are found in the counties of northern Sweden. The highest levels are found in Stockholm and Skåne counties, where the average is around 17 percent. Figures 9.4 and 9.5 show the geography of victimization among youth by county.

Local demand, global supply: when young people become cross-border commodities

Much has been in the news about human trafficking and its consequences for those involved and for society in general. In Sweden, human trafficking is thought to be the tip of the iceberg of other crimes, often organized by criminal networks that connect rural areas (in the country of origin) with urban areas (in the host country) across multiple borders. Since the Swedish crime code (human trafficking for sexual purposes) came into force in 2003, records indicate a doubling: 22 to 40 cases in 2013 (BRÅ, 2014). As much as 65 percent of the cases were recorded in the most urban counties of Stockholm and Malmö alone, one-third of these cases referring to children under 18 years old. As with any other type of organized crime, these numbers reveal only a small part of the problem.

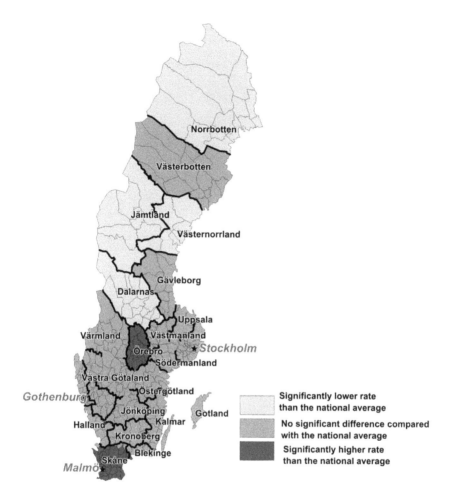

Figure 9.4 Change in percentage of youth (15 years old) who were victimized by theft, 1995–2005 (source: BRÅ, 2007).

Wennerholm (2002) suggests that the causes of trafficking are complex, inter-twined, and context-specific, with poverty and unequal gender relations the key underlying root causes. The situation of women and children in countries of origin, the profit motive, the ease with which trafficking occurs, and the demand for women and children for different exploitative purposes are principal supply and demand factors.

About 10 years ago, the Youth Shelter in Stockholm was put in touch with 71 young people with unclear identities who were apprehended committing crimes. As suggested by the report from the Administrative Board of Stockholm County (2007), one-third of these individuals were younger than 18 years old, coming from

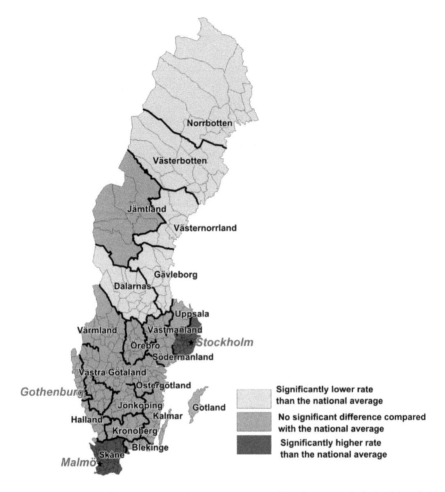

Figure 9.5 Change in percentage of youth (15 years old) who were victimized by violence, 1995–2005 (source: BRÅ, 2007).

central Europe, northern Africa, and former Soviet states, particularly Baltic countries. They were brought to steal, rob, and/or engage in prostitution. The link between rural and urban is clear in some of the cases in the report. They leave the small villages in which they are recruited to go to big cities where they find a lucrative market. One example is the case of "Maria," a young woman who was recruited in a small town in a Baltic country. In her early teens, Maria began working at nightclubs in the small town where she was born. She wanted so badly to be independent, that she was thrilled when some men asked her, "Do you want to come with us to Sweden?" But what she perhaps hoped was the road to financial independence became something completely different. Her stay in Sweden meant instead serving men in Stockholm under the control of pimps. As the report reveals, a day in Maria's life could progress in a mental vacuum created by the use of alcohol and drugs, sexual abuse, and violence of all types. It has been 10 years since this group became a symbol of the local effects of organized crime, and the problem remains. Vulnerable young people come from poor backgrounds, some having grown up in an orphanage or as street children, others perhaps sold into a criminal network by their parents. They are reluctant to cooperate with the Swedish authorities because they are terrorized by stories made up by the criminals who brought them to Sweden. "It is a fact that they do not perceive that they have something to gain by telling the truth. The threat from the adult criminal who 'owns' them is greater than the help we can offer," says a representative of the Youth Division.

Sweden is part of the northern market for prostitution. Wennerholm (2002, p. 14) states that young women from Russia and Estonia cross the border into Finland, Sweden, and Norway every weekend, sometimes encouraged by husbands or other relatives. In small villages in the country of origin, where social ties are strong, threats and harassment can have a tremendous impact on women and children, keeping them in compliance with the traffickers. Bus drivers, hotel and campsite owners, and pimps all make money on this. These informal criminal networks may be as dangerous as mafia groups. Stockholm is not the only destination in Sweden. Wennerholm (2002, p. 10) refers to other cases elsewhere in the country: "A 16-year-old Lithuanian girl found dead on a highway outside Malmö in southern Sweden. She committed suicide after escaping from an apartment where she earned her living selling sexual services."

In Sweden, prostitution is officially acknowledged as a form of male sexual violence against women and children and, since a 1999 law, sex buyers, if caught, go to jail. Just after the law took effect, the presence of foreign women in street prostitution was reported to have vanished, as the number of buyers reportedly decreased 75–90 percent (Gripenlöf, 1991–2002). Nowadays the lack of a presence of women in certain streets could be seen as an indicator that prostitution is winding down, as many contacts are made remotely and through dealers. Still, pimps, traffickers, and customers of sexual services knowingly exploit the vulnerability of young women who often come from the continent.

It is difficult to obtain precise statistics for the problem of young victims of human trafficking and sexual exploitation, especially outside big city centers. However, it is clear that this type of organized crime is often expressed at the local level, so it is important to quickly identify it when it happens. Local authorities in the host country must cooperate to identify the cases, but also authorities in the countries of origin – local and regional as well as national levels – must cooperate to fight organized crime and, in this case, the exploitation of young people.

Ekberg (2004) indicates that Sweden recognizes that, to succeed in the campaign against sexual exploitation, the political, social, and economic conditions under which women live must be improved through economic and social development action, such as poverty reduction and social programs focusing specifically on women. This political goal is legitimate but is hindered by a number of challenges, as the sources of these problems are beyond Swedish borders. Programs in countries of origin have been put in place together with nongovernmental organizations to prepare local actors to fight trafficking. These programs are shown to be fundamental to protecting young girls through information, creating national networks against trafficking in each of the origin countries (see e.g., Wennerholm, 2002). Chapters 13 and 14 discuss suggestions for preventing crime against youth and women in more detail.

Concluding remarks

Youth are a major concern for those living in rural areas. Young people need schooling, healthcare, affordable housing, and leisure activities that are not always attainable locally. The need to provide the "basics" to young people is seen as fundamental, as it keeps alive hopes for survival of the rural community. There are also other concerns associated with young people that are not primarily related to young people (drinking, drug use, acts of delinquency, and crime) but do start to appear early in life and feed the image of young people as "troublemakers." These two facets of rural youth are present in Swedish rural areas and, as shown in this chapter, elsewhere. It is suggested here that a more nuanced view of young people as a group is needed, going beyond the received dichotomy of young people as either "community saviors" or "troublemakers." This current view, it is argued here, creates unreal expectations on young people and puts them under unnecessary pressure. Chapter 13 will illustrate some actions targeting young people, which could well become intrusive in the name of the "common good" of the community.

Another conclusion that can be drawn from this chapter is that one should avoid trying to generalize about rural youth's conditions in Sweden, even in rural areas. For example, youth in sparsely populated areas in northern Sweden enjoy a number of advantages that may not be found in the south, and the opposite is also true, for those living in accessible areas. These advantages and disadvantages in terms of life opportunities are shaped by the specific dynamics of local contexts (family, school, community). The example of alcohol and drug addiction is typical. There is a need for better understanding of the community factors affecting differences in alcohol and drug use. In other words, why do communities with similar conditions end up with different outcomes in terms of drug and alcohol addiction? The same question can be posed concerning levels of offending and victimization among youth. Drug production, alcohol smuggling, and overconsumption of legal drugs among youngsters are topics that have to be included on a future research agenda.

That is not to say that we cannot find any trends that characterize both urban and rural environments. In an exploratory way, Table 9.3 shows 10 items – put side-by-side – that characterize rural youth's conditions, levels of offending, and victimization in Sweden. The patterns that emerge suggest that for six items, rural areas are better off (better mental health, less housing shortage, less alcohol and drug addiction, offending, and victimization), while for five items urban areas are better off (large share of young people, wide range of entertainment, education, job opportunities, and access to ICT). Without claiming any causal relationship between areas and conditions,

Table 9.3 Summary of the characteristics of life conditions for youth in Sweden

	Rural areas	Urban areas
Share of young people	Low –	High +
Leisure/youth lifestyle	Low –	High +
Educational attainment	Low –	High +
Job opportunities	Low –	High +
ICT infrastructure and access	Similar +	Similar +
Housing shortage/homelessness	Low +	High –
Alcohol and drug addiction	Low +	High –
Victimization	Low +	High –
Offending	Low +	High –
Mental health conditions	High +	Low –

Table 9.3 illustrates potential starting points for future research. For instance, is the attractiveness of urban areas overstated by young people? Is there a mismatch between what rural areas can offer and what youth need and expect? Or can a place be at the same time both attractive and unattractive (this ambivalence has long being indicated by the push–pull effect, as suggested by Ravenstein, 1885)? Addressing these issues requires an extension of the research that goes beyond urban–rural comparisons.

Another way of seeing the problem beyond the urban–rural divide is considering young people influenced by (very) different regional contexts. This chapter also shows that there is a north–south divide in drug and alcohol consumption, offending, and victimization among young people. Youngsters living in municipalities within the triangle enclosed by Stockholm, Gothenburg, and Malmö counties – the most urbanized area of Sweden – are often more exposed to alcohol and drugs, tend to suffer poorer mental health, and are more often involved in criminal activities and become victims of crime. It is also in this area where signs of organized crime involving young people are visible. The latter stretches beyond national borders, linking young women in the Baltic countries to large cities in Sweden, and between rural and urban areas, with recruitment of young males from suburbs to motorcycle gangs in the rural south.

The Swedish cases shown in this chapter illustrate that even the smallest communities are not immune to problems of substance use and crime. However, variability across communities makes it imperative that each individual community assesses its particular problems so that resources can be allocated appropriately. Chapter 13 takes these issues forward.

Note

1 *Dagens Nyheter*, November 19, 2007, Allt fler 80-talister bland Stockholms hemlösa [Ever more young people among Stockholm's homeless]; *Dagens Nyheter*, August 21, 2009, Lotsar ska hjälpa unga hemlösa att ändra sitt liv ["Pilots" to help direct young homeless to new lives]; SVT rapport February 1, 2011, Fattiga barn får ett utanförskap [Children in poverty made outsiders].

References

Administrative Board of Stockholm County. (2007). Organiserad brottslighet: ett hinder för långsiktigt hållbar tillväxt i Östersjöregionen. Stockholm: Administrative Board of Stockholm County.

Amcoff, J., & Westholm, E. (2007). Understanding rural change: Demography as a key to the future. *Futures, 39*(4), 363–379.

Andersson, G., & Swärd, H. (2008). Vad kan hemlösa barn berätta om dagens hemlöshet? *Socialmedicinsk tidskrift, 85*(1), 55–60.

Australian Government. (2008). Which way home? A new approach to homelessness. Canberra: Commonwealth of Australia. Retrieved April 14, 2015, from www.ag.gov.au/cca.

Bäckman, O., Estrada, F., Nilsson, A., & Shannon, D. (2013). Unga och brott i Sverige (p. 53). Stockholm: Socialstyrelsen.

Barclay, E., Hogg, R., & Scott, J. (2007). Young people and crime in rural communities. In E. Barclay, J. Donnermeyer, J. Scott, & R. Hogg (Eds.), *Crime in rural Australia* (pp. 100–114). Sidney: Federation Press.

Barton, A., Storey, D., & Palmer, C. (2011). A trip in the country? Policing drug use in rural settings. In R. Mawby & R. Yarwood (Eds.), *Rural policing and policing the rural: A constable countryside?* (pp. 147–167). Farnham: Ashgate.

Benjaminsen, L. & Dyb, E. (2008). The effectiveness of homeless policies: Variations among the Scandinavian countries. *European Journal of Homelessness, 2*. Retrieved April 14, 2015, from www.feantsaresearch.org/spip.php?article32&lang=en.

Berg, N., & Holm, A. (2004). Om niondeklassares kultur- och medievanor i stad och på landsbygd: En självrapporteringsstudie ur ett genusperspektiv (Master's degree, Örebro University, Örebro).

Biterman, D. (2013). Barns och ungas hälsa, vård och omsorg 2013 (p. 306). Stockholm: Socialstyrelsen.

Björnberg, U. (2010). Socialt kapital, tillit och resilience hos asylsökande barn och föräldrar. In H. A. H. E. Andersson, U. Björnberg, & M. Eastmond (Eds.), *Mellan det förflutna och framtiden Asylsökande barns välfärd, hälsa och välbefinnande* (pp. 111–140). Gothenburg: Geson Hylte Tryck.

Bourdieu, P. (2000). *Pascalian meditations*. Cambridge: Polity Press.

Broman, A., & Samuelsson, D. (2013). Ungdomars arbetsmarknadssituation: en europeisk jämförelse. *Statistika Meddelanden*, 1–48.

Brottsförebyggande rådet – BRÅ (National Council of Crime Prevention). (2007). Ungdomar och brott i Sveriges län 1995–2005 (Vol. 30, p. 44). Stockholm: BRÅ.

Brottsförebyggande rådet – BRÅ (National Council of Crime Prevention). (2012). Brottsutvecklingen i sverige år 2008–2011, Narkotikabrott (pp. 211–231). Stockholm: BRÅ.

Brottsförebyggande rådet – BRÅ (National Council of Crime Prevention). (2014). Police recorded statistics. Stockholm: BRÅ.

Bubenko, A. (2013). 595 skånska ungdomar i arresten 2011. *P4-Malmöhus*. Retrieved April 14, 2015, from http://sverigesradio.se/sida/artikel.aspx?programid=96&artikel=5426785.

Centralförbundet för alkohol- och narkotikaupplysning – CAN. (2013). Skolelevers drogvanor 2013. Stockholm: CAN.

Cauce, A. M., Paradise, M., Ginzler, J. A., Embry, L., Morgan, C. J., Lohr, Y., & Theofelis, J. (2000). The characteristics and mental health of homeless adolescents: Age and gender differences. *Journal of Emotional and Behavioral Disorders, 8*(4), 230–239.

Ceccato, V., & Dolmén, L. (2011). Crime in rural Sweden. *Applied Geography, 31*(1), 119–135.

County Administrative Board of Stockholm County (2007). Organiserad brottslighet: ett hinder för långsiktigt hållbar tillväxt i Östersjöregionen (Vol. 4, p. 56). Stockholm: County Administrative Board of Stockholm County.

Cruce, M. (2004). Organiserad ungdomskriminalitet i Skåne: En kartläggning av gäng-bildning bland ungdomar (p. 20). Umeå: Umeå Universitet.

Deller, S. C., & Deller, M. A. (2010). Rural crime and social capital. *Growth and Change, 41*(2), 221–275.

Donnermeyer, J. (1995). Crime and violence in rural communities. Columbus, OH: National Rural Crime Prevention Center.

Donnermeyer, J. F., Jobes, P., & Barclay, E. (2006). Rural crime, poverty and rural com-munity. In W. S. DeKeseredy & B. Perry (Eds.), *Advancing critical criminology: Theory and application* (pp. 199–213). Oxford: Lexington Books.

Edwards, R. W. (1995). Alcohol, tobacco, and other drug use by youth in rural com-munities. *Perspectives on violence and substance use in rural America.* Retrieved April 14, 2015, from www.ncrel.org/sdrs/areas/issues/envrnmnt/drugfree/v1edward.htm.

Ekberg, G. (2004). The Swedish law that prohibits the purchase of sexual services: Best practices for prevention of prostitution and trafficking in human beings. *Violence Against Women, 10*(10), 1187–1218.

European Monitoring Centre for Drugs and Drug Addiction – EMCDDA. (2012/2013). Drug use among the general population and young people. Country overview: United Kingdom. Retrieved April 14, 2015, from www.emcdda.europa.eu/publications/country-overviews/uk#gps.

European School Survey Project on Alcohol and Other Drugs – ESPAD. (2012). Sub-stance use among 15–16 year old students in the UK. Retrieved April 14, 2015, from www.espad.org/.

Estrada, F., & Nilsson, A. (2012). Does it cost more to be a female offender? A life-course study of childhood circumstances, crime, drug abuse, and living conditions. *Feminist Criminology, 7*(3), 196–219.

Findahl, O. (2013). Swedes and the Internet (p. 78). Stockholm: Stiftelsen för internet-infrastruktur.

Ford, J. O. (2008). *Rural crime and poverty: Violence, drugs and other issues.* Broomall, PA: Mason Crest.

Gripe, I., & Leifman, H. (2013). Små regionala skillnader i användning av alkohol, narko-tika och tobak [press release]. Retrieved April 14, 2015, from www.mynewsdesk.com/se/can/pressreleases/ny-rapport-om-ungas-drogvanor-smaa-regionala-skillnader-i-anvaendning-av-alkohol-narkotika-och-tobak-937794.

Gripenlöf, A. (1991–2002). Yearly reports from the Stockholm Police Prostitution Group. Stockholm: County Police of Stockholm.

Guttormsson, U., Andersson, A., & Hibell, B. (2004). Ungdomars drogvanor 1994–2003: Intervjuer med 16–24-åringar (Vol. 75). Stockholm: CAN.

Haber, M., & Toro, P. (2004). Homelessness among families, children, and adolescents: An ecological–developmental perspective. *Clinical Child and Family Psychology Review, 7*(3), 123–164.

Hanaeus, C. G., & Wahlström, F. (2014). Många svenska ungdomar pendlar till Norge. Statistics Sweden – SCB (1). Retrieved April 14, 2015, from www.scb.se/sv_/Hitta-statistik/Artiklar/Manga-svenska-ungdomar-pendlar-till-Norge/.

Hellgren, F. (2010). Ungdomsvåldets utveckling i de tre storstadslänen (Master's degree, Stockholm University, Stockholm).

Hilldén, J. (2006). Effekter av kriminella MC-gäng på brottsfrekvens i Sveriges kommuner 1996–2003 (Master's degree, Uppsala University, Uppsala).

Hoare, J. (2009). Drug misuse declared: Findings from the 2008/09 British crime survey England and Wales. London: Home Office.

Home Office. (2012–2013). Drug misuse: Findings from the 2012 to 2013 crime survey for England and Wales. London: Home Office.

Jonsson, C. (2010). I fäders och mödrars spår. Landsortsungdomars identitetsutveckling och vuxenblivande i ett livsformsperspektiv (PhD, University of Gothenburg, Gothenburg).

Karlsson, A. (2012). Unga bor i storstan: äldre i glesbygd. *Välfärd, 25.* Retrieved April 14, 2015, from www.scb.se/sv_/Hitta-statistik/Artiklar/Unga-bor-i-storstan-aldre-i-glesbygd.

Karlsson, L. (2013). Anabola androgena steroider i Sverige (Bachelor's thesis, Malmö högskola/Hälsa och samhälle, Malmö).

Kaylen, M. T., & Pridemore, W. A. (2011). A reassessment of the association between social disorganization and youth violence in rural areas. *Social Science Quarterly, 92*(4), 978–1001.

Kim, S.-W., & Pridemore, W. A. (2005). Social change, institutional anomie and serious property crime in transitional Russia. *British Journal of Criminology, 45*(1), 81–97.

Knape, A., & Strömbäck, J. (2012). Dragkampen om kommuninvånare hårdnar. *SKL-Debattartikel.* Retrieved April 14, 2015, from https://nwt.se/asikter/debatt/2013/01/10/dragkampen-om-kommuninvanare.

Magnusson, L., & Turner, B. (2000). Utarmas landsbygden? Mot nya flyttmönster. In G. B. G. Graninger & L. Nystrom (Eds.), *Vi flytt nu: Om befolkningsomflyttningarna i Sverige* (Vol. XIV). Uppsala: Stiftelsen Vadstena forum for samhallsbyggande.

National Alliance to End Homelessness. (2014). Youth homeless. www.endhomelessness.org/pages/youth.

Nilsson, S. (2013). Störst utbildningsgap mellan könen i glesbygd. *Välfärd, 84.* Retrieved April 14, 2015, from www.scb.se/sv_/Hitta-statistik/Artiklar/Storst-utbildningsgap-mellan-konen-i-glesbygd/.

Nissle, E. (2009). Organiserad brottslighet: Kriminella mc-gäng (p. 16). Umeå: Umeå Universitet.

Örstadius, K. (2014). Nu flyttar fler till än från glesbygden. *Dagens Nyheter.* Retrieved April 14, 2015, from www.dn.se/ekonomi/nu-flyttar-fler-till-an-fran-glesbygden/.

Osgood, D. W., & Chambers, J. M. (2003). Community correlates of rural youth violence. *Juvenile Justice Bulletin,* May, 12.

Payne, A., & Welch, K. (2013). The impact of schools and education on antisocial behavior over the lifecourse. In C. L. Gibson & M. D. Krohn (Eds.), *Handbook of life-course criminology* (pp. 93–109). New York: Springer.

Pettersson, E. (2013). Stanna. Flytta. Återvända? En studie av unga vuxnas reflektioner om Tärnabyområdets samhällsmiljö. Umeå: Umeå Universitet.

Pruitt, L. R. (2009). The forgotten fifth: Rural youth and substance abuse. SelectedWorks. Davis, CA: University of California, Davis.

Quilgars, D., Johnsen, S., & Pleace, N. (2008). Youth homelessness in the UK: A decade of progress? (p. 150). York: Joseph Rowntree Foundation.

Ravenstein, E. G. (1885). The laws of migration. *Journal of the Statistical Society of London, 48*(2), 167–235.

Ring, R. (2013). Brottsligheten bland ungdomar har minskat. *Nytt från BRÅ.* Retrieved April 14, 2015, from www.bra.se/bra/nytt-fran-bra/arkiv/press/2013-02-26-brottsligheten-bland-ungdomar-har-minskat.html.

Robertson, M., Harris, N., Frit, N., Noftsinger, R., & Fischer, P. (2007). Rural homelessness. Paper presented at the *2007 National Symposium on Homelessness Research,*

Washington, DC. Retrieved April 14, 2015, from http://aspe.hhs.gov/hsp/homeless-ness/symposium07/robertson/index.htm#Sociodemographic.

Rye, J. F. (2006). Rural youths' images of the rural. *Journal of Rural Studies, 22*(4), 409–421.

Sampson, R. J., Raudenbush, S. W., & Earls, F. (1997). Neighborhoods and violent crime: A multilevel study of collective efficacy. *Science, 277*(5328), 918–924.

Sandberg, P. (2012). En förening i förändring: om idrottsföreningar på landsbygden och deras utmaningar i ett postmodernt samhälle (Master's degree, Linköpings University, Norrköping)

Sermons, M. W., & Henry, M. (2010). Demographics of homelessness series: The rising elderly population national alliance to end homelessness. Homeless Research Institute. Retrieved April 17, 2015, from www.endhomelessness.org/.

Shears, J., Edwards, R. W., & Stanley, L. R. (2006). School bonding and substance use in rural communities. *Social Work Research, 30*(1), 6–18.

Socialstyrelsen (National Board of Health and Welfare). (2013). Folkhälsan i Sverige: Årsrapport 2013 (p. 92). Stockholm: Socialstyrelsen.

Statistics Sweden – SCB. (2009). Living conditions 2006–07 (Vol. 118, p. 158). Stockholm: SCB.

Stockholms stadsmission. (2011). Hemlös 2011: En statusrapport om det offentligas stöd till människor i hemlöshet, med utökat fokus på unga i hemlöshet (p. 67). Stockholm: Stockholms stadsmission.

Stockholms stad. (2010). Hemlösa i Stockholms stad. *SocialTjänst- och arbetsmarknads-förvaltningen.* Stockholm: Stockholms stad.

Swärd, H. (2001). Porträtterad nöd: berättelser om hemlösa. *Socialvetenskaplig tidskrift, 8*(1), 54–76.

Swärd, H. (2004). Att förklara hemlöshet. *Socialmedicinsk tidskrift, 8*, 8–13.

Swärd, H. (2010). Hemlös 2010: en statusrapport om det offentligas stöd till människor som lever i hemlöshet. Stockholm: Stadsmissionen.

Rikspolisstyrelsen (Swedish National Police Board). (2007). Narkotika och narkotika kemiler: Samverkan mot olaglig hantering av narkotikaoch narkotikalika droger. Stockholm: Rikspolisstyrelsen/Läkemedelsverket.

Toro, P. A., Dworsky, A., & Fowler, P. (2007). Homeless youth in the United States: Recent research findings and intervention approaches. Paper presented at the *2007 National Symposium on Homelessness Research*, Washington, DC. Retrieved April 14, 2015, from http://aspe.hhs.gov/hsp/homelessness/symposium07/toro/.

Weisheit, R. A., & Donnermeyer, J. F. (2000). Changes and continuity in crime in rural America. In G. LaFree (Ed.), *Criminal justice 2000: The nature of crime of crime, continuity and change* (pp. 309–357). Washington, DC: US Department of Justice.

Wennerholm, C. J. (2002). Crossing borders and building bridges: The Baltic region networking project. *Gender and Development, 10*(1), 10–19.

Wikström, P.-O., Ceccato, V., Hardie, B., & Treiber, K. (2010). Activity fields and the dynamics of crime. *Journal of Quantitative Criminology, 26*(1), 55–87.

Woods, M. (2011). *Rural.* London/New York: Routledge.

10 Violence against women in rural communities

Place is a predictor of victimization. Crime more often happens in places other than in the private sphere. For women, however, the home tends to be more dangerous than any other place. Women are threatened and assaulted most often where they reside, by someone they know, in acts often classified as "violence against women." In rural areas, women are less likely to report this kind of violence, for numerous reasons. For instance, long distances create isolation to a greater degree than in urban areas. This chapter points out the barriers women living in rural areas face when reporting violence, particularly when the perpetrator is known to the victim. This is followed by a brief discussion of international urban–rural trends in rates of violence against women. Then, the chapter provides a basis for the analysis of the Swedish case by presenting a list of individual and structural factors that are determinants of violence against women in rural areas.

Silence and negligence: underreporting of violence against women

> She was beaten on several occasions by her ex-boyfriend, with whom she still lives. She has bruises and cuts on her face. She decided not to report the aggression to the police because that would upset the abuser.
>
> (Weigl & Edblom, 2013)

These are the notes published in the Swedish newspaper *Aftonbladet* on a mother of three, 40 years old, from Gusum, Valdemarsvik municipality, killed by her ex-boyfriend a day before her planned escape in 2009. This case illustrates one of the reasons women in violent relationships avoid reporting such violence to the police and are afraid to seek help. In Sweden, underreporting of violence against women cannot be broken down into urban and rural areas, but researchers believe that more than one-quarter of all violence goes unreported (Lundgren, Heimer, Westerstrand, & Kalliokoski, 2002). Abroad, the situation is no different. According to DeKeseredy, Rogness, and Schwartz (2004), it is difficult to quantify the amount of female abuse in rural communities based on official data, and many believe that official data for rural areas is significantly problematic in this area. For instance, the distances between houses in rural villages are often greater than in urban centers. This fact makes it difficult for neighbors to discover violence that occurs. Also, if the woman decides to seek help, it is not always easy to get away from the house. The nearest women's shelter may be many miles away, and the distance may be exacerbated by poor or no public transportation (Lewis, 2003), limited access (DeKeseredy & Joseph, 2006), or sporadic access to the Internet or mobile phones. Websdale (1998) suggests that certain actions by the abuser, such as disabling vehicles and unplugging and removing phones, have even greater implications, isolating women in rural environments, increasing their vulnerability to violence in ways that do not happen in urban areas where public transportation and help are available. This is exemplified well by the following case described by a representative of a women's shelter in Northern Sweden.

She was from abroad, and the man was from a village, a bit outside the urban area. He met her overseas and invited her to come to Sweden and get married. She got a tourist visa, for three months, and everything went as planned until they arrived at the airport. Then, the man said that she should not expect any wedding. She was taken to his place and lived in a cottage located two kilometers away from the public road. She was abused in various ways, psychologically and physically assaulted, raped. The man threatened her, saying that she should not leave the house or else he would call the police. One day she found a bicycle in a basement, while he went to the forest where he worked. She decided to get away despite the cold weather. Without knowing where she was heading, she took the bike and found the road. Fortunately that led her to a small village outside of our town. Some local girls could speak a bit of English and talked to her and then called us at the women's shelter. She was about to freeze to death by then. She had no winter clothes. How could she cope cycling eight kilometers in that cold? She stayed at the local hotel, got food and some clothes. She was instructed by us not to call him because he would discover at once where she was, but she did. He brought some friends here and started walking around and climbing the fire escape of the hotel to check where she was. We saw him. The hotel staff called the police, but the men disappeared. When we met her again, she sat with her little bag and took out a set of papers that turned out to be her plane ticket and visa, expiring within three days. With a bit of English and sign language, she told us she had a relative in another Swedish city in the south. Then I thought, what do we do now? The solution was to take her to her relative. This turned out to be a scary situation, as when I got home, I saw that there was a car parked five feet from our garden ... I saw that it was him. Next day I managed to borrow a car and, in the middle of the night and together with a colleague of the women's shelter, we took her to her relative. "We did it!" I said loudly, but when we got on the main road, I saw in the rear-view mirror that a car was approaching fast. Then I thought, "Is it him?" Fortunately, it wasn't, but we were scared. The woman went to her relative, who took her to the airport. A few months ago, she called the shelter. Although she could not speak much

English, she thanked us, said names, and told us that she now had a job in her home country. We were happy with how things turned out.

(Women's shelter representative, northern municipality)

Not all cases have a happy ending. Burman (2012) shows that immigrant women are doubly victimized, as the Swedish immigration laws lack an understanding of gender power relations. Women, as in the case presented above, suffer from insecure rights of residence and the processes of "othering." They may be perceived as "unwanted" in Swedish society when they no longer fulfill their function as men's partners. Many enter the country with the promise of marriage. This process of exclusion of rights as citizens is far from being a Swedish problem or a problem of women living in rural areas. It is a recurrent problem in other European countries and elsewhere (Ingram et al., 2010; Orloff & Sarangapani, 2007; Raj & Silverman, 2002; Sundari, 2011).

Violence against women is a problem that affects not only ethnic minorities. In Sweden, Weigl and Edblom (2013) highlighted in a national newspaper 153 cases of women killed by their partners, the great majority native Swedes, and many living outside big cities at the time of their death.

She was careful not to show the kids any fear.... She told police about death threats, asked in vain for security alarms, and sought protection hiding in women's shelters.... They had five children, several of whom were at home when he took out a gun and shot her.

(38-year-old woman, Halland)

These two cases share common features. The women were assaulted when they were leaving the relationship and received help from women's shelters and police. Still, their outcomes were different. What are the underlying factors behind lethal violence against women? Among the societal factors that influence rates of violence are those that create a tolerant climate for violence (WHO, 2002). Social isolation is part of the dynamic of domestic violence that also affects one's decision to avoid contact with the police. In rural areas, women fear being ostracized if they speak out about male violence. Cohesive community values strengthen rural communities but may also have the unintended effect of "enabling" domestic violence to occur. In places where collective informal social control is strong (DeKeseredy & Schwartz, 2008) and may be dominated by traditional gender values of rural patriarchy (Websdale, 1998), violence against women may be acceptable at certain levels.

The underreporting of violence against women is the result not only of victims' silence but also of the silence, tolerance, and negligence of the social circles surrounding the victims (Gracia, 2004). Neighbors in rural areas may have a higher tolerance of certain acts than in urban areas (Anderson, 1999), and privacy norms dictate that they "keep their mouths shut" or "keep out of other people's business." The local culture may reflect differences in "gender contracts or regimes" (Amcoff, 2001; Townsend, 1991), which result in different conditions for women and men in various dimensions of life. Websdale (1998) provides examples of women who were afraid to call the police because they knew that their abuser was socially networked with police personnel and that little or no action would be taken in their defense. In other cases, other local women do not help because they themselves are experiencing similar problems and their own struggles prevent them from helping others (DeKeseredy & Schwartz, 2008, p. 112). In yet other cases, people may believe that a woman's "provocative behavior" causes the violence, which indicates a high prevalence of victim-blaming attitudes (European Commission, 1999).

In addition, there are issues of personal and familial dependency on the offender. Children refrain from reporting violence, because they cannot afford other familial conflicts (such as with their mother, who is also emotionally and economically dependent on the offender) or run the risk of being physically, psychologically, or economically punished by their father. In Sweden, despite the fact that youngsters often move out of their parents' home after reaching 18 years of age, for young girls, particularly those from ethnic minorities, such a move might be difficult because of cultural barriers. In rural areas, women from ethnic minorities brought to Sweden by marriage may face particular challenges (Burman, 2012; Westman, 2010). Thus, some women would tolerate violence and would not seek help or report to the police because they do not consider moving out or reporting violence as viable options.

However, in the case of Sweden, a long-standing tradition of gender equality policy and legislation, as well as an established women's movement, has greatly influenced the reporting of violence against women. According to police statistics, levels of violence appear to be related to genuine changes in levels of criminal acts, as well as various other factors such as a rise in a population's willingness to report crime to the police (Estrada, 2005), a decrease in tolerance levels as a consequence of society's increased sensitivity to violence (Jerre, 2008), and changes in the law. The Violence Against Women Act (*Kvinnofrid*)[1] adopted in 1999 is an important example. This legislation criminalized the purchase of prostitution services, provided measures to combat sexual harassment in the workplace, and successively broadened the definition of sexual violence. Although it has been argued that these legal and other factors have maximized the reporting of violence against women in Sweden, it is an open question whether these changes are sufficient to explain the disparity in reporting rates within Sweden and between Sweden and other countries.

Urban–rural trends of violence against women

In the United Kingdom, domestic violence against women appears to be concentrated in inner-city areas – indeed more than twice as prevalent as in rural areas (for violence against males, this difference is not as pronounced). Walby and Allen (2004) suggest that the higher rate of domestic violence associated with urban areas runs parallel with the finding that inter-personal violence is also higher in these areas, a trend also found in Sweden (Ceccato & Dolmén, 2009).

Domestic violence and sexual assault are crimes that are known to be under-reported (Walby & Allen, 2004). Marshall and Johnson (2005) estimate in the United Kingdom that only 21 percent of female domestic violence victims (7 percent of male victims) come to the attention of the police. For sexual assault, the reporting rate is even less: 15 percent for rape, 12 percent for serious sexual assault, and 13 percent for less serious sexual assault. Table 10.1 shows differences in victimization by area type in the United Kingdom.

In the United States, violence against women has historically been higher in urban areas than rural, but there are differences among ethnic groups. What is more interesting is that since the mid-1980s the percentage of homicides committed by an intimate (spouse, ex-spouse, boyfriend, girlfriend, same-sex partner) has been higher in rural areas than in suburban or urban areas (Figure 10.1) (BJS, 2011).

When violence happens at home, it not only affects women but also children. According to Moore, Probst, Tompkins, Cuffe, and Martin (2005), in the United States 10.3 percent of children lived in homes where disputes resulted, at least occasionally, in hitting and throwing. The prevalence of violent disputes varied slightly across different degrees of "rurality" but was lower in homes located in rural counties than in urban counties (10.7 and 9.9). About one-third of children lived in homes where disputes were expressed through heated argument and shouting. The prevalence of heated disagreement showed no clear pattern across levels of rurality or between urban and rural areas.

In the United States, ethnic minority women living in rural areas are not more likely to be assaulted by their current and former intimate partners than are their urban and suburban counterparts. A recent study by DeKeseredy, Dragiewicz, and Rennisson (2012) finds no difference in the rates at which urban, suburban, and rural racial/ethnic minority females are victims of intimate violence using the 1992–2009 National Crime Victimization Survey.

In Sweden, assaults against women have increased since the mid-1990s, particularly in rural areas (Table 10.2).[2] These increases are likely to be a result of a rise in the reporting rate of mainly single mothers and of women who are victims of abuse in the workplace (Nilsson, 2002; Selin & Westlund, 2008). The majority of women assaulted are involved in an intimate relationship with the assailant, often cohabiting with that person. Most of these women are exposed to

Table 10.1 Cases of domestic violence and sexual assault in the United Kingdom (%)

	Rural	Urban	Inner-city
Females			
Domestic violence	3.3	4.1	7.0
Sexual assault	1.2	2.2	3.0
Males			
Domestic violence	1.8	2.4	2.7

Source: Walby and Allen, 2004, quoted by Marshall and Johnson (2005, p. 18).

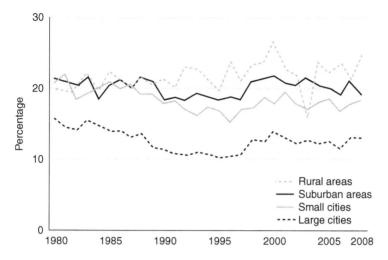

Figure 10.1 Percentage of all homicides involving intimates by urban, suburban, and rural area, 1980–2008 (source: BJS, 2011, p. 30).

violence repeatedly. This indicates that both victims and offenders differ from the population in general with respect to previous crime involvement and marginalization. Those who are foreign-born are often overrepresented, both as victims and offenders (Nilsson, 2002). It is estimated that 75,000 women are victims of violence in intimate relationships each year in the country, costing society SEK2,695–3,300 million (Socialstyrelsen, 2014).

Statistics on the geographic distribution of this type of crime are uncertain, because the "shadow figure" is high in this offense category. Even when a crime is reported to the police, it may not go to trial. According to Nilsson (2002), police reports indicate that, in about one-quarter of incidents reported to the police, the woman is unwilling to continue to assist with the investigation. The victim's refusal to cooperate makes it very difficult for the police and prosecutor to continue the investigation. One reason a woman may refuse to assist in the criminal investigation is that she is afraid of further violence from the man who has already acted violently towards her. Another obstacle may be that the woman and the man have been involved in an intimate and emotional relationship and may also have had children together.

Although legislation has recently been amended to ensure a higher degree of safety for abused women and children – by defining children exposed to violence as "crime victims" – there are still clear challenges ahead (Eriksson, 2011).

Leander (2007) estimates that about 17 women are killed as victims of domestic violence each year in Sweden. This figure is half of what it was in the 1990s. Rying (2001) suggests that about 30 women were killed in intimate relationships between 1990 and 1999. Rying (2001, p. 45) indicates that

Table 10.2 Rates and change (%) in violence against women per 100,000 females aged 15 years and older, according to police and health statistics

	Urban areas	Accessible rural	Remote rural	Sweden
Recorded violence against women, indoors, known offender – police crime statistics				
1996–2001	(8.7%)	(18.3%)	(60.0%)	(11.5%)
2002–2006	(3.4%)	(13.2%)	(46.9%)	(6.2%)
1996–2006	(15.2%)	(35.6%)	(115.6%)	(20.9%)
2009–2013*	(11.5%)	(5.6%)	(2.1%)	(7.3%)
Rate 1996	342.8	208.5	135.9	296.1
Rate 2006	394.4	282.7	291.6	358.0
Rate 2013*	582.1	567.2	478.3	470.3
Women hospitalized** as a result of violence, known offender (% increase)				
1998–2002	(21.4%)	(24.4%)	(412.1%)	(19.6%)
2003–2007	(–4.7%)	(19.3%)	(–32.6%)	(1.26%)
2008–2012	(–2.6%)	(10.6%)	(74.0%)	(1.42%)
1998–2012	(–3.9%)	(62.2%)	(443.7%)	(31.1%)
Rate 1998	7.0	4.5	1.6	6.1
Rate 2007	8.1	7.4	3.3	8.0
Rate 2012	7.4	7.3	8.7	7.4

Source: Police statistics, 1996 and 2006, and National Board of Health and Welfare (2014).

Notes
* Change in crime codes from 2009, rates based on 18 years and older female population.
** Hospitals attend patients from a widespread area, but the municipality where the hospital is located records the data.

social change and an increase in the level of attention focused on violence against women may have had an impact on these figures, as may certain law changes. Medical advances dealing with the victims … as well as the emergence of women's help-lines and shelters and the media attention.

The Swedish National Crime Victimization Surveys (SNCVS) (2006–2013) are an important data source to assess the profile of victims of crime, but they do not allow breakdown by municipality. More than one-third of women declare that they have been assaulted by an acquaintance and about one-half by someone they know. The SNCVS show that the prevalence of physical violence against women (at least one act of physical violence during the 12 months prior to the survey) was slightly higher in urban areas than in rural ones.

Healthcare statistics show a clear urban–rural disparity in rates of hospitalized women victims of violence (Figure 10.2). They confirm an increase between 1998 and 2012 in violence against women (aged 15 years and older) caused by a known offender. Although rates of hospitalization for assault were on average higher in urban areas than in rural ones, those injuries caused by a partner, husband, or other aggressor (not a friend or acquaintance) increased more in rural areas than in the countryside, particularly in accessible rural municipalities, than in urban areas. The rates of hospitalization have drastically increased in remote rural areas while in accessible rural and urban areas, rates showed minor variations.

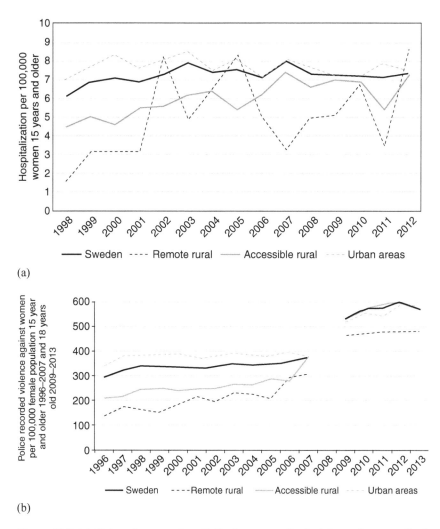

(a)

(b)

Figure 10.2 (a) Rates of women hospitalized as a result of violence, known offender 1998–2007, and (b) rates of women violence against women, 1996–2007 and 2009–2013 (data source: (a) police statistics, 1996–2006, 2009–2013 (2009 change of crime codes); (b) national patient records, National Board of Health and Welfare, 2014).

Another important difference between rural and urban areas is the increase between 1998 and 2007 of cases in which the aggressor is not revealed by the victim or recorded by the doctor in hospitals located in rural municipalities (Table 10.3). Internationally, rates of detection of this type of violence in hospitals and emergency rooms are still low, though a high percentage of women visit emergency rooms for treatment (Abbott, Johnson, Koziol-McLain, & Lowenstein,

1995). Lindblom, Castrén, and Kurland (2010) discuss the difficulties of recording cases of violence in hospitals, as most women victims of violence do not seek help for obvious physical injuries but for other, less specific symptoms such as pain or deterioration in health due to illness. They also suggest that women who die as a result of being beaten have previously sought emergency medical treatment several times.

The reasons behind these differences between urban and rural areas are difficult to ascertain, but the differences are confirmed by official police statistics. Statistics show that although remote rural areas have rates that are half the rates found in urban areas, rural municipalities show the highest increase in rates in recent decades (Table 10.2). The rise of police-reported cases of violence against women at home (by a known offender) follows the national trend of assault against women by unknown perpetrators in public places. Statistics on violence against women at home show that rates in rural Sweden are approaching those in urban areas, that is, they are increasing. It is important to note that from 2009 onwards a stricter definition of crime codes has been put in place which, although minor, can affect levels and the way violence against women is reported to local authorities.

According to Ceccato and Dolmén (2011), this trend was also found in other types of crime in rural areas, indicating that rural areas are becoming more criminogenic, particularly accessible rural areas. Note that although urban areas show higher rates of violence against women than rural municipalities do, the capital of Sweden – Stockholm – shows a lower rate on average than the adjacent southern municipalities of the metropolitan region (e.g., Botkyrka, Södertälje, and Haninge). Alcohol abuse may also be behind these differences in levels and geography of violence against women.

Outside large city regions, the geography of violence against women is far from being homogeneous (Figure 10.3), as it reflects individual and structural differences in the population as well as the local and regional abilities of criminal justice institutions and society overall to tackle the problem.

For instance, according to Ahacic (2010) alcohol consumption increased in Stockholm County between 1998 and 2008, as did the rate of men treated for addiction problems. The rise coincided with an increase in the number of licensed restaurants, while the real price of alcohol fell. More liquor stores were opened in the county as well, and sales at liquor stores increased. In the municipalities in Stockholm County, as shown in the international literature, women belonging to ethnic minorities may run a higher risk for violence than native born. In municipal-owned housing, hosts may call for help if there are signs of domestic violence in progress in the building. Moreover, some of these municipalities have police family units that are trained to deal with family violence, which in part explains their relatively high rates of reporting to the police. These municipalities are also closer to one of the main hospitals in the metropolitan area (Södersjukhuset), which has a unit specializing in gendered violence.

It is important to note that low reported rates in southern municipalities and high rates in urban areas must be interpreted with caution. Whilst they may reflect real differences in gendered violence between the regions, the reporting

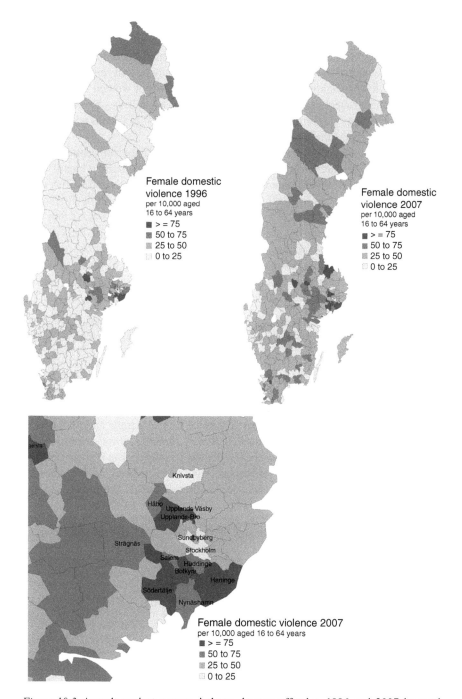

Figure 10.3 Assault against women indoors, known offender, 1996 and 2007 by total women aged 16 to 74 years old: in detail, Stockholm's metropolitan area (source: police statistics, 1996 and 2007).

236 Crime in a rural context

rate depends on local differences in support services aimed at violence against women and on features embedded in the regional gender contracts that, in turn, affect reporting rates. Little is known about what is behind low rates in municipalities that are part of the so-called "church belt." It may be that religious values lead to less violence against women, but it may also be that women are not prepared to publicly reveal partner assault or that they fear that if they reveal it, they will be ostracized by the community. Even if they reveal it to friends and family, they may never report these events to the police.

Victims of violence by partners have a number of factors in common. An important line of research on violence against women has focused on identifying these factors. Most of this literature is based on North American and British circumstances, focusing on women living in urban areas. What this literature misses is that, although rates of violence against women in rural areas may be lower, its causes may be different from urban areas and its effects on the victims may be greater. Aspects such as limited access to services, isolation, poverty, and rural cultural values make rural women more vulnerable to domestic violence than women living in urban areas. The next section highlights individual and structural factors that relate to women's abuse and violence.

Violence against women: the role of individual and structural factors in rural areas

The international literature sheds little light on geographical differences in rates of violence against women. Greenfeld (1998), for instance, suggests that in the United States women in urban environments are more likely to be victims of violence than those living in suburban and rural areas. Evidence from Australia and the United Kingdom indicates different, sometimes conflicting, findings. Rural areas show a higher reported incidence and prevalence of domestic violence than in metropolitan areas (WESNET, 2000), whilst Grossman, Hinkley, Kawalski, and Margrave (2005) show that the difference between rural and urban settings is small.

Table 10.3 Hospitalization rates* of victims of violence in 2007 per 100,000 females, and change, 1998–2007 (%)

	Urban areas	Accessible rural	Remote rural
Partners/husbands	2.8 (−9.7%)	2.8 (47.4%)	1.7 (6.2%)
Friend or acquaintance	0.5 (25.0%)	0.7 (−22.2%)	0.0 (0.0%)
Other**	4.8 (41.2%)	3.7 (105.5%)	1.7 (6.2%)
Total	8.1 (15.7%)	7.2 (64.4%)	3.4 (106.2%)

Data source: national patient records, National Board of Health and Welfare (2009).

Notes
* Hospitals attend patients from a widespread area. Women's addresses are recorded by municipality.
** Other=aggression might be caused by an ex-partner or a stranger. This category includes cases in which the doctor or the victim is not able to (or has chosen not to) declare who was the aggressor.

A problem in comparing these statistics on geography relates to the way these studies define the concept of domestic violence (such as differences in crime definitions or health statistics). Another issue relates to the way "rural" and "urban" are defined in different countries and even within single countries (see Marshall and Johnson, 2005, p. 10), which makes it difficult to compare rural and urban rates. We take the view that having a lower rate of domestic violence does not mean that the problem in rural areas is less serious. On the contrary, women in rural areas may have specific service needs and face special obstacles that are not present in urban settings (Websdale and Johnson 1998).

Table 10.4 illustrates examples of individual and structural factors behind violence against women in rural areas in different countries. As stated above, direct comparisons between studies are difficult, because studies may be based on different definitions, methods, and datasets. The purpose of this summary is to focus, when possible, on the importance of these factors in the context of urban and rural differences. This summary also provides a basis for comparison with the Swedish case study.

Geographical isolation

Geographical and social isolation characterize the lives of many rural battered women. This is the case of those interviewed in Kentucky by Websdale (1995, p. 333), who indicates that women experience a considerable amount of physical, sexual, and emotional abuse by their husbands or partners. Shepherd (2001, p. 496) also found that native women in rural Alaska suffer the consequences of domestic violence more because of the isolation of the communities where they reside, severe weather, lack of adequate law enforcement, prevalence of alcohol and other drugs, prevalence of weapons, absence of many basic public services (such as low-income housing and transportation), lack of jobs, dependence on public assistance, infrequent visits by mental health professionals, and lack of treatment programs for abusers. In a case study of remote Australian mining towns, Sharma and Rees (2007, p. 1) show signs of how sociocultural processes affect women's mental health, a finding that can be generalized to many remote areas elsewhere, where the geographic isolation of the community is a determining factor in women's victimization.

Geographical isolation also affects the legal support that women have in the countryside. Logan, Shannon, and Walker (2005) show that the process of obtaining civil protective orders varies depending on community context and that although there are barriers to obtaining and enforcing protective orders regardless of geographic region, rural women appear to face more barriers than those in urban areas. The authors show that differences exist in victimization experiences, protective orders' stipulations, violations, and perceived effectiveness among rural and urban women. Schafer and Giblin (2010, p. 283) show in the United States how intimate partner violence is perceived and policed in rural areas and small towns while highlighting some of the challenges agencies encounter in addressing these offenses within their jurisdictions.

Table 10.4 Determinants of domestic violence in rural areas: a selected review

Determinants	Area of study	Findings	Sources
Age	Urban and rural counties in Illinois, USA	Victims were younger on average in rural areas than in urban ones, regardless of their ethnic background.	Grossman et al. (2005)
	Rural West Virginia, USA	Abused women were older than age 19 (range 19–32), often abused by partners under the age of 30.	Persily and Abdulla (2000)
	Bangladesh	A slightly higher prevalence in rural than in urban areas of lifetime physical spouse violence against women.	Naved et al. (2006)
Poverty	Rural USA	Economic worries, plus other factors such as stress, boredom, and alcohol and drug use, may contribute to the overall stresses on the family, creating conditions ripe for domestic violence.	Grama (2000)
	Rural West Virginia, USA	Nearly half of partners of women had mostly low-paying, full-time jobs.	Persily and Abdulla (2000)
	Southeastern USA	Abused women and their partners were more likely to be unemployed.	Murdaugh et al. (2004)
	Urban–rural China	Women who reported incidents of violence were more likely to have grown up in rural villages and be poorer.	Tang and Lai (2007)
	Rural–urban dimension in US counties	Rural women were more at risk because they typically earned about half of what rural men earned. Some of the obstacles for women's economic self-sufficiency were rooted in structural conditions in rural areas.	Pruitt (2008)
Ethnic background	Rural USA	Limited knowledge of language, being in the country illegally made immigrant women more vulnerable to domestic violence.	Grama (2000)
	Rural South Carolina, USA	White women were at higher risk to become victims of domestic violence.	Fram et al. (2006)
	Rural–urban USA	Black women were at higher risk to become victims of domestic violence.	Lanier and Maume (2009)
	Bangladesh	Non-Muslims were at higher risk to become victims of domestic violence in rural areas than in urban ones.	Naved et al. (2006)
	Rural–suburban–urban, USA	Limited or no differences in rates at which urban, suburban, and rural ethnic minority females were victims.	Dekeseredy et al. (2012)

Theme	Location	Findings	References
Alcohol and drug abuse	Rural USA	Women were more at risk when partner was drunk or used drugs.	Van Hightower et al. (2000)
	Rural Alaska	Women were more at risk when partner was drunk or used drugs.	Shepherd (2001)
	Southeastern USA	Women were more at risk when partner was drinking and/or using drugs.	Murdaugh et al. (2004)
	Rural women in Ohio, USA	Use of alcohol and drugs increased the chances of violence for women wanting to break up a relationship.	DeKeseredy et al. (2006)
Pregnancy	Rural USA	Pregnant women were less likely to be victims of domestic violence than those who were not pregnant.	Van Hightower et al. (2000)
	Rural Bangladesh	Pregnancy was not a protective factor but violence did not escalate during pregnancy.	Naved et al. (2006)
	Urban–rural USA	Rural, low-income pregnant women faced many more stressors and more abuse than urban women.	Bhandari et al. (2008)
Geographical isolation	Kentucky, USA	Geographical and social isolation affected the potential support that women had in the countryside.	Websdale (1995, 1998)
		Men were directly or indirectly encouraged to abuse women who wanted to leave or who had left them by male peers and by neighbors who did not want to intervene.	Shepherd (2001)
	Rural Alaska, USA	Isolation of the communities, severe weather, lack of adequate law enforcement, prevalence of alcohol and other drugs, prevalence of weapons, absence of many basic public services, and lack of jobs increased the risk of abuse by partners.	
Rural culture and traditional gender roles	South Carolina, USA	Traditional gender roles facilitated by religious conservatism were often related to spouse abuse.	Fram et al. (2006)
	Rural USA	Isolation perpetuated gender inequalities and abuse (particular focus on divorce/assault). Critical theory applied to rural violence, masculinity, traditional gender roles, and rural crime prevention through environmental design (CPTED).	DeKeseredy et al. (2007, 2008, 2009); DeKeseredy and Schwartz (2008)
	Rural USA	How *rurality* affected women and the role of space and scale in supporting violence against women.	Pruitt (2008)
	Rural USA	In places where rural social and economic changes affected gender roles, social problems could arise, including domestic violence.	Olson (2011)

Rural culture and traditional gender roles

Isolation perpetuates gender inequalities because rural communities continue to define the role of men and women more narrowly than urban communities do (DeKeseredy, Donnermeyer, Schwartz, Tunnell, & Hall, 2007). As suggested by Olsson (2011), they may create unreal gender-related expectations (such as the "superwoman"). Although much has changed in rural areas, traditional gender roles still exist, in which men are the main "breadwinners" and women are limited to the domestic sphere (childrearing and housekeeping). In places where these gender roles have been affected by rural social and economic changes (such as loss of farms or other sources of income, women seeking employment or getting jobs when their husbands are unemployed or when their farms become less profitable, increases in the number of women's associations), social problems may arise, including domestic violence. DeKeseredy et al. (2007) suggest that many unemployed men deal with such challenges by spending much time with other men in similar situations, which in turn is one reason some wives leave or try to leave them. Fram, Miller-Cribbs, and Farber (2006, p. 268) also show that domestic violence is just one element in "the much larger game of maintaining the existing social order" in rural South Carolina, facilitated by religious conservatism. Similar findings were found in a rural Australian study by Wendt (2008) and in South Africa by Boonzaier and van Schalkwyk (2011).

However, traditional gender roles alone are not sufficient to explain women's victimization or stereotyped assumptions of sexual violence in rural environments. Drawing on deprivation and gender inequality perspectives, Lee and Stevenson (2006, p. 55) analyzed gender-disaggregated homicide offending rates in rural US counties. They found that "measures of both absolute and relative gender inequality had no association with female or male homicide offending in the rural context." Similar results were found by King and Roberts (2011) when they investigated stereotyped assumptions of rape ("rape myths") and traditional gender roles in a sample of university students in the United States. Contrary to previous literature on the rural culture milieu, the degree of rurality of one's hometown was not found to be statistically significant in relation to the acceptance of traditional gender roles and rape myths.

Poverty

In Sweden, the highest rates of violence caused by men are found among high- and low-income earners, according to Lundgren et al. (2002). A recent study (Trygged, Hedlund, & Kåreholt, 2014) shows, however, that women exposed to severe violence had a poorer financial situation compared to non-exposed women. Assaulted women had slower increases in income, lower odds for being in employment, and higher odds for having low incomes and means-tested social assistance in the 10-year follow-up, whether or not they had children.

Internationally many studies confirm the findings that domestic viole nce is characteristic of lower socioeconomic groups. Morley and Mullander (1994, p. 6) argue that these groups are more visible, because they lack economic resources to deal privately with their problems and are more likely to seek help from formal agencies like the police and social services from which research samples are frequently drawn. They also suggest that underrepresentation of cases among middle class and white people can be related to the fact they are less willing to admit to violence. Although not all studies have found socioeconomic differences in domestic violence (for a review see Morley and Mullander, 1994), we will discuss studies that have found links.

The nature of the links between poverty and risk of interpersonal violence is not always clear. It may be that poverty is associated with the onset of domestic violence, or it may be that in fleeing domestic violence, women are reduced to poverty (Walby & Allen, 2004). Logan et al. (2005, p. 895) show that more rural women than urban women reported that their partners denied them access to money, stopped them from seeing friends or family, interfered in relationships with others, kept them from doing things for themselves, did something to spite them, threatened or actually harmed their pets, threatened to harm their children, stalked them, threatened to kill them, or threatened them with a weapon. Walby and Allen (2004) show that in Britain women in households with an annual income less than GBP 10,000 were three-and-a-half times more likely to suffer domestic violence than those living in households with an annual income more than GBP 20,000, while men were one-and-a-half times more likely.

In the United States, domestic violence and economic hardship are correlated, as indicated in a report on the incidence of domestic violence in rural America (Grama, 2000). As it is suggested, "economic worries, plus other factors such as stress, boredom, and alcohol and drug use, may contribute to the overall stresses on the family; creating conditions ripe for domestic violence." This is also confirmed by Persily and Abdulla (2000, p. 14) in their study on violence against pregnant women in West Virginia. The majority of pregnant women were unemployed; nearly half of the partners of the pregnant women had mostly low-paying, full-time jobs. Abused women and their partners were more likely to be unemployed than non-abused women and their partners. Murdaugh, Hunt, Sowell, and Santana (2004, p. 110) also show that half of the abused women had economic concerns at the time of abuse. In China, Tang and Lai (2008) review 20 years of empirical literature and show that women who reported incidents of violence were more likely to have grown up in rural villages and tended to have low socioeconomic status. Krantz and Vung (2009) also show that women whose husbands have limited educations and are low skilled tend to be more exposed to violence in rural Vietnam, where violence perpetrated by husbands is fairly common.

In a study that assesses the rural–urban dimension of domestic violence in US counties, Pruitt (2008) shows that rural women are more at risk because they typically earn about half of what rural men earn, which puts them in a disadvantaged position. Some of the obstacles for women's economic self-sufficiency are rooted in the structural conditions of rural areas, such as a limited labor market and job-training services as well as housing and childcare options. Yet, these disadvantages may not affect women's risk to be exposed to violence. Lee and

Stevenson (2006) analyze gender-disaggregated homicide-offending rates in rural counties in the United States and find that gender-specific measures of unemployment and poverty and a measure of female-headed households exhibit no relationship with female homicide offending, whereas all three measures are associated with elevated levels of male homicide offending.

Age

Young women are more at risk of becoming a victim of domestic violence than older women are. In Sweden, a national survey on men's violence against women by Lundgren et al. (2002) shows that violence decreases with the age of the victim, but no significant difference is found between 18 and 54 years old. A later study based on cases of violence between 1995 and 2002 by Del Castillo, Heimer, Kalliokoski, and Stenson (2004) indicates that the majority of the cases are between 21 and 39 years of age. A recent study by Abramsky et al. (2011), using a WHO multi-country study on women's health and domestic violence, also shows that younger women are more at risk for violence than older ones. This is confirmed by Lanier and Maume (2009) in the United States. In Australia and Canada, young women (aged 18–24) were more at risk from all forms of violence than were older women (Bunge & Levett, 1998; WESNET, 2000). Domestic violence tends to decrease with age according to the British Crime Survey 2004/2005 (Finney, 2006). The age span may vary. In Australia, for example, data reporting domestic violence in the late 1990s shows that 40 percent of the victims were between 25 and 35 years old for both metropolitan and non-metropolitan areas, while Murdaugh et al. (2004, p. 110) show that domestic violence among Hispanics in the southeastern United States tends to happen more often among younger groups with a somewhat lower level of education. Slovak and Singer (2002, p. 53) analyze types and levels of children's exposure to violence in a rural setting. Their results indicate that "males were more likely to witness violence compared to females, and older students were more likely to witness violence compared to younger students."

Although in many countries it is not possible to disaggregate national data to compare victimization rates by age across urban and rural locations, it is interesting to note there is evidence from case studies showing that the ages of victims and offenders may vary geographically. For instance, Grossman et al. (2005, p. 75) examine individuals who were victims of domestic violence in Illinois between 1990 and 1995 in both urban and rural counties. Their findings show that victims were younger on average in rural areas than in urban ones, regardless of their ethnic background. Persily and Abdulla (2000, p. 14), in a study of violence against pregnant patients in a rural area of West Virginia, found that abused women were older than age 19 (range 19–32) and often abused by partners under the age of 30. Urban–rural differences are also found in developing countries. Using data from Bangladesh, Naved, Azim, Bhuiyaa, and Persson (2006) show a slightly higher prevalence of lifetime physical spousal violence against women in urban (40 percent) than in rural (42 percent) areas, from a large study conducted in 2000–2004.

Ethnic background

Women from minorities seem to be at higher risk for violence than other groups. A report in Australia from the Women's Services Network (2000, p. 8) indicates that indigenous women are much more likely to be victims of domestic violence than non-indigenous women are. This conclusion is based on reviews of a set of studies that look at regional differences in domestic violence.

In the United States, Grama (2000, p. 181) discusses special difficulties of rural women of color and immigrant women in rural areas. The author reminds readers that the situation of immigrant women may be more complicated by the fact that often "the domestic violence victim is dependent upon her batterer for her continued residence in the country via a conditional visa." Rural immigrant women may also be hampered by a limited knowledge of the language as well as strong cultural influences in which women are taught to obey their husbands.

Pruitt (2008, p. 407) suggests that abuse within immigrant families creates a variety of challenges, particularly in rural settings. For example, the Latino population has nearly doubled in rural and small-town America in the past 30 years. The author also refers to two other groups that have long been associated with rurality: Native Americans and native Alaskans. They are high-risk groups for all forms of violence against women, with the highest average annual rates of rape and physical assault between 1993 and 2004. Also in the United States, Grossman et al. (2005, p. 71) show that, apart from demographic differences related to race (whites and Afro-Americans), there is little difference in the circumstances of abuse when victims in the urban region are compared to rural victims of violence. Lanier and Maume (2009) show that black women in both non-metropolitan and metropolitan areas are significantly more likely to experience partner violence compared to white and other non-white women. However, the vulnerability of blacks in relation to whites was not confirmed by Fram et al. (2006, p. 256), who studied domestic violence experiences of poor women in South Carolina. Findings show that being "white, rather than black, was associated with a 0.2 standard-deviation increase in experiences of domestic violence, and never-married status was associated with a 0.17 standard-deviation decrease in such experiences." Naved et al. (2006, p. 2922) show that in Bangladesh physical abuse among the sample of non-Muslim women was higher in rural areas than in urban ones; they were exclusively Hindu, indicating a clear ethnic dimension of violence caused by the partner.

Pregnancy

In a victimization survey by Lundgren et al. (2002), 17 percent of women in Sweden declared they were victims of violence by their previous partner while pregnant and 3 percent their current partner. Prevalence figures for abuse during pregnancy are difficult to compare between countries because of differences in definitions, methods, and data used. What is common is that women who are victims of violence when pregnant have often been abused prior to pregnancy as well (for a review, see Stenson, 2004). Several studies of rural women only contain contrasting findings. Van Hightower, Gorton, and DeMoss (2000, p. 150) show that in the United States migrant and seasonal farmworker women who were pregnant were less likely to be victims of domestic violence than those who were not pregnant. Despite a negative correlation between pregnancy and abuse, nearly half of the abused respondents were pregnant in the sample. Authors suggest that this could occur "if abusers have internalized pro-natalist values that mediate against victimizing women who are pregnant." Moreover, women who have experienced abuse might choose to avoid pregnancy. In other words, "being free from abuse might have a positive influence on the decision of farmworker women to become pregnant, while experiencing abuse would have the opposite effect."

However, the protective effects of pregnancy are not confirmed elsewhere in the literature. Naved et al. (2006, p. 2922) show that although physical violence by husbands did not escalate during pregnancy, 10 percent of women in urban areas and 12 percent in rural areas reported being physically abused during pregnancy in Bangladesh. Bhandari et al. (2008) evaluate stressors experienced by rural low-income pregnant women experiencing intimate partner violence. They found that all rural pregnant women faced many stressors commonly not felt by urban pregnant women, such as when in labor having to go great distances to reach a hospital and running the risk of poor road conditions. Rural women also lacked many of the resources enjoyed by urban women, such as public transportation, access to public housing or shelters, opportunities for employment, and access to neighbors who live close enough to provide support when needed, as well as having limited possibilities of obtaining help with basic needs during financially hard times. The authors concluded that, for women experiencing intimate partner violence in rural areas, this lack of available resources may have further trapped them into staying in abusive relationships. Similar findings were found by Persily and Abdulla (2000, p. 15) in pregnant women in rural West Virginia. They also found a correlation between a history of sexually transmitted diseases and abuse, tobacco use, and abuse in pregnant women.

Alcohol and drug abuse

Although not a causal factor, alcohol and other drugs are common situational and background antecedents to the occurrence of domestic violence. In the United Kingdom, Morley and Mullander (1994) review a number of studies that, on the one hand, show an association between alcohol and domestic violence and, on the other, are inconclusive. Few differences are found between urban and rural drinkers, but substance abuse treatment services are generally less available in rural areas. Alcohol use during an assault has also been linked to an increased severity of victims' injuries. A recent study of 13 countries shows that "severity ratings were significantly higher for incidents in which one or both partners had been drinking, compared to incidents in which neither partner had been drinking. The relationship did not differ significantly for men and women or by country." The authors conclude that alcohol consumption may serve to potentiate violence when it occurs, and this pattern holds across a diverse set of cultures (Graham, Bernards, Wilsnack, & Gmel, 2011, p. 1503). The most common suggestion is that, rather than being a direct cause of violence, alcohol is better viewed as a means of gaining courage to carry out the act and/or as a convenient rationale to be excused. Kantor and Straus (1987, p. 224) suggest that "men who were classified as high or binge drinkers had two-to-three times greater rate of assaulting their wives than did husbands who abstained."

The link between substance abuse and domestic violence is corroborated by several studies from the 1980s and 1990s discussed by Logan, Walker, and Leukefeld (2001) for the North American case. More recently, Murdaugh et al. (2004, p. 110) find that nearly two-thirds of the Latino women who reported abuse declared that it frequently occurred when the abuser was drinking or, in about one-fifth of the cases, when he was using drugs, based on a sample from the rural southeastern United States. In a study of domestic violence and fear of intimate partners among migrant and seasonal farmworker women in the United States, Van Hightower et al. (2000, p. 148) show that one of the strongest predictors of domestic violence was drug/alcohol use by the respondent's partner. The factors that most influenced respondents' fear of their intimate partners were abuse, frequency of abuse, and partners' use of drugs or alcohol. Mechanisms linking alcohol/drug abuse and violence are not well understood. In interviews with women who wanted to break up a relationship, were in the process of leaving, or who had left a relationship, DeKeseredy and Joseph (2006, p. 238) find that two-thirds of the women declared that their former partners frequently drank alcohol. Shepherd (2001) reports similar findings when analyzing domestic violence among rural native Alaskan women. Lanier and Maume (2009) show an increased likelihood of violence among couples with male heavy drinking regardless of place.

In a study that examines the protective order process, barriers and outcomes in rural and urban areas in the United States, Logan et al. (2005, p. 896) report that about one-quarter of women interviewed mention that their partner was using alcohol or drugs during the incident that led to them filing the protective order. Alcohol abuse is also a predictor of domestic violence elsewhere. Tang and Lai (2007, p. 10) show that this is particularly true in China of men who lived in rural areas and had a low level of education.

One way of obtaining a less patchy picture of violence against women is to make use of all available data in the country – police statistics, health statistics, and victimization surveys – as is done in the following section for Sweden. Together, these sets of data, if not complete at least provide a complementary image of regional differences in violence against women. For example, health statistics (patient records gathered by the National Board of Health and Welfare) register the levels of hospitalization. If more female victims have to be hospitalized, then an increase in recorded health statistics should reflect a genuine rise in violence. If the violence does not require medical care, the victim might reveal her abuse in victimization surveys when she seeks help in a women's shelter, when she feels motivated to report it to the police (police records), or through victimization surveys.

The ecology of violence against women in rural Sweden

More than two-thirds of the variation in rates of violence for the whole country is associated with alcohol purchase, foreign-born population, and divorce rates. These results and the detailed methodology of this study are reported in a paper by Ceccato and Dolmén (2009). In an attempt to identify structural covariates of the geography of violence against women in rural Sweden, the authors disaggregated police-recorded data for 1996–2007 by municipalities and regressed them on demographic, socioeconomic, and lifestyle indicators, as suggested by the international literature in the previous section. A novelty of this analysis was the inclusion of JämIndex (Statistics Sweden, 2014), a gender index that indicates how municipalities perform in terms of gender equality. JämIndex consists of time series for each municipality and county for 15 individual variables such as education, average income, and use of parental leave days. The higher the index, the greater the gender equality. For instance, a municipality with a low index has few women in leading political positions in the community, a segregated labor market, large gender differences in income, and, at least hypothetically, is expected to show higher rates of violence against women. There were two model sets: one for the whole country and one applied only to rural municipalities. Results from these models were presented in Chapter 5, "The geography of property and violent crime in Sweden," Table 5.4.

Findings for the whole country show that some of the covariates were the same both for rural and urban municipalities, but they indicate that violence affects people living in these areas differently. Belonging to an ethnic minority in an urban area seems to put a woman at higher risk for partner violence than in a rural area. Moreover, the link between alcohol and rates of violence against women is dubious in rural areas and not easily interpreted. Whilst violence is weakly associated with less alcohol consumption, the proportion of outlets for purchasing alcohol has the expected (strong) effect on violence rates. Surprisingly, although the model included the JämIndex, the results did not show that municipalities with higher gender equality had a "protective effect" against violence against women.

The model for rural municipalities explains only one-third of the variation in rates of violence, compared to two-thirds for the model for the whole country. More interestingly, some indicators affect rates of violence in rural areas differently from how they do in urban areas. For instance, the ratio of the police force to inhabitants is associated with violence against women in rural municipalities but it is not in urban ones. This may indicate that the role of police in rural areas differs from those living in large cities: whilst the police are one of many possible actors to whom an assault may be reported in urban areas, in rural areas the police may be the only support to which women can turn.

Individual causal mechanisms between rates of violence against women and the use of alcohol, for instance, cannot be drawn from this study, because it is an ecological analysis by municipality. However, what is striking is that despite being an aggregated analysis (by administrative units), it predicts equally violence against women using factors that are also found in the current literature based on individual-level data (Table 10.4). For instance, studies based on individual-level data point out that the "typical" victims of violence in rural areas do not belong to the native group, are women in the process of leaving their partners, face lower socioeconomic conditions, and either they or the perpetrator make use of drugs and/or alcohol. In the Swedish case, rural municipalities with high rates of violence tend also to be characterized by a high proportion of female population with a foreign background. The link between victimization and foreign background was already pointed out by Rying (2001) when analyzing individual data of victims of homicides in intimate relationships in the 1990s. The author suggested that a large proportion of both the perpetrators and the victims were born outside Sweden, but it is common for the victim and the perpetrator to come from the same country.

Ceccato and Dolmén (2009) show that in Sweden rural rates of violence against women often go together with divorce rates (Figure 10.4). It is unclear whether broken relationships and subsequent contact with their former partners lead to more violent conflicts or if it is the other way around: greater rates of violence between partners lead to higher divorce rates. What is certain is that

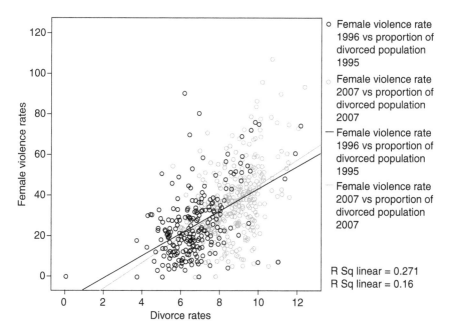

Figure 10.4 Scatter plot of female violence rates (*y*-axis) and divorce rates per municipality (*x*-axis), 1995 and 2007.

women may decide to report violence only when they have already decided to leave their partner, which explains the strong links between police-recorded violence against women and rates of divorce. Rying (2001, p. 46) indicates that in Sweden 60 percent of all cases of homicide (stemming from domestic conflicts) is motivated by jealousy or problems in connection with a separation. "The perpetrators, who are often individuals with a pronounced need to control, have killed the woman when they felt this need to be under threat." If there is plenty of evidence that some relationships lead to violence and, in extreme cases, death, why is the system not identifying these cases at an early stage? The answer, of course, is not simple, because it depends on a victim's willingness to admit the violence in the first place, which in turn depends on how culturally acceptable her admission is to the community. The answer also depends on a social network composed of friends and family as well as societal institutions (such as health and social care, police, and nongovernmental organizations) that are ready to step in and act in favor of the abused. Multiple barriers inhibit women from breaking their silence and getting the support they need to come forward. Some of these barriers are at community level. Chapter 14 will complement this discussion by reporting experiences from crime prevention initiatives in rural Sweden aimed at violence against women.

Final considerations

This chapter illustrates urban and rural differences in violence against women using Sweden as the study case. It also sheds light on possible factors behind violence against women in rural areas by examining Sweden in light of the most important international literature in the field. In Sweden and elsewhere, reporting rates for violence against women vary geographically for different reasons, which make it difficult to untangle underreported cases of violence against women between urban and rural areas. Although statistics on violence against women show more violence in urban municipalities in Sweden, rural areas are witnessing more cases of violence than in the past. Such an increase in cases of violence against women in police records was also confirmed by health statistics (hospitalization rates). This relative increase may be related to a genuine change in the level of criminal activity but also to a combination of other factors, such as a rise in victims' willingness to report to the police and other authorities, society's increased sensitivity to violence, improvements in criminal justice practices, and changes in the law.

It is important to keep in mind that the Swedish case study discussed in this chapter shares limitations with other studies based on limited data sources, which is relevant here. This analysis is based on "groupings of municipalities" as units of study. Data permitting, future analysis should explore units that make more sense for rural communities, such as rural villages within "urban" municipalities that are excluded here. For better evaluations of the prevalence of and hospitalization cases by injuries, more reliable and detailed data is necessary. For instance, the national victimization survey should increase sampling in rural areas so that violence against women can be at least reported at a municipal level. Some of the important questions on violence against women cannot be answered by quantitative frameworks. Thus, there is a need to look at case studies through surveys and interviews to examine rural regional variations in all kinds of woman abuse. It is necessary to consider the voices of victims of intimate violence as valuable information to understand its impact on their lives, such as how domestic assaults affect their levels of fear and anxiety. So far this lack of knowledge about the victim's perception of these violent events has led to a failure to learn about successful prevention strategies.

This chapter has shown that disparities between urban and rural rates of violence against women indicate that this crime may have specific determinants in the countryside at municipal level that differ from those for women living in cities (such as the role of the police in the countryside). It is unclear why indicators of gender equality do not capture the dynamics of the geography of violence against women, either in rural or in urban municipalities. One reason may be the fact that police statistics reflect society's capacity to deal with the problem and the communities' tolerance for violence as part of their daily life (embedded in the different gender contracts). This explains why municipalities with a large proportion of ethnic minorities in Sweden tend to be characterized by high levels of violence against women. They may well have a high gender index, with high gender-balanced labor market, good participation of females in local politics, support in place for assaulted women – and therefore high reporting rates for violence against women. The same reasoning may clarify the mismatch between low rates of reported gendered violence in some rural municipalities with a lower gender equality index. It may be that religious values lead to less violence against women, but it may also be that women are not prepared to publicly reveal partner assault or they have fears related to revealing it. In this case, fewer violent assaults may be just a measure of tolerance to violence, perhaps seen as part of the local gender contract and accepted norms.

Previous studies using individual-level data help remarkably in understanding gendered violence in Sweden, but in many cases they fail to distinguish between rural and urban women. New understanding that draws on rural women's perspectives of violence in the domestic realm is required to delineate a clear picture of women's needs, not only as victims but, more importantly, as agents of their life choices. Such needs pose a considerable challenge to academics, criminal justice authorities, and policy makers.

The international literature indicates that violence has a greater impact on women living in remote areas than on those living in urban centers. But is that the case in Sweden? No systematic evidence has been found on this point. At the same time, being a "welfare state" with a long tradition of a women's movement does not guarantee a homogeneous support network for women suffering violence in the domestic realm. To answer these questions, there is a need to assess whether and how different gender contracts affect local social control and criminal justice practices toward women victims of domestic violence. This includes the treatment the women receive on a daily basis, through municipal social services, healthcare, and supporting nongovernmental organizations, such as shelters.

At the national level, there are many remaining challenges in research on domestic violence in Sweden. First, there is a need to understand the nature of the violence against women, particularly focusing on potential differences between urban and rural areas. Studies elsewhere indicate that rural offenders of intimate abuse were nearly twice as likely as their urban counterparts to inflict severe physical injuries. They were also more likely to use a weapon during their assaults. Almost twice as many rural assailants threatened to kill their victims, and rural assailants were 2.5 times more likely than their urban counterparts to destroy property during the event (for a review, see Pruitt, 2008). Does geographical and social isolation contribute to more violent outcomes in rural areas than in urban ones? This is a question that can only be answered empirically, perhaps being approached as an interdisciplinary issue worthy of analysis on its own.

Second, as in other countries, violence against women in intimate relationships varies across ethnic groups, but overall in Sweden women from ethnic minorities are extra vulnerable to this type of violence. Abuse within immigrant families creates a variety of challenges; some are not unique to rural communities. However, it is unclear whether such variations differ across urban and rural areas in Sweden. Responding to them in rural context may be more difficult because of the dearth of services, particularly for those with limited knowledge of Swedish. The findings reported in this chapter also indicate that migrant women run a higher risk of victimization than their Swedish counterparts regardless of where they live. Future research should focus particularly on cases of women brought to Sweden in "marriage arrangements." It is unclear how the lack of protection these non-permanent residents suffer affect their decision to remain with their partners and cope with violence. Anecdotal evidence reported by the media illustrates cases in which the process of "othering" is used to alleviate the role of offenders in suspected cases of domestic violence and to deport women to their home countries.

Third, although violence in the private realm affects mostly women, both men and women are at risk. Knowledge of the extent to which men are exposed to domestic violence is so far insufficient in Sweden. The same applies to those who experience violence indirectly in the household, such as children and the elderly. All victims of violence, regardless of gender, gender identity, age, or ethnic background have the right to assistance and protection. Future research should investigate ways to improve the knowledge base, so a safe home environment can be ensured for all.

Finally, there is an urgent need to know more about the experiences of local crime prevention initiatives on violence against women in rural Sweden. This is important because rural areas impose challenges on women who are victims of violence. Chapter 14 contributes to this knowledge base by providing a snapshot of what is happening in terms of interventions to tackle violence against women in Swedish rural areas.

Notes

1 Literally "Women's Peace," originally from a medieval Swedish law protecting women.
2 As a result of changes in criminal codes in 2009, the data needs to be carefully analyzed when compared with data from 1996 and 2007.

References

Abbott, J., Johnson, R., Koziol-McLain, J., & Lowenstein, S. R. (1995). Domestic violence against women: Incidence and prevalence in an emergency department population. *JAMA, 273*(22), 1763–1767.
Abramsky, T., Watts, C., Garcia-Moreno, C., Devries, K., Kiss, L., Ellsberg, M., Jansen, A. F. M., & Heise, L. (2011). What factors are associated with recent intimate partner violence? Findings from the WHO multi-country study on women's health and domestic violence. *BMC Public Health, 11*(1), 109.
Ahacic, K. (2010). *Alkohol- och narkotikautvecklingen i Stockholms län 1998–2008.* Stockholm: Karolinska institutets folkhälsoakademi.
Amcoff, J. (2001). Regionala genuskontrakt i Sverige? Uppsala: Kulturgeografiska institutionen, Uppsala University.
Anderson, S. (1999). Crime and social change in Scotland. In G. Dingwall & S. Moody (Eds.), *Crime and conflict in the countryside* (pp. 45–59). Cardiff: University of Wales Press.
Bhandari, S., Levitch, A. H., Ellis, K. K., Ball, K., Everett, K., Geden, E., & Bullock, L. (2008). Comparative analyses of stressors experienced by rural low-income pregnant women experiencing intimate partner violence and those who are not. *Journal of Obstetric, Gynecologic, and Neonatal Nursing, 37*(4), 492–501.
BJS. (2011). Homicide trends in the United States, 1980–2008. US Department of Justice. Retrieved April 14, 2015, from www.ojp.gov.
Boonzaier, F. A., & van Schalkwyk, S. (2011). Narrative possibilities: Poor women of color and the complexities of intimate partner violence. *Violence Against Women, 17*(2), 267–286.
Bunge, V., & Levett, A. (1998). *Family violence in Canada: A statistical profile.* Ottawa: Statistics Canada.
Burman, M. (2012). Immigrant women facing male partner violence: Gender, race and power in Swedish alien and criminal law. *feminists@law, 2*(1).
Ceccato, V., & Dolmén, L. (2009). Violence against women in rural Sweden. Paper presented at the *International Conference Gendering Violence: Feminist Intervention in Contemporary Research*, Uppsala.
Ceccato, V., & Dolmén, L. (2011). Crime in rural Sweden. *Applied Geography, 31*(1), 119–135.
DeKeseredy, W. S., Donnermeyer, J. F., & Schwartz, M. D. (2009). Toward a gendered second generation CPTED for preventing woman abuse in rural communities. *Security Journal, 22*, 178–189.
DeKeseredy, W. S., Donnermeyer, J. F., Schwartz, M. D., Tunnell, K., & Hall, M. (2007). Thinking critically about rural gender relations: Toward a rural masculinity crisis/male peer support model of separation/divorce sexual assault. *Critical Criminology, 15*(4), 295–311.
DeKeseredy, W. S., Dragiewicz, M., & Rennisson, C. M. (2012). Racial/ethnic variations in violence against women: Urban, suburban, and rural differences. *International Journal of Rural Criminology, 1*(2), 184–202.

DeKeseredy, W. S., & Joseph, C. (2006). Separation and/or divorce sexual assault in rural Ohio: Preliminary results of an exploratory study. *Violence Against Women, 12*(3), 301–311.

DeKeseredy, W. S., Rogness, M., & Schwartz, M. D. (2004). Separation/divorce sexual assault: The current state of social scientific knowledge. *Aggression and Violent Behavior, 9*, 675–691.

DeKeseredy, W. S., & Schwartz, M. D. (2008). Separation/divorce sexual assault in rural Ohio: Survivors' perceptions. *Journal of Prevention and Intervention in the Community, 36*(1–2), 105–119.

DeKeseredy, W. S., Schwartz, M. D., & Alvi, S. (2008). Which women are more likely to be abused? Public housing, cohabitation, and separated/divorced women. *Criminal Justice Studies, 21*(4), 283–293.

DeKeseredy, W. S., Schwartz, M. D., Fagen, D., & Hall, M. (2006). Separation/divorce sexual assault: The contribution of male support. *Feminist Criminology, 1*(3), 228–250.

Del Castillo, M., Heimer, G., Kalliokoski, A. M., & Stenson, K. (2004). Den våldsutsatta kvinnan: En retrospektiv arkivundersökning av de kvinnor som behandlats på Rikskvinnocentrum 1995–2002. Uppsala: RiksKvinnocentrums rapportserie.

Eriksson, M. (2011). Contact, shared parenting, and violence: Children as witnesses of domestic violence in Sweden. *International Journal of Law, Policy and the Family, 25*(2), 165–183.

Estrada, F. (2005). Våldsutvecklingen i Sverige e en presentation och analys av sjukvårdsdata. *Arbetsrapport.* Stockholm: Institutet för framtidsstudier.

European Commission. (1999). Europeans and their views on domestic violence against women. *Eurobarometer* (Vol. 51). European Commission Directorate-General X. Retrieved April 14, 2015, from http://europa.eu.int/comm/dg10/women/index_en.html.

Finney, A. (2006). Domestic violence, sexual assault and stalking: Findings from the 2004/05 British Crime Survey. London: Home Office.

Fram, M. S., Miller-Cribbs, J., & Farber, N. (2006). Chicks aren't chickens: Women, poverty, and marriage in an orthodoxy of conservatism. *Affilia, 21*(3), 256–271.

Gracia, E. (2004). Unreported cases of domestic violence against women: Towards an epidemiology of social silence, tolerance, and inhibition. *Journal of Epidemiology and Community Health, 58*(7), 536–537.

Graham, K., Bernards, S., Wilsnack, S. C., & Gmel, G. (2011). Alcohol may not cause partner violence but it seems to make it worse: A cross national comparison of the relationship between alcohol and severity of partner violence. *Journal of interpersonal violence, 26*(8), 1503–1523.

Grama, J. L. (2000). Women forgotten: Difficulties faced by rural victims of domestic violence. *American Journal of Family Law, 14*, 173–189.

Greenfeld, L. A. (1998). Violence by intimates: Analysis of data on crimes by current or former spouses, boyfriends, and girlfriends. Washington, DC: US Department of Justice, Office of Justice Programs, Bureau of Justice Statistics.

Grossman, S. F., Hinkley, S., Kawalski, A., & Margrave, C. (2005). Rural versus urban victims of violence: The interplay of race and region. *Journal of Family Violence, 20*, 71–81.

Ingram, M., McClelland, D. J., Martin, J., Caballero, M. F., Mayorga, M. T., & Gillespie, K. (2010). Experiences of immigrant women who self-petition under the Violence Against Women Act. *Violence Against Women, 16*(8), 858–880.

Jerre, K. (2008). PM/Forskningsplan för Våld och sensibilitet. Seminar notes.

Kantor, G. K., & Straus, M. A. (1987). The "drunken bum" theory of wife beating. *Social Problems, 34*(3), 213–230.

King, L. L., & Roberts, J. J. (2011). Traditional gender role and rape myth acceptance: From the countryside to the big city. *Women and Criminal Justice, 21*(1), 1–20.

Krantz, G., & Vung, N. (2009). The role of controlling behaviour in intimate partner violence and its health effects: A population based study from rural Vietnam. *BMC Public Health, 9*(1), 143.

Lanier, C., & Maume, M. O. (2009). Intimate partner violence and social isolation across the rural/urban divide. *Violence Against Women, 15*(11), 1311–1330.

Leander, K. (2007). Mens våld mot kvinnor: Ett folkhälsoproblem (C. F. Folkhälsa, Trans.). *Stockholms Läns landsting.* Stockholm: Stockholms Läns landsting.

Lee, M. R., & Stevenson, G. D. (2006). Gender-specific homicide offending in rural areas. *Homicide Studies, 10*(1), 55–73.

Lewis, S. H. (2003). Unspoken crimes: Sexual assault in rural America. Enola, PA: National Sexual Violence Resource Center.

Lindblom, P., Castrén, M., & Kurland, L. (2010). Akutsjukvård och våldsutsatta kvinnor' i Att fråga om våldsutsatthet som en del av anamnesen. Uppsala: National Center for Knowledge on Men's Violence Against Women (NCK), Uppsala University.

Logan, T. K., Shannon, L., & Walker, R. (2005). Protective orders in rural and urban areas: A multiple perspective study. *Violence Against Women, 11*, 876–911.

Logan, T. K., Walker, R., & Leukefeld, C. (2001). Rural, urban influenced, and urban differences among domestic violence arrestees. *Journal of Interpersonal Violence, 16*(3), 266–283.

Lundgren, E., Heimer, G., Westerstrand, J., & Kalliokoski, A. M. (2002). Slagen damen: Mäns våld mot kvinnor i jämställda Sverige – en omfångsundersökning. Stockholm: Umeå.

Marshall, B., & Johnson, S. (2005). Crime in rural areas: A review of the literature for the rural evidence research centre. Jill Dando Institute of Crime Science, University College, London, p. 51.

Moore, C. G., Probst, J. C., Tompkins, M., Cuffe, S., & Martin, A. B. (2005). Poverty, stress, and violent disagreements in the home among rural families. Columbia, SC: South Carolina Rural Health Research Center.

Morley, R., & Mullander, A. (1994). Preventing domestic violence to women. London: Home Office.

Murdaugh, C., Hunt, S., Sowell, R., & Santana, I. (2004). Domestic violence in Hispanics in the southeastern United States: A survey and needs analysis. *Journal of Family Violence, 19*(2), 107–115.

Socialstyrelsen (National Board of Health and Welfare). (2014). Ensam och utsatt: Utbildningsmaterial om våld mot kvinnor med utländsk bakgrund. Stockholm: Socialstyrelsen.

Naved, R. T., Azim, S., Bhuiyaa, A., & Persson, L. Å. (2006). Physical violence by husbands: Magnitude, disclosure and help-seeking behavior of women in bangladesh. Dhaka, Bangladesh: Center for Health and Population Research.

Nilsson, L. (2002). Violence against women in intimate relationships: An overview. Stockholm: BRÅ.

Olsson, E. (2011). Hon flydde från sambon: nu ska hon utvisas. *Metro.* Retrieved April 14, 2014, from www.metro.se/nyheter/hon-flydde-fran-sambon-nu-ska-hon-utvisas/EVHndn!2V8jfhwXuFBM/.

Orloff, L. E., & Sarangapani, H. (2007). Governmental and industry roles and responsibilities with regard to international marriage brokers: Equalizing the balance of power between foreign fiancés and spouses. *Violence Against Women, 13*(5), 469–485.

Persily, C. A., & Abdulla, S. (2000). Domestic violence and pregnancy in rural West Virginia. *Journal of Rural Nursing and Health Care, 1*, 11–20.

Pruitt, L. R. (2008). Place matters: Domestic violence and rural difference. *Wisconsin Journal of Law, Gender and Society, 32*, 346–416.

Raj, A., & Silverman, J. (2002). Violence against immigrant women: The roles of culture, context, and legal immigrant status on intimate partner violence. *Violence Against Women, 8*(3), 367–398.

Rying, M. (2001). Acts of lethal violence against women in intimate relationships. Stockholm: BRÅ.

Schafer, J. A., & Giblin, M. J. (2010). Policing intimate partner violence in rural areas and small towns: Policies, practices, and perceptions. *Women and Criminal Justice, 20*(4), 283–301.

Selin, K. H., & Westlund, O. (2008). Misshandel mot kvinnor: Brottsutvecklingen i Sverige fram till år 2007. *Brottsutvecklingen i Sverige fram till år 2007* (23rd ed.). Stockholm: Brottsförebyggande rådet.

Sharma, S., & Rees, S. (2007). Consideration of the determinants of women's mental health in remote Australian mining towns. *Australian Journal of Rural Health, 15*, 1–7.

Shepherd, J. (2001). Where do you go when it's 40 below? Domestic violence among rural Alaska native women. *Affilia: Journal of Women and Social Work, 16*, 488–510.

Slovak, K., & Singer, M. (2002). Children and violence: Findings and implications from a rural community. *Child and Adolescent Social Work Journal, 19*(1), 35–56.

Statistics Sweden. (2014). JämIndex. Retrieved April 13, 2014, from www.scb.se/sv_/Hitta-statistik/Statistik-efter-amne/Levnadsforhallanden/Jamstalldhet/Jamstalldhetsstatistik/.

Stenson, K. (2004). Men's violence against women: A challenge in antenatal care (PhD Thesis, Uppsala University, Uppsala).

Sundari, A. (2011). Legislating gender inequalities: The nature and patterns of domestic violence experienced by South Asian women with insecure immigration status in the United Kingdom. *Violence Against Women, 17*(10), 1260–1285.

Tang, C. S. K., & Lai, B. P. L. (2008). A review of empirical literature on the prevalence and risk markers of male-on-female intimate partner violence in contemporary China, 1987–2006. *Aggression and Violent Behavior, 13*(1), 10–28.

Townsend, J. G. (1991). Towards a regional geography of gender. *Geographical Journal, 157*, 25–35.

Trygged, S., Hedlund, E., & Kåreholt, I. (2014). Beaten and poor? A study of the long-term economic situation of women victims of severe violence. *Social Work in Public Health, 29*(2), 100–113.

Van Hightower, N., Gorton, J., & DeMoss, C. (2000). predictive models of domestic violence and fear of intimate partners among migrant and seasonal farm worker women. *Journal of Family Violence, 15*(2), 137–154.

Walby, S., & Allen, J. (2004). Domestic violence, sexual assault and stalking: Findings from the British Crime Survey. London: Home Office.

Websdale, N. (1995). Rural woman abuse: The voice of Kentucky women. *Violence Against Women, 1*, 309–338.

Websdale, N. (1998). *Rural woman battering and the justice system: An ethnography.* Thousand Oaks, CA: Sage.

Websdale, N., & Johnson, B. (1998). An ethnostatistical comparison of the forms and levels of woman battering in Urban and rural areas of Kentucky. *Criminal Justice Review, 23*, 161–196.

Weigl, K., & Edblom, K. (2013). Dödade Kvinnor. *Aftonbladet*. Retrieved April 14, 2015, from http://dodadekvinnor.aftonbladet.se/fall/.

Wendt, S. (2008). Christianity and domestic violence: Feminist poststructuralist perspectives. *Affilia, 23*(2), 144–155.

Women's Services Network – WESNET. (2000). Domestic violence in regional Australia: A literature review. Canberra: Partnerships Against Domestic Violence, Office of the Status of Women, and Department of Transport and Regional Services. Retrieved April 14, 2015, from http://wesnet.org.au/wp-content/uploads/2012/04/WESNET-Domestic-Violence-in-Regional-Australia-A-Literature-Review.pdf.

Westman, M. (2010). Women of Thailand (Master's thesis, University of Linköping, Linköping).

World Health Organization – WHO. (2002). International classication of functioning, disability and health. Geneva: WHO.

Part V

Policing and crime prevention in rural Sweden

11 Police, rural policing, and community safety

One reason this chapter is devoted to rural policing is the difference in police work and organization. More than 40 years ago, Cain (1973) highlighted the distinctiveness of rural policing, with its isolating and lonesome nature, and the dependence on one's neighbors and community within which the police lived. Rural crime issues are very different nowadays from those in the 1970s, and certainly rurality is a complex mix that imposes new demands on policing that go beyond issues of remoteness and isolation. Policing is no longer a job for the public police force only. Yet "(t)here has always been, and still is, a difference between police work and organization in urban and rural areas" (Furuhagen, 2009, p. 13)

Mawby (2011) suggests that in many countries only a small proportion of policing is carried out by police officers especially trained by the central or local government. Alternative policing has not emerged at pace with this change or evenly distributed across or within countries. This chapter starts with an international overview of what the police have been, with particular focus on the historical development of the rural police as an institution. This is an important subject, as Mawby and Yarwood (2011, p. 1) suggest "studies of rural policing have fallen off the edge of many research agendas." This chapter also provides a detailed history of the development of policing in Swedish rural areas and discusses examples of the contemporary daily work of police with crime, crime prevention, and community safety, focusing on Sweden. Then, the chapter ends with a discussion of future challenges for policing in the Swedish countryside, as the commodification of policing has become a reality and the police organization is being centralized.

In this book, the term *police* refers to the civil force of a state responsible for the detection and prevention of crime and the maintenance of public order. In terms of actions, "police" is often associated with more traditional policing, that is, mostly reactive activities, such as patrol and direct reactions to the crimes and/or infractions being committed. Police have also been associated with proactive activities aimed at crime control as well as perceived safety. *Policing* is a broader concept that may include more than the police, often with the involvement of multiple actors, public and private ones, and citizens, all aimed at safety governance. Also referred to as *community policing*, it is more proactive than the traditional policing work of patrol. As suggested by Yarwood (2014), "community policing" usually refers to the efforts of various state, volunteer, and private agencies to police particular places in partnership with one another. Whilst police actions are typically dedicated to specific geographic areas in their jurisdiction, policing may have less distinctive territorial boundaries, as actors are not necessarily bound on a territorial basis.

Police in rural areas: an international perspective

The word police comes from the Greek words *polis*, meaning city or state, and *politeia*, management. The original meaning was the city administration or art of government. The modern police, a more "organized" police as we know them, are a relatively new phenomenon. They emerged with the development of communities where there was a clear power structure in the form of royalty or later, with independent administrative bodies. In Sweden, for example, the modern police developed in the 1800s and early 1900s as a result of industrialization and the growing need for control in cities that produced new and greater problems of order and crime. As Furuhagen (2009) states, police in a broader sense has a much longer history and is perhaps a phenomenon as old as humanity itself.

In the Middle Ages, and even in the modern era, the police played a varied role. In Sweden, police was a collective term for all public activities except the church; that is, to denote the part of the "domestic" and local management in charge of maintaining order and safety, practically everything that related to social, political, and economic life but, of course, did not have today's organization, with police departments and corps. Originally the police depended on individuals who shared the burden of ensuring collective safety. In small medieval towns, night watchmen alternated shifts monitoring the city and arresting criminals and beggars. In the countryside, peasants were assigned different roles, of village guard or parish constable. They could then also get other jobs in the local community and they worked occasionally as local agents or representatives of the king, that is, state power. Nowadays, the police reflect the state's monopoly on violence and are an institution responsible for order and security within the country (Furuhagen, 2004, 2009).

The way rural areas are policed nowadays is also a result of different traditions in policing. There are two accepted police traditions: one that follows the *Anglo-Saxon* model, which has its roots in England and in the United States, and the other, the *continental police* tradition, which prevailed in France, Italy, Germany, countries in southern and central Europe, and, to some extent, Canada. For a detailed description of Canada's and the United States' structure for rural policing, see Donnermeyer, DeKeseredy, and Dragiewicz (2011) and also later in this chapter.

The Anglo-Saxon model is characterized by decentralization and has been built on community-based and civil forms of policing with constables and guards, often unarmed. In the United States, systematic study of urban and small-town policing was almost nonexistent before the 1970s (Payne, Berg, &

Sun, 2005). Although studies were performed after that, researchers suggest that they are often descriptive and "atheoretical," with very limited attempts to link police structure and rural social structure (Donnermeyer et al., 2011; Weisheit, Falcone, & Wells, 2006). These authors suggest that the absence of research is attributable to the fact that is may be difficult to obtain an acceptable sample size of events in small municipalities. Moreover, rural residents as well as police may be less likely to accept strangers and share information with outsiders, making it difficult to conduct research in rural areas.

The continental police tradition derived originally from France, which created a *gendarmerie*, that is, armed state police on horseback, in rural areas as far back as the sixteenth century. The French police developed much stronger links with armed forces and was heavily armed. According to Furuhagen (2009), the continental police is deemed to have been, and probably still is, less civic-oriented than the Anglo-Saxon police, which is closer to the people, more service-oriented and less authoritarian. The Swedish police have been influenced in varying degrees by both traditions. The Swedish police's historical roots are local, but the state's growing involvement has been a common thread in its historical development. The next section reviews rural and small-town policing in the United States, Canada, the United Kingdom, and Australia as background for the Swedish case.

Glimpses of rural policing in the United States, Canada, the United Kingdom, and Australia

The most comprehensive research on rural and small-town policing in the United States was conducted by Weisheit and colleagues (Falcone, Wells, & Weisheit, 2002; Weisheit, Wells, & Falcone, 1994). Payne et al. (2005) report that they found that rural and small-town police departments tend to emphasize crime prevention and service activities, whereas those based in large cities focus on enforcing law and controlling crime through arrests. They also found that policing styles in rural areas largely reflect the relationship between the police and the community. Moreover, rural officers are expected to carry out a wider range of tasks than their urban counterparts do, because other social services are either nonexistent or too remote to provide timely service. Moreover, like their urban counterparts, rural police have to adapt their strategy and tactics to meet the needs of their communities (Cordner & Scarborough, 1997). Where tax bases are small, rural police departments are likely to be seriously understaffed and without important resources (Weisheit et al., 1994).

The rural setting has particular features shaping both crime and policing (Weisheit et al., 1994). Weisheit et al. (1994) give an example of what this means in the North American context. Although rural individuals are more likely to own guns, they are less likely to use guns in committing a crime. Gun ownership is much more prevalent in rural areas, where more than double the number of residents own guns than their urban counterparts. Nowadays, of the United States' estimated 13.7 million hunters, 18 percent reside outside metropolitan areas and 3 percent in big cities (Pompa & Ganier, 2013).

More recently, another face of rural areas in North America was presented by Donnermeyer et al. (2011). They highlight the complexity of rural communities in the United States and Canada and how it creates specific challenges for the police. On one hand, some of these rural areas are examples of the idyllic rural; on the other hand, some suffer from a number of problems, such as persistent poverty, depopulation, and youth drug addiction. They suggest that a way to understand the plurality of rural policing is to assume that there are several communities within a community that vary over time and space. Within these rural communities are various kinds of social orders that interplay with the formal structures of policing and deal with different types of crimes in different ways. The authors add that:

> understanding policing practices in the rural context continue down a path of testing specific actions but without ever considering macro-level forces that place strong parameters for the ways in which rural communities, peoples and police can change and work together in more effective partnerships.
>
> (Donnermeyer et al., 2011, p. 31)

In Britain, developments in policing have moved toward reactive policing, and many local police stations have been closed. Such changes are based on policing and governance at various levels as stipulated by the Crime and Disorder Act 1998. Economization in services in rural areas especially is argued to have affected some municipalities more than others, as policing has become less visible. In contrast, there have emerged in the 1990s local policing schemes based on volunteerism and community involvement. Farm Watch (FW) has been implemented across rural areas, its success in large part attributable to local police and partnership initiatives that support and maintain such initiatives. By the end of the decade, partnership initiatives had a firm place in government policy. Rural crime governance has changed in parallel with an increased emphasis on risk-based strategies that identify and police crime "hot spots" from the national to local levels, thus demoting crime in rural areas. Within the most rural regions, urban areas do exist, and these attract the bulk of available funding (Fyfe, 1995; Jones & Phipps, 2012; Yarwood, 2011). Mawby (2011) suggests that a *policing mix* has characterized community policing in rural areas in the past 20 years, through the expansion of private and state agencies involved in policing as well as volunteers and police ancillaries. The number of special constables relative to regular officers is greater in rural areas and, according to the author, has remained constant over the years despite the expansion of private and state agencies involved in policing.

In a recent study in rural Scotland, Fenwick, Dockrell, Roberts, and Slade (2012) also found that the challenges of rural police include large territorial distances, limited access to resources for support, unique community expectations, and role conflicts experienced by police officers in the social dynamics of rural communities. In these circumstances, officers learn to balance being part of the community with carrying out their policing duties, or balance policing "by the book" with community expectations. To maintain legitimacy with the community, police need to respond to and resolve minor quality of life issues. Participants suggest that this practice increases the visibility of the police and provides opportunities to gather intelligence on community activities. Fenwick et al. (2012) used focus groups to find out the unique demands on police officers following a community policing model. They found, for instance, that evidence-based practice for policing does not fit the demands of rural communities, as they present special challenges to police.

Barclay, Scott, and Donnermeyer (2011) report on Australian cases of community policing in a country where the region plays an important role in policing. To start with, the organization of policing in Australia is different from both the United States and the United Kingdom. The organization practices and laws are determined more on a regional basis in Australian states and territories, each of which is policed by a single organization that is centrally controlled. These areas are divided into regions, then police districts, and then police stations. Some rural communities are served by officers located in neighboring towns, with officers working between communities. Community policing defines important aspects of the role of the police, under the *localistic model*. Local police officers are expected to become part of the community even if it compromises objectivity. This model also has disadvantages, namely that certain groups or activities become over-policed and others under-policed. Paradoxically, as a result the model may also favor certain groups and sectional interests (Barclay et al., 2011). This may support what a more critical account of this model states: "Some communities are more willing and able to help themselves and it is an irony that those in the need of most help are unlikely to benefit from self-help initiatives" (Yarwood, 2014, p. 6).

Sweden has a long tradition of local policing, but this does not mean that it has always been decentralized. Up to the mid-1960s, Sweden had a decentralized organization (see Table 11.2, later in the chapter). Later it became more driven from the center. In the 1980s, a debate about strong governmental intervention and centralization affected many sectors of society, including the police. This development also followed trends in practices in the United Kingdom and elsewhere focused on community-based policing in Sweden. Crucial for this decentralized policing model was the 1996 national program for crime prevention, in which local police forces were central actors (Ceccato & Dolmén, 2011). Local partnerships meant that part of the responsibility of crime control and prevention was placed on the shoulders of civil society (Yarwood & Edwards, 1995) with public engagement in different levels and initiatives. This collaborative model became – and is still regarded as – important to successful crime prevention. The next section discusses the origins of modern policing, up to current developments, with a focus on rural areas.

Police and policing in Sweden: focus on rural areas

From its origins to modern policing in the 1990s[1]

The Swedish police authority's earliest origins were in rural areas, where early forms of policing likely worked in the same way as in other countries, namely the local community itself was responsible for maintaining order. It was with the nascent monarchy that pre-modern police service began to take its current form. The king's bailiffs worked in the Middle Ages with tax collection and other details of the administration but also had overall responsibility for local law and order (Sjöholm, 1941). Already in Viking times, order and law had territorial features. According to Furuhagen (2009), when Sweden was Christianized (between the eighth and the twelfth centuries), the country was divided into parishes, each one led by a priest who met with the male farmers at parish meetings to discuss local affairs, including order in the parish, such as conflicts between neighbors or problems with rowdy youngsters. To maintain order in the parish, the priest was assisted by "six men," who were elders elected or appointed by the male farmers in different parts of each parish. They would keep a close eye on local order, helping to mediate conflicts and reporting to the priest on problems of order and neglect in their villages.

It was only in the early seventeenth century that the monarchy took over and governors in each county were given the ultimate responsibility for law and order. The crown bailiffs primarily handled tax collection in their districts but they also continued to watch over law and order and prosecute crime. In practice, these tasks were handled at the local level largely by the sergeants who served under each bailiff. In addition to police-like tasks, a bailiff could act as the representative of the state in the role of "prosecutor" in some cases before district courts (lower courts in rural areas). Police chiefs were not police officers in today's sense; they were a mixture of police, tax official, and prosecutor at the lowest level. Police chiefs remained until the early twentieth century when, through a reform, they were replaced by country fiscals that basically had the same function as early sheriffs (a mixture of police, tax official, and prosecutor at the lowest level) but also had more skilled tasks (e.g., responsibility for the seizure of taxes, fees, and fines and keeping an eye on trade and industry, transport and communications, fire protection, and construction). Under the fiscals, in each rural village there were *fjärdingsmän*, or constables, elected or appointed in the local community. In practice, these were often farmers or other people in the parish who often served part-time as police.

During the second half of the 1800s, it became clear that policing in the Swedish countryside was inadequate. Cities and market towns, with concentrations of many people brought by, for instance, train stations, mills, and industries, required officers devoted exclusively to police work. In the latter nineteenth century, urban communities would hire a police superintendent and, if necessary, additional police personnel. In the early twentieth century, rural police still were not considered satisfactory, despite state funding for hiring extra police. Although there were no military police, a mounted police combined with county detectives and reserve officers was started, half financed by the state, half by counties or municipalities. According to Furuhagen (2009), mounted police had already been implemented by several counties and were called the "county police" because they were employed by the county councils. In 1920, there were 2,789 constables throughout Sweden, but only 325 of these had full-time duties. Also, they were distributed irregularly across the country, as only 383 policemen served outside the cities. At the local level, police handled tasks along with sergeants, constables, and, later, extra officers.

There were large differences between urban police forces and police in rural areas as well as between various municipalities and between towns. In the capital, Stockholm, police also had a decentralized organization. The city was divided into several districts with local police stations. Each district was headed by a commissioner, who had several detectives and a large number of ordinary constables under him. They spent most of their time patrolling on foot. Crime prevention was limited, as the emphasis was on maintaining order in a broad sense.

In 1925, a more centralized police model came into force and was supported by several sectors of society, especially police officers. Police remained essentially a municipal concern, but the state could control a local police organization. This meant that national police legislation ensured police officers' employment and working conditions, with uniform rules for wages, disciplinary punishment, and dismissal. A school was the means for centralizing training which, until then, had been spread across the country and, by today's standards, had been short and inadequate. Furuhagen (2009) reports police wages were low, especially in rural areas and small towns, where the work day was long and hard. One problem of local police had been that officers could be arbitrarily dismissed with no independent investigation. The consequences of the Police Act 1925 were largely a codification and homogenization of police work. The local connection remained strong for many small police precincts, which had considerable freedom in organizing police work. Rural areas often had only a lone constable who, in practice, was busier collecting taxes and performing sundry tasks than officially assisting in police work.

Furuhagen (2009) adds that the Police Act 1925, unlike the current Police Act, did not contain any declarations of principles that police should prevent crime. There was also no discussion about police presence in the local community, which might suggest that in practice it was not a problem and not a concern because police and police work were already strongly rooted in the local community, especially in rural areas and small towns, where much of the population lived at that time. According to Furuhagen, this reform was positive but not enough to improve and adapt the police to society's needs. The problems were mainly in rural areas, where the military had to step in. A state police, which complemented the municipal police, was established in 1932. One of the main motivations for the founding of the state police was demonstrations in 1931 when the military shot and killed five civilians. However, the shortcomings of the existing municipal police organization were numerous. The main problem was that there were too many precincts and they were too small. In 1944, there were more than 1,600 precincts (of which 123 cities and 57 towns), and rural areas had many districts with only one or two police officers. Ten years later, there were 854 precincts, and in the early 1960s there were 554. However, many districts had yet to get police officers to work satisfactorily: 70 percent of the districts had fewer than 10 police officers, some had only two. There was an increasing need for coordination over large geographical areas, particularly cooperation between police in rural areas and adjacent towns.

Personal and professional anecdotal evidence from police officers shows that the nationalization of the police meant additional resources, especially cars and other technical equipment, but also more bureaucracy and paperwork. There was now also greater consistency. In the meantime, municipal resources and circumstances for conducting effective policing still varied much between precincts. Technological developments contributed to the centralization of the police. The technology also favored a reactive approach (Furuhagen, 2009). Car patrols in the 1960s led to "alienated" police practices focused largely on event-driven emergency operations and neglect of contact with the community, because car patrolling was considered to have a deterrent effect on crime. There was an expectation that as police cars were constantly in motion, people would get the impression that the police were present everywhere. The debate about the dangers of a state police continued after nationalization. Some sectors of society alleged that the police in a centralized state could be a threat to democracy. In 1975, a police investigation led to reforms of the Swedish police in the 1980s and paved the way to a centralized model in the 1990s. With urbanization, police workloads not only increased in volume but also became more diverse. The decentralization of the police was thought necessary for the institution to adapt to more complex patterns of living and working that were emerging in larger cities at that time. This was followed in the 1980s by stronger citizen influence, as local police boards got more power to make decisions and manage their business, in terms of greater control over resource allocation. Police training also changed: the theoretical portion was expanded and contained more social and behavioral sciences. In practical everyday work, the reform advocated commitment to community policing, in which contact with the public increased while car patrols for prevention were to be avoided. During the 1990s, the reform of the Swedish police continued in the direction it began in the 1980s but faced numerous challenges as community policing reform demanded new resources that were reduced by the economic crisis of the early 1990s.

Recent developments in Swedish rural policing: 1990s onwards

As in other Western countries, in Sweden the police have undergone several transformations during the last 20–30 years. The two most important changes are the pluralization of actors exercising policing (from the hegemonic role of the police to a plethora of actors) and commodification of certain services and activities, with the expansion of private sector to traditional police roles.

In rural areas, private security companies have gained legitimacy through explicit recognition of the state, as policing models become more local-oriented. Hence, these companies operate partly in combination with other public authorities and perform legitimatized functions of security governance. In 2005, 30 percent of Swedish municipalities conducted activities that fall within the responsibilities of the police (Thelin & Svantemark, 2005). At the same time, one-third of municipalities employed private sector organizations to perform police patrols (*Kommunaktuellt*, 2002). This development is discussed in more detail in the following.

The "renewal bill 1989–1990" was the direct prelude to community police reform with the paper *Alla vårt ansvar*. The bill also suggested that most police officers be generalists, "overall police," meaning that they should be locally based officers responsible for all types of police work (criminal investigations, call-out service, crime prevention efforts). The reform was aimed at strengthening citizens' influence on crime prevention, which was considered the best way to deal with crime. Community policing would evolve to become the foundation of police activities framed by 21 police authorities (see Table 11.2, later in the chapter). The inspiration came from British and North American models such as *community policing* and *problem-based policing*. The idea was that the police should have stronger roots in the citizenry. Police work should have more contact with schools, social care, local organizations, and other agencies in the community (a predefined geographic area). Police work should also focus more than before on preventing crime. This would be achieved primarily through a systematic approach and problem-oriented policing in which police officers with good local knowledge would gather intelligence about crime and its prevention themselves. However, how many of these principles were actually put into practice?

It is clear the extent to which policing reform was not implemented in accordance with the government's intentions (Furuhagen, 2009). Several reasons obstruct the application of the model in practice. First, the reform was implemented gradually and at different times for different parts of the country. Some police authorities began to change their activities already in 1993, while others took until the late 1990s. In 2000, according to the National Police Agency, only 40 percent of all local police officers were considered "working with community policing," which was not enough to ensure plans for local policing. Second, the reform coincided with harsh economic times. Recruitment was limited. Only 20 percent of police officers were working as generalists in the 2000s, leading to the conclusion by the National Crime Prevention Council that community policing reform was not fully developed by then. Moreover, the introduction of the position of *länspolismästare* (chief commissioner of a county police department) was another form of centralization, according to Furuhagen (2009). The change meant the regional police chief was no longer part of the provincial government's organization but rather head of one of the county's police departments. In 1994, there were still 118 police regions, nearly the same number as in 1965. In 1998, there were only 21 police regions, one in each county. Furuhagen also quotes several researchers in Sweden who suggest that centralization – and not community policing – have characterized the police during the early 2000s. These researchers add that the reform led to a change in the organization alone and not in the orientation of policing services. Centralization was somehow obligatory because, as Sweden entered the European Union, better coordination at national and international levels would lead to centralization of certain routines. One example has been the need to merge the data from 21 police areas into single biometric information. By the mid-2000s, a survey (*Kommunaktuellt*, 2002) showed that half of the municipalities thought community policing worked poorly, and one-third of the municipalities employed private patrols to perform police-like work.

The political assessment was that the community policing reform would be implemented but that the police would get some new resources. However, funding for community policing reform was complicated by an acute crisis in public finances in the early 1990s. The initial idea was that there should be about 30 police officers in every community policing area, where there would be about 30,000 inhabitants; in other words, one police officer per 1,000 residents. The police were forced to cut the budget just as other public authorities were, resulting mainly in reduced staff numbers. Note that in the period 1986–2000, the number of police officers decreased (Table 11.1). Since the early 2000s, several community policing areas have merged.

Furuhagen (2009) indicates that the number of civilian employees decreased by 30 percent between 1993 and 2000. Police staff were not affected as much, but recruitment by the Police Academy stopped for three years in the mid-1990s. This trend in the police follows the overall national trend in employment by public sector entities during the 1990s (Brandt & Westholm, 2008). The number of employees per citizen dropped significantly in 1993 and then increased again. This shift has occurred in small municipalities as well as large ones. The cause of these fluctuations appears to have been weaker public finances in the early 1990s. At the same time, technological and organizational changes during the decade made possible a reduction in the number of employees, reducing in particular the need for unskilled workers.

The sharp increase in the number of police officers reflects the recent government targets of having 20,000 police officers in Sweden. The number of candidates admitted to police training each year is based on this goal. The total number of police officers a police force may be assigned depends mostly on population and crime levels. Mapping police officers per municipality can be misleading. This is not a particularly useful measure, because a "police station" in a municipality may serve only parts of the municipality (in the south) or several neighboring municipalities (in the north). Obviously, not all police employees are officers, and administrative personnel account for a large part. The latter group has steadily increased, by 36 percent from 2000 to 2012 (from 6,205 to 8,457 employees). The Swedish National Police publish the number of police out of the 21 regional police forces, but the regional police authorities determine where police employees will be stationed within their territory. This current structure will change with the police centralization and amalgamation of regional police authorities.

Table 11.1 Police officers in Sweden, 1986–2011

	1986	1990	1995	2000	2005	2011/2012	Increase 1995–2011/2012
(a) Police yearly statistics	17,193*	16,308*	16,752	16,089	17,073	20,398/19,890	18.7%
(b) Employment statistics	17,193	16,839	16,251	17,720	15,318	17,459	7.5%

Data source: (a) Rikspolisstyrelsen (2013) and (b) Statistics Sweden (2013).

Note
* 1986 and 1990 exclude police cadets.

Having a more gender-balanced police force is also part of the national goals. For instance, in 2005, women constituted 22 percent of police officers, while six years later the percentage reached 30 percent. In the late 1950s, Sweden got its first female police. Women's participation as police officers was controversial. Furuhagen (2009) suggests that at that time there were two camps: one camp felt that women meant strength for Swedish police, that both men and women could be police officers; the second camp thought that women were not suitable for practical police service. These women were called "police sisters" and had specific tasks concerning women and children. Police sisters constituted a very small percentage of the country's police force. Initially there were 26 police sisters and more than 6,000 male officers and most police sisters were based in Stockholm. The police sister designation was taken away when the same service levels and the same working conditions began to apply to both women and men. In theory, female police officers received the same training as men, but in practice there were still some differences, especially those related to weaponry and physical training. Not until the 1960s were all positions open to women. Before that, some positions were limited to male applicants.

Although the number of police officers employed reflects the degree of urbanization in Sweden (Stockholm, Västra Götaland, and Skåne, where Stockholm, Gothenburg, and Malmö – the three largest cities – are located), the increase in police officers employed was fairly even between urban and rural counties, at about 20 percent. If these statistics are broken down into smaller geographical units (counties), one notices that the largest increase in police force between 2000 and 2012 occurred in counties neighboring the two most urbanized counties (Malmö and Stockholm): Halland and Uppsala, with 53.5 percent and 40.1 percent, respectively (Figure 11.1).

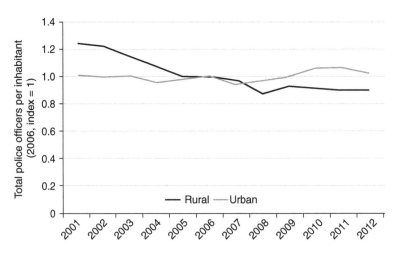

Figure 11.1 Number of police officers in rural and other municipalities, 2001–2012 (source: Lindström, 2014).

There has been a decrease in police manpower in small and rural areas in relation to urban municipalities (Figure 11.1). Lindström (2014) shows that police manpower in Sweden increased about 15 percent, but rural and small communities have not gained in police numbers since 2006, some communities even experiencing a decrease. For instance, in 2012 about one-quarter of all Swedish municipalities had no permanent police staff. These municipalities often receive police support from officers stationed in nearby municipalities. Moreover, the number of municipalities in Sweden without permanent police staff has steadily increased over time. Does an uneven distribution of police officers affect crime levels?

Lindström (2014) indicates that fewer police has meant an increase in certain types of crimes (and the opposite: relatively less crime in well-staffed municipalities). More interesting is that although crime in general has been lower in rural and smaller municipalities, increases in crime in these areas have been as large as or larger than the increases in urban municipalities. The message that emerges from this study is that the police need to be present in order to help prevent crime. However, the author calls for resident involvement in policing, because police officers are not able to do much about crime by themselves if residents are not actively involved in preventing it.

Partnerships in rural community safety

This section is divided into two. The first subsection is devoted to local crime prevention groups or councils. In 2012, there were about 300 crime prevention (CP) groups across Sweden. The role of the police is discussed here, as is the role of CP groups in rural areas. CP groups have been the main coordinators of community policing in Sweden since the mid-1990s. The second subsection discusses the expansion of the private security sector within the governance of safety in rural areas. The focus is on the increase in security private companies, either as part of public patrol or direct work with situational crime prevention. Several examples are provided in both sections to illustrate these developments.

Police and local crime prevention councils

In 2005, the Swedish National Council for Crime Prevention (BRÅ) performed the most comprehensive evaluation of CP work at the municipal level up to that time (BRÅ, 2005). The objective of the study was to investigate how CP groups had developed since the implementation of *Allas vårt ansvar*, the national CP program in 1996, which was intended to create CP groups throughout the country and support the activities of those that already existed. At that time, BRÅ found that CP groups were often directly placed under municipal councils, and, together with the police, municipal representatives had the strongest influence in the council's work. Leaders of CP groups devoted on average less than one day per week to CP activities, which were often financed by the municipality. CP members saw themselves as having a holistic perspective on what happens in the community in terms of crime and safety.

In a later study, BRÅ indicated that the role of the police was particularly important in smaller rural municipalities (BRÅ, 2006). Yet small municipalities had little chance to succeed in CP work compared to larger urban centers, mainly because of a lack of financial resources and support. It was also found that more experienced CP groups tended to work better than new ones. The experienced ones had earmarked resources and clear-cut goals. They also actively sought and used knowledge and evidence more often than other CP groups. The majority of CP groups focused on youth preventive measures against alcohol and drug addiction.

To follow up these assessments (BRÅ, 2005, 2006), this subsection reviews an analysis performed by the author in cooperation with the criminologist Lars Dolmén and published by the *European Journal of Criminology* (Ceccato & Dolmén, 2013). This subsection summarizes the discussion of the role of police in relation to CP groups' actions, organization, cooperation, evaluations, and challenges. The data was gathered using a semi-structured interview with members of local CP councils in eight rural municipalities in Sweden (for more details about the selection of these areas in previous chapters). The template for the interview constituted more than 40 questions divided into five sections. A minimum of five to a maximum of seven persons were interviewed in each municipality, in a total of 49 interviews. To obtain a comprehensive picture of CP experiences in rural areas in Sweden, data from other sources was obtained, from a database of CP projects receiving funding from the National Crime Prevention Council and from answers to an email survey to all representatives of local CP groups in Sweden (from a short email "scenario" survey submitted to all representatives of local CP groups, with a 62 percent response rate).

Crime prevention is more than volunteer action

The composition of CP groups in Swedish rural municipalities was a surprise. It was initially expected that because of strong social ties, CP groups would be composed mostly of volunteers. Contrary to our initial hypothesis, the ideal of *eldsjälar* (local enthusiasts working voluntarily) as the main drivers of CP work applied perhaps in only one case of the eight studied. Findings show that CP representatives are rarely volunteers and may not always come from existing local social networks. CP members are often employed in different areas of the municipality, police, and/or county council with roles other than CP, devoting a couple of hours per week (or less) to it. CP representatives may not even live in the same municipality as they work in, commuting sometimes on a weekly or daily basis. Their actions are much more institutionalized than was previously thought. This is certainly a development related to how *Allas vårt ansvar* has affected CP organizations and priorities since the mid-1990s. Thus, CP groups may receive funding for their activities from the municipality or by applying for external funding from regional or national sources or the European Union.

The institutionalization of CP groups may have also impacted how representatives define their CP efforts. When CP representatives were asked about their definition of "Crime prevention," they thought of a "multidimensional construct," often reflecting what they do in CP work. For instance, CP representatives from local police enforcement define CP based on the traditional role of the police (tackle crime and ensure order) but also reflecting the importance of formal social control, trust, and social networks against criminal events that take place in public places:

> CP is ... to prevent crime, reduce crime curve so the police will get a good reputation and the public has confidence in us.
>
> (Police inspector, south, high crime, old economy)

> CP is about social control. It is by far the best crime prevention effect that we have in the small community, everybody knows everybody.
>
> (Police inspector, south, low crime, old economy)

As is shown in Chapters 13 and 14, people working with youngsters with problems and/or domestic violence tend to see CP's "therapeutic" function for the community in places where violence can be a problem to be tackled in CP work:

> Successful crime prevention is about limiting alcohol to young people, finding alternatives, getting parents more involved. It's a little different culture up here in the North.
>
> (Healthcare advisor, north, low crime, new economy)

> Things happen (domestic violence) even in small municipalities. They have to be discussed. When necessary, we must act!
>
> (Crime victims association, north, low crime, old economy)

The work of CP groups in rural areas: are rural issues demoted?

On a daily basis, CP tackles problems of perceived safety, often relying on safety and night and security walks, involving the local community in general. Through partnerships with schools, CP members may be involved in programs aimed at integrating refugee children who come to these municipalities. Farm crimes (e.g., theft of trucks, fertilizers, cattle) and environmental and wildlife crime do not belong on the main agenda (see Chapter 13). Jones and Phipps (2012) and other British researchers quoted in their article found similar results. As initially expected, CP groups concentrate their work on problems of the "urban core" of the rural municipality and therefore rarely focus on environmental crime, with very few exceptions.

Youth is unanimously the most important issue in rural areas for CP councils, according to representatives (this topic will be further discussed in Chapter 13). All eight municipalities highlighted the problems of alcohol and drug addiction as well as related problems, some being seasonal and associated with violence in the public and private spheres, vandalism, and, to a lesser extent, property crimes.

Though youth-related problems may be found in the most remote rural areas in Sweden, they are often taken as a typical big-city problem. The focus on "big city problems" in CP work in rural areas is also found when looking at the projects nationally funded. Why is this so? Partnerships have been central in the national CP model that tends to prioritize urban problems. As an example, the majority of projects funded by BRÅ are in urban areas, and if they are based in rural municipalities, they still focus on issues that are more often found in large cities, such as youth violence, preventive measures against drug and alcohol addiction, or situation-based solutions to improve perceived safety. This is not specific to Sweden. In the United Kingdom, Gilling (2011) suggests that recent developments in national crime governance and policing have by default negated rural crime. In the British case, this is because the new risk-based strategies preclude many rural crime issues from meeting the nationally defined "crime problem" benchmark. The author suggests that until relatively recently, responding to "headline" crime occurring in more populous areas has the priority in performance terms (Gilling, 2007). In Sweden, this might also be the case, but certainly this biased model also reflects a national top-down model of CP that identifies several target areas and establishes frameworks for action often focused on big cities' problems, disregarding rural diversity. This is further reinforced by a scheme of prizes awarded to CP projects assessed as "best practices" following these guidelines, which may be replicated in other municipalities. Whether they make sense in a (different) rural context is difficult to say, but it seems reasonable to expect that there is a need to re-examine the current model. Even if the causes of crime in rural areas are the same as those in urban areas, it seems in-depth knowledge is necessary to tackle problems that are expressed differently depending on where they occur, as crime and perceived safety might depend on context.

Partnerships, knowledge, and resources

Several interviewees suggested that a large share of their activity is devoted to achieving a satisfactory local partnership per se, as community policing is supposed to be based on information sharing (Figure 11.2). In practice, this means a large part of their time goes into taking courses on crime prevention to improve knowledge among CP representatives and attending lectures and meetings. This has become the main goal of some CP groups, which is problematic, of course, because partnership and collaborative work, as submitted here, are a means to help CP work, not the end itself. Such work should lead representatives to better understanding of the problems and causes with which they must deal, and which interventions should be put into practice.

Most CP representatives declared good internal collaborative work, but not all did so. Some groups show signs of a sectoral split between those who work with social CP, often with more long-term strategies, and those who work with situational crime initiatives. Overall, community policing seems to be facilitated by strong social ties in rural communities. Some suggest that being small is an

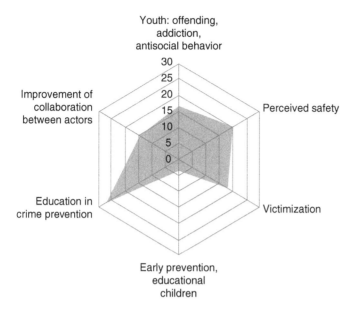

Figure 11.2 Issues addressed by the CP projects financed by BRÅ (%) (data source: projects granted funding by the Swedish National Council for Crime Prevention (BRÅ), 2004–2010, in Ceccato and Dolmén, 2013, p. 101).

advantage, because a "problem" can be solved quickly since "unofficial talks" may become "official" just because "one happens to run into someone else." This is perceived to be an advantage by most but not all respondents. What may be an advantage in community policing can be perceived as a sign of unbalanced power relations that, in a small community, may lead to exclusionary practices (see e.g., Yarwood, 2010). These strong social ties may be a hinder for CP work when conflicts between safety and economic goals become a fact. The police inspector quoted below illustrates this case:

> I can think it is a disadvantage at times that those who have control over the money also "sit on" the CP council. If you take the economic point of view instead of the CP one, you may "sit on two chairs."
>
> (Police inspector, south, low crime, old economy)

Not surprisingly, the police have been an essential part of the projects which got support from BRÅ during 2004–2010. A brief analysis of these partnerships shows that they tended to be headed either by local or regional police forces or members of the municipal councils themselves, while other CP actors formally have a more auxiliary role. Figure 11.2 shows that improving collaboration between CP partners is often a reason for requesting external funding. An obvious source of funding is BRÅ.

Collaboration within CP work is not only limited by funding. Interviewees suggested that regulations regarding data secrecy and handling within the organization and between partners, although necessary, is a major hindrance to CP work. For instance, police officers may have access to individual data on suspects that cannot be shared with those in the CP group. Some suggest that the confidentiality regulations are misunderstood or misused. Particularly in rural areas where "everybody knows everybody," individual information can become a sensitive matter. This becomes more complicated when CP members in neighboring municipalities cooperate (often within their own field).

Assessment of CP groups' initiatives

Most of the CP projects do not include any precise follow-up, which makes difficult any pre- or post-assessment of the implemented crime prevention measures. Figure 11.3 illustrates that this is the case for the sample of projects financed by BRÅ between 2004–2010. About half of the CP groups performed some kind of evaluation of their activities, and one-third had an action plan. Many collaborated with neighboring CP groups, but only a few had established cooperation with universities, creating a poor knowledge basis for action and assessment. Poor assessment routines characterize CP work in rural municipalities in Sweden.

Swedish rural CP groups are not alone. The assessment of CP actions in rural areas follows the overall international trend in CP. As suggested by previous research, knowledge about which CP interventions work and which do not work

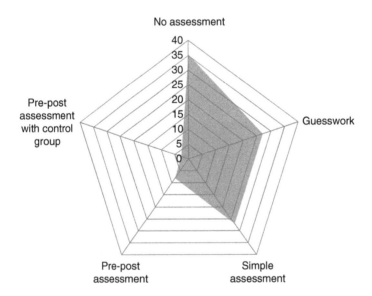

Figure 11.3 Type of evaluation in CP projects financed by BRÅ (%) (data source: projects granted funding by the Swedish National Council for Crime Prevention (BRÅ), 2004–2010, in Ceccato and Dolmén, 2013, p. 101).

remains fragmentary and patchy, even in other contexts than the rural (Wikström, 2007). In Sweden, CP initiatives in rural municipalities may never be assessed to the same extent as those in urban areas because of limited funding in the first place. Moreover, as suggested by Bullock and Ekblom (2010), the problem of assessment of CP actions may suffer from the fact that they do not always contain the right information to help practitioners select and replicate projects to their own context. There are exceptions, though. Several CP initiatives have been replicated as examples of good practices. The Kroneberg model and EFFEKT, for instance, have been associated with a long-term assessment showing the particular impact of these CP programs both nationally and internationally. These examples are discussed in detail in Chapter 13.

Although most CP groups declare that they make use of crime statistics or other equivalent relevant information, a small proportion of their work is declared to be evidence based. Lack of skills among those involved in CP work seems to be the root of the problem of poor assessment – from the conception stage, to actions and evaluation. Recall that a significant amount of CP activity relates to individuals' own training (Figure 11.2). CP groups tend to keep initiatives that have already been in place elsewhere and are well accepted by the community (e.g., youth recreation centers). When CPs are innovative, they tend to invest in projects that were applied elsewhere (e.g., safety walks, drinking limitations) by importing models and assuming they are "good practice."

Joint police and customs station: an example from Ydre

The range of basic services offered in rural areas in Sweden has been significantly reduced in the past 20 years. This trend accelerated in the 2000s, and in many parts of the country the degradation of basic services has reached such a level that the basic functions of society are being called into question (Degerlund, Jansson, & Lönnqvist, 2010). Sweden is not alone in this development. In the United Kingdom, for instance, the rationalization of public services has been keenly felt by those in rural areas, as crime rates have risen in supposedly "crime-free" areas and policing has become less visible (Jones & Phipps, 2012).

What is interesting is that at the same time that basic services have been shut down, new forms of service provision have been put into place. The example discussed in this section illustrates how the process of amalgamation of the police and customs authorities in the rural municipality of Ydre suggests that both policing and customs services have improved.

Ydre Municipality is in Östergötland County, in southeast Sweden. For the past 10 years, a joint office has been located in Ydre. It currently consists of 10 employees: four employed by the customs authority, five by the police, and one shared (receptionist). In the early 1990s, the Ydre police had only two police employees and could stay open only two hours each week. In Flötningen, a few miles from Ydre, there was a customs station (especially for the Norwegian border) that had been open for clearance of goods for business hours every weekday. By moving the customs station to Ydre and co-locating the two authorities, the hours were extended, and services to citizens improved. One bonus of the relocation was that it led to cooperation between customs and police in external services to an extent that had not happened before. Collaboration consists of joint patrol operations when possible, depending on the mission. They may involve drug issues, crime prevention, monitoring of hunting and fishing issues, control of dangerous goods, passport and immigration controls, and customs and traffic controls. They assist each other whenever possible to provide service to citizens. The cooperative agreement is periodically updated when changes in each organization make it necessary.

> Of course, expenses are lower with the same office, as we can split the costs, but the best thing about the partnership is that we are now cooperating with the police. This has resulted in a number of successful initiatives.
>
> (Customs representative in Ydre: Schmidt, 2013)

The co-location makes it easy to exchange information, which is important. The result of collaboration between authorities on police matters has yielded excellent results a number of times, such as when several church burglaries were cleared up following a joint operation. The assessment by the authorities is that these crimes would have been difficult to clear up if not for the cooperation between the authorities (Brandt & Westholm, 2008).

The volunteer sector in policing

In Sweden, as previously suggested, volunteer work appears to account for a minor portion of direct CP efforts. Members of CP groups are often employed in different areas of the municipality, police, and/or county council, having roles other than CP and devoting a couple of hours per week (or less) to it. However, it is submitted here that this is only a partial view of rural communities that are based to a large extent on complex networks of social relationships linked through local social associations, interest groups, and support groups. Thus, there is a need for a nuanced perspective on volunteer work in rural areas, one that stretches beyond – perhaps not too far – the traditional work of police and CP groups. For instance, close to the work of police are active support groups such as those working with homeless and missing people, discussed below.

In the United Kingdom, a better understanding of the work done by volunteer groups together with the police has been achieved by Parr, Stevenson, Fyfe, and Woolnough (2012). Six varied cases were selected for in-depth examination, to understand how police resources are deployed and the decision-making processes within police organizations and to focus on what spatial assumptions are made and acted upon during missing events. Missing people represent a significant challenge for the police due to the volume of cases and the potential risks missing people face. A recent study in the United Kingdom looked at numerous cases to add to the knowledge-base about missing person behavior but also to support the best approaches when dealing with missing persons operationally.

Yarwood (2014) considers searches for missing people one aspect of rural policing. The author illustrates how a search for a person relies on a relationship network that has wider significance than existing formal networks. Concentrating on search dogs, attention is given to the ways that non-human agencies are enrolled in policing networks. This not only broadens understanding of policing but also contributes to the wider debate in rural studies. The author suggests that community-based policing in rural places must similarly recognize how it is linked to wider networks and work in relation to them.

In Sweden, volunteers organized to search for missing persons are not a new phenomenon but could be considered a recent trend when considered as an organized movement under the national group Missing People. When *Missing People Sweden* formed in 2012, it was a small group of volunteers. Nowadays, Missing People is a popular movement with thousands of volunteers across the country. After solving several cases, the organization has been honored with police medals and important sponsorships. Yet not much in-depth study has been done to understand their methods and how they can be coupled with traditional community policing.

Another stream of volunteer work that has increased in Sweden revolves around those who live as homeless. The media has shown examples of a split debate between groups who favor support to the homeless and those opposed. The homeless are often associated with mendicancy in the streets and often considered a problem of "social order" in large cities, particularly in public places such as at train stations and bus stops. Even in big cities, direct conflict between locals and people found in the street are reported in national newspapers (Sundberg, 2014). For instance, a man accused of assault by several witnesses has himself brought charges against a woman for assault. He shoved her away because he felt he was under attack. The local police officer declares she has never experienced anything like it during her years on duty. This is seen as a counter-reaction to a dramatic increase in homeless EU migrants that often turn to mendicancy to survive.

On a positive note, people are not waiting for formal volunteer organizations to help. Some support is being provided by individuals themselves (see for instance, Hökerberg, 2014). A recent report by Stadsmission (2014) indicates almost half of homeless mendicants sleep outdoors. The majority state that they live in homelessness in their home country. Because of the way Swedish social services interpret current regulations, help is mostly offered by churches and volunteer organizations, sometimes in cooperation with municipalities. This includes practical assistance with food, clothes, and somewhere to sleep, but also information, advisory services, language instruction, and schooling for their children. Homeless EU citizens present their own range of problems, having different difficulties and needs (Socialstyrelsen, 2013). The number of homeless people is greatest in urban areas (this applies particularly to EU migrants and non-EU citizens who have lived in an EU member state as long-term residents and therefore have rights similar to those of EU citizens), but homelessness is also found in rural areas.

Policing and the expansion of private security companies

Private security companies provide services for private enterprises, government bodies and municipalities, and individuals. Private security is not a new phenomenon, nor has its expansion gone unnoticed, but they have taken over several responsibilities that in the past were associated with the public sector. As the presence and impact of commercial security actors increases, the roles and functions conventionally ascribed to the state are being transformed as new geographies of power and influence take form (Berndtsson & Stern, 2011). As we shall see below, rural policing is no exception.

Private guards have become an ordinary part of the landscape as they go almost unnoticed. Their presence has become part of everyday life in public places (Button, 2007). In Sweden, the number of private security companies increased 161 percent between 1993 and 2013 (Figure 11.4). Although most private security companies in Sweden are found in the regions containing the three largest urban areas (Stockholm, Gothenburg, and Malmö), there has been a significant increase in the number of private security companies in smaller municipalities, particularly in a few counties such as Kronoberg, Kalmar, Götaland, Halland, and Norrbotten, in northern Sweden.

Apart from the increase in the number of private security companies in Stockholm, Skåne, and Västra Götaland, the private security sector has expanded substantially in counties such as Halland, Kronoberg, and Gotland, counties that have also experienced a relatively sharp increase in police officers (Figure 11.5a and 11.5b). This simultaneous increase is difficult to explain at this aggregate level, but as police officer assignment is often a function of crime rates and

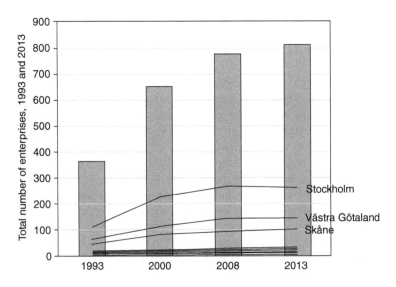

Figure 11.4 Number of enterprises in the security sector between 1993 and 2013, Sweden (bar) and by county (lines) (data source: Statistics Sweden, 2013).

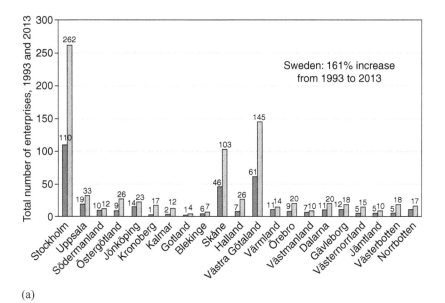

(a)

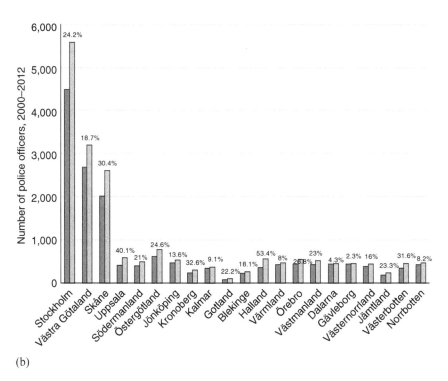

(b)

Figure 11.5 (a) Number of enterprises in security sector by county, 1993 and 2013, and (b) number of police officers and increase (%), 2000–2012 by county (data source: (a) Statistics Sweden, 2013; (b) Swedish National Police Agency, 2013).

demography in an area, the increase in the private security sector may reflect an increase in criminogenic conditions in the area. Alternatively, the increase in the private security sector could reflect a set of priorities that are set at regional and local levels that may not be linked to a crime increase per se.

Police and private security company in Söderköping

Söderköping is an example of a municipality in which the private sector has become integral to policing and safety governance. The municipality has the police and a private security company that combats and prevents crime. The County of Östergötland, where Söderköping is located, has experienced an increase in police officers of about 25 percent of the total and a rise of almost 200 percent in the number of enterprises in the security sector during the past decade (Figure 11.5a and 11.5b).

Key actors in the security partnership for this rural municipality perceive their roles as safety service providers differently and are accepted by the local community in different ways. The private company in this case is run by a former police officer. The company directly provides services to increase safety and security, with staff that walk around in the municipality and talk to young people – primarily and traditionally a job for the police. The company's work is intertwined with work developed by the local CP group. As shown below, people continue to expect the police to be more visible even though they believe the police are not as efficient as the private security companies. The municipality is a typical middle-sized town with burglaries, thef, and vandalism accounting for most victimization. This example questions how the lines of distinction between the public and the private are challenged by the needs of rural communities.

A survey conducted by Lundin (2006) shows that the majority of respondents had not seen the police at all recently and were dissatisfied with police work, particularly those outside the urban core. Responses included, "What cop?" and "Söderköping has no police." Many stated that they had never seen any police in Söderköping. "Yes, sure there is a police officer, but they're probably just here sometimes?" As a result, as many as 75 percent of respondents declared not being satisfied with the police presence, 52 of the respondents were dissatisfied with the way the police prevent crime, and 40 percent of respondents felt private security was needed in the area where they live.

In rural areas, the dissatisfaction with the police seemed greater, as only 18 percent of respondents declared satisfaction with how the police work against crime; almost the same proportion is pleased with the police presence. However, a higher proportion of respondents in the outer areas than in the urban area preferred not to comment on police actions. A few respondents were concerned whether the police would actually make it to the crime scene if something happened. Statements that have emerged during the interviews in the outer areas were that the police were not as visible as they would expect, the police were under-resourced and should be working in a more preventive way (Lundin, 2006).

Hiring private security companies is seen by a share of the interviewees as a reasonable solution to prevent crime (theft, burglary, and vandalism), as the police are not as present as they would expect. However, this opinion was not shared by all; it depended on place of residence. For instance, in the Broby–Norra district, two-thirds of respondents saw no need for a security company, as the area was a quiet area, or they believed that security companies should not perform police tasks. In another part of Söderköping, in Eriksvik–Södra, respondents had a more positive view of private security companies: half of respondents saw a need for a private security company as a way to increase perceived safety and deter crime. According to them, the private security company seemed more reliable, as the police have limited resources. The "efficiency" and "reliability" of the private security sector has already been noted in the literature as one reason for its expansion at the expense of the police in fighting crime and ensuring community safety (Berndtsson & Stern, 2011; Loader & Walker, 2007). However, the type of work done by security companies in Söderköping and/or other rural municipalities is not generally well known, nor is it known whether their activities are submitted to any type of supervision or, in that case, by which authorities.

It can no longer be expected for security to be provided or controlled by either public or private actors anymore. If this was the case, this assumption would be an oversimplification of the current policing model in rural areas that obfuscates an existing interplay between private security companies and the police. If policing is performed in other rural municipalities in the same way as it is done in Söderköping, the role of public (police) and private (security companies) actors would not be so easily separated. However, neither this fact nor the lack of police resources – a common excuse for hiring private companies – contribute to improve the private sector legitimacy as key actors in ensuring security to those living in rural areas.

With the imminent police centralization in Sweden, a new community policing model has to be in place to accommodate the current expansion of the private security sector. The challenge is how to ensure that security remains a public good once private sector security providers have established themselves. First, the role of private security companies, either as patrols or engaged in crime prevention work, has to become more transparent. Private security companies have become arms of the state by developing their role as guarantor of security as a public good (Loader and Walker, 2007). Second, the engagement of private security companies should happen in a wider context of community policing, in which CP groups play a central role as coordinating bodies together with the police. Epstein (2007, p. 150) suggests that the state governs through private security actors, but is that so in rural areas? Third, the commodification of security involves a large number of actors beyond private security companies. In rural areas, they may take different forms (e.g., security technology companies, security networks), so obtaining a better understanding of the private sector as security provider is desirable in both rural and urban contexts.

Chapter 13 returns to the case of Söderköping to illustrate the layers of social control that exist to tackle vandalism and to provide details about residents' satisfaction with the police and private security companies.

Private security networks and policing

Private security networks offer an alternative way of reporting crime and promoting remote surveillance. The system is separate from the emergency telephone number or other standard methods of contacting police that allows a member of the community to supposedly provide anonymous information about criminal activity. The network is funded by members of the network, such as trucking companies, forest contractors, excavation contractors, retailers, and homeowners. In Sweden, there is also a company specialized in situational crime prevention in several different areas but heavily focused on issues that rural areas suffer most: crime against transport and vehicles (goods), building companies, and homeowners.

The private network is devoted to crime against vehicles and goods. The company supports a network using different forms of preventive initiatives. Thousands of people are said to be active in crime prevention, as more than 4,000 vehicles are connected to the network through an app that can be used to report crime, serve as remote surveillance, and receive real-time information about crime in progress. As a crime occurs in an area, data is reported to the network of members. The system works with informal reporting of events as they occur either by testing or sending images linked to x-y coordinates. All information sent to the private security network by email or through the app is protected by the Personal Data Act (PDA), ensuring anonymity. Ongoing crimes or information about ongoing crimes must also be submitted to the police. For more details, see Chapter 12, which exemplifies the work done by private security networks to combat diesel theft in remote rural areas in Sweden.

Future of rural policing: what happens with police re-organization?

On January 1, 2015, 21 police authorities will be merged to form a single national police authority in Sweden (Table 11.2). What will the new police organization mean for policing in rural areas? The reform signals a centralization of the vital functions of the police at the same time as it is intended to keep community policing alive. The model imposes new demands on the current traditions and culture of police work in various sectors and at various geographic levels. As it is now, the 21 police authorities work fairly independently. As such, the lack of standardization makes difficult the daily routines of police work as well as collaboration between authorities. Lindström (2014) also suggests that the police have been severely criticized for not being able to clear up more offenses though their resources have been increased. This is also one reason why the country's 21 police authorities will be consolidated into a single police service by 2015.

The new police authority is expected to increase consistency and uniformity, promoting clear guidance and control with short decision paths over seven police regions. These police regions are planned to have a similar basic structure and organizational units with similar tasks under the same denominations (SOU, 2014). It is expected that this uniformity in the organization will strengthen opportunities to explore similar approaches across police activities. The aim of unifying the organization this way is a more flexible use of resources and thus increased efficiency. At the regional level, analytical entities will investigate crimes that require special skills or are infrequent, such as cybercrime or child pornography. At the local level, knowledge of local communities is crucial for effective police work. The police chief's responsibility is to ensure that there are sufficient police resources in every municipality for police work and in relation to the police's commitments in community policing schemes. This support is expected to ensure that local police authorities can fulfill the commitments made to the local community. To ensure the continued development of crime prevention and community safety, the Police Authority should also allocate resources for these tasks based on key performance indicators. An instrument for this work will be safety surveys that, starting in 2015, will be conducted in all municipalities (SOU, 2014).

The police reform builds on the previous work and experience acquired since the implementation of local police (*närpolisen*) in the mid-1990s. About 85 percent of municipalities already have a collaboration agreement with the police (BRÅ, 2006). The BRÅ report reveals that this agreement is considered to have great potential for successful policing, but in many municipalities there are a number of problems to making it work. Both the police and the municipalities declare that they face difficulties keeping the agreement alive. An important factor for successful collaboration is reportedly to be the existence of a coordinator who can drive collaborative work forward.

From the police side, the current proposals for the police organization are creating anxiety among police employees (SOU, 2014), especially in relation to their role in community policing. For instance, some people suggest that there is a risk that it may provide a pretense, internally and externally, that crime prevention and intervention are two different "boxes" associated with different human resources when in fact these roles will be performed by the same individuals in some parts of Sweden. This is certainly true for the case of rural and small municipalities. This might give rise to unrealistic expectations on the number of police officers in the main office and the number of tasks that can be performed (SOU, 2014).

Rural areas are often associated with strong social links and networks which can be perceived as a resource in policing as well as a hindrance. In this respect, the report by SOU (2014) shows that some police officers in collaborative schemes have been concerned that they may feel that citizens should decide what they should do. There is also a concern that further attachment to the community can be perceived by police officers as an extra workload and generate feelings of inadequacy.

Contrary to the new reform, old challenges are associated with the size of the police forces and remoteness of some parts of the country. For instance, in an

Table 11.2 Historic development of police organization 1965–2015: profile and challenges

Time	Police organization	Police profile in rural areas	Challenges
1960s	 119 police authorities	Police and police work was already strongly rooted in the local community, especially in rural areas and small towns, where much of the population lived at that time. Urbanization imposed new demands. Technology also contributed to development toward a more centralized police. Municipal resources and opportunities to conduct effective policing still varied greatly between precincts.	• Large differences in police performance across the country. • Inefficiency in police routines as the need for coordination over large geographical areas increased, particularly the need for cooperation between police in rural areas and adjacent towns. • Detachment of police from local issues, as police patrols in the 1960s adopted what were perceived by the population as "alienated police practices," focused largely on event-driven emergency operations and passive car patrol, neglecting interaction with the community.
1990s	 21 police authorities	Community policing was implemented in the 21 police authorities. Guidelines were drawn up for creating local crime prevention councils. The number and kind of actors exercising policing proliferated, and certain services and activities were commodified with the expansion of private sector companies into traditional police roles. Police education changed. Police work involved more crime prevention activities than previously. Perceived safety became part of the police agenda.	• Gradual/irregular implementation of community policing schemes across the country. • Adverse effects of economic crisis in 1990s on public resources and full implementation of community policing schemes. • Conflicting policy measures at regional level counteract attempts to make policing local. • Institutionalization of local crime prevention councils. • Top-down national crime prevention policy focusing on big-city problems, leading to neglect of sparsely populated and remote rural areas.

2015

1 police authority, seven regions: North, Central, East, West, Bergslagen, Stockholm, South

The new police authority is expected to increase consistency and uniformity, promoting clear-cut guidance and control with short decision paths in 7 police regions with a similar structure and organizational units with similar tasks. At regional level, analytical entities will investigate crimes that require special skills. At local level, the police chief's responsibility is to ensure sufficient police resources for the police work in every municipality and in relation to the police's commitments in local participation schemes.

- Highly dependent on collaborative work by the previous 21 police authorities in the first years of implementation.
- Extra resources required (funding/manpower) to maintain service quality in the most rural areas of the country.
- Concerns about safety as an individual right when private/public partnerships take over police work where police have no permanent presence.
- Requires a national crime prevention policy adapted to the needs of rural areas (less urban-centric).

international perspective, Sweden, like the other Scandinavian countries, has relatively few police officers per capita (Lindström, 2014). The same author indicates that as late as 2012 about one-quarter of all municipalities did not have a permanent police staff. Currently, these communities receive police support from officers stationed in nearby municipalities. Contrary to the political vision, he adds, there has been a steady increase in non-permanent policed municipalities in Sweden since the 2000s, and they tend to be concentrated in smaller municipalities.

On top of this, the supply of police manpower in rural areas has become a problem in the 2000s. As shown in previous sections of this chapter, the number of police officers in Sweden has increased since 2006, but this increase has been concentrated in larger urban areas, not reaching the rural and small municipalities. In this context, it is worth noting that some municipalities have a surplus of police, whereas others are being under-policed. Still, as shown below, sharing police manpower seems to be the future of dealing with policing challenges in rural areas. Of course, this goes against the principles of community policing as stated in the 2015 police organization:

> Ensuring police presence and local support is often a challenge in rural areas.... [A]s regards police intervention, there may be geographic and demographic reasons to deviate from the main principle that the police have to act and have responsibility for the local communities (the lowest geographical level). This may for example be necessary in rural areas where there is a need to share responsibility for emergency intervention – at least during some part of the day.
>
> (SOS, 2012, pp. 12–13)

However, some rural and small municipalities run a higher risk of being under-policed even with these alternative solutions (such as sharing police manpower between municipalities). Part of patrol work has already been taken over by private security companies. As was shown in previous sections, situational crime prevention is nowadays supported by ICT and active surveillance by residents and passers-by, but the framework for receiving this information has yet to be put in place. For social crime prevention, municipal authorities and social services can carry on the work of preventing crime and delinquency, as is already done, together with schools and individual organizations. How this mix can be used to produce the desirable results in rural areas is still to be seen.

Concluding remarks

It is unclear to what extent policing reform in the mid-1990s was fully implemented in accordance with the government's intentions. A good sign is that nowadays there are about 300 community partnerships (crime prevention groups) around the country. They are often composed of a core of representatives from the municipality, police, and schools. This homogeneous format for crime prevention was inherited from the traditional decentralized municipal planning system in Sweden but, more importantly, from the structural changes imposed by police reform around local crime prevention. The economic downturn in the 1990s affected public resources and most likely the full implementation of community policing schemes. Top-down national crime prevention policies focusing on big-city problems neglect the special demands of sparsely populated or remote rural areas. For instance, property crimes targeting enterprises, farm crime, environmental and wildlife crime often fall outside a crime prevention group's agenda. Members of crime prevention groups who were interviewed unanimously designated youth issues as the most important in rural areas for crime prevention councils. Most of the work by such groups does not include any strict follow-up. When it does, the evaluation is characterized by simple assessment procedures. Different types of crime prevention models are usually "imported" from other municipalities as examples of good practices. Little thought is put into the adequacy of these remedies in a particular rural context.

With the new police authority coming into force in 2015, it is expected that the consistency and uniformity of routine police work will increase, as the existing 21 police authorities disappear. The centralization of certain functions should make police work more effective and economically viable. The 2015 model also relies on intentions to keep strong links to local policing alive. At the local level, future work will build on experiences with existing local partnerships between the police, municipal authorities, the private sector, and citizens that stem from experiences from community policing reform in the 1990s and onwards.

What are the challenges and opportunities of the new police in rural areas?

With centralization, there is a risk that links to rural (sparse/remote) regions will weaken over time, as permanent police positions decrease in small and rural municipalities – a trend that has been reinforced in the past decade. The intention to keep community policing strong demands extra resources, in terms of direct funding as well as manpower to maintain the quality of service in the most rural areas of the country. To make community policing more sensitive to the needs of rural areas (e.g., a less urban-centric model), a national crime prevention policy needs to incorporate clear roles for new safety providers, particularly private security companies, volunteers, and other actors in local safety partnerships. The rapid increase in private sector security in small and rural municipalities in the past few decades generates concerns about "safety as an individual right," as private/public partnerships take over the police work when the police are no longer present.

The police reorganization generates a number of opportunities, of course. For instance, at the same time that basic services are closed down, such as a police office, new forms of service provision can be put in place. The example discussed in this chapter illustrates how the process of amalgamation of the police and customs can trigger better services by both. Another opportunity emerging as the police as an authority are no longer present full time is to engage other actors in community policing. This is nothing new, but exemplary volunteer organizations can fill the gap and provide the insurance that the community needs (e.g., successful cases driven by Missing People). In some cases, the synergy between these "new actors" and police is said to help strengthen existing social bonds through the creation of hybrid networks of information in rural areas. People living in rural areas need better understanding between themselves and police that will change the image of the police as the only safety provider.

In addition, policing in rural areas has the potential to become more sensitive to continuously changing urban–rural relationships. The incorporation and use of ICT to improve surveillance and crime detection in areas where guardianship is low is an example of such potentiality. In terms of surveillance, the capacity of geo-referencing events by texting, voicing, or imaging as crime happens is new in policing but it is here to stay. The use of social media in community policing may be particularly important in rural areas, because of the long distances, which have traditionally been one of the barriers for police work in rural areas. Still, this transformation will only be possible with a long-term involvement of key actors in community policing, in which the police has a central role.

Note

1 This section relies heavily on the written work and personal contact with the Swedish criminologist and historian Björn Furuhagen – for a complete reference to his work, see the reference list. This author is grateful for the permission granted by Furuhagen to translate his work, here partially reproduced.

References

Barclay, E., Scott, J., & Donnermeyer, J. (2011). Policing the outback: Impacts on integration in an Australian context. In R. Mawby & R. Yarwood (Eds.), *Rural policing and policing the rural: A constable countryside?* (pp. 33–44). Farnham: Ashgate.

Berndtsson, J., & Stern, M. (2011). Private security and the public–private divide: Contested lines of distinction and modes of governance in the Stockholm–Arlanda security assemblage. *International Political Sociology, 5*(4), 408–425.

Brandt, D., & Westholm, E. (2008). *Statens nya geografi.* Stockholm: Högskolan Dalarna.

Brottsförebyggande rådet – BRÅ (National Council of Crime Prevention). (2005). Ett steg på väg. Kartläggning av de lokala brottsförebyggande råden (Vol. 15). Stockholm: BRÅ.

Brottsförebyggande rådet – BRÅ (National Council of Crime Prevention). (2006). Redovisning av uppdraget att analysera vilka samarbets: och arbetsformer som skapar förutsättningar för goda resultat i lokalt brottsförebyggande arbete. Stockholm: BRÅ.

Bullock, K., & Ekblom, P. (2010). Richness, retrievability and reliability: Issues in a working knowledge base for good practice in crime prevention. *European Journal on Criminal Policy and Research, 16*(1), 29–47.

Button, M. (2007). *Security officers and policing: Powers, culture and control in the governance of public space.* Aldershot: Ashgate.

Cain, M. (1973). *Society and the policeman's role, London.* London: Routledge & Kegan Paul.

Ceccato, V., & Dolmén, L. (2011). Crime in rural Sweden. *Applied Geography, 31*(1), 119–135.

Ceccato, V., & Dolmén, L. (2013). Crime prevention in rural Sweden. *European Journal of Criminology, 10,* 89–112.

Cordner, G., & Scarborough, K. (1997). Operationalization community policing in rural America: Sense and nonsense. In Q. Thurman & E. McGarrell (Eds.), *Community policing in a rural setting* (pp. 11–20). Cincinnati, OH: Anderson Publishing.

Degerlund, B., Jansson, B., & Lönnqvist, B. (2010). *Lokala Hållbara Servicelösningar.* Stockholm: Hela Sverige Ska Leva.

Donnermeyer, J., DeKeseredy, W. S., & Dragiewicz, M. (2011). Policing rural Canada and the United States. In R. Mawby & R. Yarwood (Eds.), *Rural policing and policing the rural: A constable countryside?* (pp. 23–32). Farnham: Ashgate.

Epstein, C. (2007). Guilty bodies, productive bodies, destructive bodies: Crossing the bio-metric borders. *International Political Sociology, 1*(2), 149–164.

Falcone, D. N., Wells, L. E., & Weisheit, R. A. (2002). The small-town police depart-ment. *Policing, 25*(2), 371–384.

Fenwick, T., Dockrell, R., Roberts, I., & Slade, B. (2012). Rural policing: understanding police knowledge and practice in rural communities. *Annual Report 2011.* Dundee: Scottish Institute for Policing Research.

Furuhagen, B. (2004). *Ordning på stan: Polisen i Stockholm 1848–1917.* Trelleborg: Brutus Östling.

Furuhagen, B. (2009). Från fjärdingsman till närpolis: en kortfattad svensk polishistoria. Växjö: Växjö universitet Polisutbildningen.

Fyfe, N. R. (1995). Law and order policy and the spaces of citizenship in contemporary Britain. *Political Geography, 14*(2), 177–189.

Gilling, D. (2007). *Crime reduction and community safety: New Labour and the politics of local crime control.* Cullompton, Devon: Willan Publishing.

Gilling, D. (2011). Governing crime in rural UK: Risk and representation. In R. I. Mawby & R. Yarwood (Eds.), *Rural policing and policing the rural: A constable countryside?* (pp. 69–80). Farnham: Ashgate.

Hökerberg, J. (2014, May 30). Det var som att hitta hem. *Dagens Nyheter.* Retrieved April 14, 2015, from www.dn.se/sthlm/bienvenido-flores-det-var-som-att-hitta-hem/.

Jones, J., & Phipps, J. (2012). Policing farm crime in England and Wales. Paper presented at the *Papers from the British Criminology Conference, 12,* 3–24.

Kommunaktuellt. (2002). Närpolisen i din kommun. *Kommunaktuellt,* 35–36.

Lindström, P. (2014). Police and crime in rural and small Swedish municipalities. *Journal of Rural Studies,* doi:10.1016/j.jrurstud.2014.12.004.

Loader, I., & Walker, N. (2007). *Civilizing security.* Cambridge: Cambridge University Press.

Lundin, T. (2006). Safety survey in Söderköping (p. 53). Söderköping: Söderköping kommun.

Mawby, R. (2011). Plural policing in rural Britain. In R. Mawby & R. Yarwood (Eds.), *Rural policing and policing the rural: A constable countryside?* (pp. 57–67). Farnham: Ashgate.

Mawby, R., & Yarwood, R. (Eds.). (2011). *Rural policing and policing the rural: A con-stable countryside?* Farnham: Ashgate.

Parr, H., Stevenson, O., Fyfe, N., & Woolnough, P. (2012). Geographies of missing people: Processes, experiences and responses. *Scottish Institute for Policing Research: Annual Report* (p. 81). Dundee: Scottish Institute for Policing Research.

Payne, B. K., Berg, B. L., & Sun, I. Y. (2005). Policing in small town America: Dogs, drunks, disorder, and dysfunction. *Journal of Criminal Justice, 33*(1), 31–41.

Pompa, F., & Ganier, D. (2013, February 27). In gun debate, it's urban vs. rural. *US TODAY.* Retrieved April 14, 2015, from www.usatoday.com/story/news/nation/2013/02/27/guns-ingrained-in-rural-existence/1949479/.

Schmidt, N. (2013). De känner sig hotade. *Dalarnas Tidning*. Retrieved April 17, 2015, from www.dt.se/allmant/dalarna/de-kanner-sig-hotade.

Sjöholm, E. (1941). *Lagstiftningen om polisväsendet*. Stockholm: Norstedts.

Socialstyrelsen (National Board of Health and Welfare). (2013). Homelessness among EU citizens in Sweden. Stockholm: Socialstyrelsen.

Statens Offentliga Utredningar – SOU. (2012). OP-1 Den lokala polisverksamheten. Stockholm: Genomförandekommittén för nya Polismyndigheten, 16. Retrieved April 17, 2015, from www.polissamordningen.se/.../OP_1_Den_lokala_polisverksamheten.pdf.

Statens Offentliga Utredningar – SOU. (2014). Beslut om huvuddragen i den nya polismyndigheten detaljeorganisation (p. 66). Stockholm: Regeringen.

Stadsmission, S. (2014). Hemlöshetsrapport. *Stockholms Stadsmissions hemlöshetsrapport* (p. 36). Stockholm: Stadsmission.

Statistics Sweden. (2013). Employment statistics database (code SSYK 3450). Stockholm: SCB.

Sundberg, M. (2014, April 1). Man knuffade ut tiggare i gatan. *Dagens Nyheter*. Retrieved April 17, 2015, from www.dn.se/nyheter/sverige/man-knuffade-ut-tiggare-i-gatan/.

Rikspolisstyrelsen (Swedish National Police Board). (2013) Police officers in Sweden, 1986 to 2011 [Database]. Stockholm: Rikspolisstyrelsen.

Thelin, K., & Svantemark, K. (2005). Polis i kris: har kommunerna kraften. Stockholm: Timbro.

Weisheit, R. A., Falcone, D. N., & Wells, L. E. (2006). *Crime and policing in rural and small-town rural America.* Prospect Heights, IL: Waveland Press.

Weisheit, R. A., Wells, L. E., & Falcone, D. N. (1994). Community policing in small town and rural America. *Crime and Delinquency, 40*(4), 549–567.

Wikström, P.-O. H. (2007). Doing without knowing: Common pitfalls in crime prevention. *Crime Prevention Studies, 21*, 59–80.

Yarwood, R. (2010). An exclusive countryside? Crime concern, social exclusion and community policing in two English villages. *Policing and Society, 20*(1), 61–78.

Yarwood, R. (2011). Whose blue line is it anyway? Community policing and partnership working in rural places. In R. Mawby & R. Yarwood (Eds.), *Rural policing and policing the rural: A constable countryside?* (pp. 93–105). Farnham: Ashgate.

Yarwood, R. (2014). Lost and found: The hybrid networks of rural policing, missing people and dogs. *Journal of Rural Studies, 39*, doi:10.1016/j.jrurstud.2014.11.005.

Yarwood, R., & Edwards, B. (1995). Voluntary action in rural areas: The case of neighbourhood watch. *Journal of Rural Studies, 11*(4), 447–459.

12 Prevention of farm crimes and crimes against nature

This chapter takes the issues of Chapter 8 forward by discussing the main crime prevention initiatives related to farm crimes and environmental and wildlife crimes (EWC). These crimes and their prevention are rarely in the headlines, which is not surprising given that in most countries crime control and prevention strategies focus on big-city problems. The role of community in dealing with farm crime and EWC in rural municipalities through crime prevention initiatives is given special attention. First, farm crimes and EWCs are framed taking into account a selection of international studies followed by examples from Sweden. Then the chapter turns to new forms of surveillance and protest against farm crime and EWC using ICT and social media.

Preventing farm crimes

Preventing crime is difficult, but it is even more challenging to prevent farm crime. One of the main difficulties is lack of useful data, especially from official sources. If data is not available, it is difficult to implement actions aimed at reducing and preventing crime. Even in early stages, if a crime cannot be reported, the police cannot catch criminals. In Australia, Sweden, England, and Wales, farmers state that they do not report farm crime, either because they accept a certain level of theft and damage on their properties or they believe that going to the police is a waste of time (Barclay, Donnermeyer, Doyle, & Talary, 2001; Jones & Phipps, 2012; Lantbrukarnas Riksförbund, 2012). This raises questions about the community's confidence in formal policing. When statistics are available, such as those recorded by the police, they may be too broad in scope to allow analysis based on crime type or comparative trends, either spatially or temporally. Consequently, crime prevention strategies become limited and rarely lead to generalization (e.g., Ceccato & Dolmén, 2013). When data exists, it may be selective, covering experiences of victimization in certain groups, such as only farmers. In the United Kingdom, Jones and Phipps (2012) exemplify a number of data sources and the limitations, from police statistics, to data registered by insurance companies.

Another issue is that farm crime and its prevention may depend more on context than other forms of big-city crime do. Chapter 8 showed that most farm crimes follow regional patterns, indicating the need for specific intervention in terms of prevention. In Sweden, low temperatures in the north limit the type of farming, so intervention against tractor theft is particularly important in southern Sweden, where most agricultural properties are located. As suggested by Donnermeyer, Barclay, and Mears (2011), although the specific circumstances or risk factors associated with farm crime appear to be similar, it cannot be assumed that issues related to the policing of farm crime are similar. The authors also highlight the importance of considering potential differences in the organization of law enforcement at different places. They note that in US counties where agriculture is economically important, it is likely that more attention is paid to the safety and security needs of farmers. The availability of resources among police forces as well as the profile of police officers on each police force (O'Connor & Gray, 1989) can also influence whether farm crime is on the daily police agenda.

Experience from the United States suggests that a lack of data is not the only problem when dealing with farm crime, as better data sharing among actors and organizations is needed, too. Better crime prevention would be in place if farmers would report all types of farm crime, which does not always happen. Mears, Scott, and Bhati (2007) indicate that the police should consider collaborating with law enforcement agencies within and between counties to deal with existing crime and to deter would-be offenders. Collaborative work by police is essential, as suggested by Donnermeyer et al. (2011), when dealing with organized drug production and agro-terrorism, when it may include state-level police and various law enforcement agencies at the national level.

Before adopting any models of intervention toward farm crime, it is necessary to consider differences in police organization, particularly those stemming from international experience. As suggested in Chapter 11, what is defined as relevant in crime control (and by whom) depends on the police organization, which in turn affects what works and what does not work in preventing farm crime.

Despite these challenges, a number of studies report experiences preventing farm crime. Donnermeyer et al. (2011) summarize in detail experiences in Australia and the United States. The authors conclude that there are two types of problems in dealing with farm crime in Australia. The first relates to the challenges of enforcement in remote areas where guardianship is poor, by farmers as well as society in general. The second relates to specificities of local cultures found in any rural community that make crime prevention and crime control difficult. In Sweden, slow police response times have affected satisfaction with the police in most Swedish remote areas (SOU, 2002). The size of local police areas also varies. Southern areas are relatively easy for police forces to cover because of the relatively high population density, whilst in the north some police areas are very large.

A study from Australia assessed the work done by police squads or crime investigators who specialize in rural crime (Donnermeyer & Barclay, 2005). According to this analysis, the most common obstacles to effective policing were the lack of time and resources to deal with farm crime and the difficulty of effectively patrolling large areas, according to police officers. Officers also found it difficult to deal with several calls for service, for instance, when they suspected that farmers were reporting a theft for the purpose of tax evasion.

In other cases, it was difficult to make a case, because farmers were negligent. Poor management practices include rarely locking gates, sheds, and fuel tanks, lack of identification on livestock, farm produce, machinery, and equipment, and poor recordkeeping on stock numbers and stock movements. They also felt that gathering enough evidence to prove a case beyond a reasonable doubt was one of the most challenging tasks by the police dealing with farm crime.

In the United States, the literature on farm crime and how to deal with it is limited. One exception is a recent research project conducted by Mears (Mears et al., 2007). The initiative was called the Agricultural Crime, Technology, Information, and Operations Network (ACTION), located in California's Central Valley. The study assessed the effectiveness of a number of activities aimed at preventing and reducing farm crime. These activities involved actions such as collecting and analyzing crime data, encouraging information sharing among law enforcement agencies, and marking equipment and livestock. The study shows that although farm crimes were common, they were rarely reported. Some crimes follow seasonal patterns, sometimes depending on the demand for products in the market. The authors also show that "one solution fits all" in terms of farm crime prevention does not work, as some farm crimes are unique, requiring specific actions. As farmers are vulnerable to victimization from multiple sources, a crime prevention initiative has to follow a multi-pronged approach.

In the United Kingdom, the use of private policing against farm crime has figured less in rural areas, compared to the use of more formalized public volunteering, police ancillaries, and safety walkers (Mawby & Yarwood, 2011). There are few systematic evaluations of these initiatives. One was done in the mid-1990s by Yarwood and Edwards (1995), assessing the importance of neighborhood watch schemes in rural areas. Although authors did not look at farm crime only, their study confirms the importance of neighborhood watch schemes in reducing fear of crime and improving police–community relations but warns that such schemes could reinforce social bias, a recognized problem associated with voluntary action.

Several initiatives devoted to farm crime in England and Wales are reported by Jones and Phipps (2012). These initiatives vary, from "volunteer arms" and farm watch schemes, to labeling of products and security measures developed against the theft of machinery and livestock. One farm watch scheme makes use of an online "watch link" that allows two-way communication between police and people in the community, via telephone, fax, email, or mobile phone. Although new channels are potentially available via ICT technology, the authors reveal some concerns. One concerns the viability of such technologies in rural areas, as broadband technology has not been developed to its full potential and 3G signals may be out of reach for emails. The other refers to the need for community participation to make these initiatives possible.

Farm crime in Sweden: the perspective of crime prevention groups

The way police are organized influences policing work and whether or not farm crime becomes a priority on a daily agenda. In the past two decades, in Sweden and elsewhere, partnerships between the police and other local authorities have been characterized by community safety initiatives in both urban and rural areas (Ceccato & Dolmén, 2013; Yarwood & Edwards, 1995). There is consensus that this community safety model has evolved but that a fully collaborative framework between police and local actors remains to be seen (BRÅ, 2009). In the 2010s, the winds of centralization led to the reorganization of the police (currently ongoing), which is expected to affect policing across the country. However, as yet no one knows for certain whether these changes will affect the day-to-day work of the police and crime prevention (CP) groups in rural communities. As it is now, the police play the leading role in controlling and reducing farm crime. Theft of diesel machinery and tools has become burdensome in many rural areas (Lantbrukarnas Riksförbund, 2012). So how do these local partnerships deal with farm crime? What is the role of CP groups in rural areas in dealing with this offense?

To answer these questions, a short email survey was sent to all municipalities in rural Sweden that have a CP group, with a response rate of 62 percent. Members of CP groups were invited to describe the most important short- and long-term actions they would take as a group to tackle the following problem.

> *Five cases of theft have been reported to the police recently. Tractors, tools and generators have been stolen from farms outside the city. It is suspected that the perpetrators come from a nearby town. What would your local crime prevention councils do to address the problem and ensure it does not recur? Please describe the most important actions you take.*

CP groups in rural areas appear to be prepared to tackle farm crime "if something happens," or at least they have the organization to deal with this offense. The scenario above is much more part of the reality of communities in southern Sweden than in the extreme north, where agriculture is limited by long cold winters. However, the way CP representatives reacted to the above scenario differed little regardless of where they lived. Interestingly, a few representatives believe that their CP group would not bother to react to such a small number of crimes.

The large majority of representatives regard farm crime as a "police issue" (Figure 12.1). As in the case below, CP representatives highlight the importance of reporting the crime to the police (if the police do not know yet). Similar to findings in the United States (Mears et al., 2007), a couple of CP representatives would highlight the need to establish cooperation with other police forces beyond the boundaries of the local police district to tackle farm crime:

> This is a police matter, not an issue for the CP council.
>
> (CP representative, municipality in central Sweden)

> Have a dialogue with the police in the first place. This is a police matter. The police, in turn, may have to work over the boundaries of jurisdictions. Important to inform residents about the importance of police reports.
>
> (CP representative, municipality in southern Sweden)

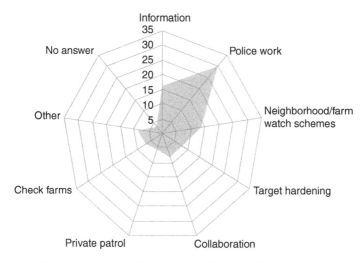

Figure 12.1 What would your local crime prevention councils do to address farm crime? (source: own survey, *N*=60 local crime prevention councils).

Echoing findings in Australia and in the United Kingdom (Donnermeyer et al., 2011; Jones & Phipps, 2012), CP representatives who answered the survey indicated that poor willingness to report minor farm crimes was a problem. Some representatives highlighted the need to inform residents about the importance of reporting all kinds of crime to the police, as there is "a local culture of acceptance" of minor thefts, vandalism on roads, and littering in forests.

Most representatives consider the partnerships within the CP groups important to support preventive actions to control and prevent farm crime. Improving guardianship and strengthening information channeled by passers-by are often considered important in tackling farm crime.

> Keep alive the positive social networks…. It may be important that postmen, paperboys and other people moving around [rural] areas can report what they see.
>
> (CP representative, municipality in southwestern Sweden)

Unfortunately, representatives tended to react to the scenario by suggesting actions toward properties in urban areas rather than considering the challenges on farms or in areas outside the urban core. For instance, some suggested implementing neighborhood watch schemes, instead of farm watch, or installing CCTV cameras. It was notable that very few CP groups had representatives from farms.

> We inform residents, property owners and others so they can prevent burglary, check locks, possibly alarm, tell neighbors when you go away, have lamps turned on, etc.
>
> (CP representative, municipality in southwestern Sweden)

A CP representative from a municipality in central Sweden suggested a fairly complete range of measures to be tackled, from farm watch schemes and labeling and registering theft-prone goods, to educational programs to help farms discourage offenders from steal off their property. Collaborative work between the police, CP members and relevant organizations is considered important, though the interviewee was not completely certain about engaging safety walkers, or "vigilante groups."

> [W]e make sure that a police report is made, otherwise we help with that. Collaborate with appropriate organizations, such as insurance companies, The Federation of Swedish Farmers locally and create educational programs to disseminate information on how to protect their property.... The experience we have here in the county is from many thefts of snowmobiles and ATVs. In the long run, we would continue working with and supporting farm watch schemes.
>
> (CP representative, municipality in central Sweden)

Even though the police are regarded as the main player in preventing farm crime, CP representatives suggest hiring private companies to help with patrol work. Beyond groups performing private patrols, there are also companies that work together with the police, other local actors (e.g., trucking companies, forest contractors, backhoe operators, and retailers), and CP groups on situational crime prevention in rural areas as illustrated in Box 12.1.

The use of ICT in rural areas is allowing new forms of surveillance, especially in remote areas and during times nobody is around. Partnerships between private and public actors have been fundamental to this development, coordinated by CrimeStoppers Sweden (CrimeStoppers, 2014). These partnerships involve the police, the Farmers' Association, construction companies, and insurance and telecom companies. These particular partnerships with CrimeStoppers Sweden showed a rapid expansion in Sweden. They have been working with target hardening and increasing the risk for offender detection on three main fronts.

Crime reporting. A cell phone app called CrimeAlert has also become popular for reporting crime as it happens. Development is underway of new services with new features, such as multi-language support and uploading movies and notes from the crime scene.

Product marking. Crimestoppers Sweden cooperates with an insurance company on the product Datatag, a British marking method that utilizes microchips, etching, special decals, DNA, and microdots. As in the United Kingdom, Datatag has built-in registers that the police and insurance companies can use to search misappropriated equipment and accessories. A liquid DNA for diesel is also being implemented that will facilitate finding the rightful owner of diesel stolen from machinery.

Crime detection. Cameras (e.g., hunt trail camera) that are used in places with machines and sheds are showing good results. (A good camera costs about €400 or US$550.) If someone burgles the premises, for example, an image or movie is

Box 12.1 Checklist to reduce the risk of diesel theft in rural areas

Diesel theft is on the rise. What can you do to prevent it?

It is estimated that the cost of diesel theft was around SEK200 million in Sweden in 2013. In the construction industry, the cost of stolen materials reached SEK1.5 billion. Many of these thefts are cleared up thanks to tips, cameras, alarms, and other good preventive measures. Unguarded places are often the target of fuel thieves. You can protect your property with simple means. Here are a few suggestions that can make it difficult for thieves to succeed.

1 Plan your protection based on where you work (the greater the risk of detection, the less the risk of theft).
2 Find out if the place you will be working at is a crime "hot spot."
3 Based on information from the police, take appropriate security measures.
4 Place machinery, sheds, and tools in highly visible places, as transparency and lighting discourage thieves.
5 Ensure that your diesel tank has an alarm or is monitored.
6 Close shelves and personal property with approved locks and chains. Do not buy cheap locks, as they are not rated for heavy damage.
7 Do not leave any property visible in a vehicle. It only takes a minute for a thief to empty the cab.
8 Use alarm, complete with multimedia camera, and put up a sign that the area is under surveillance.
9 Let the police know that you have implemented security measures and that they are welcome to stop by your workplace.
10 A guard patrol sometimes can be a good solution. Check if your colleagues can join in and share patrolling duties.
11 Label your theft-prone equipment and machinery.
12 Try to leave as little diesel fuel as possible in each machine.
13 Enlist the help of neighbors and landowners in the place where you're working. They can certainly pay attention to what happens in the area.
14 If you monitor your machine with a camera, follow current rules on general camera surveillance.
15 Report all kinds of crime!

Source: CrimeStoppers (2014).

sent to contractors via cellphone. According to CrimeStoppers (2014), in recent years a number of offenders have been caught thanks to these cameras. Signage is required, as is compliance with national regulations about where the camera can be located and filming only in places to which the public should not be allowed access.

Prevention of environmental and wildlife crime

The need to protect nature from damaging action by humans has long been recognized. Prevention of environmental harm can be defined, according to White (2007,

p. 36), "in terms of ensuring future resource exploitation and dealing with specific instances of victimization that have been socially defined as a problem." This means that protective actions are directed at preventing or minimizing certain destructive or injurious practices into the future based upon analysis and responses to damage identified in the present.

Environmental crime prevention in rural areas faces a unique challenge – its location. The contamination of a lake in an urban area is easily noticed and perhaps quickly repaired, while an oil spill or deforestation in a remote area may go unnoticed for years. The recognition of the harm depends also on awareness of the problem, which in part can be linked to proximity to the environmental damage itself.

Several issues are listed by White and Heckenberg (2014) to indicate how environmental crime prevention is more demanding than traditional crime prevention. For instance, environmental crime prevention has to deal with acts and omissions that are already criminalized and prohibited but it also has to identify events that have yet to be designated as harmful. Many areas of harm are not yet criminalized. Moreover, interventions often collide with economic interests and growth, as compliance with precautionary principles will almost always reduce current profit margins. Environmental crime prevention also has to negotiate different kinds of harm, which affect humans, at different scales, local and global environments, and non-human animals. Thus, while the specificity of the harm demands a tailored response, there are some forms of environmental harm that cannot be contained, requiring coordination at supranational levels. This is particularly important when the harmful effects are not homogeneously distributed geographically or across social groups, such as those based on gender (e.g., Arora-Jonsson, 2011).

Presumably tightening regulations in one area may lead to displacement of the problem elsewhere. Thus, the attitude of "not in my back yard" (NIMBY) among countries in the Global North runs the risk of perpetuating environmental harm in countries in the Global South. Moreover, environmental crime prevention deals with actors of different agencies, which means in practice that only a few voices are heard. However, these differences in power are no excuse for not incorporating the activities of ordinary people and the involvement of diverse communities in crime prevention. Likewise, environmental crime prevention requires multidisciplinary approaches to the study of the environment that goes beyond the boundaries of traditional disciplines.

Most environmental problems have an identifiable location associated with place characteristics – a quality that for crime prevention is an important resource. Knowing the type of place means that harm can be easily predicted and different actions can be taken to solve the problem or prevent it from happening in the future. Theories that start from an opportunity perspective, the characteristics of the place, and time that crime occurs, such as routine activity theory, crime pattern theory, and situational crime prevention theory, focus on the specific characteristics of a situation. Thus, situational crime prevention strategies can be particularly useful when the place or site of environmental harm is known, as these strategies are based on removing the opportunity to commit crime and increasing the likelihood of apprehension. The design of prevention strategies may follow the five categories of opportunities (effort, risks, rewards, situational conditions, and neutralizations). A number of recent examples in the international literature report the use of situational crime prevention applied to EWC.

Lemieux (2011), for instance, exemplifies the case of elephant poachers in Africa, suggesting a number of measures to limit the number of criminal opportunities, such as limiting access to areas where wildlife live, controlling weapons, increasing police patrols, and using technology to enhance the monitoring capabilities of wildlife authorities. Another, more difficult, suggestion is to reduce consumption of wildlife products, demanding measures against traders and consumers by systematic screening of exports and imports.

On the other side of the Atlantic, Pires and Clarke (2011) study the situational conditions of parrot poaching in Bolivia. They found that parrot poaching was consistent with parrot poaching in Mexico, which is predominantly an opportunistic activity performed by *campesinos*, local farmers who have easy access to bird nests and are motivated by poor economic conditions. The authors suggest increased penalties, more enforcement, and more protected areas but also a number of other strategies based on situational crime prevention. They suggest that intervention should be focused on the most poached species with protection of their nests during the breeding season. This could be accomplished through the use of nets and other physical barriers, CCTV surveillance of open areas with termite mounds, and installation of nesting boxes at a height too great for poachers. Reducing poaching requires engaging local communities in conservation and generating revenues through alternative livelihood, such as ecotourism or regulated trade, and employing poachers as rangers.

White and Heckenberg (2014) illustrate the use of situational crime prevention combined with more long-term actions applied to illegal fishing in Australia and other types of EWC. They suggest tackling illegal fishing by providing alternative sources of revenue for traditional fishers, working with changes in attitudes and community mobilization, such as by educating children about species decline and implementing coastal watch schemes, increasing efforts by fencing off key areas, increasing the risk of apprehension by installing CCTVs, increasing patrols, and reducing rewards, such as by disrupting markets and strengthening moral condemnation of overfishing. Authors highlight that they are suggested actions, not one-size-fits-all. The suggestions only make sense when put into a specific context, requiring close analysis of the different dimensions of each type of environmental problem.

Following a similar line of thought, Huisman and van Erp (2013) state that the prevention of environmental crime requires, in addition to situational crime prevention measures, a more macro approach. The authors analyze 23 criminal investigations of environmental offenses in the Netherlands, claiming that to understand opportunities for environmental crime one cannot rely on a situational analysis of criminal opportunities of individual cases alone. One must also take into account the political and regulatory culture and socioeconomic context of environmental crime. Despite criticism of using situational crime prevention on environmental crime (e.g., Huisman & van Erp, 2013), the attractiveness of this approach lies in its potential for the design of simple yet effective preventive measures (Clarke, 1997). Taking into account the current international evidence, the next section focuses on EWC prevention in Sweden.

Environmental crime prevention in Sweden

In the 1960s, environmental harm started to be perceived as a serious problem for society. At the same time, there was a shift, from the notion of *protection*, to *conservation* of nature. According to that notion, individuals should be able to benefit from natural resources at the same time that they should care for them. This shift in the perception of environmental harm, however, did not change the view of value and consumption of nature.

In the 1970s, Forsling and Borgblad (1978, p. 54) indicated that the challenge in Sweden was still a "balanced vision" in society that would equalize things that were not actually equivalent (for instance, monetary returns of water use and value of clean water). A number of steps forward were taken when the Swedish minister of justice demanded international action against environmental crime and economic crime among multinational companies.

In 1972 a conference was held in Stockholm which became a milestone for the international environmental movement (UN, 1972), and in the 1980s and 1990s interventions against nature gradually had to be assessed from an ecological point of view, following standards of use of natural resources and environmental assessment protocols. Since then, there have been major changes in criminal law and environmental regulation, following the conferences in Rio, Kyoto, and Johannesburg (e.g., UN, 1992). Shifts in public perception of environmental problems globally impose new values on natural resources and demand preventive measures.

In Sweden, environmental issues and environmental harm became the central focus in the 1990s with the introduction of the Environmental Code in 1999 and the establishment of a new organization in the police and the prosecution service for combating environmental crime (Korsell, 2001). The Environmental Code states that agencies exercising a control function have a duty to report suspected environmental offenses to the public prosecutor. Moreover, such agencies were empowered to impose administrative sanctions. According to Korsell (2014), although crime registers show an increase in environmental crimes recorded, only a few criminals have been sentenced to prison. As Chapter 8 showed, the most common sanctions for crimes against the Environmental Code are fines.

Nowadays, in order to ensure that environmental laws are observed, authorities divide their tasks into three types: regulatory, supervisory, and self-monitoring. The self-monitoring is performed by the entity itself and aims to create systematic work procedures, risk management, and other precautions within their own operations. The authorities who are responsible for supervision have the task of providing the operational regulatory support and advice regarding how to apply environmental regulations. Furthermore, they ensure the coordination of operational supervision, so that environmental laws are applied in the same manner by the various operational supervisors. The Inspections Ordinance (Naturvårdsverket, 2011a, p. 13) states that government authorities should give guidance to operational supervisors. Sweden currently has 16 supervisors. The Inspections Ordinance (p. 13) also indicates how oversight work between the state and municipal authorities is allocated. The most common case is for a municipal authority to be responsible for the supervision and inspection at the municipal level (Naturvårdsverket, 2011b).

Municipalities are the main framers of the tasks of the environmental inspector, whose job is to give notice of cases that do not follow the law and environmental requirements, though the county administration and other state authorities may also be involved, depending on the case. Given such importance in the detection of EWC, what is the professional profile of these environmental inspectors?

In an attempt to answer this question, the duties and expected qualifications of environmental inspectors in two rural municipalities of about 30,000 inhabitants were selected from daily newspaper job ads searching for these professionals. There is fair demand for environmental inspectors, a job regarded as extra demanding. One reason is that the work of an environmental inspector, together with police officers, health and animal inspectors, and other similar professionals in Sweden, is regarded as particularly stressful. The scientists' union studied whether and how often various inspectors are intimidated in their work. The survey shows that the worst affected category is animal welfare inspectors; about 70 percent state they have been threatened and are threatened when performing their duties. It is estimated that four out of 10 environmental inspectors have been threatened in the past year (Warne, 2013).

Table 12.1 provides two recent job descriptions for environmental inspectors in rural Sweden. Though they are fairly similar in terms of duties and qualifications, note that for Municipality 2 the advertisement explicitly requests an individual who can cooperate across departmental and other agency lines (county and local authorities) as well as can handle "stressful situations." As suggested by Korsell (2001, p. 133) those who probe environmental crimes face a problem that investigators of other economic crimes do not face. The majority of environmental harm is, according to Korsell, legal and takes place with the consent of society. Only when environmental harm involves breaches of rules and permits does it become an issue. For this reason, it is difficult to prosecute many environmental offenses.

Another challenge is that in Sweden (e.g., Korsell & Hagstedt, 2008), as in Scotland (e.g., Fyfe & Reeves, 2011) and certainly many other places worldwide, the definition of an EWC crime is contested on a daily basis by those from the community and elsewhere. For instance, if livestock are in danger because of an increase in the population of large predators, illegal hunting of these animals

Table 12.1 Examples of job descriptions in two rural municipalities, 2014

Municipality 1 and Municipality 2 seek an environmental inspector

Municipality 1 – northern Sweden	Municipality 2 – southern Sweden
Duties	**Duties**
We are looking for an environmental inspector for a permanent position. The tasks involve the examination and supervision of environmental and health protection under the Environment Act. Responsibilities include independently conducting and administrating cases. Desired skills are in any of the areas of waste management, vehicle service and fuel, contaminated soil, solvent management, engineering workshops. The business focus will depend among other things on the candidate's skills and experience.	As Environmental Inspector in the municipality, you will work mainly with testing, supervision, advice, and information under the Environmental Code. You should also handle complaints, orders, and prohibitions. Projects and investigation, preliminary tests, and sampling/measurement are other duties that may be included in the work. You will work with sewage, but the service may also include other tasks. *You should be able to work across departmental and administrative boundaries and with other agencies.*
Qualifications	**Qualifications**
The candidate has to have environmental and health inspector education or other appropriate higher education in the environmental field. Long-term experience of environmental work and leadership are an advantage. The candidate must be able to express himself/herself orally and in writing and be able to independently formulate and make his/her own decisions. Driver's license required.	You must have relevant academic training in the environmental health field and good knowledge of the Environmental Code and its rules and regulations. Good computer skills are essential, as well as working with public sewage systems. It is an advantage if you have previously worked in ECOS, which is our case management system.
	A driver's license is a requirement, since the position involves field work. *We are looking for someone who is confident, purposeful, and can handle stressful situations but be calm and work in an objective manner.*
	You should have good social skills and ability to operate and structure your work. We assume that you have the ability to express yourself orally and in writing and that you are committed to your field of specialization.

Sources: NetJobsGroup (2014); Röhne (2014).

may become socially accepted, locals may turn a blind eye, and may even support it in the community, despite the act being illegal. Tradition and "the way things are done in the countryside" trump criminal law, a thing that is defined by groups living far from the local reality. This form of disputation is portrayed by von Essen, Hansen, Källström, Peterson, and Peterson (2014) as a form of resistance to imposed external values. They suggest that a recent phenomenon of illegal hunting of protected species has been observed in Scandinavian countries. Von Essen et al. (2014) suggest that as an everyday form of resistance, illegal hunting provides a continuity of livelihood practices while at the same time providing the group with the means of challenging the legitimacy of the regime in subversive ways in the struggle for recognition. These forms of disputation are against the state, the European Union, and also locals who represent "mainstream values."

The next section discusses who is responsible for dealing with EWCs in selected rural municipalities in Sweden. To assess the actions of these groups against farm crime and EWC, data from two different sources was analyzed: semi-structured interviews with representatives of CP groups in eight rural municipalities and responses from an email survey to all representatives of CPs. The short email survey was based on hypothetical scenarios and sent to all municipalities with a CP group in rural Sweden.

EWC and the role of CP councils

EWC is not regarded as an issue for CP councils. The large majority of CP representatives in Sweden think that it is up to the municipal and county authorities, especially environmental inspectors, together with the police to deal with EWC in first place. Based on responses from police officers, local police forces do not feel comfortable in this role and point to the environmental inspectors as key in the process. Interestingly, this seems to be replicated elsewhere. For example, White (2008, p. 197) suggests:

> for the police … dealing with environmental harm is basically dealing with the unknown … environmental law enforcement is a relatively new area of police work … and it is at a stage where perhaps more questions are being asked than answers are provided.

To assess in detail the role of a CP council if an environmental crime were to happen in their municipality, an email survey was sent to all representatives of CPs in Sweden (62 percent response rate). The email survey contained a hypothetical EWC scenario, and CP members were invited to describe the most important short- and long-term actions they would take as a group to tackle it.

> You have learned that an unknown quantity of toxic waste has been dumped near a large river at the border of your municipality on several occasions. Two other municipalities were also affected by the waste. You suspect that

the waste comes from a company in your community. What would your local crime prevention council do to solve the problem and ensure that this crime does not happen again?

Less than one-quarter of the interviewed CP representatives would not know what to do or would not take any action if the case concerning toxic waste described above occurred in the municipality (Figure 12.2a). The main reason they would not act, is that they do not think CP should deal with EWC. However, even if they believe that EWC is not a matter for CP work, two-thirds of them can easily identify the authorities that are responsible for the problem. These respondents pointed out who should investigate the suspected toxic waste, to whom they would report the case (the environmental authorities and the police), and, in case of a crime, they would make sure that the offenders would be taken to court. Some representatives would also list ways to repair the damage and activate insurance for those affected by the crime (*skadestånd*). They also believe that the general public should be informed as soon as possible either by media or Internet. If the damage would affect other municipalities, the county should be involved as well as the local authorities of each municipality concerned.

> this must primarily be a matter for the police and the county (länstyrelsen), as well as for municipal environmental authorities (miljöförvaltningen).... I do not believe this type of crime is a matter for a local CP council, as there are other authorities that monitor, supervise and investigate environmental crimes. In the long run, together with the Environment Agency, the energy company (and possibly county) I would drive a campaign and also organize information sessions. Try to develop checklists or the like, which can be an aid to entrepreneurs in the management of hazardous waste.
>
> (CP representative, municipality, central Sweden)

One-third of the CP members interviewed would not take any action in the long run (Figure 12.2b) or did not answer the question. Most of them see establishing a long-term plan as crucial to ensuring the problem does not happen again. Others believe that improving information about handling toxic waste would be necessary. Education programmes toward companies, especially small ones, was suggested, as was overall improvement of control checks by the local authorities.

As reported by the CP representatives interviewed, the local environmental inspectors and the police still face significant challenges in dealing with EWC at the community level. Overall there is a lack of knowledge about EWCs. Some types get more attention from the media and, in subsequent years, have tended to be easily identified by the same environmental authorities. It seems that in some municipalities, toxic leaks and construction in protected areas are often the problem, while in others, offenses involve littering or illegal hunting.

As previously shown in Chapter 8, there is some sort of regional specialization of EWC. Such specialization is partly a result of the ecosystems

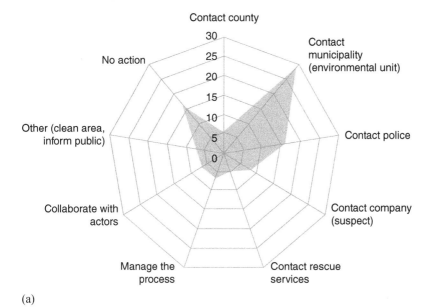

(a)

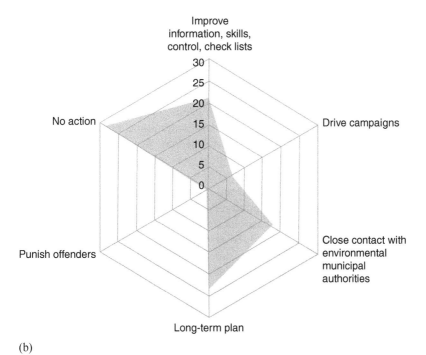

(b)

Figure 12.2 (a) What would your local crime prevention council do to solve the problem of EWC and (b) ensure that this crime does not happen again? Percentage of valid answers (source: own survey, $N=83$).

themselves (and what they contain across the country, including how accessible they are) but also results from the practices of environmental authorities in detecting EWC. However, it is unknown how the interplay of these two factors affects EWC detection.

Even if EWCs are detected and cases are sent to court, very few offenders are found guilty. If they are guilty, the penalty usually consists of fines, not prison sentences. In the early 2000s, Korsell (2001, p. 134) suggested that the sanctions imposed for environmental crime in Sweden were mild. The explanation was that "agencies that control environmental crime find it difficult to uncover the more serious incidents," especially because companies work close to the allowed prescribed limits. If there is any deviation, they are often small, so the offender is bound to incur a minor penalty. In certain cases, the crimes may not be reported, as minor violations against nature are often considered acceptable or the price to be paid for the sake of keeping jobs. Those who discover these violations may turn a blind eye despite the crime.

Protest to protect the rural environment

Protesting is regarded in this context as a way of denouncing an environmental harm. Protesting is thus an act of crime prevention and as such can be considered part of rural policing. Paradoxically, protesters and police are rarely on the same side. Though the role of the police is to ensure safety and the common good, it is rare that protesters are placed side by side with the police. On one side are the police, keeping order and protecting public and/or private property. On the other are protesters. This is not only typical for Sweden, of course.

A number of similarities emerge when Woods (2011) presents the history of protests in the countryside in the United Kingdom since the early 1970s. The author suggests that the policing of protests has not traditionally been high in the priorities of rural police forces in the United Kingdom. Woods classifies protests into two types. One type is those genuinely born of a local cause, such as farmers' protests or protests against mining or hunting. The second type is those that happen to occur in rural areas by chance but are triggered by urban or other types of movement composed of protesters from elsewhere (such as protests against nuclear power or military bases located in a rural area).

Protesting has a long tradition in Sweden. More commonly, protests take shape as face-to-face encounters, on the streets with banners in hand in big cities as well as in rural areas. Although this form of street protesting is rare, it may take on other forms in everyday life. It is part of the Swedish democratic process to react to decisions by protesting through opinion pieces in newspapers or participation in programs on radio or television. More recently, there has been an explosion of blogs and other specialized Internet sites. Most are open forums, but a few call attention to different types of environmental issues.

Throughout the twentieth century, it was common for farmers to go to the Swedish capital to protest against an agreed policy action. More unique was when angry women in the 1960s made their way to central Stockholm to protest – an event that became a cornerstone in the history of women's political participation. They were not there as wives only but rather as consumers to protest against rising prices. According to Forsberg (1997), this demonstration would have great significance for the conduct of pricing policy (milk prices) in Sweden. Researchers still talk about this protest as a symbol of public reactions that showed links between the countryside and urban areas.

Since the 1990s, the Swedish media has shown examples of scandalous reports about abuses in the food system. Swedish radio and television reported unethical and disreputable treatment of animals that awoke strong public reactions, such as the treatment of cows and pigs, salmonella outbreaks, and the like, some following the international mad cow disease debate (Forsberg, 1997). In today's global community, protests deal increasingly often with issues that go far beyond national borders. More recently, social media has become a new arena for protesters. Protesting has provided new ways to flag global problems with a local impact and vice versa.

The police have a role to play in street demonstrations. Apart from the riots in big cities such as Malmö and Stockholm in 2013, when force was used by the police to handle burning cars and contain violence, protests are less violent events.

Speaking for the forest

Some protests reach the national media, as they have had a long life of dispute. One recent example is the protests about iron ore mining in Kallak, Jokkmokk, in northern Sweden. These rural protests are small events and rare in Sweden. The reaction of the police has been reported by the newspapers as non-violent but reports from these events made in the area show that protesters are pulled away from the road by the police and then dispatched by bus.[1] These rural protests are considered peaceful by the media when compared to events that have happened recently in urban areas in Sweden (the confrontations between police and youngsters in riots in Malmö and Stockholm in 2013 mentioned above). Yet, in reality they may also involve a great deal of violence.

In Kallak, there are at least two conflicting interest groups. On one side stand the critics, made up of representatives from Sami groups (the indigenous Finno-Ugric people inhabiting the Arctic area that encompasses parts of far northern Norway, Sweden, Finland, and Russia) as well as tourism entrepreneurs and environmental activists and scholars who emphasize the mining industry's negative impact on the local environment and the whole river valley.[2] On the other side stand local politicians and sections of the population who see mining as a positive force that has the potential to create hundreds of new jobs and attract people to Jokkmokk, which currently has around 5,000 inhabitants. Jokkmokk's association, "Allmänningen," which is an economic association with all individuals who are owners of forest, owns most of the area staked for the Kallak mine, but part of the land is privately owned. Some suggest that the board of Allmänningen is pro-mining, despite there being members who are against it. The company has rights to prospect, but in this case the landowners and reindeer herding complained in the media that the company dug beyond the area where they had permission. Newspapers also reported that the landowners and reindeer herding made a complaint about protesters to the police as they felled trees in the area.

The role of police is often to maintain the peace by avoiding direct conflict between employees and protesters. Confrontations between police and protesters in the area of the planned mine at Kallak went on throughout 2013 (Figure 12.3) and, according to news reports, is still ongoing in 2014. The last police intervention was less violent, but it was still brutal to witness an 85-year-old Sámi reindeer herder being taken away from the area.[3] These confrontations are not problem free. It is unknown how the protesters feel about the police when in place. As often happens in the United Kingdom (see e.g., Woods, 2011), rural police officers are also usually residents and may sympathize to some extent with the causes espoused by protesters.

Environmental experts suggest that blasting in the mine can form cracks in the ground and affect the hydropower dam a few kilometers away. There is risk for drinking water contamination, and, in a worst case scenario, downstream villages may be swept away by flooding if anything happens to the dam. A nationwide Swedish newspaper reports the environmental harm is undeniable but is not the only impact. A protester, whose family has reindeer grazing in the area, was lifted away by police and placed in the trench. She says that it's an abuse of her people. She adds "in Sweden we denounce the oppression of indigenous peoples in other countries but oppress its own indigenous people."

Figure 12.3 Protesters against iron ore mine will continue: our fight has just begun (source: Anette Nantell, *Dagens Nyheter*, 2013).

Together with other protesters, this person turned to international law, the ILO Convention, which deals with indigenous people's rights to land and water. Along with 40 other activists, she formed a barricade against the police officers who let the mining company's trucks drive the ore down the road bit by bit.

Undoubtedly, much has changed since the first cries for change in natural conservation approaches and animal rights against economic interests in the 1960s and 1970s. However, cases like the one described above make us return to what Forsling and Borgblad (1978, p. 54) wrote nearly 40 years ago:

> As it is today, the short-term economic interests weigh much heavier than, for example, nature conservation interests. Nature cannot be valued in money.... The consequence of adopting this "balanced vision" is that in reality not all interests are not at all equal.

It is perhaps true that the value of untouched nature may not raise the GDP of a country, but steps have been taken since the 1970s to protect natural environments. In the European Union, since the 2000s incentives have been paid to farmers who preserve nature areas. Of course, there are numerous cases in which the process and the decisions are still anchored on an outdated tradition of justice that put in doubt the defense of the community's sustainability. When harm and damage are imminent, it may be too late to undertake mainstream intervention. The only alternative then may be taking more tangible, perhaps drastic, measures such as protesting.

Protests in newspapers

Most local newspapers have a letters column (*insändare*), now also digitally accessible via the Internet. Newspapers have special sections for these types of arenas. In such columns, hundreds of letters may be found denouncing environmental harm across the country: from oil spills and chemical waste dumping, to animal abuse. A recent case of a fishing farm in the northeast of the country became nationally recognized when the company had to look for a new location following protests by the local population in local newspapers. Protests in this case happen without the direct involvement of the police, but the municipality and environmental inspectors were involved after public complaints. Another case exemplifies the dubious role local authorities may play in cases of environmental harm. On one side, the environmental inspectors represent the local authorities who safeguard environmental rights. On the other side, the municipality itself is accused of unlawful actions against the environment by approving the disposal of wastewater into a lake.

> How can you dump wastewater in Hamstasjön? Obviously that is an environmental crime.... School kids are taught not to dump waste in nature, but what will they think if the municipality directs wastewater into the lake.... Wake up and act!
>
> (*Sundsvalls Tidning*, February 7, 2010)

Protests can also be made by formal authorities. Five of the northernmost counties have jointly protested recently against the government ICT development proposal. In a protest letter published in several newspapers (e.g., Lindgren, 2014), the counties claim that rural municipalities are at a disadvantage, as the population outside towns with 3,000 residents and fewer are not included in the program, which will ensure access and updates to broadband support for the future. As the communications landscape gets denser, the networked population is gaining greater access to information, opening up opportunities to undertake collective action. In the environmental arena, as a number of examples in Sweden have demonstrated, this participation can help impose demands for change.

Protests in the Internet era

Since the rise of the Internet in the beginning of the 1990s, the population with access to the Internet has increased dramatically, even in the most remote rural areas in Sweden. Over the same period, social media has become a fact of life for civil society worldwide, with the use of different tools: text messaging, email, photo sharing, social networking, and the like. Social media often involves many actors – citizens, activists, nongovernmental organizations, software providers, governments (Shirky, 2011). The possibilities for building networks of information and capacity to quickly influence public opinion have also dramatically changed.

In Sweden, blogs and other forums are often used to inform and mobilize individuals around different types of environmental harm/crime (see, for example, animal rights, www.djurensratt.se/, or the Ministry of the Environment's blog, http://blogg.miljodep.se/). The beauty of social media is the independence of location. Protesters fuming about local causes can trigger a movement beyond national boundaries. Enjolras, Steen-Johnsen, and Wollebæk (2013) show that, as a tool for protest, social media represents an alternative structure alongside mainstream media and well-established political organizations and civil society that recruit in different ways and reach different segments of the population.

An agenda to tackle EWC: littering, chemical waste, and illegal trade in endangered animal and plant species

Littering and car dumping in the wild

According to figures presented in Chapter 8, littering accounts for the second largest share of EWC in the police statistics in Sweden. This category is dominated by the disposal of garbage in forests and on the outskirts of main urban areas and tends to be detected close to roads. This includes domestic waste, old furniture and cars. Some cars are burned on-site (Ceccato & Uittenbogaard, 2013).

Levels of littering and garbage dumping are potentially associated with garbage collection fees. As indicated in Chapter 8, the difference in garbage collection fees among municipalities is SEK25,003 per year, according to the Swedish Homeowners Association's 2012 survey. The difference, however, is bound to affect both those that own their homes as well as those who rent (costs are shared by rent tenants).

The increase of vehicle dumping in nearby forests has often been associated with the lack of incentives for car owners to take their cars to the closest junkyard (the incentive expired in the 2010s). Instead, many vehicles are left in the woods or along roads, or parts of them are, as some parts are sold in the secondhand market. This is an example of the complexity of defining actions to prevent this type of harm. An apparently isolated decision taken at the national level of eliminating incentives for car owners has motivated vehicle dumping in the forest. In a single rural municipality in northern Sweden, more than 30 cars are left each year for the municipality to take care of. This problem is not divorced from other types of crime, such as theft of car parts later sold elsewhere.

For the communities in these targeted areas, more awareness would be necessary to report cases of domestic waste dumped into the wild and its impact. Spills of fuel and other chemicals are left with old cars. The detection of these crimes depends on the accessibility of the area by road or through an urbanized area. Recorded cases depend on detection, and detection is based on what people witness on a daily basis. Some of these areas are difficult to access, and garbage and waste in the forest may go undetected for much of the year, as the area is covered by snow, particularly in northern Sweden.

Fencing off properties goes against *allemansrätt*, the Swedish tradition of the right for anyone to use other people's property. However, areas that are constantly targeted by waste dumping should be exempted from the rule. While suggestive of possible intervention, the following list of measures to tackle waste dumping has to be considered in the specific Swedish context.

Note that some of these specific measures include changes in fees and incentives at national level, while most are directed at regional and local actions with the full engagement of the local community. Although local authorities may not have the power to make structural changes that affect the long-term conditions for environmental harm, this chapter offers a number of indications of how conditions may be reconsidered so as to enhance the prevention of waste dumpage in nature in rural communities most targeted by the problem. These suggestions are not organized according to order of priority but rather are linked to the attributes of situational and social crime prevention principles.

Incentive schemes
- Decrease garbage collection fees for domestic waste at national level.
- Increase frequency of collection of domestic waste in tourist areas/"cottage belt."
- Prevent discharge in forest by offering public recycling stations in rural locales.

- Promote public campaigns to reduce waste and encourage re-use and recycling materials.
- Reinstate national system of incentives for old car return.

Improve public awareness
- Inform individuals about consequences of inappropriate garbage dumping in nature.
- Post information about garbage dumping/littering restrictions in nature.
- Education in schools about consequences of waste dumping.
- "Cash and release" media advertising including through social media.

Mobilize community
- Awareness of the problem by visiting the damaged areas.
- Adoption of the problem by crime prevention groups (CP).
- Litter watch schemes (LWS) by grown-ups and schoolchildren.
- Promote coordinated actions by CP, LWS, and other local actors.
- Confidential hot-line and app systems linked to denouncement of garbage and litter.

Increase the difficulty of committing crime
- Identify particular targeted areas/forests/rivers and prevent access to these areas with fences and gates.
- Limit pathways into the wild and nature conservation areas.
- If targeted, make it difficult for outsiders to access natural areas protected by law.
- Remove places that can be used for littering/dumping.

Maximize the risk of detection
- Install CCTV cameras.
- Increase patrols in targeted areas/forests/rivers.
- Disrupt markets for second-hand car parts.
- Investigate origin and identity of previously dumped vehicles.
- Motivate guardianship by transients of suspects along roads.
- Identify unauthorized transients in areas protected by law.
- Report suspect purchases of fuels used to burn cars and other materials.

Reduce the rewards
- Quick removal of waste and dumped materials in nature (avoid "copy cats").
- Refocus the problem in the media by showing cases when offenders are caught.
- Increase fines for garbage dumping in nature.
- Induce guilt by strengthening moral condemnation of garbage dumping into the wild.
- Spread pamphlets/media about the impact of garbage dumping in the area.

Reporting waste dumping should happen regardless of whether it conforms to the definition of a crime. Dumping domestic waste, for instance, may not be regarded as a serious crime but should be pointed out for its potential harm in a form of chemical pollution to soil and water or plastic materials that are not biodegradable.

Unlawful handling of chemicals/chemical pollution

EWC records of unlawful handling of chemicals present a concentrated pattern in rural areas spread over the country. Remote rural municipalities in Sweden have a significantly high percentage of these crimes: unlawful handling of chemicals, disruption of control, and disregard of regulations and permits for the use of chemical components. Newspaper articles show several cases of inactive businesses that leave machines and products that are the source of the problem. In contrast with littering and car dumping, chemical pollution is often perpetrated by a business (e.g., industry, mining, or farming).

Incentive schemes
- Tailored information to local companies about handling and managing chemicals.
- Control access to prohibited chemicals through import via Internet or tips from police or customs (border patrol).
- Information to personnel on how to handle and manage chemicals in the production process.

Improve public awareness
- Inform individuals about consequences of unlawful handling of chemicals.
- Certification scheme for businesses that are environmentally friendly that can be flagged in their products.
- Create "code of good practices" in managing waste among company associations.

Mobilize community
- Assist compliance through coordinated action at local (CP, police, environmental inspectors) and regional levels, business and environmental authorities.
- Confidential hotline and app systems linked to whistleblowing on chemical pollution and other environmental problems.
- Creation of public–private partnerships to educate appropriate use of chemical handling and management of toxic waste.

Increase the difficulty of committing crime
- Seal production process to reduce the risk of chemical spill.
- Frequent inspections of production system by environmental inspectors and the like.

Maximize the risk of detection

- Trade union representatives can ensure working conditions adhere to rules.
- Companies that shut down are responsible for what is left on the grounds of the company, including chemical waste and other potentially damaging product.
- Improve knowledge of environmental inspectors to increase instances of detection.
- Police officers may be engaged in detection and the investigative process when there is suspicion of crime together with environmental inspectors.
- Collection and analysis of crime data.
- More resources toward the investigative process and during production of evidence (qualified biologists, toxicologists, or epidemiologists).
- Better information sharing along the process and between different actors.

Reduce the rewards

- Increase sanctions to unlawful handling of chemicals/pollution.
- Zero tolerance to businesses that do not comply with environmental norms, including minor deviations.

Illegal trade in endangered animal and plant species

"The global trade in illegal wildlife is a multi-billion dollar industry that threatens biodiversity" (Rosen & Smith, 2010, p. 24). Current evidence shows that regulation and enforcement have been insufficient to effectively control the global trade in illegal wildlife at national and international levels.

Sweden imports and, to a lesser extent, exports endangered animals and plants. As an importing country, endangered species most trafficked from other parts of the world are used as pets, in collections, or in the form of tourist objects and as ingredients for health foods.

Globally southeast Asia is a hub of illegal activity (Rosen & Smith, 2010). As an exporting country, there are cases of poaching large predators, such as bears and wolves, but also bird eggs, mostly for trade. As Chapter 8 suggested, illegal trade conducted by organized criminal networks is more difficult to investigate and is often rejected by public prosecutors on the grounds that the offense cannot be proved because of lack of evidence (Korsell & Hagstedt, 2008; Sazdovska, 2009).

According to Rosen and Smith (2010), the effective control of illegal trade in endangered animal and plant species requires a multi-pronged approach including community-scale education and empowering local people to value wildlife, coordinated international regulation, and a greater allocation of national resources to on-the-ground enforcement. At regional and national levels, nations without the independent capacity for enforcement will require help from other nations in the form of partnerships to be able to control trade. White and Heckenberg (2014) suggest also that to control illegal trade as an organized crime, it is necessary to share knowledge of perpetrators, involving the investigation of chains of damage and the network of players, which may involve corruption of authorities as part of the organized crime system.

Chapter 8 suggested that a slightly higher percentage of cases of animal abuse, illegal animal possession, and disregard of protected species are recorded in remote rural municipalities than in accessible and urban municipalities. Together with illegal trade, this calls for preventive action at national, regional, and local levels, where environmental authorities can act upon the problem. Suggestions put forward below to tackle illegal trade in endangered animal and plant species in Sweden focus on issues that have a local dimension, though some indicate the need for structural changes in national and global regulation and planning.

Incentive schemes
- Secure reserves and conservation areas.
- Increase the natural habitat for endangered species.
- Reward vigilance from patrols, voluntary poaching control units.
- Compensation when endangered species destroy crops or livestock.
- Invest in community-based eco-projects in origin countries (as alternative to poaching).

Improve public awareness
- Inform individuals about consequences of inappropriate consumption of endangered animal and plant species.
- Media advertising including through social media about the local and global impact of the trade (both origin and host ecosystem).
- Incentive for consumption of certified products only (e.g., wood, fur).

Mobilize community
- Adoption of the problem by crime prevention groups (CP).
- Promote coordinated actions – more explicit customs declarations.
- Popularize the database of national endangered species.

Increase the difficulty of committing crime
- Identify and protect particular species of animals and plants.
- Limit pathways into the wild and nature conservation areas.
- More rangers and patrols on the ground (origin country).

Maximize the risk of detection and reduce rewards
- Disrupt market for commercialization of endangered animals and plants.
- Investigate origin and identity of animals by using micro-chipping, DNA forensic techniques.
- Motivate guardianship by locals, including by purchase of animal medication.
- Report suspect purchases of organic/biological materials through customs.
- Better information sharing along the process and between different actors.
- Bilateral government agreements to tackle illegal trade.

- Increase sanctions and fines on convicted offenders.
- Refocus the problem in the media by showing cases when offenders are caught.

Concluding remarks

Farm crime and EWC are not considered a priority in CP councils' agendas or by the police. Exceptions are municipalities that are targeted by these problems, where environmental inspectors and the police play an important role in crime detection. Although local CP councils demonstrate good knowledge of what to do in the case of a farm crime or EWC occurring in their municipality, there is an overall lack knowledge about what works and what does not work when tackling farm crime as well as EWC among those interviewed from CP councils. Such crimes normally are not followed up and are considered one-off events detected by environmental inspectors and police. There are indications that public (including CP groups) and private partnerships are blooming in municipalities that are often targeted by farm crime and EWC.

Environmental inspectors, who might detect such offenses, cannot be expected to take over the role of the police as criminal investigators; so many cases never reach trial. At the same time, CP groups in each municipality should be more aware of, and perhaps be more curious about, these events than they are nowadays. There is a clear scope for further research here. First, research can be helpful in improving crime prevention practices by taking a closer look at the barriers (legal, organizational, economic, and cultural) that make the detection of farm crime and environmental violations difficult as well as the reasons why they rarely go to trial. It is possible that there are geographical differences across the country that explain levels of detection and conviction rates. As most community practices to prevent these crimes fall outside the range of responsibilities of the traditional actors engaged in crime prevention (such as the police and CP councils), a good start is to find out ways to keep the new public–private partnerships alive as legitimate actors in rural policing. With clearly defined roles, there is no doubt about who is in charge when dealing with farm crimes or EWCs.

A model of a rural CP that takes into account the needs in the countryside must capture the changing urban–rural relationships. These relationships are currently being redefined as the use of ICT makes crime less dependent on space. ICT can be used to increase efficiency in crime detection and the reporting of criminal events, as suggested by the use of CrimeAlert, tagging, and specialized cameras. The use of CCTV to detect criminals on building sites or in forests, a common target of thefts in rural areas, is an example of how the technology can be used in areas where guardianship is low. The use of social media in community policing may be particularly important in rural areas because of the long distances. The powerful capacity of georeferencing social control by texting, voicing or imaging as crime happens is new in policing, but it is here to stay as a new expression of surveillance (Ceccato & Dolmén, 2013). In a more general account, for prevention and reduction of farm crime and EWC, the collection and analysis of crime data must be improved via police records and partnerships, followed by information sharing throughout the process and among different actors. In the future, national victims' surveys should incorporate questions that are more appropriate for rural areas, with samples that allow meaningful analysis across rural municipalities and regions, which, for the time being, is not possible.

Indeed, the sharing of information is an important activity in order to raise awareness of farm crime and EWC occurring in particular areas. Public awareness is also important, education about the issues for children, and engagement in safety walks and watch schemes are potential ways to get the community involved and prevent crime. For farm crime, especially concerning machines and tools, marking equipment and promoting harder sanctions and more aggressive enforcement may be effective in high targeted areas.

It is not known why remote rural municipalities show higher shares of chemical environmental crimes, but lack of support by environmental authorities and lack of adequate information about how to handle chemical waste is certainly a major contributor to the problem. Better information from environmental authorities on handling chemical components should be in place. Municipal authorities should impose better control of waste left by inactive companies. Small businesses, perhaps the most important group of offenders, should get better information from environmental authorities on handling these components. Resources should be earmarked from the national to the local levels to provide educational programs that prevent the problem in the first place.

EWC records, in particular for garbage dumping and littering, show that such crimes often occur in accessible areas, such as near roads, though not too close to urban areas, as that may increase the risk of being detected or recognized. Police records also show that larger municipal areas can lead to an increase in cases of dumping. The adoption of electronic surveillance along roads could, for instance, be an alternative to increasing surveillance in areas more targeted by garbage dumping. Routine activity principles can be the basis for assessing detection schemes and EWC concentrations. Popular places may see more EWCs, which then can be easily combated by improving surveillance and security at that particular spot. Public campaigns can suggest that such dumping spots should be better supervised and may be under indirect social control of the local community. Future research should focus on finding ways to deal with the problem and better implementing preventive schemes using current public and private partnerships, such as the ones found in rural Sweden.

To restrict the illicit market in plants and animals, information should reach the general public, as many crimes of this type are committed "by mistake" or ignorance of the current environmental laws. In Sweden, Customs has a key position in preventing protected plants and animals from entering the country. Within the country, the rate of detection of these environmental violations can be improved by increasing surveillance at suspected locations. At the individual level, consumers can be vigilant of ingredients in food and medicines that can arise from illegal trade. For example, furniture can contain types of wood that are threatened in their local habitat or fur from endangered species. So consumers should avoid buying products that are not certified. The same can be said about other products of suspicious origin.

Nature is a means for economic sustainability but it is submitted here that EWCs cannot be excused for the sake of keeping the rural economy alive. The issues of the social and economic sustainability of rural areas must be assessed in relation to the needs of the environment. To make things more difficult, some of these recorded environmental crimes are caused by businesses such as sawmills and more traditional enterprises that have been part of the community for a long time and are now targeted by new environmental rules. Most people in the community do not view these activities as crimes. Perhaps this is a reflection of the fact that society is still adopting a "balanced vision" noted already in the 1970s by Forsling and Borgblad (1978). And yet, natural resources are exploited individually, while the costs of harm to nature are shared collectively.

Protesting, either through the media or face-to-face, is an example of people's capacity to mobilize around a specific cause. So far, protests in rural areas, either for inherited causes or new externally imposed ones, are for the time being seen as exogenous to crime prevention actions and policing. As illustrated in the Swedish mining case, although the police may sympathize with the causes of protesters, as some police officers are locals, structural barriers keep their actions apart. Cases like this one call for a discussion of the police's role and legitimacy in rural communities, particularly now when Swedish police centralization will soon be a fact.

Notes

1 Polisingripande i Kallak. Retrieved April 17, 2015, from www.youtube.com/watch?v=YhhFdLvPinU.
2 Gruvbrytning kan orsaka dammhaveri. Retrieved April 17, 2015, from www.nsd.se/nyheter/gruvbrytning-kan-orsaka-dammhaveri-7659120.aspx.
3 The old man in Gállok. Retrieved April 17, 2015, from www.youtube.com/watch?v=kLCiKXsui_k.

References

Arora-Jonsson, S. (2011). Virtue and vulnerability: Discourses on women, gender and climate change. *Global Environmental Change, 21*(2), 744–751.
Barclay, E., Donnermeyer, J. F., Doyle, B. D., & Talary, D. (2001). Property crime victimisation and crime prevention on farms. In N. A.-G. C. P. Division (Ed.), Institute for Rural Futures, University of New England.
Brottsförebyggande rådet – BRÅ (National Council of Crime Prevention). (2009). Samverkan i lokalt brottsförebyggande arbete. Stockholm: Rikspolisstyrelsen, Sveriges kommuner och landsting.
Ceccato, V., & Dolmén, L. (2013). Crime prevention in rural Sweden. *European Journal of Criminology, 10*, 89–112.
Ceccato, V., & Uittenbogaard, A. C. (2013). Environmental and wildlife crime in Sweden. *International Journal of Rural Criminology, 2*(1), 23–50.

Clarke, R. V. (1997). *Situational crime prevention: Successful case studies*. Monsey, NY: Willow Tree.

CrimeStoppers. (2014). Allt fler drabbas av kostsamma dieselstölder, vad kan man göra åt detta? Retrieved May 3, 2014, from www.crimestoppers.se/2014/03/08/forebygg-pa-ratt-satt/.

Donnermeyer, J. F., & Barclay, E. (2005). The policing farm crime. *Practices and Research, 6*(1), 3–17.

Donnermeyer, J. F., Barclay, E. M., & Mears, D. P. (2011). Policing agricultural crime. In R. I. Mawby & R. Yarwood (Eds.), *Rural policing and policing the rural: A constable countryside* (pp. 193–204). Farnham: Ashgate.

Enjolras, B., Steen-Johnsen, K., & Wollebæk, D. (2013). Social media and mobilization to offline demonstrations: Transcending participatory divides? *New Media and Society, 15*(6), 890–908.

Forsberg, G. (1997). Jordbruk som tjänsteproduktion: en ekologisk välfärdssektor. *Tidskrift för Genusvetenskap*, 30–38.

Forsling, A., & Borgblad, M. (1978). Konflikten mellan jordbruket och naturvården i markavvattningsfrågor. Uppsala: Institutionen för markvetenskap, Avd. för lantbrukets hydroteknik.

Fyfe, N. R., & Reeves, A. D. (2011). The thin green line? Police perceptions of challenges of policing wildlife crime in Scotland. In R. Mawby & R. Yarwood (Eds.), *Rural policing and policing the rural: A constable countryside?* (pp. 169–182). Farnham: Ashgate.

Huisman, W., & van Erp, J. (2013). Opportunities for environmental crime: A test of situational crime prevention theory. *British Journal of Criminology, 53*(6), 1178–1200.

Jones, J., & Phipps, J. (2012). Policing farm crime in England and Wales. Paper presented at the *Papers from the British Criminology Conference, 12*, 3–24.

Korsell, L. (2014, May 28). Number of convicted and imprisoned by environmental crime in Sweden. Personal conversation.

Korsell, L., & Hagstedt, J. (2008). Illegal handel med hotade djur- och växtarter: En förstudie (Vol. 14). Stockholm: BRÅ.

Korsell, L. E. (2001). Big stick, little stick: Strategies for controlling and combating environmental crime. *Journal of Scandinavian Studies in Criminology and Crime Prevention, 2*(2), 127–148.

Lantbrukarnas Riksförbund. (2012). Brott på landet: En undersökning bland lantbrukare. (J. Johansson, Ed., p. 40). Stockholm: Sveriges Lantbruk.

Lemieux, A. M. (2011). Policing poaching and protecting pachyderms: Lessons learned from Africa's elephants. In R. Mawby & R. Yarwood (Eds.), *Rural policing and policing the rural: A constable countryside?* (pp. 183–192). Farnham: Ashgate.

Lindgren, J. (2014, May 19). Glesbygden missgynnas. *Norrländska Socialdemokraten*. Retrieved April 17, 2015, from www.nsd.se/nyheter/lulea/glesbygden-missgynnas-8491728.aspx.

Mawby, R., & Yarwood, R. (Eds.). (2011). *Rural policing and policing the rural: A constable countryside?* Farnham: Ashgate.

Mears, D. P., Scott, M. L., & Bhati, A. S. (2007). A process and outcome evaluation of an agricultural crime prevention initiative. *Criminal Justice Policy Review, 18*(1), 51–80.

Naturvårdsverket (Swedish Environmental Protection Agency). (2011). Utvärdering av tillsynen över verksamhetsutövarens egenkontroll (p. 79). Stockholm: Naturvårdsverket.

NetJobsGroup. (2014). Lediga job: Miljöinspektör. Retrieved May 28, 2014, from www.miljojobb.se/miljoinspektor.html.

O'Connor, M., & Gray, D. (1989). *Crime in a rural community.* Sydney: Federation Press.

Pires, S. F., & Clarke, R. V. (2011). Sequential foraging, itinerant fences and parrot poaching in Bolivia. *British Journal of Criminology, 51*(2), 314–335.

Röhne, J. (2014). X kommun söker Miljöinspektör. Miljöaktuellt. Retrieved May 28, 2014, from http://miljoaktuellt.idg.se/2.1845/1.560146.

Rosen, G., & Smith, K. (2010). Summarizing the evidence on the international trade in illegal wildlife. *EcoHealth, 7*(1), 24–32.

Sazdovska, M. M. (2009). Elimination of ecological crime as a part of organized crime in the former Yugoslav Republic of Macedonia. *Review of International Affairs, 60*, 80–91.

Shirky, C. (2011). The political power of social media: Technology, the public sphere and political change. *Foreign Affairs (article summary),* February, 12.

Statens Offentliga Utredningar – SOU. (2002). Polisverksamhet i förändring. Stockholm: Delbetänkande från polisverksamhetsutredningen, Justitiedepartementet, Statens offentliga utredningar, 70.

Naturvårdsverket (Swedish Environmental Protection Agency). (2011a). Tillsynsmetoder och inspektörens roll (The Inspections Ordinance). Retrieved April 17, 2015, from www.naturvardsverket.se/sv/Lagar-och-andra-styrmedel/Tillsyn-och-egenkontroll/Att-bedriva-operativ-tillsyn/Tillsynsmetoder-och-inspektorens-roll/.

Naturvårdsverket (Swedish Environmental Protection Agency). (2011b). Utvärdering av tillsynen över verksamhetsutövarens egenkontroll (p. 79). Stockholm: Naturvårdsverket.

United Nations – UN. (1972). Declaration of the United Nations Conference on the Human Environment. Retrieved April 17, 2015, from www.unep.org/Documents.multilingual/Default.asp?DocumentID=97&ArticleID=1503.

United Nations – UN. (1992). Rio Declaration on Environment and Development. Retrieved April 17, 2015, from www.un.org/documents/ga/conf151/aconf15126-1annex1.htm.

von Essen, E., Hansen, H. P., Källström, H., Peterson, N. M., & Peterson, T. L. (2014). The radicalisation of a counterpublic: The case illegal hunting in the Nordic countries. *Journal of Rural Studies,* doi:10.1016/j.jrurstud.2014.11.001.

Warne, K. (2013). Hot vanligt bland inspektörer. *Vision.* Retrieved May 28, 2014, from http://vision.se/nyheter/2013/juni/hot-vanligt-bland-inspektorer/.

White, R. (2007). Green criminology and the pursuit of social and ecological justice. In P. B. a. N. South (Ed.), *Issues in green criminology: Confronting harms against environments, humanity and other animals* (pp. 32–51). Cullompton, Devon: Willan Publishing.

White, R. (2008). *Crimes against nature: Environmental criminology and ecological justice.* Portland, OR: Willan Publishing.

White, R., & Heckenberg, D. (2014). *Green criminology: An introduction to the study of environmental harm.* Oxford: Routledge.

Woods, M. (2011). Policing rural protest. In R. Mawby & R. Yarwood (Eds.), *Rural policing and policing the rural: A constable countryside?* (pp. 109–122). Farnham: Ashgate.

Yarwood, R., & Edwards, B. (1995). Voluntary action in rural areas: The case of neighbourhood watch. *Journal of Rural Studies, 11*(4), 447–459.

13 Crime prevention in rural areas

Youth-related challenges

To frame the Swedish case, this chapter briefly reviews some of the current international literature in criminology on crime prevention activities aimed at youth in rural settings. The role of community in dealing with the problem in rural municipalities through crime prevention initiatives is given special attention. The chapter closes with examples from the Swedish rural context and concluding remarks.

Crime prevention and youth in the rural context: an international perspective

Violence and addiction to alcohol or drugs are often common concerns in crime prevention worldwide. Rural areas do not appear to provide strong deterrence to these problems for young people (Johnson et al., 2008). Although different strategies are implemented to tackle crime, violence, and addiction, the role of community is identified as fundamental to the prevention of crime and substance abuse among youngsters. Some actors, such as schools (e.g., Shears, Edwards, & Stanley, 2006) and local collaborations (e.g., Albert et al., 2011), have a direct effect on preventing substance abuse, disorder, and crime. The role of community is argued to also have an indirect effect, through culture and norms that may discourage or encourage addiction and crime. International examples of crime prevention (CP) initiatives based on community engagement, though not extensive, are briefly discussed in the next few paragraphs.

In the United States, Hawkins (1999) suggested a system that empowers communities to organize themselves to engage in outcome-focused prevention planning. This model for prevention planning uses the tools of prevention science and is called Communities That Care (CTC). The method includes school surveys that reliably measure risk, protection, delinquency, and drug use outcomes across states and ethnic groups applied to a number of study areas in the United States. In Europe, CTC has been tested in England, Wales, Scotland, and the Netherlands. A more recent example in the United States was reported by Albert et al. (2011), who assess community-based programs against overdose among youth in western North Carolina, where unintentional-poisoning mortality rates had drastically increased since 2009. The overdose prevention program involved five components that rely heavily on community involvement through monitoring and surveillance data, prevention of overdoses, and face-to-face meetings.

Community norms against substance abuse play an important protective role against drug use (Collins, Harris, Knowlton, Shamblen, & Thompson, 2011). While little research has looked at the indirect impact of community, Beyers, Toumbourou, Catalano, Arthur, and Hawkins (2004) find that in the United States community norms favorable to substances such as cigarettes, alcohol, and marijuana affect use among young people. Changes in the community culture are crucial to obtain good results in prevention. Another example in this direction is reviewed by Payne, Berg, and Sun (2005). The authors discuss the results of a youth violence prevention plan using a rural and growing community in the United States. They discuss the advantages of adopting an "empowered approach" to develop youth violence prevention, together with policy makers, practitioners, and citizens. Details of the approach are presented along with issues that arose during the research and planning process.

Johnson et al. (2008) suggest that community prevention efforts should focus on reaching rural areas and segmenting program content based on youngsters' needs, which might differ from group to group. The authors found, for instance, that white teenagers from that particular region of the United States would benefit from an emphasis on preventing tobacco and alcohol use, whilst non-white teenagers would benefit from an emphasis on preventing violence and victimization. In the United Kingdom, youth crime and anti-social behavior are common problems associated with crime prevention in rural areas, also linked to alcohol and drug addiction (e.g., Forsyth & Barnard, 1999).

Internationally, CP initiatives have been criticized because they implement interventions that may negatively impact young people (White, 1998). Interventions are often not intentionally directed at young people alone, but young people still feel most affected by them as they tend to "hang around" together in groups in public places, especially teenagers. White (1998, p. 131) points out that some CP strategies run the risk of over-controlling young people rather than addressing the structural causes of youthful offending or antisocial behavior.

Keeping these issues in mind, the next section reports on experiences with crime prevention devoted to young people in selected rural areas in Sweden. Email surveys, an analysis of a crime prevention database, media excerpts, and face-to-face interviews were used to capture examples of current CP initiatives.

Addressing youth problems in rural Sweden

Youth-related problems are the main CP concern, transformed into different types of intervention, from early offending careers, to violence and alcohol and drug addiction. CP projects funded by the Swedish National Crime Prevention Council (BRÅ) between 2004 and 2010 were evaluated by the types of municipalities that receive funding, the types of projects, and whether any assessment of these projects was done by the group.

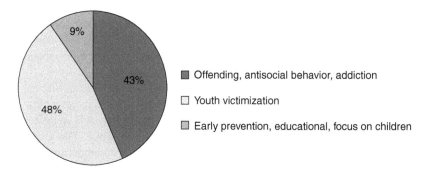

Figure 13.1 Issues addressed by the CP projects financed by BRÅ (%) (source: own graph from BRÅ database).

CP projects funded by BRÅ focused mostly on youth-related issues ($N=37$). Within those projects that deal with youth problems, 48 percent deal with victimization (violence), about 43 percent are related to offending, antisocial behavior with drug and alcohol abuse, and about 10 percent are devoted to early offending prevention focused on young children (Figure 13.1). Note that the funding is directed to CP interventions in both large and small towns.

To investigate further how CP groups in these projects work on a daily basis with youth-related problems, a short email survey was sent to all CP groups in rural municipalities. The email survey helped to select eight municipalities which were further investigated for case studies using face-to-face interviews, as discussed in the next section. Members of CP groups were asked to discuss the most relevant short- and long-term actions they would take to solve the problem below.

> *A small group of young people are causing various disturbances in various public places. (They were found drinking alcohol outside their school and they have been engaged in acts of vandalism on public property, fights with other youngsters and minor thefts.) Residents in the area are very upset by the young people's lack of respect for others. Although they have a foreign background, they were born and grew up in the municipality. Residents have now come to see you as a representative of the local crime prevention council (or equivalent) asking for help to solve the problem. What does your local crime prevention council do to address the problem and ensure that it does not happen again?*

Getting youngsters "busy" is declared to be a common long-term action to prevent youth problems. Youth problems are composed of a variety of issues, alcohol and drug addiction, truancy, acts of public disorder, thefts. However, it is surprising how unvaryingly CP members declare addressing the hypothetical youth problem in their community. Most CP councils declared that they would rely on cooperation between police, school, social services, and youth recreation centers. There are some specific features in the way they interpret the scenario. Some of these CP groups would call for involvement of young people themselves and their families to solve these problems. Others suggest more social control in the form of security guards, police, and safety walkers.

> We usually put in extra security, in the form of guards. This is to get a clear picture of the problem ... we talk with staff, municipal police, it is an agreement between the police and the local crime prevention group. The group discusses how to deal with the problem and arrives at a common decision about what to do, and based on it we act. In this case, contact with the families is essential. We try to break the pattern. In the long run, we inform teachers and recreation staff, talk to the safety walkers and allow security guards especially to check out the area.
>
> (CP representative, southern Sweden)

> Existing collaboration between schools, police, social services and youth center would be important, although we should have that at a much earlier stage. In this case it seems to have gone too far! The municipality has a combined entity for social services and health in schools for children up to 19 years old. This unit should work hard with these young people and their families.
>
> (CP representative, northern Sweden)

Many representatives could relate the scenario to the everyday reality they face in their municipality. For those who already deal with such youth-related problems, collaboration between local actors is considered essential.

> This scenario is our reality today in one of the villages we have here in the municipality. It is a complex problem, and the residents of the village feel that the police never come to them. We called a meeting with residents in the area so they could talk about their frustration. Schools, social services, police and recreation will collaborate on urgent individual cases. Then we had a meeting with the young people and listened to them.
>
> (CP representative, northern Sweden)

> We have had a similar problem here. The individual actors in the network have the foundation of their expertise and resources in working to resolve the issue.... Efforts have solved the problem and are expected to ensure that problems of this kind do not arise again.
>
> (CP representative, southern Sweden)

Surprisingly, the CP representatives do not address the potentially special needs of young people with parents who are foreign born (the scenario specifically highlights this group). Some CP representatives were upset by the formulation of the hypothetical scenario, calling it offensive and particularly "picking on young people with a foreign background." However, even this group of representatives could not conceive the idea that youngsters with a foreign background may have at that particular stage of their lives special needs of schooling, socialization, and community participation. It was initially expected that CP groups would engage these youngsters more often in order to identify their needs and arrange appropriate actions. For example, limitations to the Swedish language might be a problem to be tackled by the school if the youngsters had a foreign background, as it was the case in the hypothetical scenario. The homogeneity in the answers from the CP representatives is certainly associated with the "infrastructure" in place and service routines rooted in Sweden's welfare system at municipal level. They tend to answer in a similar way because they tend to follow BRÅ guidelines as well as a number of CP models that tend to be used nationwide as examples of "good practices." Examples of these models are the Kronoberg model and EFFEKT, both discussed in the next section of the chapter.

Interviews with CP representatives

Semi-structured interviews were conducted face-to-face in 2010 (in Swedish) with representatives of local CP councils in eight municipalities (49 interviews in total, about six individuals per study area). They were policy officers, school representatives, members of women's shelters, county council members, social services, other NGO members, and citizens. Findings indicate that CP groups approach youth problems in rural areas in two ways.

The first way that CP groups deal youth problems in rural areas is by focusing on young people who are already causing concern (e.g., because of truancy or fighting) and may be labeled locally as "troublemakers," perhaps similar to the group described in the hypothetical scenario in the previous subsection. Targeted action is therefore directed at this group only, often involving school, parents, and, in more serious cases, the police and social services. Among those with confirmed problems of addiction, there is a specific drug abuse program with frequent checks, in at least two municipalities. Collaborative work between police, school, families, and social services is declared essential for this group.

The second way is to implement preventive actions directed at all youngsters in the municipality. In this case, the goal of these actions is to keep young people entertained, away from the "boredom of the countryside," involved in structured or semi-structured activities, under the supervision of adults. Events conducted in these meeting places may not be associated with crime prevention per se, but most believe that "keeping youth busy" is a good way to prevent crime. These events can be festivals and, on a daily basis, youth recreation centers, common in rural municipalities.

Youth activities at recreation centers are still considered the most popular type of action adopted by CP groups to prevent youth problems (Figure 13.2). These centers play an important social role, because they may constitute the only "parent-free" zone devoted to leisure in the community. No doubt that these

Figure 13.2 Examples of places for youth leisure activities in rural Sweden.

recreation centers indisputably play an important role in the social life of the community, however, the role of these youth recreation centers for CP has been long disputed. For instance, Mahoney and Stattin (2000) show in a Swedish case study that youth participation in low-structure leisure activities, such as the ones that take place in youth recreation centers, was associated with high levels of aggressive behavior, alcohol/drug use, delinquency, and crime. Internationally, Bursik (1999) concludes that better knowledge is needed about "communities' supervisory and socialization capabilities" of which these recreation centers are part. There is no agreement among those interviewed. One CP representative argues in favor of this approach, whilst another highlights the challenges of organizing youth recreational activities within this framework. In the Swedish study areas, interviewees believe that CP activities play an important role for the health and quality of life of local youth:

> The first time we had [the festival] we thought it should be drug free ... and it did not work so well. We ended up with drunk people and/or drugs anyway.
> (Church representative, the north, high crime, new economy,
> quoted in Ceccato and Dolmén, 2013, p. 105)

> We have to reach out to young people, for children and young people who really need us and believe in what we say.... It's definitely a challenge!
> (Politician in the Police Board, the north, high crime, old economy)

In terms of organization, CP groups in northern Sweden diverge from those in southern groups. It is unclear at this stage how much these differences affect the crime preventive work directed at young people.

Three important differences can be identified. First, whilst all southern CP groups indicate having a formal structure, no northern municipality has a group working under the name "local crime prevention council." Moreover, northern municipalities have a looser organization (for details see Ceccato and Dolmén, 2011). Second, CP groups in the north also declare lower levels of cooperation within and outside the group. Also, CP activities driven in northern municipalities tend to be often motivated as a general health and social service and less as crime preventive actions than they do in the southern CP groups.

One of the barriers mentioned by the interviewees was the Swedish legislation on data secrecy and handling. Information-sharing between local authorities supports the family and the school, so they can prevent children from embarking on a possible criminal career. Most of the CP representatives believe that although necessary, data secrecy is a major hindrance to CP work. Ceccato and Dolmén (2011) confirm that there are complaints that social services fail to get permission to share information between authorities which impede them to help youngsters at risk.

CP groups deal with youth problems by implementing similar types of projects, yet, some of them are organized differently. There are no apparent differences between municipalities with relatively higher crime rates from those with less crime. There are, of course, exceptions. Ceccato and Dolmén (2011) exemplify that chronic addiction problems common in some northern municipalities demand a constant constellation of experts in CP groups that are found more sporadically in the southern municipalities. More CP groups in the south declare that they deal with conflict between youth groups which is ethnically motivated more than in the northern case studies. Most of these projects directed at youth do not involve any formal assessment. Any follow up, if it happens, is limited to simple assessment procedures or reports describing the activities. In Sweden, CP initiatives in rural municipalities may never be assessed to the same extent as those in urban areas because of limited funding and skills of the CP members. One difficulty in following up is that in certain cases, CP groups haven't stated the initial goals for the local actions in the first place.

I: The plan that you use, have you set any specific goals with the work?
R: We have no goals of our own. We have a drug and alcohol policy action. It is not completely implemented. So I use more crime prevention goals where I work, so it's very diffuse...
I: No milestones either?
R: No measurable milestones, no plan for follow-up more than the follow-up and the reports that I write here every year.
(Safety coordinator, the north, high crime, new economy)

Seasonal problems (violence during the tourist season, for example) impose specific demands on CP work, requiring more concentrated action during particular events or seasons. This was expected particularly for the so-called "new economy" municipalities, those that are more service-oriented and regularly receive an inflow of tourists at particular times of the year. One of the interviewees in the south describes the challenges with seasonal problems related to youth in the summer, whilst in the north it seems to be considered in the framework of daily CP activities.

We try to do some stuff with this summer mess.... It's about serving alcohol, information on the prohibition of alcohol consumption in the city.

There must be a functioning sobering unit. It's about police patrolling operations, supervision of taverns, etc.

(Safety coordinator, the south, high crime, new economy)

I cannot say that we are targeting a winter season here, but it's probably more about looking at our own youth, what goes on around schools.

(Alcohol manager and safety coordinator, the north,
high crime, new economy)

Efforts are made to improve personal skills and improve the knowledge base among those involved in CP but also for parents and other adults working directly with children and youth. About one-third of the interviewed representatives spend time improving their skills, especially to deal with "new" challenges, such as drugs and alcohol sold over the internet.

We are partly adopting the EFFEKT Model (Örebro Prevention Program), and my colleague was the one who trained us, so we can support our own community with the skills. But we're not there yet. Another is to have a structured training program for drugs of abuse and a clear program of action when they suspect abuse of any kind.

(Alcohol coordinator, the north, high crime, new economy)

We need to take a long perspective of 20 years in CP, for children and their families.... We gather skills and knowledge and have a common strategy – counties, municipalities and NGOs ... to minimize the risk factors.

(Youth coordinator, the north, high crime, old economy)

Drugs. From alcohol to harder things.... We get depressed because it is easy to find websites where you can order drugs on the internet. Things happen fast. When [the government] does not have time to classify them as drugs, there are new ones to buy online.

(Alcohol coordinator, the north, high crime, new economy)

It is therefore not a surprise that the southern high-crime, new-economy municipality shows a high degree of collaborative work in CP with other municipalities, regions, and organizations also universities; an exception when compared to the other studied municipalities. The same applies for the northern high-crime municipality in preparation for the winter season (Ceccato & Dolmén, 2011). Table 13.1 summarizes the main characteristics of CP groups' activities in the eight municipalities.

Experiences from CP work with young people

The Kronoberg model on Gotland

To curb violence in public spaces, the police in the region of Växjö, in southern Sweden, developed the "Kronoberg model." Although applied in most of the

Table 13.1 Youth-related problems and CP activities: case studies in northern and southern rural municipalities in Sweden

Case studies – north			Problems	Local CP	Internal cooperation	External cooperation	Good examples	Situational CP	Evidence-based CP	CP challenges
High crime	New	Åre	Youth violence, alcohol, drugs (including illegal alcohol), graffiti, theft (winter)	No (but SamBU)	Police, social services, child and youth services, leisure activities, school, church	Municipal, regional	"Rondellen projekt," Busstrafiken, Fryshusen cooperation, Aunt Anna's Café, STAD projekt	Police walks, cooperation with pubs	Limited, police data, reports at national level	Economic resources, better cooperation, better skills and knowledge
	Old	Arvika	Alcohol, drug consumption, youth violence, motorcycle gangs, domestic violence	No (only in Karlstad – Center for Crime Prevention)	Police, social services (focus on women's violence), leisure activities, school, pubs, church, witness support organization	Municipal and regional, particularly with Karlstad	"Skan projekt," Kommet project, parent support (Samtal om Barn & Ungdom), klass morfar, offender support back to society	Parent and police walks, lectures in schools, CCTV	Limited, police data, reports	Better consensus on goals of CP, economic resources for family interventions, measures that reach children and young people, drugs require more support from police and social services
Low crime	New	Storuman	Alcohol, drugs, criminal damage, youth violence, seasonal problems (winter), temporary labor force (summer, berry pickers), domestic violence	No (FRIDA and LINNEA group)	School, police, health care, psychiatric care, social services, children's and mothers' care, church, women's shelter organization	Municipal, regional	"FRIDA," LINNEA, LINUS, Stad project (limited alcohol purchase), "sick cottage," "Storuman's safety model," Salut project	Parent support, invited lectures in schools, CCTV mostly in private places	Limited, used in specific projects, including maps, drug use survey	Better contact with youngsters, liberal attitude toward alcohol use, limited economic resources, better engagement of representatives of each group
	Old	Dorotea	Theft, criminal damage, alcohol, violence between youngsters in school (including ethnic minorities), drugs, domestic violence	No (Samrådsgrupp)	Police, social services, leisure activities, child care, health care, church, student association	Limited municipal and regional	"Safety walks," Ungdomstjänst, specific actions against drugs, "TRIO projekt"	Parent support, CCTV, invited lectures in schools	Limited	Economic resources, secrecy law, better cooperation including regional council, improve skills of CP actors

continued

Table 13.1 Continued

Case studies – south			Problems	Local CP	Internal cooperation	External cooperation	Good examples	Situational CP	Evidence-based CP	CP challenges
High crime	New	Gotland	Youth isolation, violence, alcohol, drugs, vandalism, seasonal problems (spring/summer)	Yes, SafeGotland	School, police, leisure activities, social services, health department, churches, witness support association, Red Cross, Save the Children Sweden	Municipal, regional, national (e.g., university) and international	"Wonderful youth," "Theme weeks" by recreation groups, "Every other water," safety walks	CCTV in schools, safety walks, invited lecturers, children's home	Limited, reports, crime statistics	Secrecy law, cooperation (seasonal problems), better CP organization, Internet crime, economic resources
	Old	Markaryd	Social disturbance, ethnic conflicts (anti-Semitic groups) burglary, drugs and alcohol, street racing, vandalism, seasonal problems (Markaryd market, summer)	Yes	School, police, leisure activities, social services, witness support association	Municipal, regional, national	"Moped project," neighborhood watch	Safety walks, police, CCTV, neighborhood watch schemes, "Moped project"	Police data, safety survey, CAN survey	Better cooperation, regional council, and school
Low crime	New	Söderköping	Vandalism, car theft, youth violence, public disorder (chicken races)	Yes	School, police, social services, child and youth services, municipality, tenants' association headed by a safety coordinator	Limited	"Dare to be," leisure associations, patrol reports, CCTV, schools, vandalism	Private guards, CCTV, police, safety walks	Limited, police data reports, safety surveys	Organization less dependent on one actor, better internal cooperation, economic resources, drugs
	Old	Gnösjö	Vandalism, alcohol, drugs, youth violence, theft	Yes	Police, emergency services, social services, churches, industry, pensioners' association, Järnbäraren	Limited, municipal and regional	"Youth at risk zone," "Coolt-projekt," "Tjejmässan," safety walks	CCTV in schools, safety walks, security guards	Police data reports	Short-term projects, attract youngsters, Internet crime, practical actions toward high perceived lack of safety

study areas, we selected only Gotland as an example, as this case has been externally assessed by BRÅ.

The Kronoberg model aims to prevent young people from drinking alcohol in public places and ultimately helps to reduce youth violence in these settings. The method involves the police intervening systematically with young people in town who are drunk or carrying alcohol and pouring out the alcohol onsite. Meanwhile the police call the parents, for instance, to take their children home. If the parents are not around, the next step is to contact social services. This also applies to those under-age young people who find themselves with other young people carrying alcohol. The model also involves long-term measures such as having meetings with parents about young people and alcohol. The police also focus on those who illegally sell alcohol to or procure alcohol for young people. This is important, given that organized crime is responsible for a significant proportion of smuggled liquor. The second component is the police's investigative measures against those supplying alcohol to young people, that is, against alcohol peddlers. This is done by defining a special chain of responsibility, which is established in the procedure for investigating alcohol offenses, to make sure that the investigative work is staffed by police who also take part in the field operations followed by a report. These procedures are followed for every suspected alcohol offense. The alcohol that is forfeited is documented and followed up. An investigation is carried out to take legal action against people committing alcohol peddling offenses and other alcohol offenses that occur. While this may seem an obvious enforcement of the law, the Kronoberg model offers a structure for working more systematically and demands resources devoted to actually investigating such crimes.

The Kronoberg model has been implemented in five of the eight areas of study, fully or partially. Gotland was one of the municipalities evaluated by Brottsförebyggande rådet (2009). Table 13.2 shows the number of reports (and percentage change) on alcohol forfeitures, alcohol-related offenses, and assault among young people in each district during the months of the project in 2008, and the corresponding months in the years 2006–2007. According to the Kronoberg model, resources should be set aside especially to carry out initiatives in the field and perform investigations into alcohol offenses. Through this, information is concentrated to a group of police officers. However, in Gotland no special investigation organization was created, and the investigations were distributed and handled as before. As expected, the police have been more active in detecting alcohol-related offenses (illegal sale or possession of alcoholic drinks), and forfeitures and their efforts are reflected in changes in statistics before and after the application of the model, including the reduction in violence involving young people.

Although not all municipalities studied showed a reduction in assault, the experience shows that when young people were prevented from drinking in a public setting, fewer young people needed treatment for alcohol poisoning. Police working with the Kronoberg model are more active in places where young people consume alcohol and, therefore, come into contact with and open more

Table 13.2 Before and after the Kronoberg model in 2008: Gotland and Karlstad

Police district	2006		2007		Change 2006–2007		2008 (change 2006–2008)	
	Gotland	Karlstad	Gotland	Karlstad	Gotland	Karlstad	Gotland	Karlstad
Alcohol forfeitures	132	63	93	53	–59%	–66%	127 (4%)	163 (158%)
Alcohol-related offenses	7	51	34	107	385%	110%	49 (44%)	144 (182%)
Assault among young people	48	61	36	53	–29%	–13%	34 (29%)	53 (–13%)

Source: Adapted from Brottsförebyggande rådet (2009, pp. 11–15).

reports concerning a greater percentage of the cases of assault that occur. This would, in turn, mean the statistics on offenses reported capture a greater number of the actual crimes of violence than before. Overall, according to BRÅ (2009, p. 16), the experiences from the police districts that have worked in accordance with the model show that

> [t]he fact that young people are prevented from drinking in a public environment has also led to fewer young people needing treatment for alcohol poisoning. The statistical results strongly suggest that this may, in turn, contribute towards reduced crimes of violence in a public environment.

In 2012, the Swedish parliament suggested to the government that the Kronoberg model be implemented nationwide (Sveriges Riksdagen, 2012).

Youth in Gnösjö: social control and local collaborative initiatives

Gnösjö is a municipality in southern Sweden that has relatively low crime rates but, as with many other rural municipalities, has youth-related problems. Gnösjö is an interesting case because it and its neighboring municipalities are characterized by successful small businesses often associated with the existence of strong ties in informal networks (Karlsson & Larsson, 1993), including a large number of free churches, athletic movements, and a relatively large share of population composed of migrants (Brulin, 1998; Johannisson & Wigren, 2006). Traditional gender contracts are also part of the "package" that characterize Gnösjö culture (Forsberg, 1998; Pettersson, 2002). Gnösjö is somehow geographically secluded, which seems to have a protective effect against crime, at least combined with its relatively healthy economy and strong levels of social control that characterize the local culture.

> Social control here means that they [young people] avoid wrongdoing when a neighbor or someone nearby sees what they are doing. They cannot be anonymous. Also, people go to church, and it is probably critical not to steal if you belong to church. We have low unemployment, so we do not have much social exclusion, alcohol or drugs. Sure they exist, but less than in other places.
>
> (CP representative, Gnösjö)

The Gnösjö spirit (*Gnosjöandan*, as it is called in Swedish) is a feature of the local culture, dominated by a few actors, which is well illustrated by the answers from another interviewee who works directly with youth-related problems (in this case, religious institutions).

> Youth is probably our biggest concern. People see that there is a need for them; otherwise we would probably not need three recreation centers in a small place like this.... Young people have to have somewhere to go ...

they are visible outdoors, in the parks, youth clubs. There are a lot of churches. Two recreation centers are completely non-profit and supported by voluntaries.... We are passionate about everything that has to do with young people.

(Fieldworker, Gnösjö)

The fieldworker's comments illustrate a number of formal and informal collaborative efforts that characterize CP actions toward youth in Gnösjö. Some build upon volunteer work, others rely on support from different local actors or in cooperation with external stakeholders, such as the universities. Some of these initiatives are discussed below.

In Gnösjö, fieldworkers are essential in CP work with young people. Fieldworkers are employed by the local community to work with outreach, prevention, and advisory. Fieldworkers work with youth age 13–21. Experience in both large and small communities across the country shows that adult role models on the street, especially during evenings and weekends, can contribute to safe setting for young people (e.g., BRÅ, 2010). In these frameworks, citizens work together with the staff of schools. Police and representatives of recreational associations visit the places where young people normally gather, such as recreation centers, schools, public places, and the Internet. Safety walks may also be part of their work together with other adults, which occurs on every Friday and Saturday evening and night. The goal is to walk and prevent vandalism, brawls, and booze – but above all for everyone to feel safe in the community. An interviewee found the initiative valuable but judged not free of problems. Migrant parents, for example, are often underrepresented on safety walks or at parent–teacher meetings, partially because of a lack of language skills. The interviewee also highlighted other barriers. The community is dominated by a culture that is difficult to penetrate for an outsider or even a native Swede.

We have about 800 people from Southeast Asia, about 10 per cent of the municipality's population. Not everyone can speak Swedish. I do not think they're people who like building "groups of interests, associations" in the same way as we Swedes do. We've got a lot of associations in Sweden.... It is terribly difficult to engage [the foreigners]. Then, it's hard to get Gnosjö residents into life. We came here in the early 1970s, and it took several years before we got to know each other. *They* are not so easy.

(CP representative, Gnösjö)

In past years, there have been a number of projects, some evolving into other initiatives, among them the drug prevention project called "Coolt," which organized different drug-free events and leisure activities directed at young people nearby. The project was based on the collaboration of schools, social services, and culture and leisure departments. Young people got membership cards which gave them free access to different activities, such as Café nights and a Female fair ("Tjejmässan") about every third weekend. The card was personal and swiped in a reader at the entrance to each event, each swipe gives a stamp. After a certain number of stamps, members would have a chance to win prizes. This initiative was organized with local recreational associations, giving young people the opportunity to try different activities. Other initiatives involve courses directed at children, young people, and adults who have difficulty controlling their impulses (e.g., re-Pulse).

To reduce the use of alcohol and other drugs by teenagers, Gnösjö has been applying together with a number of other municipalities in Sweden a prevention program that empowers parents to publicize zero tolerance to the use of alcohol and drugs (EFFEKT, formerly the Örebro Prevention Program run by Örebro University, Sweden). EFFEKT is designed to fit into an ordinary community structure, without any significant expense, by using existing personnel or actors within the community. A number of studies show encouraging results from the method: drunkenness, frequent drunkenness, and delinquency rates were lower in the intervention group than in the control group of students after the intervention (Koutakis, Håkan, & Margaret, 2008) (Figure 13.3). Authors also tested whether the intervention effects were moderated by community type (inner city, small town, housing project), but findings show that the intervention's effects on drunkenness and delinquency were the same everywhere. A re-evaluation of the data using frequency measures shows a significant program effect on lifetime drunkenness and a marginal effect on past-month drunkenness over time (Özdemİr & Stattin, 2012). For detailed information about the project, see Koutakis (2014).

According to the EFFEKT website, the program content is delivered to parents twice a year through short presentations with the goal of maintaining parents' restrictive attitudes toward youth drinking. First, parents are provided with information on how drinking has potential short- and long-term consequences for young people. Then, parents are made to understand that they can still influence their children's attitudes and behavior and that their expectations make a difference. Hence, parents are advised to explain that they expect their children not to use alcohol. Finally, the program provides parents with concrete tools to make their views clear, and to set rules on youth alcohol drinking (for more details, see Koutakis, 2014).

Layers of social control to tackle vandalism in Söderköping

Söderköping municipality also has an idyllic appeal,[1] with relatively low crime rates in the county of Östergötland, the southern Stockholm area and the capital of Sweden. However, vandalism in schools and in outdoor public places has been a recurrent problem in the municipality often associated with young people. Around 20 percent of the interviewed population in the local safety survey declare being afraid of having their property damaged by vandals, which are often local youngsters living in the municipality. A number of interventions have been implemented in recent years; for example, "safety line" seems to have increased social control in public places.

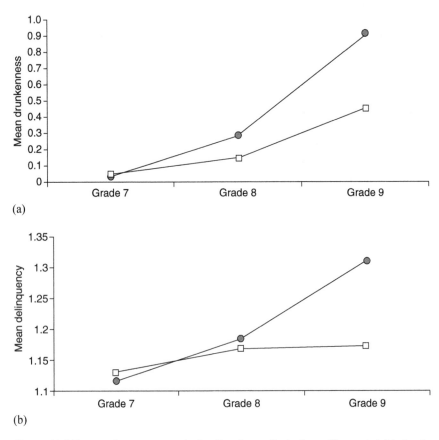

Figure 13.3 Repeated-measures analysis of variance displaying self-reported (a) drunkenness and (b) delinquency by youth in the intervention (square) and control
conditions (circle) (source: Koutakis et al., 2008, p. 1634).

"Safety line" is a phone number that can be used to report minor or less acute
events, such as damage to property, hazardous outdoor environments, unsafe
places, traffic safety problems, blocked emergency exits, and similar events.
When someone calls, the call ends up at SOS Alarm, which forwards the call to
the appropriate organization. If the case is deemed urgent, the emergency oper-
ator can turn it into a regular emergency call. The service has expanded to
include an agreement with the social services department for people to get basic
assistance, for example in case of minor accidents. In 2009, 220 calls were
recorded, of which 183 resulted in some form of action. Safety line has been
helpful in tackling property damage, impacting on the costs devoted to vandalism. Damage reports for 2009 show encouraging figures on overall insurance
claims. A compilation of the past three years shows that claims costs for the
municipality resulting from vandalism decreased, from SEK220,000 to

SEK49,000, between 2007 and 2009. As a complement to tackle vandalism, CCTV cameras were approved by the municipality and installed to promote surveillance of properties owned by the municipality or other properties such as schools and public places (Hagström, 2009). However, not all types of interventions were well received. An interviewee recalls that checking ID cards at the entrance of the school was not a popular measure.

> Right now CCTV are installed in X school, and we're going to put them up on the municipal building and in another school. There has been quite a lot of vandalism there, too. Then we decided that guards should work in a different way. Now they go around and check whether the doors at the schools are locked. It was a lot of work from the start to lock all the doors and send all the reports to the principals, but it was worth it, as vandalism decreased.... I also forced everyone entering the school premises to show identification. That measure was not popular, but stubborn as I am, I got them to do it, and now everyone realizes that it was a good thing.
>
> (CP representative, Söderköping)

Söderköping is an example of a rural community where security companies provide part of the services that in the past were performed by local police. "Layers of social control" are revealed by one of the interviewees when referring to crime prevention and work performed by parents and teachers. In this case, the layers of social control follow a hierarchical structure, from the police and security guards, to members of safety walks and neighborhood watch schemes as well as the overall community.

R: To be honest, I don't think safety walks work as they should. They have not been as crime-preventive as I wanted them to be.
I: Why? How would you like to change it?
R: Say you and I hang out all the time. Then your ideas and mine are the ones applied, and perhaps they are not the best ones, especially if we don't know young people at all.... But I can't say that to them.
I: Why not?
R: No, because then safety walks will vanish. And that is not what I want. ... I have security guards who have an eye on them, and if I would not have the guards on them, I would not even know whether or not they are there, what they are doing.

(CP representative, Söderköping)

According to the municipal safety survey, the work performed by the patrol and security guards is highly appreciated by the community in the urban core of the municipality (Lundin, 2006). Part of this work involves the work of adult citizens either through neighborhood watch schemes or safety walks and both are also regarded as important efforts to maintain town safety. The same group of respondents' experience increased collaboration between security guards and representatives of different municipal agencies in the community as fundamental in keeping the streets safe.

Paradoxically, most people are not happy with the work done by the police but are positive toward the tasks taken over by the security company, which patrols and walks around the city, talking to youngsters. However, inhabitants interviewed believe there is no need for security guards in their residential areas. Note that these responses refer to all types of crime (Figure 13.4).

Dealing with social exclusion, truancy, and drinking in Arvika

Discrimination and social exclusion can also be found in rural communities. As in any other municipality in Sweden, schools have guidelines for preventing discrimination in all its aspects. A plan for these efforts comes from national legislation against discrimination and degrading treatment. The plan indicates efforts the school can make to create a safe environment for everyone. Responsibilities

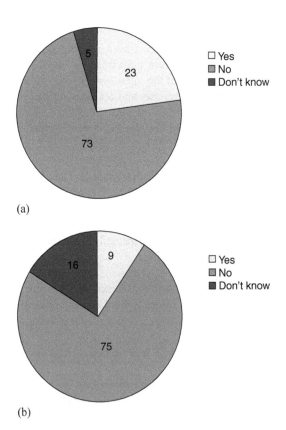

(a)

(b)

Figure 13.4 (a) Are you satisfied with the police presence in Söderköping as a whole? (b) Do you think there is a need for a security company where you live? Percentage of respondents (data source: Lundin, 2006, pp. 23–24).

for action are therefore shared between the principal and the staff in the school, including a statement of promotion and preventive measures to be initiated or implemented during the school year. An evaluation of these measures is expected to be included in the plan for the following year. However, it is uncertain whether these evaluations are done and how. Arvika has worked with multiple actions to prevent discrimination of any type and avoid truancy and other more serious problems (see e.g Arvika kommun 2014b). The school is seen as central in this preventive work, as are recreation centers.

> We use the recreation center in a more concrete way, too. We had a group that was a bit strong about "white power" and was there.... We took the boys and created a boys' group where value issues were discussed to ensure that they would not get onto the same path again.
>
> (CP representative, Arvika)

> A big task we have now is to work with monitoring responsibilities around the school. There are probably as many reasons for truancy; it's a sense of alienation that one can experience.
>
> (CP representative, Arvika)

Closely associated with the school's work, there are the activities run by Arvika Youth Center, which are believed to be crime preventive, with activities and special initiatives on weekends. The youth center has activities for boyS and girls with themed weeks. On special weekends, such as the Walpurgis Night celebrations (April 30) when many people drink to excess, and at secondary school graduations, people collaborate with safety walkers, social services, church police, and NGOs. For instance, in 2014 Arvika Youth Center, the CP group and social services held a competition among youth that rewarded those adolescents who abstained from drinking alcohol. This is a drug prevention activity called Blowing Green (Blås Grönt). The competition takes place throughout 2014 with different stages of competition. Each stage ends with the delivery of first, second, and third prizes for the winners. The youth who has played the most rounds for Blowing Green during the year will win a prize (Arvika kommun 2014a). Despite its good intentions, one of the drawbacks of this type of initiative is that it can be perceived as a coercive measure that limits youth's right to leisure activities, which may include moderate drinking. Another problem is that those who participate are often adolescents who would not drink regardless of the initiative. Those who may be at risk already are not attracted to participate in the competition in the first place. The remaining challenge is to find ways to attract youngsters who are at risk of addiction.

Arvika is also part of the national project "Small municipalities against drugs." The community is actively involved in a project with other municipalities in the country, in which all teachers in primary and secondary schools are trained in various methods of prevention. On a more permanent basis, Arvika also implements what is often called in Sweden "Komet Education." The course is directed at parents with children from three to 11 years old and teenagers 12 to 18 who want help managing conflicts successfully (Comet Groups – "Parental Komet Kids" and "Parental Comet Teens"). Parents get concrete suggestions and exercises to try at home between sessions. The meetings are based on active participation and contain many examples, discussions, and ideas for how to respond to their child. The content is geared to seeing opportunities and solutions to daily problems. In this direction, a new project, *Muraren*, aims to provide greater access to psychiatric services for assessments and addiction treatment. The project is tailored to young adults (18–29 years old) and is perceived by the county as promising (Brönnert & Näsström, 2014). The work is based on tight cooperation between local actors. They meet on a few occasions a year to discuss solutions and improvements on various issues, especially to reassess and develop local guidelines. Arvika has also implemented the EFFEKT program (Örebro Prevention Program), started by training personnel in their own municipality to work with parents and schools.

Concluding remarks

Keeping youngsters entertained during their free time is suggested as a common long-term action to prevent youth problems. Drawing on data from Ceccato and Dolmén (2011), this chapter show that most crime prevention aimed at young people revolves around recreational centers and activities. Findings indicate that the role of these recreational centers as a crime preventive measure should be better understood if the future of CP work with young people in rural areas will rely on them.

In the Swedish context, knowledge is needed about the nature and quality of these youth recreation centers and social activities, for instance, whether or not these recreational centers (and the activities they offer) fulfill the demands of youth groups in contemporary rural environments. Another issue is whether they have any influence on individuals' predisposition to offend, particularly for those that are already at risk.

However, it is unclear how much social control driven by CP initiatives affects young people's quality of life. In many rural communities where the need for "parent-free spaces" is limited, emphasizing the need for parents to police their offspring may not be perceived as a positive action by young people, including those who would not consider getting involved in trouble. Spaces for young people may be jeopardized by extending police powers to safety walkers and parents that suddenly feel they own the spaces being regulated and controlled. Local recreational centers may be the only locale for entertainment for young people but may also be perceived by some as spaces that exclude and/or contain their means of expression. In the long run, well intentioned CP actions may be perceived by youth as coercive, having the potential to impact young people's decisions to move out and seek anonymity.

What works and what does not work in terms of crime prevention toward youth in rural municipalities is not always properly assessed or even reported.

This is by no means solely a problem of rural areas. Evaluation of CP actions in rural areas follows the overall trend in CP assessment that knowledge remains patchy and incomplete (Wikström, 2007). The literature of crime prevention indicates that successful partnerships are often characterized by strong leadership and regular exchange of relevant information among members (Berry, Briggs, Erol, & van Staden, 2011). Because of limited funding and skills, evaluations of CP interventions are rarely followed up when applied to rural contexts, and if they are, the assessments do not always contain the proper information to help other practitioners to replicate projects in their own contexts.

Privatization of security has reached rural areas, and some of the work once performed by the local police force is nowadays taken over by security guards in partnership with other local actors. Although this shift is inevitable in many rural areas and does not necessarily imply a decrease in security services, further investigation is needed, particularly on the role of the private sector in CP work in rural settings. Yarwood (2011) suggests that potential problems of collaboration are how to determine responsibility for action and, when the roles of actors are not well defined, whether this may create a "nobody in charge world."

Finally, crime prevention does not happen in a vacuum. Whatever approaches are taken by CP groups, interventions are bound to have consequences for the groups that they are aimed at, in this case, young people. White (1998, p. 135) reminds us that "how we engage in crime prevention has real consequences for real people." Thus, perhaps a good way forward is to take the voices of young people into account before, during, and after interventions are made. Their views and expectations about the programs for which they are often the targets can shed light on the consequences and appropriateness of the interventions in their everyday lives and their rights as citizens. This is particularly important where the application of crime prevention measures has been perceived by youngsters as restrictive and unintentionally reinforced class and ethnic divides that might already exist in these communities.

Note

1 For details, watch www.youtube.com/watch?v=3u8ziN3islI&feature=youtu.be, retrieved April 20, 2015.

References

Albert, S., Brason Ii, F. W., Sanford, C. K., Dasgupta, N., Graham, J., & Lovette, B. (2011). Project Lazarus: Community-based overdose prevention in rural North Carolina. *Pain Medicine, 12*, S77–S85.
Arvika kommun. (2014a). Blås Grönt på Valborgsmässoafton! Retrieved April 25, 2014, from www.arvika.se/kommunochpolitik/pressochinformationsmaterial/nyheter/nyhetsarkiv/blasgrontpavalborgsmassoafton.5.3278eb23144b2e75ebe32a9.html.
Arvika kommun. (2014b). Trygghet, ansvar och respekt på Glava skola, 2013–2014 (p. 25). Retrieved April 17, 2015, from www.arvika.se/.../Plan+mot+diskriminering+och+kränkande+behandling.

Berry, G., Briggs, P., Erol, R., & van Staden, L. (2011). The effectiveness of partnership working in a crime and disorder context: A rapid evidence assessment. *Research Report* (Vol. 52). London: Home Office.

Beyers, J. M., Toumbourou, J. W., Catalano, R. F., Arthur, M. W., & Hawkins, J. D. (2004). A cross-national comparison of risk and protective factors for adolescent substance use: The United States and Australia. *Journal of Adolescent Health, 35*, 3–16.

Brönnert, L., & Nässtrom, L. (2014). Granskning av vård, omsorg och stöd för personer med missbruks- och beroendeproblematik. *Revisionsrapport, Arvika kommun* (p. 12).

Brottsförebyggande rådet – BRÅ (National Council of Crime Prevention). (2009). Evaluation of the K-model (the Kronoberg model) (Vol. 5, p. 19). Stockholm: BRÅ.

Brottsförebyggande rådet – BRÅ (National Council of Crime Prevention). (2010). Trygghetsvandring tankar på vägen. Stockholm: Tryggare och Mänskligare Göteborg, Boverket och Brå.

Brulin, G. (1998). How to shape creative territorial energy: The case of the Gnosjö region. *Concepts and Transformation, 3*(3), 255–269.

Bursik, R. J. (1999). The informal control of crime through neighborhood networks. *Sociological Focus, 32*(1), 85–97.

Ceccato, V., & Dolmén, L. (2011). Crime in rural Sweden. *Applied Geography, 31*(1), 119–135.

Ceccato, V., & Dolmén, L. (2013). Crime prevention in rural Sweden. *European Journal of Criminology, 10*, 89–112.

Collins, D., Harris, M. A., Knowlton, J., Shamblen, S., & Thompson, K. (2011). Non-medical use of prescription drugs among youth in an Appalachian population: Prevalence, predictors for prevention. *Journal of Drug Education, 3*, 309–326.

Forsberg, G. (1998). Regional variations in the gender contract: Gendered relations in labour markets, local politics and everyday life in Swedish regions. *Innovation: The European Journal of Social Science Research, 11*(2), 191–209.

Forsyth, A. J. M., & Barnard, M. (1999). Contrasting levels of adolescent drug use between adjacent urban and rural communities in Scotland. *Addiction, 94*(11), 1707–1718.

Hagström, H. (2009). Verksamhetsberättelse för kommunens säkerhetsarbete 2009. Söderköping: Söderköping kommun.

Hawkins, J. D. (1999). Preventing crime and violence through communities that care. *European Journal on Criminal Policy and Research, 7*(4), 443–458.

Johannisson, B., & Wigren, C. (2006). The dynamics of community identity making in an industrial district: The spirit of Gnösjö. In C. Steyaert & D. Hjorth (Eds.), *Entrepreneurship as Social Change: A Third New Movements in Entrepreneurship* (pp. 188–208). Cheltenham: Edward Elgar.

Johnson, A. O., Mink, M. D., Harun, N., Moore, C. G., Martin, A. B., & Bennett, K. J. (2008). Violence and drug use in rural teens: National prevalence estimates from the 2003 youth risk behavior survey. *Journal of School Health, 78*(10), 554–561.

Karlsson, C., & Larsson, J. (1993). A macro view of the Gnosjo entrepreneurial spirit. *Entrepreneurship and Regional Development, 5*(2), 117–140.

Koutakis, N. (2014). EFFEKT. Retrieved April 24, 2014, from www.effekt.org/english.4. 56dc814a133a2dbc05580003223.html.

Koutakis, N., Håkan, S., & Margaret, K. (2008). Reducing youth alcohol drinking through a parent-targeted intervention: The Orebro prevention program. *Addiction, 103*, 1629–1637.

Lundin, T. (2006). Safety survey in Söderköping (p. 53). Söderköping: Söderköping kommun.

Mahoney, J. L., & Stattin, H. (2000). Leisure activities and adolescent antisocial behavior: The role of structure and social context. *Journal of Adolescence, 23*(2), 113–127.

Özdemİr, M., & Stattin, H. (2012). Does the Örebro prevention programme prevent youth drinking? *Addiction, 107*(9), 1705–1706.

Payne, B., Berg, B., & Sun, I. (2005). Policing in small town America: Dogs, drunks, disorder and Dysfunction. *Journal of Criminal Justice, 33*(1), 31–41.

Pettersson, K. (2002). Företagande män och osynliggjorda kvinnor: Diskursen om Gnosjö ur ett könsperspektiv (PhD, Uppsala University, Uppsala).

Shears, J., Edwards, R. W., & Stanley, L. R. (2006). School Bonding and Substance Use in Rural Communities. *Social Work Research, 30*(1), 6–18.

Sveriges Riksdagen (Swedish Parliament). (2012). Kronobergsmodellen och ungdomsvåld. Retrieved April 17, 2015, from www.riksdagen.se/sv/Dokument-Lagar/Forslag/Motioner/Kronobergsmodellen-och-ungdoms_H002Ju353/?text=true.

White, R. (1998). Curtailing youth: A critique of cohercive crime prevention. *Crime Prevention Studies, 9*, 117–137.

Wikström, P.-O. H. (2007). Doing without knowing: Common pitfalls in crime prevention. *Crime Prevention Studies, 21*, 59–80.

Yarwood, R. (2011). Whose blue line is it anyway? Community policing and partnership working in rural places. In R. Mawby & R. Yarwood (Eds.), *Rural policing and policing the rural: A constable countryside?* (pp. 93–105). Farnham: Ashgate.

14 Challenges to preventing women abuse in rural communities

The purpose of this chapter is twofold. First, the chapter discusses the actions under way to address violence against women in Sweden, following the conclusions about violence against women presented in Chapter 10. To frame the Swedish case, this chapter briefly reviews some of the current international literature in criminology on actions countering violence against women. Particular focus is on the role of the community through crime prevention initiatives to tackle the problem in rural municipalities. Secondary data, email surveys, media excerpts, and face-to-face interviews are used to illustrate current initiatives to prevent violence against women in rural settings. The chapter concludes with examples of good practice in Swedish rural contexts and closing remarks.

Addressing violence against women in an international perspective

Providing help in a shelter may be the first step in establishing a safe environment for women victims of domestic violence but it is not the solution. Police and criminal justice interventions are crucial to stop violence against women, though they may result in the unintended consequences of more violence to both victims and offenders (Danis, 2003). A successful intervention may require the involvement of police, healthcare, judicial, and legal services, shelters and protection services, schools and other educational institutions, religious or cultural groups, and others. The United Nations for Gender Equality and the Empowerment of Women (UN, 2011) strongly recommends that to effectively combat violence against women, community support is needed.

Danis (2003) indicates that the coordinated community response strategy has had success by showing that a combination of legal interventions has better outcomes than the use of one strategy alone. If community plays an important part in prevention, the "local culture" has to be aligned in favor of gender equality and against women's abuse. In Chapter 10, we discussed how ignorance or neglect of violence against women is far too often part of the rural culture, in some cases allowing violence to escalate to a level at which women are killed. The police must be backed up with systematic knowledge to act in cases when repeated violence has already occurred. The community can play an important role in supporting women who need to leave relationships that are abusive. Resources at different levels have to be in place to make available women's shelters and enable criminal justice procedures that can protect a woman while she is starting a new life, away from an abusive partner.

Prevention of violence against women occurs in two ways: either by preventing repeated attacks (e.g., by tackling the abusive partner) or, in the long run, by changing values and social structures which promote violence. The majority of work worldwide has focused on attempting to reduce the incidence of repeat victimization by providing legal, welfare, and social support for women and, to a more limited extent, by attempting to control and change gender differences (Home Office, 1994).

An important body of research focuses on the UN-inspired coordinated community response programs which intend to establish support networks for victims and their families. How they work depends on each community's capacity to protect victims, hold perpetrators accountable, and reinforce the community's intolerance of violence against women. Becoming free from a partner's violence is not an easy process – whether by leaving an abusive partner or otherwise. Previous research recognizes that both social isolation and an effective community response contribute to a woman's increased risk of violence by partners and ex-partners (Aguirre, 1985; Sullivan & Bybee, 1999).

In the United States, there have been three types of intervention against women's violence: intervention focused on men in batter-men's groups, on couples counseling, and on community intervention projects. Despite the growing use of both criminal justice and social service interventions, the evidence for their efficacy in the 1990s is not clearly established (Tolman & Edleson, 1995). Tolman and Edleson suggest that although research contributed to an ongoing dialogue about how best to meet the challenges related to violence against women, there are as yet no conclusive findings about the best way to respond to male violence, and research rarely provides a clear-cut direction in policy and practice. More recently, Bennett and Williams (2001) report on the overall effectiveness of these programs, while others (Sullivan & Gillum, 2001) refer specifically to the quality of advocacy for battered women in these frameworks.

In the United Kingdom, there is also a growing body of research on crime-centered approaches and mandatory policies toward domestic violence and how they affect women negatively (Coker, 2004; Mills, 1998). Stover (2005, p. 452) suggests that although recent studies have focused on beginning to evaluate domestic violence interventions and their effects, "there is still a great deal of work to be done to understand how to implement effective interventions to reduce domestic violence and improve outcomes." In the United Kingdom, the recent introduction of risk assessment and management processes in domestic violence cases has taken place at a time of concerted efforts by the British government to raise the profile of domestic violence and improve the response of all agencies, including the most significant overhaul of the law on domestic violence since the 1970s (Hoyle, 2008).

However, studies that report experience combatting violence against women in rural settings are still the exception. In the United States, for instance, Benson (2009) reports the Illinois experience in dealing with domestic violence and concludes that police officers are not responding adequately to domestic violence situations, especially in rural areas. Concerning rural Australia, Bull (2007) highlights the limitations and challenges of providing services for women in rural areas, whilst Carrington (2007) associates violence in rural areas with a crisis in rural masculinity. Owen and Carrington (2014) examine domestic violence service provision in rural Australia and conclude rural service models are urbancentric and ignore the architecture of rural life.

One of the most recent examples is provided by DeKeseredy, Donnermeyer, and Schwartz (2009) in a discussion of how key principles of Crime Prevention Through Environmental Design (CPTED) can be applied to help design appropriate community-based prevention strategies to improve the security of women living in rural places from abuse by spouses and partners in both ongoing and terminated relationships. Beyond "modifying the built environment" to reduce crime opportunities in public places, as often postulated by first-generation CPTED studies, DeKeseredy et al. (2009), focus on communities' capacity and readiness (Donnermeyer, Plested, Edwards, Oetting, & Littlethunder, 1997) to propose actions to prevent abuse of women in rural settings. Second-generation CPTED, as it is called, is about developing and improving forms of defensible space (in this case, perhaps the private sphere, too) through community-level activities that generate locally based discourse on norms, beliefs, and values related to various security issues which can serve to deter abusers. The authors suggest four overlapping strategies to combat violence against women and to improve their safety: community culture, connectivity and pro-feminist masculinity, community threshold, and social cohesion.

a   *Community culture.* The development and reinforcement of local shared culture that makes people aware of gender-related violence and decreases their tolerance for domestic violence. Festivals, sporting events, music, and art enjoyed by the local community with the assistance of community members can be used for breaking down rural patriarchy and promoting greater awareness of women abuse by giving voice to the issue and confronting public expressions of rural patriarchy (DeKeseredy et al., 2009).

b   *Connectivity and pro-feminist masculinity.* There is a need for initiatives that support women (e.g., easily accessible women's centers/shelters in rural communities) as well as interventions directed toward men, such as a pro-feminist men's movement, that argue for more action by men to stop women abuse and violence. These initiatives aim at changing in the long run the attitudes of men who are already violent toward women but also at encouraging others to break the silence when violence occurs or to avoid behaviors based on gender discrimination, such as boycotting strip clubs and confronting men who make sexist jokes.

c   *Community threshold.* Fear among victims of violence isolates them, making it difficult for victims to develop social ties with neighbors who might be willing to confront a man who is violent and for victims to learn about services available to them. Community threshold can be enhanced and violence reduced in places where people come together for informal social control and act for the common good, such as activities against abusive behavior or supporting interventions that reduce women abuse.

d   *Social cohesion.* Second-generation CPTED studies show that positive communication skills and conflict resolution enhance cohesiveness (Saville & Clear, 2000). Thus, schools could be a natural arena for courses and information for all, young and old, in many rural communities.

We now turn to actions for victims of violence in rural Sweden, those provided by social welfare, police, and non-governmental organizations as well as the work organized around local crime prevention councils. As highlighted in Chapter 10, there has been an increase in reported cases of violence against women as well as the number of women searching for hospital care for domestic violence in rural Sweden. There are indications that this increase is not geographically homogeneous across the country and can be related to the levels and quality of the assistance provided in these communities. Appendix 14.1 lists the main sources of data used in the study.

The Swedish national action plan against violence against women

Sweden has a long tradition of gender equality policy. Early on, Sweden criminalized the purchase of prostitution services, enacted measures to combat sexual harassment in the workplace, and successively broadened definitions of sexual violence. Sweden constitutes an interesting case because the country has the highest figures of reported rape in Europe but one of the lowest conviction rates (Lovett & Kelly, 2009). Sweden has a strong reputation for addressing violence against women, which partially explains its high rape-reporting rates. These recent reforms were influenced by a tradition of gender equality policy and legislation, as well as an established women's movement, that culminated with the 1990s *Kvinnofrid* (protection of women) legislation and changes in the penal code after April 1, 2005. This introduced a holistic package of measures intended to address violence against women. These measures include crime definition, improvement of support to victims, knowledge building, and public debate about violence. Although it has been argued that these legal and other factors have maximized the reporting of violence against women in Sweden, it is an open question whether these changes alone are sufficient to explain the disparity in reporting rates within Sweden and between Sweden and other countries.

In practice, this urgency turned into the largest fiscal commitment to equality issues ever carried out in Sweden. The parliament approved SEK1.6 billion directed to gender equality, a tenfold increase in resources compared to previous years. Of these funds, around half a billion have been used to combat men's domestic violence against women. According to the national Swedish newspaper *Dagens Nyheter*, the government invested a total of nearly SEK1.1 billion from 2006 to 2012. Money has been used in a variety of actions (Figure 14.1).

Yet there is no indication that fewer women are subjected to violence. On average, 17 women are murdered at home each year. It is estimated that around 12,000 women are beaten in their homes by the person closest to them. In 2002, 1,571 cases of gross violations against women were registered by the police, while 2,513 cases were registered in 2011. Although this may suggest that little has been done to prevent violence, it can also paradoxically mean that now the means are in place that allow women to come forward and report violence. What goes against this positive assumption is the fact that although large sums have been invested in countermeasures since 2006, the number of cases seems not to be strongly affected by them. The National Council of Crime Prevention assessed the national action plan, stating that an "impressive amount" of activities have been carried out, "but the impact on target groups is more uncertain" BRÅ (2009). Rying (2012) highlights the central role of local actors/communities in preventing this type of crime.

> I suggest a central authority in each municipality where women can turn to and get help from one and the same person, so that they do not have to run around. We constantly see cases of lethal violence against women that could have been avoided with better cooperation among authorities.
>
> (Interview with Mikael Rying, 2012)

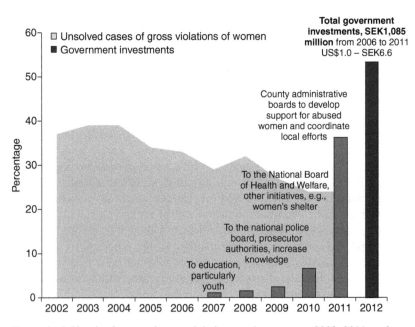

Figure 14.1 Unsolved cases of gross violations against women, 2002–2011, and government investments, 2006–2011, in Sweden (data source: National Council of Crime Prevention, published by *Dagens Nyheter*, see Beausang, 2012).

A number of suggestions have been put forward, from more active and rapid action by the police and other criminal justice agents such as prosecutors, to improved and continuous knowledge-sharing by all actors involved at all levels.

Women's shelters in Sweden

For many women, leaving their partners is their last option, not because they do not want to but because they feel trapped and cannot see a way out of their abusive relationships. One problem is that people still think that battered women could simply leave if they wanted to. This assumption not only ignores many structural obstacles preventing women from leaving (e.g., geographical and social isolation) but also neglects the fact that many women really want to leave their abusive partners, at least temporarily, for a shelter. This section focuses on the urban–rural distribution of women's shelter in Sweden.

Support for women victims of domestic violence can be provided in Sweden by social welfare and related services, police, and non-governmental organizations in each municipality. According to the Swedish Association of Local Authorities and Regions (SKL, 2009), municipalities report particularly good experiences from collaboration among women's shelters, police, and municipal governments when dealing with violence against women. But it was not always like that. In 2001, more than 60 municipalities in Sweden (out of 290) gave no support to women's shelter organizations (NCK, 2001)

According to SKL's 2009 report, municipal support is now higher: at least 96 percent of those municipalities participating in the survey offer some sort of counseling in the acute phase of violence and at least 75 percent offer more long-term counseling. In the case of counseling for children and youth who have experienced violence in intimate relationships, at least 92 percent of the municipalities offer emergency support calls and at least 80 percent offer more long-term counseling. An absolute majority of the municipalities also offers risk assessment and support to police trial. Of the municipalities that responded to the survey, 89 percent said they offer protected accommodation for victims, and as many as 80 percent said there was a women's shelter in the municipality (Andréasson, Stenson, Björck, & Heimer, 2006; Weinehall, 2005).

Internationally, shelters are the cornerstone of services offered to victims of domestic violence. These agencies typically offer crisis intervention services and may or may not provide immediate shelter, long-term counseling and support (Sullivan & Gillum, 2001; Allen, Bybee, & Sullivan, 2004).

The process of creation of women's shelter was similar in Norway, Denmark, and Sweden and shows similarities with the process in the United Kingdom, the United States, and Canada since the early 1970s. At that time, women's shelters were places with emergency phones and beds where women and children could seek shelter from a violent man. Nowadays, shelters are not regarded as institutions, but as a place where women can get help and support and meet women in similar situations. Healthcare, police, and social services are important partners but they cannot replace the shelter's crucial work. In Norway and Denmark, municipalities are responsible for financing these centers, though the state contributes. In Denmark, the state pays half of the municipality's expenditure. In Norway, the funding of these shelters is integrated into state block grants to local governments. Funding in Sweden is more complex. Some shelters are run by the municipality and financed by one or more municipalities, possibly with the addition of daily fees, while others are privately run with daily fees. A majority is run by non-profit organizations such as women's and girls' shelters. They are often financed by a combination of operating subsidies from the municipality, daily fees, and donations (Socialstyrelsen, 2013).

In the Swedish case, the Swedish Association of Women's Shelters and Young Women's Empowerment Centers (SKR) is a national organization for local women's shelters and other organizations that work primarily against men's violence toward women. The shelters were started by volunteers, always women. Today, they are run by volunteers, sometimes together with paid employees, and there are shelters for about 190 of Sweden's 290 municipalities; some of the major municipalities have several shelters. They are organized in two national associations: the National Organization for Women's Shelters and Young Women's Shelters (ROKS), which organizes 126 shelters, and SKR, which has 32 member organizations. Women may seek a shelter for several reasons. The most common is that they need to talk to someone who understands the problem of domestic violence. Quite often women flee to shelters to escape a man's violence, often in dramatic circumstances. These women may be offered shelter and sometimes protection. Many of them bring children with them (NCK, 2001).

The President of ROKS has worked with abused women for more than 30 years. Beausang (2012) is rather pessimistic about what still lies ahead:

> Many programs have come and gone, we've had new legislation and awareness of this type of crime has increased but the violence has not decreased.... Police and prosecutors must learn the special problems of these crimes.... The problem is that there is a lack of continuity of knowledge.

Women's shelter organizations are often concentrated in urban municipalities, often large cities, and vary in terms of the services they offer (Figure 14.2). What is worse is that most rural municipalities have none. According to SKR's database, only three out of 22 remote rural municipalities in Sweden have any record of having women's aid organizations (rate of 0.14). They are located in northern Sweden and are geographically large municipalities: Storuman, Överkalix, and Pajala. In accessible rural municipalities, a bit more than one-third of them have records of having at least one organization of this kind (rate of 0.43). Half of the municipalities regarded as urban have at least one women's shelter and/or organization that supports victims of domestic violence (rate of 1.09). Some urban areas have none, while others have more than two, such as Stockholm, Gothenburg, Malmö, Lidköping, Skövde, and Eksjö. Whilst the great majority of women's shelters and supporting organizations are registered in SKR's database, a small number of independent shelters are not recorded in the national database.

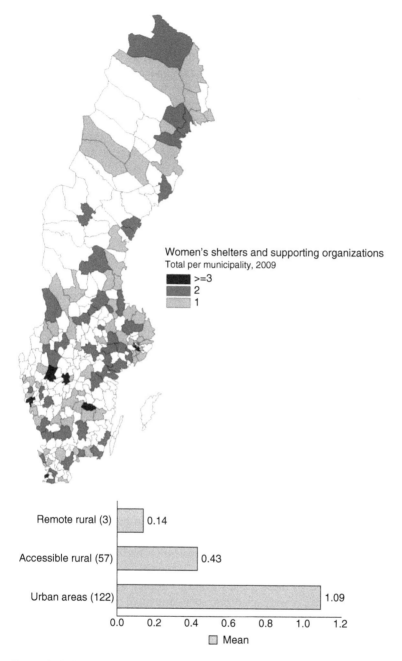

Figure 14.2 Geographical distribution of women's shelters by Swedish municipalities and rates, by municipality by type (data source: SKR, 2009).

Note
The remote rural municipalities with a women's shelter are Överkalix, Storuman, and Pajala.

Since the mid-1990s, the Victim Support Association has also developed activities with a special focus on violence against women often (but not only) after the victim has been to the police. The Association currently consists of approximately 100 local Victim Support units that cover all the country's police districts. Victim Support is a non-profit association, independent of religious and political affiliations. Their task is to support and help victims. Regardless of where one resides in the country, support is provided by *Kvinnofridlinjen*, which is a national helpline set up in 2007 in multiple languages for those who have been subjected to threats, violence, or sexual assault. They are open around the clock, and calls to them are free of charge and do not appear on the caller's phone bill. All these services characterize the kind of support that can be found in Sweden.

In the next section, we discuss the role of local crime prevention councils (and other related groupings) in relation to violence against women in Swedish rural areas.

Local partnerships against violence against women

In Sweden, the implementation of community safety schemes based on local partnerships (crime prevention groups, or CPs) went hand-in-hand with overall decentralization of the police in the mid-1990s. Violence against women was put on the agenda of these partnerships in the mid-2000s often involving social welfare and healthcare, police, and organizations supporting women. This development has been pushed forward since the creation in 1994 of the national women's center (Rikskvinnocentrum). In 2006, this was augmented by the national knowledge center (Nationellt Kunskapscentrum, or NKC) on violence against women. Equally important since the 1970s has been the women's movement, through support groups that work with victims of violence against women, such as ROKS. Important in this development was also the *Kvinnofrid* (protection of women) legislation implemented in 1998, which turned repeated violence against women into an offense in its own right. So far, the role of individual actors in dealing with cases of violence against women has been assessed separately, such as the role of healthcare (Andréasson et al., 2006), municipalities, and police (Weinehall, 2011). These assessments rarely look at the role of local crime prevention partnerships as a whole at the municipal level.

To assess the actions of these groups against violence against women, data from three different sources were analyzed: semi-structured interviews with representatives of CP groups in eight rural municipalities, analysis of SKR database, and responses from an email survey to all representatives of CPs. The email survey helped to select the eight case-study municipalities that were further investigated using face-to-face interviews, as discussed in the next few pages. Semi-structured interviews were conducted face-to-face (in Swedish) with members of local CP councils in eight selected municipalities. The questions were adapted to accommodate the difference in expertise of each CP member. A minimum of five and a maximum of seven people were interviewed in each municipality (49 interviews in total; about six individuals per study area). These people included policy officers, school representatives, representatives of women's shelters, county council representatives, social services, other NGO representatives, and citizens.

In addition, a short email survey was based on hypothetical scenarios and sent to all municipalities with a CP group in rural Sweden. The response rate was 62 percent. CP members were invited to describe the most important short- and long-term actions they would take as a group to deal with the following scenario.

Domestic violence is a problem in your community. Some residents have lately heard of violent events in one particular family. The woman shows signs of having been exposed to violence (bruises and other physical marks) but has not reported these to the authorities. Neighbors and residents nearby would rather not "interfere" or they think that they prefer to concentrate on their own family business. Some people think that domestic violence is not something to worry about. If such a matter is brought to your attention, what would the local crime prevention council do to tackle this problem and to prevent similar problems occurring again in the future?

According to the survey and interviews, domestic violence is a question that requires coordinated actions among different local actors. Good coordination and sharing knowledge are often highlighted as important ingredients to tackling violence in the private sphere and were the most common action CP members stated they would take.

Strikingly, domestic violence was not considered part of the "daily" agenda in one-quarter of the local crime prevention groups that answered the email survey. (They either stated it clearly or did not answer the question.) Most of the groups see themselves as "a coordinating organ" which has a comprehensive view of what can be done to support the victim in the short and long run.

Social services (first) or other members of municipal social boards or experts are regarded, in 85 percent of the cases, as important actors to deal with domestic violence (Figure 14.3a). Commonly, those who are active members of crime prevention groups are themselves responsible for these specific tasks in the municipalities. They would probably make home visits, report the events and begin an investigation. They also highlight the need to create a secure relationship with the woman in question and, in some cases, offer the possibility of establishing an immediate contact with the women's shelter. The clear links between women's shelters in this process seem to be fundamental for half of the respondents. If beatings occur, they have to be reported, so bruises and other injuries can be documented by a doctor and healthcare center and the case can be reported to the police. Many argue that different actors and authorities cooperating in cases of violence prevent the situations from "falling between the cracks" in the system.

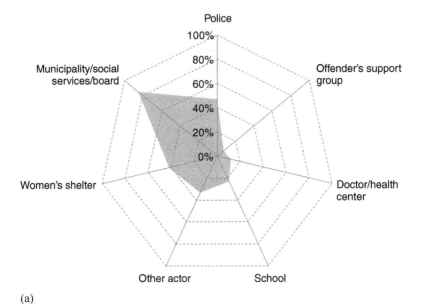

(a)

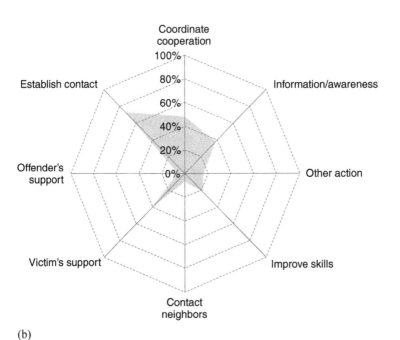

(b)

Figure 14.3 (a) Who should address domestic violence? (b) How would CP groups address domestic violence? (source: own survey, $N=60$ local crime prevention councils).

Although a majority of respondents declare that the role of crime prevention councils in cases of domestic violence is only to coordinate, they still show signs of having a clear strategy on how they would tackle the problem if it appeared in their community (Figure 14.3b). Two-thirds of crime prevention groups would establish contact with the relevant local authorities in an institutionalized way, using channels of support that already exist for victims. Improving the existing networks linking local actors is also regarded as important. In the long term, improvements in personal skills for handling violence and providing information are also considered relevant. Support for both victims and perpetrators is regarded as a must in some municipalities. Unexpectedly, very few declare that they would rely on strategies based on informal social control of neighbors and friends of victims.

Half of the respondents think that domestic violence has to be brought to the attention of police (the others declare that it is the woman's right to decide whether she registers the crime) and in nearly all cases the relationship between victims, local community, and authorities is regarded as unproblematic. As suggested by DeKeseredy, Schwartz, and Alvi (2008), strong social control, common in rural areas, might inhibit women from reporting events or even prompt them to hide such events from neighbors or local authorities, particularly the police. However, one of the respondents reflected upon the current barriers a woman may face when victimized and what is needed to improve the current conditions:

> Helplines can get them to dare to report. There may be reasons why many do not dare to report ... I guess they do not want to end up as a little item in the newspaper ... or they don't want to go to hospital (large women's workplace) because they don't want to show their injuries. The municipality must have a plan to support everyone involved ... perpetrator, victim, children and others. A joint plan with the police, prosecutors, healthcare and others.
>
> (A respondent from southern Sweden)

Many representatives highlight the need for a long-term strategy to support victims, particularly for social services to assist in making a plan for what the family needs and may be willing to receive, possibly supporting the woman in a separation. The role of the school in this process was highlighted in two ways: first, by supporting the children as they might be witnessing these violent events at home; second, by educating and improving gender awareness for school-aged children as a preventive measure. Some respondents highlighted the importance of providing education to those who can actively intervene if violence breaks out at home, such as the caretaker in a housing association.

Emphasizing the role of the police in prevention

Although the Public Prosecution Office in Sweden has invested heavily in fighting violence against women, the number of reports of violence and threats against women has increased while charges have decreased. Some prosecutors believe the problem lies with the police:

> I feel that the judicial police training should be improved. The police would be better at interrogation and treatment. There's a shortage of trained police that can quickly get into the problem.
>
> (A prosecutor in the Stockholm region, in Stengård, 2009)

Recent discussion in the media about women's homicides indicated the role of the police is fundamental in preventing women abuse in rural areas. Jönsson (2013), from the police in Västernorrland, whose team analyzed dozens of cases of homicide in the past 12 years in an area of southern Sweden, says in a radio interview that she believes the police should play a more important role in combating violence against women. Jönsson suggests that, to improve the prevention of violence and killings in close relationships, the police must work more systematically. There is a need to create a database of addresses where there have been repeated calls of fights and/or domestic violence. Such information could provide patrols with more knowledge about what to expect from a particular case in what Jönsson calls "flat fights." She points out that this is particularly crucial at critical stages of victims' lives, such as when women want to separate from their partners or husbands or leave their parents' homes against their will:

> Had we taken these more proactive actions, using skills that are actually in place, we could have certainly prevented a number of murders.
>
> (Jönsson, 2013)

In addition to gathering evidence, there is also a need to ensure that battered women do not withdraw complaints or notifications made to the police, especially in situations in which the separation process is under way and when quarrels are more frequent. Another proposal entails the creation of counseling support for those who have a past of violence and are in the process of separation, to avoid situations that can escalate into violence and murder. Another important component of prevention is the way a restraining order is put into practice by criminal justice. A restraining order (prohibition of contact between a perpetrator and the victim) is said to be insufficient. In the future, a restraining order should be combined with electronic surveillance, with electronic differential tagging on the perpetrator at the same time that the restraining order comes into force. Long-term intervention which does not necessarily involve the police also ought to be put in place to support women to dare to leave a destructive relationship, avoid violence, and, in the worst case, to avoid being murdered. This means that women must get more help than is currently the norm in Sweden, as in some cases they need help finding a new home, a school for their children, and maybe even a new job – all these places far from the abuser.

Unlocking women's violence in the rural context

I: What about men's violence against women? Is this something you see a problem with?

R: No, not really. We discussed it at the previous meeting when X brought the statistics ... there was no case. It is one thing here and another assault case there, but domestic violence or violence against children, or rape.... We are pretty spared from it actually. Luckily. Why? I don't know if women don't dare to report it or if the "free church belt" makes you have a different view of it.

Although not specific to Sweden, the case above illustrates one of the most important challenges in tackling violence against women in rural areas: to get evidence that violence is actually taking place. Can violence against women be truly addressed if there is a "cultural blindness" that does not recognize the problem?

Answers from interviews show signs that domestic violence goes underreported in some of these municipalities. Although there seems to be a tight network between social and health services, police, and women's shelters, cases reported to the police are termed "low" in certain parts of Sweden. As pointed out in Chapter 10, differences in reporting rates of domestic violence may reflect differences in "gender contracts or regimes" (Amcoff, 2001; Townsend, 1991) that creates different conditions for both women and men. In places where more modern gender contracts dominate, there is "the right background" for women to feel accepted even if they report violent actions by their partners. In more traditional gender contracts, however, domestic violence may go undetected for different reasons. On the other hand, high levels of domestic violence in larger cities in the country might be a result of the supply of services, particularly police units, specialized in family conflicts to detect and register family violence.

When a victim actually reaches a women's shelter, she may not want to report to the police or social services. Some believe that the only way to change women's attitudes toward their partners is to invest in awareness and information through lectures in the community. Since it is a small community, information often passes mouth-to-mouth, which is sometimes more effective than the lecture itself. Others think that it is easier to approach abused women when there are children involved, since these women may have a larger interface with the local community and services than others who do not have children. Trust must be established, otherwise women do not dare to tell.

> What we have seen in the women's shelter is that women would not report to the police or social services. Many times they come and talk about "friends" who have problems, and when they come a few times, then it turns out that their friends are actually them. We get it at once but we wait until they can tell their own story themselves.
>
> (Women's shelter representative, northern municipality)

After reporting an incident, a woman may still refuse to participate in the investigation, which is perceived by the criminal justice system as a problem. There are many different explanations for this. Women avoid reporting the case because of social and economic dependence on the perpetrator. Other explanations are that a woman's primary goal is to get out of the abusive relationship and not put the abuser in jail or that she was ill-treated by police or not believed (Weinehall, 2006). Despite being an exception, one respondent mentioned that women are guaranteed the possibility to choose their own contact person at the police, so they do not need to disclose themselves to more than one person after the first incident has been registered.

Identifying "sectoral blindness"

Crime prevention is rarely defined from a gendered violence perspective by those who work directly with violence against women in crime prevention partnerships. Our analysis shows that when local crime prevention partnerships deal with women's safety, the common agenda is to deal with fear of crime in public spaces (using safety audits or safety walks), not with violence that happens in the private sphere.

Although those living in rural areas feel safer in public places in their neighborhoods than those living in urban areas (BRÅ, 2008), interventions against aggression toward women in rural areas still focus on perceived safety in public places. Thus, as in urban areas, in rural areas the actions of crime prevention groups often tend to be guided by the dichotomy of discourse between *private* versus *public spaces*, neglecting the problem of domestic violence and giving priority to (fear of) violence in public places. Moreover, the priorities of crime prevention groups are often the result of an interplay of the interests of representatives in the local community in which the police still play an important role, which often results in less focus on violence by partners or family in the private sphere.

Of course, safety in public places is very important as it deals with a woman's right to move about safely in society. Decades of research have shown that the fear of being victimized by a crime is more prominent among women than men, but crime is just one factor that affects women's perceived safety (Ferraro, 1995; Lagrange & Ferraro, 1989). Other types of behavior – such as intimidation, groping, sexual comments, harassment, and threats – also affect women's mobility. According to Loukaitou-Sideris (2014), fear leads women to utilize precautionary measures and strategies that affect their travel patterns. Whether traveling by bus, automobile, or other mode, women's fear of public transportation facilities (e.g., parking structures, buses, train carriages) affects the way they engage in travel and may preclude them from a basic right: the ability to move undisturbed from origin to destination without worrying that a "wrong choice" of mode, transit setting, or time of travel might have consequences for their safety. Women living in rural areas, particularly in countries with long travel distances like Sweden and Australia, may be extra dependent on private vehicles and public transportation to allow individuals to go to work or ask for help if anything goes wrong. For instance, a study of teenagers' movements in the suburbs of a middle-sized Swedish city reported a fear of traveling or of being alone in transit environments late in the evening (Aretun, 2009). Our case studies in Sweden show that violence against women is dealt with separately from other issues of outdoor safety and rarely relates to women's mobility. The dichotomy of actions between *private* versus *public spaces* is more often found among those crime prevention actions in southern municipalities than in the northern study areas, where alcohol and drug consumption and addiction are targeted by joint efforts against violence.

Although those who deal with violence against women may work separately from traditional activities in crime prevention, they do show signs of cooperation with neighboring municipalities both in southern and northern study areas on some gender issues. The type of support may vary. For instance, all studied municipalities are aware of and work to implement the regulations in the legislation to protect women (*Kvinnofridslagen*). The work done by the selected municipalities in the south and north of Sweden may be similar but, in terms of organization, they are different. In the north, the groups have a looser organization and work based on their individual responsibilities (e.g., the Linnea group is devoted to gender violence), whilst in southern municipalities the groups have a formal crime prevention alliance.

Although nearly all respondents describe their activities as being prescribed either at the national or regional level, there are indications they have some room to affect what happens locally. For instance, a group in southern Sweden decided, parallel to their current support to women victims of violence, to start a men's forum.

> We have established a men's forum. It is a preventive effort aimed at violent men. They must first be able to contact us.... It is an outlet for their aggression before they hit their partner or wife. It is difficult to measure its success. They come to a special apartment that we have set up and then there is the opportunity to meet them anonymously.
>
> (Coordinator, southern municipality)

Changes in priorities have now put the focus on domestic violence with more comprehensive involvement of multiple actors, but it seems that actions are taken without knowing how big the problem is at the local level. These groups' actions and the type of help they provide have become more institutionalized over the years, often following a top-down approach, from regional to local levels. Interestingly, there was not a single case in which any real records of domestic violence were declared as the basis for starting their activities.

I: But why did you start the project?
R: New law, the law changed.
I: So it was not as if you started the project because some statistics (on violence) increased?

R: I'm no feminist as such, but no, there is nothing that we have seen here but you know that there is [violence].

(Project leader, northern municipality)

It is unclear why local actors do not track cases of violence against women if they "know" that they exist. If police statistics may fail to capture "the real numbers," health statistics (number of admissions/hospitalization) should reveal how serious the situation is. The same could be argued for women's shelters and local social services. Violence may extend to children, which could also be identified as a problem at school or day care.

Tackling specific rural challenges

Reaching all those in need and locating them are often regarded as difficult tasks in small municipalities. Some of these rural areas have women from ethnic minorities, from Thailand for instance, often brought to Sweden through marital ties or "marriage arrangements." Westman (2010) shows examples of how migrant women in rural areas exploit their positions and try to challenge the traditional norms in the Swedish countryside. Overall, for those who work with gendered violence, the challenge is greater when victims belong to ethnic minorities who may not speak the language or do not want to seek help for fear of being expelled from the country.

We have a lot of migrant women in the villages.... It is not easy. You need to reach everyone. We have women with addiction problems who are abused, we have women that we do not reach, who do not know the language. We have to get out the information that we exist.

(Project leader, northern municipality)

While it is important to note that abused women with a foreign background are a heterogeneous group with different social backgrounds, they may share a number of vulnerabilities: lack of knowledge of their rights, heavy dependence on the perpetrator, and limited social networks. Studies show that abused women with a foreign background often get incorrect information from the perpetrator. Threats such as that she would be deported if she left him or that her children would be taken away from her were common. Ethnic discrimination is another factor that can make foreign women especially vulnerable. When this happens there is a risk that the woman will be seen primarily as a representative of a culture and secondarily as an individual (Socialstyrelsen, 2014).

The women may also need emotional support and help to process events and find a way forward. Women who are not accustomed to living independently or who are new to the country may need help with practical tasks when they have left their partner and must create a life on their own. Good and competent treatment is a prerequisite for a violence-prone woman to receive community support and help. If the woman has limited language skills and limited knowledge of Swedish society the process can be even more difficult.

More often in the north than in the south, Swedish respondents report the difficulty of dealing with domestic violence and addiction (especially alcohol addiction, sometimes by both victim and abuser) (Weinehall, 2011). The police highlight that some problems are "chronic" in rural communities and, although they follow routines, they lack total commitment when they are called several times to the same address (Weinehall, 2011).

There are also problems associated with long distances to services and support. As in many other rural areas (see e.g., Pruitt, 2008), local governments in rural places often struggle financially to maintain basic public services and resources. Respondents also indicate their own lack of skills and the group's poor resources for tackling violence in the private sphere. They travel to neighboring municipalities to attend courses and establish collaborative work. Cooperation between municipalities is an essential part of their work, especially in attempts to protect victims' privacy and anonymity. However, long distances may play a positive role in the process of looking for support. Anonymity can be safeguarded by "sending women to the neighboring municipality" where better resources can be found.

> We found out that it is impossible to have women's shelters in small municipalities … because everybody knows everybody…. So you have to cooperate. When we have no money to hire someone, we must find ways within existing resources. It is not easy. We must help each other. That is why we will work together with X, Y and W municipalities. When something happens, it's primarily to X municipality that we sent women.
>
> (Project leader, northern municipality)

Some are more active than others in working on issues to prevent long-term domestic violence. Information and education of young people, and of parents, is part of the agenda in nearly all study areas in northern Sweden. These lectures are often financed with joint support from the municipality, county council, and NGOs and encompass a range of issues, from drug and alcohol addiction (which is a problem particularly in northern municipalities), to changes in attitudes to traditional gender roles.

> We had a play about boys' violence against young girls…. We will also go up to T-municipality and H-municipality to hold lectures for parents of young people's habits on the Internet, because parents have no idea what the young people are busy with online.
>
> (Safety coordinator, northern municipality)

An interviewee also mentioned that they found a course at the closest university on men's violence against women and children. They applied for money from the County Council so the police, women's shelter representatives and the municipality had the opportunity to take the course. In summary, there have been a number of initiatives from local crime prevention representatives to improve and spread new knowledge about gendered violence and its prevention.

Avoiding "acting in the dark"

Those who work with issues related to violence against women face a number of other challenges in Swedish rural areas. Although local crime prevention councils show examples of good practice in a number of areas (Ceccato & Dolmén, 2013), there is an overall lack of knowledge about "what works" and "what does not" in countering violence against women. However, this is not a problem exclusively of those who deal with domestic violence. The examples provided by those who participated in the survey show that the majority of the activities and projects conducted within a CP framework rarely reach the point of being assessed. Most of the "success stories" are often told in the form of anecdotes about people's struggles with poor resources to deal with gendered violence, the structural barriers they face, and how their work has made changes in the victims' lives (e.g., by providing shelter or making it possible for women to leave their abusive partners).

Many of those who were interviewed would also argue that being in a "small community" is an advantage for the type of work they do. They claim that any "problem" may be solved quickly because "unofficial talks" may become "official" just because people know each other. However, not everybody agrees. What is perceived to be an advantage by some may be an indication by others of unbalanced power relations. In cases where women abuse occurs, this may lead to what was termed by Barclay, Donnermeyer, and Jobes (2004) the "dark side" of *gemeinschaft*: violence against women is tolerated and conflicts are resolved "within the group."

Aligning national goals to regional programs and local actions

The great majority of respondents expect more resources to become available for long-term action, funding that can be earmarked at the national and regional levels for local action at the community level. They suggest that they need extra resources not only for their current activities but also for new ones (e.g., a girls' forum in a northern municipality, pro-feminist men's movement, such as a males' forum in the south). Better guidelines and knowledge of how to work together with other local actors to tackle violence against women is also desirable.

More knowledge could perhaps explain large regional differences in the number of domestic violence cases that go to trial. In some northern counties, only 20 percent of complaints of women abuse were prosecuted in 2012, whilst in counties with the best clearing percentages, Gotland and Jämtland, the figure was 69 percent (Beausang, 2012). In addition, the whole criminal justice system must be adapted to quick response in extreme cases of women's abuse. Restraining orders should be implemented more often, together with electronic tagging in extreme cases. Relocation of the woman to another community can be an alternative, but it requires resources and the coordinated actions of different actors. As suggested by Jönsson (2013) in a radio interview, actions like these may keep women from dying at the hands of violent partners.

Some claim there is a mismatch between national and local policy, and also poor support for putting national guidelines on violence against women into practice locally. Some in the north also argue that "things decided in Stockholm do not take into account the conditions and resources of remote rural municipalities." The effect of this disconnect between national and local scales in policy has already been pointed out elsewhere by Pruitt (2008, p. 413). Referring to North American conditions, Pruitt argues that

> challenges associated with domestic abuse are unlikely to be solved by action at any one scale. They also are not likely to be addressed effectively with national policies that ignore space- and place-based differences. Nor are they likely to be resolved entirely at the local level, particularly in light of the lack of resources.

This calls for responses that represent collaboration between national and regional levels on the one hand, and local on the other.

Two examples of good practices

These two examples were selected because they are interventions that combine individual and community-based actions. These initiatives intend to establish networks of support for victims, offenders, and their families, which has been an important goal in the UN-inspired coordinated community response to gender violence.

Moreover, the selection of cases is limited by the views, experiences, and perceptions of those who work with crime prevention in eight rural municipalities in Sweden. Although they may reflect a rich variety of rural municipalities in the country, conclusions cannot be generalized for all rural areas, with similar types of initiatives. Despite these limitations, we believe it is important to be able to report on the experiences of those working with women's abuse in these two examples. In the future, it is important to focus on the views of those who seek support either as victims or perpetrators of violence.

Women's shelter in Storuman

The women's shelter called "Kvinnojouren i Storuman" started in 2004 by local nurses who had experienced many cases of abuse against women. They took the idea to a member of the community council, who was later backed up by social services, and then the group was formed. Since then, they have had a good response from the authorities and society at large. When they started their activities, neighboring municipalities (e.g., Sorsele) wanted to get involved. Nowadays they share the apartment and running costs. They now have seven people who work on a number of cases. Some of the work is done at the *individual level*.

R: Yes, the problem is psychological abuse, you know, to access it, and reduce it. It is a preventive program that you do not know how long it can last.

I: How do you work with it?

R: By boosting women's self-esteem and gaining confidence. It is extremely important; it is what is lacking in them. They must be aware that they have self-worth. It is so easy to become depressed. If you are confident in yourself, you dare to go against [your oppressor]. One should not simply put up with crap.

Activities run by the women's shelter organization in Storuman also represent good examples of a community-based approach toward prevention of gender violence. The group attempts to develop and reinforce a shared long-term culture that does not tolerate women abuse and constantly tries to prevent it through training and information. As Saville and Clear (2000) indicate, positive communication skills and conflict resolution enhance cohesiveness. Thus, schools and local community centers can be used to provide information and training in rural communities. One of the members of the group gives examples of how they work in a preventive way together with the community:

> On March 8, the women's shelter usually sponsors free bowling and coffee for women and girls, and this year, the girls invited boys. We had 100–110 people there. It was amazing for such a "little Storuman." Out in the schools, we must do this. We have to reach out to young people.
>
> (Women's shelter)

In Storuman, they are constantly searching for resources, to invite people for lectures on the theme "gender and violence." At the time of the interview, they had applied for funding from the County Council and received enough to hold a number of lectures and training courses for people in the community but also for inhabitants of neighboring municipalities.

However, such preventive work faces challenges. Although various forms of violence against women share a number of commonalities, there is a common belief among women working at the women's shelter that the effective long-term prevention of the problem demands a better understanding of women's needs and their cultural contexts (Ingesson, 2012). A group that is relevant in northern Sweden is the Sami. The leader of the women's shelter, who has been active more than 20 years, says that in her experience the Sami society is patriarchal, consisting of a male-dominated power structure and individual relationships, with a systematic bias against women. Even within the Sami group, there is friction on values related to gender roles, such as between those who take care of reindeer and other Sami groups. As part of their work with prevention, the women's shelter in Storuman received funding from the County Council for interviews to assess Sami women's needs and life situations. Working against this progressive background is the local culture, which reminds us of its patriarchal values in the middle of the town (Figure 14.4).

Men's forum and women's safety walks in Gotland

Gotland has one of the highest rates of clearing of domestic violence cases that go to trial (69 percent) in Sweden (Stengård, 2009). In Gotland they implement the ideals of a pro-feminist men's movement as described by DeKeseredy et al. (2009). The Men's Forum (*Mansforum*) was started in 2007 by men working with family therapy for social services (municipal) and with no connection to the various women's supporting groups that also exist in the municipality under the action program called *Kvinnofrid på Gotland* (legislated protection of women on Gotland). The Men's Forum was initially intended to be a place for men to talk, including those who had a history of domestic violence (men convicted of crimes). The Men's Forum also has a helpline. Eriksson (2011, pp. 24–25) reports on local initiatives against violence against women.

Figure 14.4 "The wilderness man": an ideal of masculinity or a symbol of patriarchal society? Storuman, Lappland, Sweden (photograph source: Carin
Lånersjö, 2011).

Most men who come to a meeting at Men's forum want more than just talk on the phone.... Those who are violent often come back several times as they feel they have difficulty controlling their anger and know that they scare people with it.

However, the initiative is not free from challenges. Since Men's Forum is not a completely formal activity within social services, it is always uncertain from year to year whether the forum will continue because of limited funding.

Another challenge is the lack of male personnel working in social services. As pointed out by Eriksson (2011), 25 women and one man are employed in family care services. Those men who come to the forum may agree with the participant at Men's Forum who said, "It's only girls there and they don't understand us." Almost all departments in social services are dominated by women. As in many other rural communities, attracting qualified personnel is a challenge, and often other priorities go before gender equality when new staff is hired for municipal services.

Since 2013, the group is functioning with three persons. They are part of the family support unit. Nowadays they devote about three hours a week to the Forum within normal working hours. That includes email contact, phone messages, and booking times for meetings (once a week). Persons referred to the Forum are obliged to come. They are usually men who have problems managing their anger. Others, who come on their own, are often men who got trapped living with a mentally ill partner, have a custody battle going on, or feel steamrollered by officers at social services and need someone to whom they can vent their problems.

All calls so far have been individual. The group's representative suggests that their challenge in the future is to initiate discussion groups. The municipality is a small place – everybody knows everybody – and there is a resistance among individuals to open up and talk about their problems with violence to a group, as chances are that others in the group know the person, their partner, or a family member.

There are also initiatives directed at women's safety in public places. A "safety walk" (or "safety audit") is an inventory of the features of an area (or a park) that affect individuals' perceptions of safety. Safety walks were introduced on Gotland in the beginning of 2009 with the objective of identifying physical environments that are perceived as frightening for women. They are also a way to engage and empower local women. Safety walks have initially been used to demonstrate how daily fears translate into concerns about the physical environment, which is useful information for planners (WACAV, 1995, p. 1). Safety walks have led to changes in the physical environment. At the time of the interviews, new safety walks were planned to tackle the problem of safety in the center of the city. Housing companies improved surveillance conditions (installed new lights, replaced broken ones, trimmed bushes), but interviewees believed that changes depended greatly on budgets. Bicycle sheds and park areas will also get extra lighting in the near future.

Sandberg (2010, p. 21) reports examples that these changes were not free of controversy, including comments by the person responsible for the outdoor environment in the inspected residential areas.

> They have cleared a dense forest which was located in the middle of the block ... the measure was met with resistance. Almost 100 per cent of the disaffected were men who made their voices heard ... but many women came forward with encouraging comments about the changes.
> (City Garden on Engineering Management, Gotland)

In Gotland, the public has been invited through advertisements on the municipality's website, newsletters distributed by the housing companies (distributed to all residents in the area), and information posted on notice boards in the areas to be inspected. Local community actors also took part: police, social services, leaders of local associations. According to the interviewees, the response from the public varied by residential area but has usually been low. This is a recurrent problem with safety walks (Ceccato & Hanson, 2013). Ceccato and Hanson suggest that, although safety walks encourage communicative planning, the limited participation of individuals runs the risk of reflecting the views of only a specific group whose voices may be easily heard. If a biased assessment from a safety survey is used as grounds for changes in the built environment, it may unexpectedly help consolidate gender stereotypes – something that goes against the most fundamental goals of the safety survey. Despite potential methodological challenges, safety walks provide valid evidence to be taken into account when the goal is to plan for safe environments.

Final considerations

What do the Swedish cases tell us about overall violence against women in rural areas? The underreporting of this offense results from the victim's silence, and from the tolerance and inhibition of the social circles surrounding the victims. If rural crime prevention deals with women's safety, it often focuses on perceived safety in outdoor environments. It seems that, so far, interventions against aggression toward women are often guided by the dichotomy of discourse between private versus public spaces that also guide the work done by local CP groups and, to some extent, also the police.

Violence against women is regarded as an important issue by all individuals working in local CP groups who were interviewed. However, these professionals believe that social services or other members of municipal social boards or healthcare experts are the key actors in dealing with domestic violence at the local level. They also highlight the importance of women's shelter organizations (which are rarely found in remote rural areas) and, most importantly, that domestic violence is a question that requires coordinated action among local actors.

Women's shelter organizations are a cornerstone of efforts to deal with victims of violence in Sweden. However, they are concentrated in urban areas, one-third are in accessible rural municipalities and only three in remote rural municipalities in Sweden. Limited by resources, the type of help they offer varies greatly, from call lines to protection for the victims and housing.

Networking and sharing knowledge are often highlighted as important ingredients in tackling violence in the private sphere when lack of resources is a fact. Our analysis shows that when local partnerships for crime prevention deal with women's safety, the common agenda is to deal with victimization and fear of crime in public spaces (using safety audits or safety walks) and neglects violence in the private sphere. In certain northern rural municipalities, women's violence is regarded as an important issue by CP groups (often associated with alcohol addiction problems). Often however, the priorities of crime prevention are the result of interplay of interests on the part of representatives from the local community, in which the police still play an important role, and may not always focus on violence in the domestic sphere.

Crime prevention groups in northern Sweden differ in terms of organization from those in southern municipalities. All act as crime prevention groups, but northern municipalities clearly have a looser organization, which may not facilitate the challenges they face on a daily basis. Some report problems of dealing with addiction and violence, reaching ethnic minorities that are victims of domestic violence and treating chronic cases as well as problems related to long distances to services and support. They also indicate their own lack of skills and the group's poor resources for tackling violence in the private sphere.

In a more structural account, some claim there is poor support to put into practice national policy guidelines on violence against women, as many problems are multidimensional, touching upon various areas (addiction, unemployment, ethnical minorities, migration laws). This fact reminds us that domestic violence is a product of multi-scale factors and that responses to it should also be multi-scale, requiring better collaboration between national (e.g., Swedish National Council for Crime Prevention – BRÅ), regional (e.g., county), and local scales (e.g., local police force). In the specific case of Sweden, a more accurate inventory of the types of services and support (including financial ones) for women facing violence in the domestic environment in rural areas is necessary. The problems of geographical isolation and remoteness of rural areas, in particular, make public awareness and education campaigns fundamental to transmitting the idea of social responsibility in issues of gendered violence. These changes mean that more resources need to be allocated at different levels, such as healthcare, law enforcement, community services, and support programs for the victims and their children.

Any action ought to be embedded in long-term support for battered women based on the cooperation of local actors at different levels, but some actors believe that the criminal justice system as a whole should play a more central role than it does today. For instance, many believe that creating a database of women who repeatedly call for police help in the case of family quarrels will enable police officers who deal with domestic disturbances to follow a more systematic procedure. Of course, the need for local police to be more present and work proactively locally goes against the "centralization winds" that blow in Sweden and characterize the current police reorganization.

Social services also play a role in focusing attention on those who directly experience violence or witness violence against a loved one, such as children and the elderly. In extreme cases, protection of identity and housing are the only solution. Foreign women require special attention, as these women are often highly dependent on the perpetrators, may not be aware of their rights, and have limited language skills. In rural contexts, these barriers can become amplified by geographical and social isolation.

A special group consists of women brought to the country in marriage arrangements. This group of women may need extra support to process events and find a way forward. Women who are not accustomed to living independently or who are new to the country may need support with practical tasks after they have left their partner and are creating a life of their own. A better understanding of the current migration laws is necessary to track cases of violent men who import a "series of wives" from abroad and make use of the current system to send them back as soon as the relationship comes to an end.

Crime prevention of gendered violence has long been based on principles of behavior avoidance, demanding from women the difficult decision to leave their homes to stop violence. Interventions directed at potential perpetrators (men at risk), such as the example from Gotland, can also help prevent violence in a more pro-active way. In the long term, it would be better to have an open discussion of what the current norms of socialization and gender roles are among adults at various levels in society. This is perhaps one of the most important structural challenges in preventing violence. Although violence in the private realm primarily affects women, both men and women are at risk. Knowledge of the extent to which men are exposed to domestic violence is so far insufficient in Sweden. All victims of domestic violence, regardless of gender, gender identity, or gender expression, have a right to assistance and protection.

Information and education programs, especially those directed at young people, improve the odds for change in gender stereotypes and diminish tolerance for gendered violence. The examples discussed here show that there are also initiatives among those dealing with gendered violence in trying to improve their skills and improve the knowledge base to deal with the specific challenges of gendered violence in rural areas. Although many challenges remain untouched, examples of good practices, such as those discussed in this chapter, give hope that change is under way.

Appendix

Table 14.A.1 Description of data sources

Type	Description	Data	Source
Media	Print and Internet articles as well as radio programs	2005–2012	*Aftonbladet, Dagens Nyheter*, Swedish radio
Women's shelter database	Number of women shelter organizations per municipality	2009–2010	Women's shelter
Email survey: "the scenario study"	Scenario study using email survey sent to representatives of local crime prevention councils in rural Sweden (60% of those rural CPs answered the email survey)	2010	Own survey
Face-to-face survey conducted with eight local crime prevention councils in rural areas	Eight rural municipalities selected according to their location (north/south), type of economy, and degree of urbanization/levels of crime.	2010	Own interview

References

Aguirre, B. E. (1985). Why do they return? Abused wives in shelters. *Social Work, 30*, 350–354.

Allen, N. E. N., Bybee, D. I., & Sullivan, C. M. (2004). Battered women's multitude of needs evidence supporting the need for comprehensive advocacy. *Violence Against Women, 10*, 1015–1035.

Amcoff, J. (2001). Regionala genuskontrakt i Sverige? Uppsala: Kulturgeografiska institutionen, Uppsala University.

Andréasson, C., Stenson, K., Björck, A., & Heimer, G. (2006). Den svenska hälso- och sjukvårdens arbete inom kompetensområdet våld mot kvinnor: nationell kartläggning. Uppsala: Rikskvinnocentrum.

Aretun, Å. (2009). Ungdomars utsatthet i bostadsområden: Trygghetsprinciper för fysisk planering. Linköping: Linköping University Electronic Press.

Barclay, E., Donnermeyer, J. F., & Jobes, P. C. (2004). The dark side of gemeinschaft: Criminality within rural communities. *Crime Prevention and Community Safety, 6*(3), 7–22.

Beausang, A. (2012). Satsning mot kvinnovåld resultatlös. *Dagens Nyheter*. Retrieved April 17, 2015, from www.dn.se/nyheter/sverige/satsning-mot-kvinnovald-resultatlos/.

Bennett, L., & Williams, O. (2001). Controversies and recent studies of batterer intervention program effectiveness. Harrisburg, PA: National Electronic Network on Violence Against Women. Retrieved April 17, 2015, from www.vawnet.org/applied-research-papers/print-document.php?doc_id=373.

Benson, S. R. (2009). Failure to arrest: A pilot study of police response to domestic violence in rural Illinois. *American University Journal of Gender, Social Policy and the Law, 17*, 685–703.

Brottsförebyggande rådet – BRÅ (National Council of Crime Prevention). (2008). Nationella trygghetsundersökningen 2007: Om utsatthet, trygghet och förtroende. Stockholm: BRÅ.

Brottsförebyggande rådet – BRÅ (2009). *Våld mot kvinnor och män i nära relationer* (Vol. 12). Stockholm: BRÅ.

Bull, M. (2007). Alcohol and drug problems in rural and regional Australia. In J. F. D. E. Barclay, J. Scott, & R. Hogg (Eds.), *Crime in rural Australia* (pp. 71–85). Sydney: Federation Press.

Carrington, K. (2007). Crime in rural and regional areas. In J. F. D. E. Barclay, J. Scott, & R. Hogg (Eds.), *Crime in rural Australia* (pp. 27–43). Sydney: Federation Press.

Ceccato, V., & Dolmén, L. (2013). Crime prevention in rural Sweden. *European Journal of Criminology, 10*, 89–112.

Ceccato, V., & Hanson, M. (2013). Experiences from assessing safety in Vingis Park, Vilnius, Lithuania. *Review of European Studies, 5*(5), 1–16.

Coker, D. (2004). Race, poverty, and the crime-centered response to domestic violence: A comment on Linda Mills's insult to injury: rethinking our responses to intimate abuse. *Violence Against Women, 10*, 1331–1353.

Danis, F. S. (2003). The criminalization of domestic violence: What social workers need to know. *Social Work, 48*, 237–246.

DeKeseredy, W. S., Donnermeyer, J. F., & Schwartz, M. D. (2009). Toward a gendered second generation CPTED for preventing woman abuse in rural communities. *Security Journal, 22*, 178–189.

DeKeseredy, W. S., Schwartz, M. D., & Alvi, S. (2008). Which women are more likely to be abused? Public housing, cohabitation, and separated/divorced women. *Criminal Justice Studies, 21*(4), 283–293.

Donnermeyer, J. F., Plested, B. A., Edwards, R. W., Oetting, G., & Littlethunder, L. (1997). Community readiness and prevention programs. *Journal of the Community Development Society, 28*(1), 65–83.

Eriksson, M. (2011). Contact, shared parenting, and violence: Children as witnesses of domestic violence in Sweden. *International Journal of Law, Policy and the Family, 25*(2), 165–183.

Ferraro, K. F. (1995). *Fear of crime: Interpreting victimization risk.* Albany, NY: State University of New York Press.

Home Office. (1994). Preventing domestic violence to women (R. M. Morley & A. Mullender, Eds.). London: Home Office.

Hoyle, C. (2008). Will she be safe? A critical analysis of risk assessment in domestic violence cases. *Children and Youth Services Review, 30*, 323–337.

Ingesson, M. (2012). Mer kunskap om samiska kvinnor: Viktigt för kvinnojouren i Storuman. Retrieved April 17, 2015, from http://sverigesradio.se/sida/artikel.aspx?programi d=2327&artikel=983273.

Jönsson, B. (2013, November 8). Kvinnomord hade kunnat hindras. Sveriges Radio (Producer). Retrieved from http://sverigesradio.se/sida/artikel.aspx?programid=104&artikel =5698685.

Lagrange, R. L., & Ferraro, K. F. (1989). Assessing age and gender diferences in perceived risk and fear of crime. *Criminology, 27*(4), 697–720.

Loukaitou-Sideris, A. (2014). Fear and safety in transit environments from the women's perspective. *Security Journal, 27*, 242–256.

Lovett, J., & Kelly, L. (2009). Different systems, similar outcomes? Tracking attrition in reported rape cases across Europe. London: Child and Woman Abuse Studies Unit.

Mills, L. G. (1998). *The heart of intimate abuse: New interventions in child welfare, criminal justice, and health settings.* New York: Springer.

Nationellt centrum för kvinnofrid – NCK. (2001). Kommunerna som blunder för mäns våld mot kvinnor (p. 28). Stockholm: National Council for Women's Freedom (NCK), Victim Support Association.

Owen, S., & Carrington, K. Domestic violence (DV) service provision and the architecture of rural life: An Australian case study. *Journal of Rural Studies*(0). doi: http://dx. doi.org/10.1016/j.jrurstud.2014.11.004

Pruitt, L. R. (2008). Place matters: Domestic violence and rural difference. *Wisconsin Journal of Law, Gender and Society, 32*, 346–416.

Rying, M. (2012, June 3). Satsning mot kvinnovåld resultatlös. *Dagens Nyheter.* Retrieved April 17, 2015, from www.dn.se/nyheter/sverige/satsning-mot-kvinnovald-resultatlos/.

Sandberg, K. (2010). Ett tryggare Gotland: En studie om trygghetsarbete i den offentliga miljön. *Arbetsrapporter.* Uppsala: Department of Human Geography, Uppsala University.

Saville, G., & Clear, T. (2000). Community renaissance with community justice. *Neighborworks Journal, 18*, 18–24.

Stengård, M. (2009, December 5). Färre åtal för kvinnovåld. *Aftonbladet.*

Stover, C. S. (2005). Domestic violence research: What have we learned and where do we go from here? *Journal of Interpersonal Violence, 20*, 448–454.

Sullivan, C. M., & Bybee, D. I. (1999). Reducing violence using community-based advocacy for women with abusive partners. *Journal of Consulting and Clinical Psychology, 67*, 43–53.

Sullivan, C. M., & Gillum, T. (2001). Shelters and community based services for battered women and their children. In J. L. E. C. M. Renzetti & R. Bergen (Eds.), *Sourcebook on violence against women* (pp. 247–260). Thousand Oaks, CA: Sage.

Swedish Association of Local Authorities and Regions – SKL. (2009). Utveckling pågår En kartläggning av kvinnofridsarbetet i kommuner, landsting och regioner. Stockholm: SKL.

Tolman, R. M., & Edleson, J. L. (1995). Intervention for men who batter: A review of research. In S. R. S. M. A. Straus (Ed.), *Understanding partner violence: Prevalence, causes, consequences and solutions* (pp. 262–273). Minneapolis, MN: National Council on Family Relations.

Townsend, J. G. (1991). Towards a regional geography of gender. *Geographical Journal, 157*, 25–35.

United Nations – UN. (2011). What is a coordinated community response to violence against women? *The United Nations for gender equality and the empowerment of women.* Retrieved April 17, 2015, from www.endvawnow.org/en/articles/127-what-is-a-coordinated-community-response-to-violence-against-women.html.

Women's Action Centre against Violence Ottawa-Carleton – WACAV. (1995). Safety audit tools and housing: The state of the art and implications for CMHC. Ottawa, Canada: Canada Mortgage and Housing Association, Victim Support.

Weinehall, K. (2005). Mäns våld mot kvinnor i nära relationer Polisens hantering av en brottslig handling (p. 85). Umeå: Umeå universitet, Pedagogiska institutionen.

Weinehall, K. (2006). Räkna med kostnader: en fallstudie om mäns våld mot kvinnor. Paper presented at the *Brottsoffermyndighetens konferens på Internationella brottsofferdagen*, Stockolm. Retrieved April 17, 2015, from http://urn.kb.se/resolve?urn=urn:nbn:se:umu:diva-32094.

Weinehall, K. (2011). Mäns våld mot kvinnor i nära relationer Polisens hantering av en brottslig handling. Umeå: Umeå universitet, Pedagogiska institutionen.

Socialstyrelsen (National Board of Health and Welfare). (2013). Skyddat boende: en jämförelse med Danmark och Norge. Stockholm: Socialstyrelsen.

Socialstyrelsen (National Board of Health and Welfare). (2014). Ensam och utsatt: Utbildningsmaterial om våld mot kvinnor med utländsk bakgrund (p. 60). Stockholm: Socialstyrelsen.

Svenska kvinnorörelsen – SKR. (2009). Women's shelters by Swedish municipalities [Database]. Stockholm: National Organisation for Women's Shelters and Young Women's Shelters (ROKS).

Westman, M. (2010). Women of Thailand (Master's thesis, University of Linköping, Linköping).

Part VI

The difference that rural makes

15 Lessons from rural Sweden and looking ahead

This chapter brings together the content of this book and gives an overview of the main conclusions drawn. This chapter pays special attention to issues of youth in rural areas, farm crime, and crime against environment and wildlife, as well as cases of violence against women, with particular focus on Swedish rural areas. Crosscutting issues are summarized in this chapter before new research frontiers are suggested and conclusions drawn.

Lessons from the book

Part I – Introduction

This part introduces the reader to the book's aim, scope, and structure. Chapter 2 presents arguments for why rural areas matter in a criminological perspective. The chapter attempts to unravel simplistic views of rural areas as crime-free and/or "strange" or dangerous by discussing a number of issues that reveal rural areas as both safe and criminogenic. Low crime rates, typical of rural areas, do not necessarily mean safety for all when victimization is unequally distributed, perhaps concentrated in a specific group. This part concludes with a review of the theoretical framework adopted in the research on which the book is based and reflections on the process of doing research, including issues related to the data.

Part II – Trends and patterns of crime

Chapter 4 compares crime rates and prevalence in Sweden with those in the United States and the United Kingdom. In all three countries, urban crime rates are higher than rural ones, regardless of definitions of crime types and how rural areas are conceptualized. The comparison of the international data shows mixed but often declining trends for rural areas but especially for urban areas. The hypothesis that urban and rural crime rates in the United States and Sweden are converging is also discussed. Then, the analysis focuses on specific types of violent and property crimes in rural areas, drawing conclusions for rural areas in multiple countries whenever possible. Inequality of victimization by groups is still a major challenge when crime trends for different areas are compared. Most groups that are overrepresented in repeat victimization are found in urban areas, but for certain crimes and for frequent victimization the differences between those living in urban and rural areas are small or nonexistent. As is discussed in this chapter, the analysis of inequality of victimization demands an approach that is informed by crime, group, area, and time.

Chapter 5 takes the first step toward a more nuanced picture of crime in rural areas by modeling the geography of property and violent crimes in rural Sweden. Results from the regression models indicate that accessible rural municipalities were more criminogenic in the late 2000s than they were in the 1990s, particularly municipalities located in southern Sweden. Crime rates are higher where urban criminogenic conditions emerge, not necessarily in urban areas but in settings that have strong links with urban centers. These results show increasing dependencies between the city and the countryside, not only with regard to the population's demographic and socioeconomic characteristics but also lifestyle and criminogenic conditions. Changes in routine activities associated with existing and new risk factors are indicated as potential causes of the increased vulnerability of accessible rural areas in recent decades. Moreover, some evidence of anomic conditions is found when a population increase in municipalities affects crime rates. Yet, it is still unclear whether pro-social institutions moderate or mediate the impact of economic conditions on the crime rate. Chapter 5 finishes with reflections on why new theoretical frameworks are needed to help interpret a multinational comparison of rural–urban dependencies, some of which are evident through changes in rural residents' consumption, lifestyles, and victimization.

Part III – Perceived safety in rural areas

Chapter 6 attempts to illustrate that the safety perceived by people living in rural areas is a more complex phenomenon than overall expressions of fear of crime suggest. The implication of this is that there is no single remedy for the problems of crime and perceived safety, let alone a single actor (such as the police) that can tackle such problems. The book argues that perceived safety is a collective project that requires constant assessment by those who produce it: those who are in fear, the community itself, and other stakeholders. Perceived safety is both the cause and the product of people's everyday life practices and experiences, embedded in a context that is not politically neutral, or limited to the village, rural areas, or individual nations. Undoubtedly some tangible attributes of perceived safety stem from local conditions, where daily anxieties arise from victimization, discrimination, economic change, and other root causes of fear.

Instead of reducing the issue of perceived safety to the risk of victimization, Chapter 7 looks beyond actual statistics on perceived safety between rural and urban areas to shed light on the nature of fear among people living in rural areas, with particular attention to rural areas in Sweden. Several groups of individuals declare themselves to be more fearful than others. This group may be composed of those who are more vulnerable to crime in the first place, for a number of reasons, and therefore more fearful, reflecting concerns about crime, stability, and social change. Since 2006, certain measures of perceived safety have decreased among the poor in Sweden. For them, poor perceived safety affects their mobility patterns and quality of life. Inequality in victimization may also explain the pattern. The poor are victims of crime more often and reveal more anxieties than wealthier groups in Sweden. However, as elsewhere in the international literature, fear of victimization in Sweden does not reflect the severity of the crime. Rather, fear of crime appears to reflect reductions in perceived crime risk, that is, changes in the situational conditions for crime, especially for car-related crime. A more nuanced picture of perceived safety in rural areas is presented in chapters 8–10. In these chapters, victimization and fear are discussed in relation to, for instance, young people and women.

Several lessons may be learned from these patterns of perceived safety in Sweden. One lesson is that urban–rural divides in perceived safety (with more people being fearful in urban environments than in rural) represent a rough picture of reality, because there is inequality in both victimization and perceived safety by groups. This is exemplified in Part IV of this book. Chapter 7 concludes by questioning the role of police and policing in reducing fear of crime and boosting perceived safety in rural areas.

Part IV – Crime in a rural context

Chapter 8 focuses on farm crime and environmental and wildlife crime and to a lesser extent, it touches on rural production of narcotics. The chapter has two sections, and both place Sweden in an international context. Farmers are victimized mostly by theft of diesel and other fuels, machinery, and tools as well as by different types of fraud. As many as three out of 10 farmers or their properties declared to be a victim of crime in 2012–2013. Farmers in the south have been exposed to crime two or more times more than the national average, but there are differences by type of crime; for example, theft of fuel is slightly higher in northern Sweden than in the south. Underreporting is a problem with these offenses. Findings also show that despite community efforts to deal with farm crime, victimization has not decreased.

This chapter also provides a glimpse of environment and wildlife crime (EWC) in Sweden. Police records and newspaper articles indicate an increase in EWC in the past decade. It is important to note that before 2007 only crimes with a suspect were recorded by the police, which partly explains the rise between 2006 and 2007. Although crimes against the environment and wildlife are rural phenomena, the geography of EWC varies by crime type. The proportion of serious EWC, unlawful use of chemicals, and crimes related to nature and wildlife is similar in both urban and accessible rural municipalities. Urban and accessible rural municipalities also show high numbers of minor EWC reported, such as littering, garbage dumping, and illegal waste transportation. Remote rural municipalities have a significantly higher percentage of chemical environmental crimes, comprising unlawful handling of chemicals, disruption of control, and disregard of regulations and permits for the use of chemical compounds. For crimes against the protection of nature and wildlife (animal abuse and illegal animal possession as well as disregard of protected species), a slightly higher percentage is recorded in remote rural municipalities than in accessible and urban municipalities.

Drug production attracts less attention than farm crime does in Sweden, compared with the United States or Australia. According to police records, drug production in Sweden tends to be concentrated in rural areas. Media articles report cases of cannabis cultivation in apartments and cellars but also on farms in southern Sweden. Production of synthetic cannabis has also been reported in northern Sweden. However, it is unclear how these reports relate to levels of drug addiction, and much less is known about the nature of users and potential dealers in the rural context. Little is also known about the potential links between drug producers/dealers in rural Sweden and international drug providers through, for instance, the internet.

Chapter 9 turns to a more familiar issue: the paradox of young people, seen either as the "saviors of the countryside" or "the agents of local trouble." This chapter attempts to illustrate both sides of the coin using available official statistics. First, demographic, socioeconomic, and lifestyle differences among young individuals in Sweden are introduced as a background for understanding regional differences in offending and victimization among youth. This is followed by a discussion of factors associated with youth crime and victimization in rural areas; apparently they are similar to those in urban areas. As much as possible, the Swedish case is compared with the international literature, often with examples from British and North American research.

The chapter closes with a discussion of two superficially divergent issues: motorcycle groups that have confirmed links to numerous criminal activities, and young women who come to Sweden after being recruited in remote areas in neighboring Baltic countries. The impact of the motorcycle groups and their networks of influence in rural areas is controversial, as younger members may belong to the community, and therefore their actions are somewhat tolerated by locals. For a certain group of women, the chapter traces individuals' journeys from regions in the Baltic countries to urban Sweden, illustrating the rural–urban link. Young people often become cross-border commodities, forced to engage in activities orchestrated by groups that look like criminal networks. Police statistics of these cases are inexistent or incomplete. Evidence used here is based on interviews (with young people brought to the country, mostly to big cities) and other data sources gathered by supporting organizations.

Chapter 10 points out the barriers women living in rural areas face when reporting violence, particularly when the perpetrator is known to the victim. Following a brief discussion of international urban–rural trends in rates of violence against women, the basis for an analysis of the Swedish case is provided, a list of individual and structural factors pointed out in the international literature as determinants of violence against women in rural areas. In Sweden and elsewhere, reporting rates for violence against women vary geographically for different reasons, which makes it difficult to disentangle "shadow figures" of violence against women between urban and rural areas. Statistics reveal more violence against women in urban municipalities in Sweden, and yet in rural areas more cases of violence against women are being recorded by the police, which is also confirmed by health statistics (hospitalization rates). The increase may reflect a genuine change in the level of criminal activity but could also result from a combination of other factors, such as a rise in victims' willingness to report to the police and other authorities, society's increased sensitivity to violence, improvements in criminal justice practices, and equally important, changes in the law. It is unclear why indicators of gender equality do not capture the dynamics of the geography of violence against women, either in rural or in urban municipalities. One reason may be the fact that police statistics reflect society's (in)capacity to deal with the problem and the communities' tolerance for violence as part of their daily life, embedded in different gender contracts. The international literature indicates that violence has a greater impact on women living in remote areas than on those living in urban centers. In the case of Sweden, no systematic evidence has been found on this point. At the same time, being a "welfare state" with a long tradition of a women's movement does not guarantee a homogeneous support network for women suffering violence in the domestic realm.

Part V – Policing and crime prevention in a rural context

Part V is divided into four chapters: Chapter 11 discusses issues of rural policing, Chapter 12 is devoted to youth-related problems, Chapter 13 focuses on environmental and wildlife crime (EWC), and Chapter 14 builds on Chapter 10 by discussing crime prevention against violence against women, with the focus on rural areas.

One reason Chapter 11 is devoted to rural policing is the difference in police work and organization. International literature long highlighted the distinctiveness of rural policing, with its isolating and lonesome nature, and the dependence on one's neighbors and community within which the police lived. Rural crime issues are different nowadays from those decades ago, and certainly rurality is a complex mix that imposes new demands on policing that go beyond issues of remoteness and isolation. Policing is no longer a job for the public police force only. A good sign is that nowadays there are about 300 community partnerships (crime prevention groups) around the country. They are often composed of a core of representatives from the municipality, police, and schools. This homogeneous format for crime prevention was inherited from the traditional decentralized municipal planning system in Sweden but, more importantly, from the structural changes imposed by police reform around local crime prevention in the mid-1990s. The economic downturn in the 1990s affected public resources and most likely the full implementation of community policing schemes. Top-down national crime prevention policies focusing on big-city problems neglect the special demands of sparsely populated or remote rural areas. For instance, property crimes targeting enterprises, farm crime, and environmental and wildlife crime often fall outside a crime prevention group's agenda. Police-recorded crime does not allow typical rural crimes (e.g., farm crimes) to be registered. Members of crime prevention groups who were interviewed unanimously designated youth issues as the most important for crime prevention councils in rural areas. Most of the work by such groups does not include any strict follow-up. When it does, the evaluation is characterized by simple assessment procedures. Different types of crime prevention models are usually "imported" from other municipalities as examples of good practices. Little thought is put into the adequacy of these remedies in a particular rural context. This weak attachment to local needs imposes further challenges to crime prevention after the new police organization come into force in 2015. With the new police authority more consistency and uniformity of routine police work is expected, as the existing 21 police authorities disappear. The centralization of certain functions should make police work more effective and economically viable. The 2015 police model also relies on intentions to maintain strong links with local policing. Future work is expected to build on experiences with existing local partnerships between the police, municipal authorities, the private sector, and citizens that stem from experiences from community policing reform from the 1990s on.

Chapter 12 takes the issues of Chapter 8 forward by discussing the main crime prevention initiatives related to farm crime and EWC. The role of the community in dealing with farm crime and EWC in rural municipalities through crime prevention initiatives is given special attention. Farm crime and EWC are not a top priority on crime prevention (CP) councils' agendas or by the rural police. Exceptions are municipalities that are targeted by these problems, where environmental inspectors and the police play an important role in crime detection. Although local CP councils demonstrate good knowledge of what to do when a farm crime or EWC occurs in their municipality, there is an overall lack of knowledge among those interviewed from CP councils about what works and what does not work when tackling farm crime and EWC. Because they are rare (or not easily detected), such crimes normally are not followed up and are considered one-off events detected by environmental inspectors and police. Public (including CP groups) and private partnerships appear to be flourishing in municipalities that are often targeted by farm crime and EWC. The chapter reviews new forms of surveillance and protest against farm crime and EWC using ICT and social media, then discusses in detail an interesting case of protest against EWC. An example is the protests about iron ore mining in Kallak, Jokkmokk, in northern Sweden.

Chapter 13 turns to crime prevention activities aimed at youth in rural settings. The role of community in dealing with the problem in rural municipalities is given special attention. Findings show that crime prevention groups in rural areas appear to be well prepared to deal with daily youth problems, or at least they have the organization to deal with individuals who run a higher risk of offending or to prevent other children and teenagers from engaging in risky behavior. Keeping youngsters entertained during their free time is often suggested as a long-term action to prevent youth problems. Most crime prevention aimed at young people revolves around recreational centers and activities. However, it is unclear how much social control driven by crime prevention initiatives affects young people's quality of life. In many rural communities, where "parent-free space" is limited, emphasizing the need for parents to police their offspring may not be well received by young people, including those who would never consider getting involved in trouble in the first place. Spaces for young people may be jeopardized by extending police powers to safety walkers and parents that suddenly feel they own the spaces being regulated and controlled. In the long run, well intentioned crime prevention actions could be perceived by youth as coercive, potentially influencing young people to move away and seek anonymity. Whatever approaches are taken by crime prevention groups, interventions are bound to have consequences for the groups that they are aimed at – in this case, young people. Another problem is that little knowledge exists about what works when dealing with youth-related problems. When they are assessed, they do not always contain the proper information to help other practitioners replicate the projects in their own contexts.

Chapter 14 illustrates challenges in preventing women abuse in rural communities. It starts by discussing current activities that address violence against women in Sweden, following the diagnosis of violence against women presented in Chapter 10. Secondary data, email surveys, media excerpts, and face-to-face interviews capture examples of current prevention initiatives against women's violence in rural settings. Underreporting of this offense is the result not only of the victim's silence but also of the tolerance and inhibition of the social circles surrounding the victims and responsible organizations – perhaps starting with the subtle role local crime prevention councils play in dealing with this particular type of violence. If rural crime prevention deals with women's safety, it often focuses on perceived safety in outdoor environments. It seems that, so far, interventions against aggression toward women have often been guided by the dichotomy of private versus public spaces that also guides the efforts of local crime prevention councils and, to some extent, the police.

Violence against women is regarded as important by all interviewed individuals working on local crime prevention councils. However, they believe that social services, other members of municipal social boards, or health experts are the key actors to deal with domestic violence at the local level. They also emphasize the importance of women's shelter organizations (which are rarely found in remote rural areas) and, most importantly, that domestic violence is an issue that requires the coordinated actions of local actors. Women's shelter organizations are a cornerstone of efforts assisting victims of violence in Sweden. Yet, they are concentrated in urban areas. One-third are in accessible rural municipalities, and only three in remote rural municipalities in Sweden. Crime prevention has long been based on principles of behavior avoidance, demanding from women the difficult decision to leave their homes to stop violence. Interventions aimed at potential perpetrators (men at risk), as the example from Gotland shows, can help prevent violence in a more pro-active way. The view is that all victims of domestic violence, regardless of gender or age, have the right to assistance and protection.

Future research questions

Several themes emerged throughout the book. Some of these are highlighted here, as they represent remaining research questions in the field and provide new direction for future research.

Although crime in rural areas may not always be specifically rural, its nature fails to be fully understood by the current urban-based theories. A key issue for future research is to understand the causes of changes in crime rates in rural areas and how they relate to specific rural conditions for each area. Crime trends have to be considered against a background of what is happening in these areas: changes in their economic base, each population's socioeconomic and demographic challenges, and people's routine activities – just to name a few issues. Such conditions affect levels and processes of social control in these areas and, consequently, crime.

Following Donnermeyer and DeKeseredy's (2013) suggestions, the role of social organization on the formation of criminogenic conditions of rural areas (as opposed to social disorganization) is a fundamental research question to be further investigated in the future. As these authors well observe, crime manifests itself in rural localities in ways that both conform to and challenge conventional theory and research, thus the next step is to empirically test some of the alternative approaches to crime in rural areas.

Another important area of future research is the concept of population at risk, using both resident population and floating population (by vehicle traffic or alternative sources such as opportunistic sensors in mobile phones), as affected by high and low seasons (e.g., summer vs. winter). The book highlights the need for more nuanced evaluations of whether crime affects rural municipalities, as much of the debate on the impact of temporary population on local communities is often based on perceptions of increased crime during high seasons.

In terms of the geography of crime, upcoming studies should attempt to include indicators of social change rather than the ones used in this book. In addition they should also test the importance of differences in regions' functionality on crime levels (e.g., if they contain capital cities, holiday resorts, or industrial towns), because this affects human interaction and, as a consequence, conditions of crime. The testing of variables that serve as indicators of pro-social institutions as moderators of inequality on crime is one example.

Another important question in rural areas is whether thefts are committed by local offenders or are the actions of outsiders coming from neighboring communities. Traditionally, outsiders are often blamed for certain types of crime. Of course, this is an empirical question that can be checked looking at how the flow of information from the targets reaches potential offenders, supposedly living outside the community. It is possible that some offenders travel between municipalities to commit a crime, but no evidence is available for how far offenders travel in Swedish rural context. Past research on urban environments suggests, however, that the majority of criminals commit a crime close to where they live which, for most crime types, is an area smaller than municipal boundaries. Data on the location of offences, offenders and victims and/or targets is necessary to assess whether rural crime is committed by locals or by those travelling to such municipalities for the purpose of committing an offence.

This research shows some factors that affect perceived safety are associated with individual, group, and/or area characteristics. Moreover, some processes triggered by fear seem to have the same impact on people's lives regardless of whether they take place in an urban or a rural area or elsewhere. Future studies should be devoted to the nature of perceived safety in rural areas. Given the multifaceted nature of perceived safety and the complexity of fear of crime, a relevant question is, how can fear be informative to those living and working with safety issues in rural communities?

Another remaining question refers to the current and future challenges for rural policing and crime prevention in rural areas. Crime has become less dependent on space, so the fear of being a victim of crime may be fed by borderless "glocal" forces. An individual living in in a remote rural area of Sweden may run the same risk of being victimized by computer fraud as someone living in New York City. New types of computer-based communication may become facilitators for traditional crime in the physical world, such as pedophiles looking for potential victims on youth chat forums. Information technology also connects people without regard to their physical location but may leave tracks as soon as they move in (real and virtual) space. This imposes new challenges for crime prevention, because law enforcement authorities have to find online criminals that may reside far from the police authority's territorial jurisdiction. Moreover, further investigation should look at the profile of victims of fraud in rural areas, to shed light on why farmers are often vulnerable to this type of crime. Note that many Swedish rural communities have an overrepresentation of elderly, a group often targeted by telephone calls from strangers, some leading to fraud.

In relation to farm crimes, larger properties are more certain attractors than smaller ones, as they often have more locations to steal from, and if they are fairly accessible they make the right target if nobody is around, such as in remote areas and accessible rural areas. Little is known about the situational crime conditions of farm crimes. In order for a crime to occur there must be an intersection of a potential target (e.g., a tractor), a motivated offender passing by and poor guardianship – at the 'right place' (tractor is visible from the road) at the 'right time' (vacation time, no-one is around). The combination of these conditions are expected to provide the necessary situational conditions for far crime. A question remaining for future research is the assessment of how seasons regulate the flow of people, activities, and consequently crime. In addition, there is a need also to investigate the existence of a demand for drugs in rural contexts among youth that seem to be both producers and users of popular synthetic drugs. The relationship between alcohol and drug consumption should be further investigated in a broad social and cultural context for rural communities. There are reasons to believe that, in certain rural contexts, both alcohol and narcotic use is accepted within certain limits.

With regards to youth problems, researchers should strive for a more nuanced view of young people living in rural areas as a group. It is also important to obtain better knowledge about the nature and quality of youth recreation centers and social activities, for instance, whether or not these provisions fulfill the demands of youth groups in contemporary rural environments. Another issue is whether the provisions have any influence on individuals' predisposition to offend, particularly for those that are already at risk.

In terms of violence against women, a more accurate inventory of types of services and support for women facing violence in the domestic environment in rural areas is needed. New understanding that draws on rural women's perspectives of violence in the domestic realm is required to delineate a clear picture of women's needs, not only as victims but, more importantly, as agents of their life choices. Such needs pose a considerable challenge to academics, criminal justice authorities, and policy makers. Also, there is a need to assess whether and how different gender contracts affect local social control and criminal justice practices toward women victims of domestic violence. This includes the treatment that women receive on a daily basis, through municipal social services, healthcare, and supporting nongovernmental organizations, such as shelters.

Safety is often linked to the image of rural idyll, a refuge from urban life. The literature on the attractiveness of rural areas points out the importance of safety as an asset that attracts not only tourists but also new residents and businesses. An interesting research question would be the one that connects safety to rural development and social sustainability of rural communities. Is safety a component of rural attractiveness? And how does it take root in different types of rural areas?

As with the research in this book, any future research must deal with data accessibility and quality. Current research is limited by what official statistics can offer to cover the types of crimes that are relevant for rural areas. Another problem is underreporting of certain types of offenses. Current sampling used in crime victim surveys does not allow breakdowns of groups of interest within rural areas, which is a limiting factor for rural criminology. These data-related problems limit the advances that can be made in research and, more importantly, affect the scope of crime prevention and safety interventions.

Concluding remarks

The main goal of this book is to contribute to the knowledge base on crime, perceived safety, and crime prevention in rural areas, putting Sweden in an international perspective. These issues are often neglected in both criminology and rural studies. Rural areas' relatively low crime rates have been thought to be the main reason for the neglect of the topic. Another reason is that patterns of crime are believed to be homogeneous across rural areas, because "rural" is everything that is not urban, which is another misconception. This book attempts to challenge the rural–urban dichotomy that far too often leads to a disregard for the impact of different rural contexts on crime and safety and neglects the dynamics of rural areas as arenas composed of active agents.

Several principal themes recur throughout this book. They can be summarized as follows. Crime does not happen in a vacuum. Crime is the result of historical, political, demographic, socioeconomic, and cultural processes that characterize a specific place at a specific time. The implication of this is that safety in rural environments depends on context, so it should be analyzed using caution. In each country, or in each framework (e.g., legal, political, historical), the underlying factors that trigger crime may be different. Crime per se may be just the "tip of an iceberg" of different social problems. One can hardly claim that there is something in particular about rural areas to explain why an individual commits a crime, yet, there are reasons to assume that there are features of rural areas that differently affect the situational conditions of crime. For instance, geographical isolation is part of the dynamic of crime in rural areas.

Another recurring theme is that safety in rural areas is a multi-scale process. More than ever before, rural areas are exposed to external influences – some global – that directly affect localities. In the past, media played the key role in shaping stereotypes of rural safety, as my UK experience showed me. However, the process going on now is not quite the same. The new social order affects the way the productive system shapes the supply of jobs (e.g., laborers coming from abroad) and makes patterns of consumption independent of geography, for instance, through the widespread use of ICT. As most crimes depend on human interaction, crime takes new shapes, victims, and places – some virtual. This means that even in rural areas, safety may not follow homogeneous trends or patterns. Unequal victimization makes certain groups and places more vulnerable than others at certain times. Any attempt to generalize about "what rural safety may be" runs the risk of neglecting whose safety is in focus. This leads to the next recurring theme in this book.

Perceived safety has a reflexivity component, which means that its nature depends on those who produce it. Reflexivity takes place when the observations or actions of individuals in the social system affect the very situations they are experiencing (Loader & Walker, 2007). Thus, although security services are becoming tradable commodities in today's market economies (e.g., commodification of police services by security companies), they are still seen (and demanded) by individuals as basic components in a collectively defined social contract, that is, as a public good. Security provision is also an arena for the involvement of civil society, a development that is positive (BRÅ, 2009; Yarwood, 2011, 2014). Overall this development has unintentionally created a *gray zone* of action between actors, in which assigned tasks are no longer obvious from the point of view of the observer (e.g., a rural resident). This uncertainty of "who does what" in security provision may be triggering anomic feelings and legitimizing criminal actions.

The international evidence on crime prevention in rural areas is limited. Local crime prevention groups are, as far as the Swedish case is concerned, composed of a hard core of representatives from the police, the municipality, and schools. This "institutionalized" model is partially inherited from the traditional decentralized municipal planning system in Sweden but also a result of, among other things, structural changes in the police (and policing) since the mid-1990s. Moreover, crime prevention guidelines and practices overlook the nature of rural crime, its seasonality, and what happens outside the urban core of rural municipalities. Evidence from rural Sweden shows that local crime prevention groups face a number of challenges (e.g., appropriate skills, resources) but show indications of being well prepared to address youth-related problems more than any other crime- and safety-related problems. Yet, their practices are guided by routines that do not give priority to rigorous evaluation of interventions.

This book analyzes crime, perceived safety, and practices in crime prevention in rural areas using a toolbox of quantitative and qualitative methods within a Crime Science framework, here presented separately in each chapter. It is important for researchers to select methods of analysis that are appropriate to the goals of each research project, related, of course, to the theoretical framework guiding that particular analysis. The analytical challenges posed by currently available data and previously applied methods should be further investigated.

Finally, the findings here raise questions of whether there is a need for criminological theories (or new theoretical frameworks) that can grasp large-scale crime patterns. As it is now, most environmental criminology theories fit the analysis of intra-urban underlying forces of crime, at best, but do a poor job identifying criminogenic conditions that extend over large geographical areas. This is particularly true for areas that are sparsely populated, rural, and cover large extensions of the country, and where human interactions happen in nodes in space. Is there a need for theories, methods, and data that can better fit the rural context? In essence, Crime Science allows the distillation of knowledge from a large array of divergent disciplines into a coordinated response to crime. How can Crime Science contribute to both theoretical and empirical development in rural criminology? This book is an attempt to start to answer that question.

References

Brottsförebyggande rådet – BRÅ (National Council of Crime Prevention). (2009). Samverkan i lokalt brottsförebyggande arbete. Stockholm: Rikspolisstyrelsen, Sveriges kommuner och landsting.

Donnermeyer, D., & DeKeseredy, W. S. (2013). *Rural criminology*. Abingdon: Routledge.

Loader, I., & Walker, N. (2007). *Civilizing security*. Cambridge: Cambridge University Press.

Yarwood, R. (2011). Whose blue line is it anyway? Community policing and partnership working in rural places. In R. Mawby & R. Yarwood (Eds.), *Rural policing and policing the rural: A constable countryside?* (pp. 93–105). Farnham: Ashgate.

Yarwood, R. (2014). Lost and found: The hybrid networks of rural policing, missing people and dogs. *Journal of Rural Studies, 39,* doi:10.1016/j.jrurstud.2014.11.005.

Index

Lightning Source UK Ltd.
Milton Keynes UK
UKHW02f0151150618
324248UK00003B/147/P